CALVIN P. OTTO
Bolt Beranek and Newman Inc.

ROLLIN O. GLASER
Morse Shoe, Inc.

The Management of Training

A Handbook for Training and Development Personnel

ADDISON-WESLEY PUBLISHING COMPANY
Reading, Massachusetts
Menlo Park, California • London • Amsterdam • Don Mills, Ontario • Sydney

Printed in the United States of America. Published simultaneously in Canada. Library of Congress Catalog Card No. 71-100876.

ISBN 0-201-05510-4
DEFGHIJKLM-CO-798765

"He that hath wife and children hath given hostages to fortune."
— Francis Bacon

To our hostages then . . .
Pat, Jim and Sharon.
Chris, Barbara and Brad.

Preface

Prefaces are for serious-minded people who want to know in advance what your book is all about and why you've gone to the trouble of writing it. Assuming that you are both serious and curious, here it is in a nutshell.

As practicing training men we have always felt the need for a single source of basic information about the everyday management of a training department. It seemed to us that the newly appointed training director, as well as the man who has made his career in this field, might have frequent use for such a tool.

Accordingly, we have sought to pull together the fundamentals of the training job and to introduce a pragmatic approach to solving training problems that has worked well for us. We have tried to build a foundation for work with other more specialized and detailed materials currently available to the training department. To our way of thinking, the contents of this handbook should be part of the minimum qualifications required of every training specialist. We do not pretend to have the answer to every training problem that training personnel encounter. Instead we have tried to provide a framework upon which the training man can build.

We are particularly indebted to Dr. Robert E. Silverman, Chairman, Department of Psychology, New York University College of Arts and Science, for his chapter, "Learning Theory Applied to Training." Our thanks also to Dr. Phil Sleeman, Boston University School of Education, for letting us borrow liberally from his 1968 spring course in television. Arthur J. Tobias, Director of the Management Training Institute in New York, gave freely of his time in the preparation of Chapter 23, "Getting Started in Management Development." We owe a great deal to the many unidentified people in the training profession for the countless ideas and suggestions which have become the common currency of the training business and appear in this book.

We are especially appreciative of the assistance given us by Kay Decker and Kathi Freitas in the preparation of this manuscript.

Cambridge, Massachusetts — C.P.O.
Canton, Massachusetts — R.O.G.
February 1970

Contents

Part 1

The Training Director, His Department, and His Organization

Part I presents a detailed look at the training director's major responsibilities in any enterprise. The basic teaching/learning activities focused on in these chapters are ones which the head of a training function must give considerable attention to before he can effectively plan, develop, or administer his programs.

1

The Training Director's Job

TRAINING, DEVELOPMENT, AND EDUCATION

Training, development, and education – what, if anything, distinguishes each? "Training" originally referred to the communication and learning of the manual skills necessary to perform an economic task. Gradually, the term came to include a broader spectrum of activities, ranging from skill training to individual development to organizational change. The broader definition is usually meant when the word "training" is used today.

While training is directly concerned with improving people's performance with regard to economic activities, education is not generally thought of in such narrow terms. Alfred North Whitehead, the great educational philosopher, defined education as "...the acquisition of the art of the utilization of knowledge." "Education" is an all-inclusive term, taking into consideration *all* learning activities, including those oriented toward profit.

A national organization for professional training people recently changed its name to include the term "development" in addition to training. Development may be thought of as industry's synonym for education. Both education and development go beyond the traditional restrictive parameters of training.

These distinctions become blurred, however, when one considers the wide range of teaching/learning needs of the typical organization. We think that it is enough to be aware of the meanings the terms carry with them. Then, like practically everyone else, we ignore the fine points as long as we are understood, and use whichever label seems to best describe our meaning in a given frame of reference.

For the purposes of this book, we will stick to the conventional term "training" mainly because we are so used to it. Our definition will contain elements of training, education, and development, however. Training, to our way of thinking, refers to the teaching/learning activities carried on for the primary purpose of helping members of an organization to acquire and apply the knowledge, skills, abilities, and attitudes needed by that organization to carry out its mission.

WHAT SHALL WE CALL HIM?

The title of this book reflects the majority view. The man responsible for the teaching/learning activities of an organization is usually called a training director or director of training. As early as 1919, Charles Allen, in his book *The Instructor, the Man and the Job*, referred to the man who had "full charge of all matters regarding the training and breaking in of workers in addition to the general supervision of the training department" as the training director.*

Recently, changing attitudes toward the training director's responsibilities have been translated into changes in his title. He is sometimes called a training manager, a manager of personnel development, an education and training officer, a manager of learning systems, and so on. The traditional title "training director," however, is still the rule, and the variations are the exceptions.

We will follow the majority in this respect, although we will be describing a man with the full range of teaching/learning responsibilities. We will use "training" to include development and education, and we will use "directing" to include guiding, assisting, motivating, actuating, stimulating, encouraging, communicating, persuading, leading, and inspiring. For consistency and convenience, then, we will stick to the conventional label.

While training people use the term "training" in its broader sense, we wonder if everyone in the organization does. It has been estimated that expenditures on training during business recessions are cut on an average of 30 percent. We suspect that some of the reasons for the vulnerability of the training function are tied to corporate misconceptions of the objectives of this department. If training is looked upon as a nice but unnecessary extra, it may be a result of the mental set of the organization's managers and the past performance of the department.

---

*Charles Allen, *The Instructor, the Man and the Job,* Chicago: J. B. Lippincott Co., 1919, pp. 299-300, as quoted in Donald W. Devine, *The Critical Requirements for Training Directors,* Philadelphia: University of Pennsylvania School of Education, 1962, p. 9.

Possibly the training director and the department should be described in terms which would more directly relate the objectives and the work of the department to those of the organization. For example, in the case of a profit-making organization, the title would suggest the training director's contribution to the profit objective.

WHAT DOES A TRAINING DIRECTOR DO?

But let's get down to specifics. A good starting point for talking about any job is a straightforward job description. The following is a list of the major responsibilities of the typical training director. The list is not in any particular order and no attempt has been made to give the items on the list relative value or emphasis.

1. Maintains a continuous audit of organization's training needs.
2. Develops training philosophy, policy and procedures in writing.
3. Prepares objectives for department's work and communicates them to his staff.
4. Prepares department's budget and periodically evaluates value received from budget expenditures.
5. Develops and applies administrative controls to the work of the training department.
6. Researches learning theory for applications to organization's teaching/learning problems.
7. Supervises the work of the training staff.
8. Plans developmental activities for his staff, and periodically appraises their professional growth.
9. Arranges for training materials, equipment, and facilities.
10. Supervises and assists in the production of audiovisual materials for training.
11. Edits all written materials produced by the training department.
12. Analyzes and refines the organization's systems.
13. Organizes and executes special training programs for disadvantaged and technologically displaced workers.
14. Organizes and participates in developmental programs for top management.
15. Develops and applies methods for checking the effectiveness of all training programs.

The above list tells us nothing about how well these tasks must be performed. Later in this chapter we will discuss the setting of performance standards for training directors. The job description is the first step which must be taken before standards can be successfully developed.

Let us take some of the key elements in this description – not necessarily in the order given – and look at them more closely.

THE TRAINING DIRECTOR IS A LEARNING SPECIALIST

The training director in any type of organization – business, industry, education, government, or military – has similar fundamental responsibilities. One of these is to know and bring about those conditions which will produce optimum learning at the lowest possible cost to the organization.

Learning may be broadly defined as a more or less permanent change in behavior which occurs as the result of some form of practice. The learning process itself is an unobservable intervening variable which links practice to behavior change. The training director must know what kind of practice to provide and how much of it is necessary to bring about the behavior changes critical to the organization's success. Not only will he need to know something about the concepts of conditioning, reinforcement, reward, extinction, motivation, discrimination, and generalization, but he will also need to know how to apply these concepts to the practical constraints of the organization's learning environment. In short, he needs to know and be able to provide whatever it takes to get a man to learn efficiently and effectively.

One of the claims made about teaching machines when they first appeared on the market was that they were developed in the learning psychologists' laboratory, and therefore were based on the "scientific" principles of learning. Many training people accepted and still accept these claims uncritically. They invested and continue to invest thousands of dollars of their organization's assets in teaching machines. In many cases, the training director had not taken the trouble to carefully evaluate the principles of learning used by the machines, or to find out if they really were at work in the learning process. There were, as a result, many disappointments because of the lack of knowledge on the part of the man who had the responsibility for being the organization's repository for this kind of information.

No one expects the training director to go about discoursing on Skinner or Hull or other learning theorists. This subject matter has limited appeal to people outside the field, anyway. However, the training director must have a basic understanding of learning theory so that he can effectively guide the teaching/learning activities of the organization. This is simply a dollars-and-cents approach to an organizational task which puts responsibility on the director for getting maximum results for the organization's investment in behavior change activities. This is his and every other department head's responsibility – to give the company a maximum return on its investment. It is up to the training director to acquire and apply expertise in learning so that he can get the best classroom environment, the best sound-slide show, or the best role-play to accomplish the organization's objectives.

THE TRAINING DIRECTOR IS A SYSTEMS ANALYST

The training director and his staff are in a unique position to contribute to systems analysis and development. The analysis of a current system or nonsystem is one of the first steps that must be performed in developing any program. The training director in the following story used this type of analysis to help develop his company's program.

When the store he worked for opened a new retail branch, it was proposed that the new store be equipped with the latest in cash register systems. The training director was asked to prepare a manual for instructing new employees in the operation of these registers. The assignment would have been easy if four distinct systems for other types of registers did not already exist in the other branch stores. The first job was to analyze what was already being used, and then to determine how the radically different new register could be integrated into the on-going system. Only after this careful and exhaustive research had been performed was it possible to go on and develop the materials required for training the new salespeople. Prior to giving the assignment to the training department, the help of the accounting department and the computer people was sought. While each group contributed information and a point of view, it was the training group, because of its relatively bias-free point of view and understanding of the human problems encountered in using the system, which was finally able to develop a successful subsystem to mesh with the existing system.

THE TRAINING DIRECTOR IS A COMMUNICATIONS EXPERT

Many line people think of training as something that happens when an instructor lectures a class or a trainee reads a printed manual. True, these are two common forms that training takes, but certainly not the only two, nor even the best two. A training director we know had taken on the assignment to train new people to correctly distribute large quantities of toys to leased toy departments throughout the country. As the toys were sold, the distributor in the home office adjusted each store's inventory by shipping more of the same from the warehouse. The training director began work by collecting opinions from experienced distributors on what a new man needed to know to correctly perform the job.

Once this had been accomplished, the training director expanded his information into a written narrative. He then went back to the line manager who had originally requested the training and showed him his progress. The manager was satisfied that he now had his training program, and that nothing further needed to be done.

It took a great deal of discussion and persuasion to convince the manager that the narrative was merely a step in the total process of developing materials to communicate the information necessary to train an effective distributor. The next phase of the training director's work was to develop the most appropriate means for getting the information to the trainee. This might take the form of assigning sections of the narrative to read, completing sample forms, telephone role-playing, filmstrips, and so on.

The training director, then, must be an expert in the ways of communicating information to people. He need not be a technical expert in the operation of a movie camera, but he must know enough about the medium so that he can decide if and when it is the most efficient and effective means of handling a specific training problem. This job is becoming increasingly more difficult as communications methods and devices proliferate. Even as we wrote some of the later chapters on audio-visual equipment and techniques, there were changes which required the rewriting of some materials. Regardless of the difficulty, the training director must be able to select the best means of transmitting information to be learned by others in the organization.

THE TRAINING DIRECTOR IS A CONSULTANT TO HIS ORGANIZATION

The training director's work cuts across all lines in the organization. One moment he may be having a telephone conversation with the president about the need for training supervisors in basic labor relations in anticipation of a union drive, and the next hour he may be supervising the training of stockboys in the safe handling of stock trucks on the selling floor. Sooner or later the requirements of his job place him in contact with all segments and all levels of the organization.

His relative freedom to move and become involved in other people's problems can probably be attributed to his nonthreatening role in the organization. Supposedly, the training director has no direct authority over anyone except those on his own staff. He has no special axe of his own to grind. His purpose is to help others in the organization do a better job. For this reason he often finds himself being used as a sounding board for complaints, ideas, and problems. He becomes a collector of opinion and fact about all of the nooks and crannies of the organization. He becomes a man in whom a great many people place their trust and confidence for a great many reasons.

Because of this unique position the training director has the opportunity to function much as an outside consultant would. From his broad knowledge of his environment, he can advise, and work through those he advises, to help the organization carry out its work.

THE TRAINING DIRECTOR IS AN ADMINISTRATOR

While it is not his primary or most important task, the training director has the responsibility for administering training programs, his staff, space, and equipment. He must have all of the administrative skills of other department heads. These skills include handling the financial matters of his department; supervising the use of the training areas; recruiting, selecting, training, and supervising his own staff; maintaining training records; and developing systems to handle his department's administrative routines.

It is important to note at this point that the administrative function must be kept in perspective. It is all too easy to become wrapped up in the details of running a department and miss the reasons why the department exists in the organization. The only justification for people, equipment, space, and program control is that control usually produces greater efficiency in reaching organizational objectives. Administration may be looked upon as a vehicle for getting a job done; it is not the job itself.

The training director may take a lesson from the public school system in that it is all too easy for him to slip into the role of "keeper of the classroom." Too often the training director and his staff see themselves, and are in turn seen by the organization, as extensions of their high school and college academic counterparts. We believe that the association is unfortunate and sometimes detrimental to the training department.

TRAINING PHILOSOPHY, POLICIES, PROCEDURES, AND PRACTICE

The term "philosophy" often arouses some very strong and negative feelings among training people. We suppose that this is the result of the widely held stereotype of philosophy and philosophers. The training director, however, must start from a philosophical base before he or his staff can develop programs to give practical assistance to the organization. The theoretical constructs developed by the training director should provide his staff and the consumers in the organization with day-to-day operating guidelines.

Two basic philosophical questions must be considered by every training director: first, what are the ultimate ends of training in my particular organizational setting, and, second, what are the fundamental principles underlying training and how can these be utilized, given the constraints of my organizational environment? There are other questions, but these are the basic ones.

Answers to these and other questions will not come quickly or easily. They are questions which must be grappled with when the training director first takes over his department. Tentative answers must be found. The training director will probably spend his entire career searching for better answers.

From a philosophical base the training director will develop policies and procedures affecting the training department. Simply defined, a policy is a statement of intent by top management reflecting in broad terms what it proposes to do. It is meant to be a guide to thought and action in the organization. While only top management can set training policy, the training director should play a key role in its original formulation. He should take the initiative and, working directly with management or through his boss, help set the policy he feels is essential to helping the organization in its work. Training policies should include such subjects as who gives and receives training, what courses and programs will be offered, when training will be conducted, how it will be conducted, why it should be given in the first place, and where it will be given.

These policies should be in writing so that everyone concerned can read them, understand them, and suggest modification where necessary. Written policies will also help provide the necessary continuity to an organization's training efforts should there be changes in circumstances and/or personnel.

Procedures are ways of accomplishing the goals set by policies. These, too, should be in writing to ensure uniformity. Practice is what actually takes place in the "real world" of the organization. The training director's never-ending task is to look at policy, procedure, and practice and attempt to keep them in line with philosophy.

THE TRAINING DIRECTOR IS A TEACHER

The training director may from time to time take over the actual teaching in a given learning situation. This will depend upon his staff size and limitations on his free time. It is certainly recommended that the training director at least observe the work of his staff in the classroom.

The training director is a teacher in another sense. Besides teaching in meetings, he teaches in brief encounters in the hallways and offices, and sometimes during coffee breaks and lunches. In other words, he is constantly looking for opportunities to help people do a better job in both formal and informal situations. It goes without saying that the training executive must find unobtrusive ways of doing this kind of teaching so that it will not be offensive to those it is intended to help.

PROGRAM PLANNING

Whether the training director develops a training department from scratch or inherits an on-going operation, one of his first tasks will be to undertake an audit or survey of his existing services, and then to consider those that will be needed in the future. This means that the training director must first identify the organization's goals, get the necessary agreement to the validity of the goals he identified, establish a priority for the work, establish a budget, and finally begin to develop programs to help the organization achieve these goals.

The audit or survey should be periodically reviewed and updated. Once management has given its stamp of approval to the plans, individual goals and projects may be assigned. No special form is required for the survey. The items should clearly relate the programs to be continued or developed to the goals of the organization. Once accepted by management, the survey can be used as a blueprint for action by the training department and the director. Without an approved audit the training director's efforts are likely to be scattered. Management and the organization will have no clear idea of the department's work. This makes programs vulnerable to attack by others in the organization. A well-formulated survey and approved plan will eliminate most of this, leaving the training director free to make his contribution without wasting undue time in defending his work and explaining his expenditures.

TRAINING FOR THE TECHNOLOGICALLY DISPLACED AND THE DISADVANTAGED WORKER

The training director must assume the responsibility to plan for and retrain those workers in the organization whose jobs become automated. He must be aware of impending changes in work routines. Although information will not always come to him, he must be sensitive to what is happening in his company. He should be continually asking questions, planning, watching for situations which are likely to turn workers out of their jobs, and offering a plan to "retread" a man so that he can continue to be productive for the organization.

The training director also has a responsibility to those would-be workers who are handicapped by reasons of their social class, educational level, skin color, and so on. During the past few years the unemployment rate has continued to drop from a national average of 5.7% in 1963 to 3.8% in 1967. In some areas of the country the percentage has dipped even lower. This means that many of the applicants an employer is now forced to consider will not have the desirable work habits and personal qualifications an employer is accustomed to finding in the labor force. This situation will continue to worsen from the employer's standpoint.

Problems, however, are merely opportunities turned upside down. The bringing of more and more unskilled, disadvantaged workers into an organization will provide a tremendous chance for the training director to apply his knowledge and skill to a great human cause and to make a real contribution to the organization as well. The training executive will do well to explore such federal programs as the MA-4 (the Fourth Manpower Administration Program), which was adopted to train and integrate the "hardcore" unemployed into the workforce. MA-4 is a federally funded program which pays the employer to train, prepare, and retain a disadvantaged worker for a permanent job. Payment is made on a fixed-cost basis which reflects the employer's cost in developing training materials, staff salaries, rental of training space, and wage differentials while the disadvantaged worker is being brought up to the organization's standard, etc. In short, the director of training has a crack at one of the most challenging tasks ever offered to him – a chance to help correct the physical, educational, psychological, social, and training deficiencies of a large segment of our population.

DESIGNING A USABLE RESEARCH PROGRAM

The training director is concerned with the future as well as the present training needs of his organization. He should be constantly checking the effectiveness of his methods and materials. Unfortunately, the task of researching present practice is given short shrift or no shrift at all by most training people. The reason – management does not appear to place much value on work it cannot see immediate use for. The training department is off on another project and much too busy to take the time necessary to monitor a program's effectiveness. Even the gathering of simple data through tests to see whether a course is accomplishing what it was designed to accomplish is neglected.

Program effectiveness cannot be taken for granted. The training director must establish a selective continuing program of research which will help him solve the practical problems he will encounter. We are not talking about research for the sake of research. We are thinking of the kind of analysis that will pay off in training dollars and cents.

HOW WILL WE KNOW WHEN THE TRAINING DIRECTOR IS DOING ALL OF THESE THINGS WELL?

Measuring performance is not as difficult as it sounds. Once we have identified the training director's responsibilities, the next step is to set a standard of performance for each one. If we say, for example, that a training director should be responsible for developing and applying administrative controls to the work of his department, we need to find a way to objectively determine whether this is being done. The training director, his boss, and perhaps a member of the personnel department must sit down and jointly define exactly what is meant by administrative controls. This may include such tasks as preparing progress reports, training records, and other kinds of paperwork. All of these administrative tasks must be clearly identified. Once this is done to everyone's satisfaction, the next step is to agree upon the ways both the boss and the subordinate will be able to judge the quality of work being done. If we look at training records, for example, we may ask if they are up to date, accurate, and useful to the organization. The extent to which the records meet these criteria tells us how well the training director is performing in this area of his responsibility.

The whole job of setting performance standards is a matter of taking the time and making the effort to find measurable ways of determining how well work is being done. In most cases, managers are content if they have simply listed a subordinate's duties. The second and most important step, that of creating standards for each duty, is usually neglected. If we are to know how well our training executive is performing his job, we will need to have both quantitative and qualitative standards.

The subject of setting performance standards deserves much more space than we can give it in this book. If you are interested in this vital subject, we would suggest that you read a book by Virgil F. Rowland, entitled *Managerial Performance Standards.* *

WHAT DOES THE TRAINING DIRECTOR NEED TO DO HIS JOB?

If you were the personnel director or some other executive responsible for hiring the next training director, what qualifications would you look for in your man? Here are a few guidelines based on the kind of work the head of the training function is required to perform. Bear in mind that these generalizations have the same weaknesses as all generalizations. There are successful training people who do not have all of these qualifications. If you pick a man with most of them however, you will increase the probability of your choosing a man who will be an asset to your organization. No attempt will be made in this section to describe how you evaluate these qualifications in a candidate. We will content ourselves with simply identifying them.

Personal Characteristics

The following set of personal characteristics seems to cover some of the more important qualities of men we have seen become successful training directors. The list has not been empirically determined; it is based on prejudice and intuition. The pattern of traits will vary depending upon the nature of the organization doing the hiring or promoting. The training executive of a sales-oriented corporation, for example, will have different characteristics than the training executive of a bureaucratic organization such as the government.

1. *Ability to speak articulately.* The training director's job demands high verbal ability. Each day he will be working with people at all levels of the organization. He must be able to give clear directions, explain difficult concepts, argue persuasively, question thoroughly, and motivate others through speech. The training director will need to be able to converse effectively with individuals, discuss problems with small groups such as his own staff, and speak publicly to large audiences.

---

*Virgil K. Rowland, *Managerial Performance Standards,* New York: American Management Association, 1960.

2. *Ability to write correctly and convincingly.* A training executive spends much of his time communicating in writing. He needs to be able to write clear and correct expository prose. His writing tasks will take the form of memos, pamphlets, manuals, scripts, training reports, and so on. If he does not personally write in the above forms, he will probably need to know enough to be able to constructively criticize assistants producing written material for him.

3. *Ability to organize the work of others.* Like all executives, the training man must be a good organizer. He must think clearly and logically. Often he will be working in areas where he has had no direct experience. The only way he will be able to make a contribution will be through his ability to help subject matter experts to organize and give form to their experiences for the purpose of training others.

4. *Capacity for frustration.* The name of the training game is frequently frustration of well-intentioned efforts. The training director may see clearly what people need, but getting them to accept it may be difficult. The training director must have a high tolerance for frustration and at the same time be able to maintain an optimistic and positive attitude toward his work. He needs to be able to "hit 'em again harder," even if he has suffered repeated disappointments.

5. *A willingness to submerge his own ego.* All staff people have bruised egos. It is the nature of the job. Line people are always quick to criticize staff work, and often question the necessity for it at all. The training director and his staff must be able to derive satisfaction from work well executed, even though little recognition is given by anyone else in the organization. An important requirement of staff work is that line managers be allowed and even encouraged to take the credit for successful training programs. The training staff must support the line. If the line succeeds, the staff succeeds. The training director must have the maturity necessary to submerge his own ego in order to build the line manager's.

6. *Inventiveness.* All executive positions require a high degree of creativity. The training job is no exception. Training people are called upon to use their imagination to structure effective learning situations on a moment-to-moment, day-to-day basis. They must be able to improvise, while at the same time using resources available within the organization, keeping costs down, working with all types of students, and producing measurable results when the programs are finished.

7. *Persistence.* Good ideas often do not receive immediate acceptance. If the idea is really worth something and the training director is convinced of its value, he must be prepared to persist until either the idea is accepted or he is proved wrong.

8. *A strong interest in the growth of individuals and organizations.* The observation that the training director is an agent of change within the organization has been expressed again and again during the past few years. Many of the training director's efforts are focused on helping individuals grow so that the organization can grow. Often this growth is not linear in direction. It proceeds by fits and starts with occasional back-pedaling and treading of water. A training man must gain his satisfaction from assisting growth, however slow and painful it may be.

9. *The ability to inspire others to greater achievements.* A training director is often the man behind the scenes. He may not be on the front line, but he is vital to the success of the battle. The training director must be able to offer inspirational leadership to all levels of the organization in order to help them express their abilities to the fullest.

10. *Flexibility.* Few plans come off as they are originally conceived. Broken field running is often the only way to get a touchdown. The training man must be highly flexible and sensitive to the need to change his course if it is for the good of the organization.

These, then, are some of the characteristics successful training executives have exhibited. Probably no man has all of them to any great extent. When considering a man for the position, however, you will do well to give these traits some consideration before making your decision.

Educational Background

The educational background a man should have for the training director's job is not yet settled. There are some who believe that a college degree is not even necessary. We think, however, that a man without at least a bachelor's is at a definite disadvantage if for no other reason than the fact that the training director often deals with college educated men and needs to feel that he is at least their equal.

Assuming a college degree to be essential, the particular degree that will best suit a man for the job is still open for discussion. A major university offering a graduate degree in employee development includes the following courses in its curriculum: the counseling of adults, the evaluation of adult education programs, current issues in adult education, the adult as a learner, and so on. Whether this program and others offered by large universities can contribute to the development of potential training people has not yet been conclusively demonstrated. University education for training people suffers from the same weaknesses as the education given other professionals. It tends to be removed from the actual on-the-job situation, and little attempt is made to relate theory to organizational practice. Also, instructors vary radically in experience and ability, and programs lack continuity. Unfortunately, the training man, like many others, is trapped by the organization's demand for academic credentials for the sake of academic credentials. Most organizations are interested in the fact of graduation and not in the quality of the learning experience or its relation to the work to be performed. In all probability the training director will be no better at performing his job with a master's degree than he would be with a bachelor's. Academia has much work to do before it can honestly say that it can make a contribution to the training director's ability to do his job.

Work Experience

Training executives can and do come from all kinds of work experiences. There are four work patterns which we think make a man a better candidate for the job: a variety of work assignments, experience in managing others, a communications-oriented job, and administrative experience.

The potential training director should have had a number of different types of jobs. These jobs need not be directly related to the jobs in which he or his staff will provide training. What is important is that the jobs provide insights into the nature of work, a feel for what people need to do a good job, how people work in groups, etc. Mere quantity of work experiences is not, of course, the answer.

The training director should have had some experience in handling people under a variety of conditions. Military experience can be invaluable in this respect. The training director's responsibilities will require him not only to supervise his own training staff, but also to be able to train others in the art of effective supervision.

Teachers often make good training directors. They have had the experience of trying to communicate their ideas to others. They have also felt both the frustration of not coming across and the exhilaration of effective communication. Teachers are not the only ones engaged in communications work. Sales managers, radio/TV announcers, writers, media producers, all have communications experience which may be useful.

Handling the problems of administration is the fourth area of useful work experience. Much of the training executive's time is spent in the details of administering programs, space, and equipment. Previous experience in this area will be helpful in handling the paperwork and procedures necessary to running an efficient department.

WHERE DOES THE TRAINING DIRECTOR FIT IN THE ORGANIZATION?

Training is traditionally looked upon as a staff function. Most frequently it is one of the jobs performed within the personnel department. Training logically follows hiring and is one of the means the personnel department uses to improve the productivity of the organization's workforce. Training directors, therefore, often report to personnel directors.

Some people disagree with this arrangement. If training is too closely allied with personnel, there may be a strong temptation on the part of personnel people to push personnel type training to the neglect of the other needs of the company. In some organizations, the training function has been completely separated from the personnel department to avoid this possibility.

This objection may be disappearing. It seems to us that there is a new emphasis developing in personnel departments. While they were once heavily weighted in favor of labor relations and employment, many are now being organized around the concept of personnel development. The efforts of the entire personnel staff are geared to improving the productivity of the organization's workers. Legal and administrative functions are being pushed into the background while the focus is on employee development. In this type of department the training director has a stronger voice.

It seems to us that training problems arise in all of the personnel department's functions. The operation of the typical employee-benefits subdepartment of the personnel department provides a good illustration. Benefits people are usually entombed in the microscopic details of their benefits plans. The work is largely done on paper by following pseudo-legalistic procedures. Some of this is undeniably necessary. Too often, however, this becomes the whole job. The employee for whom the whole insurance program ostensibly exists is left to stumble through contract language in wordy, dull pamphlets. As a result, most employees have no idea of the value or cost to the company of their benefits. The real job of the benefits person is to effectively communicate what it is all about. This means that more time must be spent teaching supervisors to answer questions which are basic to the plan, counseling employees, and developing aids such as filmstrips. Adding frills to benefits is not half as useful as effectively explaining to the employee what he already has. Training concepts can and should permeate the entire personnel function of an organization.

What Did You Do For Me Today?

We once knew of a line manager who made it his business to stop by the training director's office each day and ask this question. Annoying as it was, the question was actually proper. The training department provides services to the line departments. As a service department it must satisfy its users. If it is not meeting the needs of the line departments, then it is properly open to criticism.

What often happens is that the training department becomes inbred and perpetuates its own interests rather than those of the organization. It forgets the mission of the organization and becomes like a bureaucracy feeding on its own rituals and taboos.

Training is usually looked upon by line departments and management as an expendable. The training department must continually prove its usefulness to the organization. The training director cannot sit behind his in-basket and react only to requests that are sent to him. He cannot be simply an order taker. He must go out into the organization and create a need for his services. A recent survey of training methods being used by large companies revealed that 62% of the training directors surveyed did not know what the in-basket technique was all about.* If 62% of the training people do not know this, imagine the ignorance of the rest of the organization. There is much to be done.

The training director and his department will fail if they are simply passive instruments in the company. Support comes from a broad base – not simply from one's boss. Training must stop protecting its domain and aggressively go out and sell its services. If it is rejected, it must return again and again.

The Relationship of Training to Top Management

Few managers really know what they should expect from their training departments. Training is alternately seen as a frill, an in-thing, and a panacea for all organizational ills. It seems to us that under normal

*"Industrial Training Survey," Kennilworth, Illinois: Sharp and Oughton Inc., 1968.

circumstances the training director should work with management in the following seven general ways: to help examine organizational problems, to help develop objectives for solving these problems through training techniques, to explore alternatives to training, to develop training plans, to explore the appropriate resources to implement plans, to evaluate the results, and to help take follow-up measures to reinforce the problem solutions.

Until management recognizes the relationship between the function of the training department and the bottom line on the company's financial report, training will always be misunderstood, and either too much or too little will be expected from it.

Whose Responsibility Is It To Train?

Is training solely the responsibility of the training department? We do not think so. Even if it had the staff necessary to handle all of the training the organization needs, it probably would not have the know-how. Training falls into two general categories: common denominator training, and specialized training. Common denominator training is training consumed by many employees in the organization. It is of a general nature, requiring no special expertise. Orientation training falls into this category. Specialized training must usually be handled at the department level. It is specific job training which is best given by someone who is close to the work on a daily basis. Operating a specific model of punch press would be an example of this type of training. As a rule of thumb, the training department should probably handle the common denominator training, using line people wherever possible, and line managers should handle the specialized training, getting guidance in methods and materials from the training department. In general, the training director should build as much of the training responsibility back into the line organization as is practical. This will automatically build support for training on the broadest base in the organization. The training director should operate with the leanest possible staff. His purpose is not to create dependency upon him and his department, but to make the organization self-sufficient. His goal should literally be to work himself out of a job. Realistically, this will never happen, but it is a useful operating principle.

2

How to Prepare and Present a Training Forecast

Have you ever considered what it would be like to drive cross-country without a good road map? Even with today's well-marked highway systems, chances are you would get lost five or six times. Training directors often try to drive their departments for years at a time on poorly marked roads without adequate maps to guide them. They say they are too busy with urgent business to take the time to plan a route; they think they can fly by the seat of their pants; or they are not really concerned with the length or the cost of their trips.

The seasoned driver, however, knows that the most pleasant and the fastest trip is a well-thought-out, well-organized venture. A little time spent in carefully mapping out the route pays large dividends for everyone. This analogy, simple as it is, holds an important lesson for the training director. This lesson is the subject of this chapter.

One of the first tasks of a newly installed training director is to survey or audit the organization's environment and the contribution his department is presently making to the organization's mission. This is a job which must be repeated periodically by all training directors. Once the survey is made, the training director must develop a plan of action to direct the resources of his department to assist the institution in reaching its goals.

Let us broaden this concept a bit and call the plan a training forecast. The training forecast involves seven basic steps:

1. Looking at the total organization and each of its parts to determine what the training department can contribute to the overall mission.
2. Evaluating the present formal and informal training activities, if any,

to determine how successful these activities are in helping the organization in performing its work.

3. Identifying present and potential organizational problems which the training department may help rectify.
4. Assessing the capabilities of the present training staff, equipment, and space to handle the goals of the plan.
5. Preparing a written plan of action based on a specified period of time the plan is to cover.
6. Preparing a budget which spells out in detail how much the planned training activities will cost.
7. Establishing criteria which can be used to measure how well the forecast has been carried out and what remains to be accomplished.

Let us take a look at each of these seven steps and explore their meaning for the training director. It is important to note that the preparation of training forecasts is in reality a continuous process; but it is one that must be formally undertaken periodically, probably once each year.

HOW TO LOOK AT YOUR ORGANIZATION

In some ways new training directors have a distinct advantage over old. They approach organizational problems with clear eyes. The fact that something has been done in a certain way for years has little meaning to them. They are in fact usually bent on overturning sacred cows and replacing them with their own. Recall your own experience in a new situation. You saw things with crystal clarity – a clarity which began to dull even after only a few days of exposure. In the beginning, your approach should be to immerse yourself in the organization's environment. Record your observations. Make your judgments and your plans later. Collect your facts like a scientist. Go to as many diverse sources as time will allow. Watch out for your own predispositions and favorite solutions.

1. Begin by talking with your staff (if you have one). If you are a new training director from the outside, this may be more enlightening than if you come out of another department in the same organization or out of the ranks of the department itself. You may be lucky enough to have long-service employees on your staff. While their view of their responsibilities and their outlook on the organization may seem rigid and soured from experience, they will be repositories of what has been tried

and how well it has worked. They will, of course, reflect all of the past frustrations which the department has met, their own petty concerns, and perhaps jealousies over not having been selected to fill your job.

2. Obviously, your boss will have his own set of observations and concerns. He may even have kept a folder of thoughts and ideas about your job, which he will present to you with a flourish and a sigh of relief now that you have arrived to solve his problems. He will also be in a position to advise you on the character of the organization, expectations for your role, and possible pitfalls to be avoided. All of this you will respectfully consume, bearing in mind that your boss may have misjudged the situation and that you will need to hear many sides of the story before you can reach meaningful conclusions.

3. Talk with other department heads to find out how their departments fit into the flow of organizational activities. Coffee is a great catalyst for getting ideas out on the table for consideration. Be wary of the department or division manager who appears to have ascertained the "most important" program for you to develop. It may be a favorite axe which he has already brought out on other occasions for grinding with your predecessors.

4. Sample the opinion of all levels of the organization. Talk with the chairman of the board as well as with the lowest-paid hourly worker. Each has insights and blind spots which will provide you with the raw data for reaching your own conclusions.

5. Examine, if possible, the efforts of others in similar organizations. No need to reinvent the wheel. Others have probably faced the same problems you are about to uncover. Consider yourself lucky if your company belongs to a trade organization or other group that carries on an exchange of information. The opinions of the members can be a genuine asset in your struggle to develop your own plan of attack.

6. Read a wide variety of the available organizational literature, from the annual report to orientation booklets for new employees. The house organ, if there is one, will be a revealing source of the spirit and intent of the organization in the past.

All of the above methods of "immersion," plus any others you can devise, should lead you to some basic understandings about your company. Plunge in and sort out your impressions later. This first step is critical to everything you will try to accomplish later. Don't close off any avenues for data collecting. Hold off your final conclusions as long as humanly possible. The time for pouring the cement in the form will come soon enough.

Fig. 2-1. Checklist for evaluating present training activities.

Type of training	Purpose	Formal/ Informal	Number Hours	How Performed	Where	Est. Cost
Orientation	For new rank and file	Formal	2	Lecture with instructor	Company cafeteria	3.00/ trainee
Job Training						
First-Line Supervisors	All warehouse foremen	Formal	12	Classroom group discussion	Training room	110.00/ trainee
Middle Management Development						
Top Management Development						
Systems and Procedures						
Sales Improvement	Refresher training for salesmen	Formal	8	Four 2-hour class sessions	Field sales offices	32.00/ trainee
Security						
Safety						
Training Under Poverty Programs						

A CHECKLIST FOR EVALUATING YOUR PRESENT TRAINING ACTIVITIES

Having looked at your organization, it is now time to study your own department to find out what it is currently contributing to the overall mission of the corporation. The checklist shown in Fig. 2-1 will help you to systematize your observations. The list has been organized along the lines of the training that is typically done in organizations. You may wish to refine it so that it corresponds more closely to what is being done in your own company.

IDENTIFYING PROBLEM AREAS FOR TRAINING

The third step in preparing your forecast is the identification of organizational problems which the training department is equipped to help solve. Pieces of problems will come to you from the very beginning from many sources. Some problems may even have been outlined to you during the selection interview. Others will emerge during discussions with your boss, other department heads, your staff, and top executives. Do not automatically assume that you have a problem which training can solve. Training is too often looked upon as an organizational cure-all. It may not in fact be able to provide the best treatment for the problem. It will not, for example, solve your customer service problems if your salesforce has been poorly selected. Supervisory training is of little help if the boss of the supervisors is too weak to follow through when you finish. Problems which at first look like training problems may be ones which training cannot even begin to solve. Solutions could require a redesign of existing systems – for example, firing the top man, or a host of other actions in which training will take little part. The trick, of course, is to wait long enough for the ballots to be counted before reaching your final conclusions and distributing your written training forecast to the management board.

CAN YOUR PRESENT DEPARTMENT HANDLE THE NEW FORECAST?

Once your forecast has been developed, you will need to take a close look at your present staff, equipment, and facilities and decide whether your department in its present condition will be able to carry out the plan. Will you have enough people on your staff? Are they flexible enough to undertake new programs? What are their strengths and weaknesses? Will new equipment be necessary? Will you have a space problem? If so, can other space be used on an occasional basis or will new training areas need to be contructed? All of these questions must be answered in your written forecast. Management must have all of the data before it can reach an intelligent decision about your plans.

PREPARING A WRITTEN TRAINING FORECAST

When all of the evidence is in, you will want to prepare a written plan. Why go to the trouble of setting everything down in writing? Here are some important reasons:

1. Putting something in written form forces the writer to think systematically through all of his plans and examine their consequences.
2. A written plan gives the department's members a chance to look at the scope of your thinking and make additions, subtractions, and changes if appropriate. They will also become knowledgeable about the direction in which you intend to take the department.
3. A written plan gives management an opportunity to see your thinking and know what they should be getting for their money and how much they will be expected to spend. This also gives them the opportunity to approve or disapprove of your plans. Six months later they will not be able to say that they didn't know your intentions.
4. Your written plan can provide you and management with a tool for later evaluation of the department's effectiveness.

Your written forecast should probably take the form of two reports: the first, a description of the current and proposed work of the department; the second, a summary of the first, identifying the work to be done, who will perform it, and how much it will cost. The descriptive document can be organized along the lines of the typical functions performed by the training department such as new employee orientation, policy training for front line supervisors, communications skills training, etc. Or it may be organized by problem areas such as excessive inventory shortages, recurrent safety hazards, cash register operation, etc. A third way of organizing the descriptive document is by employee populations in the organization which are to be trained such as sales managers, new welders, life insurance salesmen, file clerks, etc.

The following examples show how you might lay out the descriptive document and its summary. This example is organized by employee population within the organization. Note that priorities for training have been assigned.

Training Department's Forecast
For Calendar Year

Training for Sales Personnel

1. Orientation for New Salespeople. We presently provide 7-1/2 hours of orientation for new salespeople. The time is allotted as follows:

Welcome to company	15 minutes
Work rules	1 hour
Benefits	1/2 hour
How to write saleschecks and operate the register	5-3/4 hours

Complaints from supervisors and the new salespeople themselves indicate that too little time is spent on the most important aspect of their job, the art of selling fashion merchandise. We propose to increase the time spent in learning to sell and develop the following program:

The welcome, work rules, and benefits would be allotted the same length of time. The use of the register would also receive about the same amount of attention. Greater attention will be given to customer approaches, merchandise presentation, customer courtesy, increasing sales, closing sales, etc. The final one hour of training will be spent in individualized training in the department to which the salesperson will be assigned. Total time needed for the new program – 15 hours.

2. Sales Seminars. We presently spend more than $5000 annually on shopping reports. Our reports are well prepared but are not being put to sufficient use to justify such a large expenditure. During the next six months we will tabulate the results of these reports and develop training materials to improve areas of general sales weakness. We further anticipate a four-hour seminar for all salespeople receiving shopping reports below a minimum grade.

3. Seasonal Sales Rallies. In the past we have held seasonal sales rallies to charge up the salesforce just prior to the back-to-school season. We will continue this practice and concentrate on selling coordinated items for the fall campaign.
. . . etc.

The summary of the same material might appear like this:

Summary of Training Department
Forecast for Calendar Year

I. Training for Sales Personnel

A. Orientation for New Salespeople
1. Continue methods and materials presently used. Improve salesmanship.
2. Increase classroom time from 7-1/2 to 15 hours.
3. Cost of training each new salesperson will be $43.25.

B. Sales Seminars
1. Develop training materials for seminars based on research of salespeople's shopping reports.
2. Retrain salespeople with poor shopping reports.
3. Cost of four-hour seminar per trainee will be approximately $12.00.

C. Seasonal Sales Rallies
1. Continue two seasonal rallies each year.
2. Fall theme should be selling coordinates.
3. Cost of rally, approximately $375.00.

. . . etc.

COSTING OUT YOUR FORECAST

For many this is the most difficult part of planning. Actually, it is more time-consuming than difficult. The total cost of training to industry has been estimated to be about 18 billion dollars annually. By 1970 it is expected to rise to 25 billion. That is obviously a substantial sum. You and every other training director will be forced to justify your requests to commit increasingly heavy corporate expenses to training. You may as well get used to thinking of training in economic terms, for that is the only reason for providing your service in a profit-making organization.

The last step in the preparation of your training forecast will be the costing out of the whole package. This is usually referred to as preparing a budget. Simply defined, a budget is nothing more than a financial plan for attaining the objectives of an organization, in your case, the training department.

How does one begin to prepare a budget? Some people think that you begin with what was spent last year. All that you need to do to get your budget accepted by management is to stay fairly close to what was appropriated the year before. Suppose, however, there was no last year for your organization. Suppose you were over-funded last year. While last year's expenses offer some help in planning for the coming year, that is not necessarily the place to begin work.

The best and only defensible place to begin budget planning is with the programs you intend to develop and execute for the coming budgetary period. If you have followed the previous steps in developing your forecast, you have already worked out your programs and their objectives. The rest is simply a matter of determining what it will cost to produce the programs. There is nothing mysterious about that.

The value of approaching the budget from the standpoint of programs should be clear. Instead of offering management a budget, you offer them a set of programs, which if they agree they need and want, they will buy. The budget then becomes a price tag. If the price is too high, then a program or two may need to be excluded for the next period. But if you kept the organization's goals clearly in mind and used good judgment in developing your programs, you are not likely to suffer great budget cuts. This point is important: never present training costs isolated from what these costs are expected to accomplish.

Some department heads feel that padding the budget is the only way to end up getting approximately what is really needed to run the department. This may in fact happen in some corporations. Aside from being dishonest, padding should be unnecessary if you follow the formula of selling a program first and a price tag second. If management does not agree that the program is necessary to the organization's success, it should not be budgeted for anyway.

Often training directors get hung up on the cost/quality relationships of their programs. Spending more money may produce a more effective piece of training or it may not. There is probably no conclusive way to prove what quality of program is needed to accomplish a given learning task. It comes down in the end to the training director's judgment and the professional stamp management feels is in keeping with the corporate image. Your starting point should be to produce a program of just sufficient quality to accomplish the learning task. Because programs are only means to ends, they should reflect only that degree of sophistication absolutely essential to reach those ends.

Many department heads worry excessively about getting management support for their budget proposals. The real worry should focus on getting support for the programs themselves. If the programs are wholeheartedly endorsed by management, then logically, management will support those programs financially. The point here is that training directors should concentrate on the relationship of their programs to organizational objectives. Politicking to obtain financial support is of secondary importance.

The training director should look upon budget preparation as a continuous process involving the following six activities:

1. The determination of the objectives for training programs.
2. The development of a training plan to achieve these objectives.
3. The preparation of a budget document to forecast the expenditures to implement the training plan during the stated period of time.
4. The presentation, considerations, and adoption of the budget.
5. The administration of the budget.
6. The appraisal of the budget in relation to achievement of training objectives.

Budgeting should be viewed as an on-going activity, not as a frantic, every-six-months type of scramble. The training director should get in the habit of maintaining a folder in which he collects data for the next budgetary period. His departmental records should reflect with reasonable accuracy how the money was actually spent.

For simple and efficient budgetary control, the accrual accounting system shown in Fig. 2-2 is recommended.

Fig. 2-2. Training budget form (accrual system).

Account Number	Budget Appropriation	Encumbrances	Payments	Unencumbered Balance

Under accrual accounting, as soon as purchases are made, or orders signed, or services agreed to, the obligations are charged to the affected account as encumbrances. When the corresponding bill is paid, the procedure is to credit the account with the original encumbrance and charge the final payment to it. In this way the state of the budget is always accurately known. In other systems, entries are made in the expenditure ledger only when payments are actually made. The real balance cannot be ascertained by simply subtracting the total of payments to date from the amount budgeted because commitments may have been made but not accounted for. How much is still in the budget can only be guessed, and the man charged with responsibility for the budget will frequently find himself in hot water with his boss or the controller because he has spent more than he had in his budget. Accrual accounting will help you avoid that unpleasant situation.

In setting up your original budget categories the following coding system or a variation of it will be helpful. A decimal system such as this one can be expanded or contracted to fit individual requirements.

Basic Programs (100 Series)

110 Rank and File Orientation
120 Front Line Supervisory Training
    121 Basic Supervisory Techniques
    122 Communications
    123 Personnel Policy and Procedure
130 Job Training
140 Middle Management Development
etc.

Special Programs (200 Series)

210 T-Group Pilot Program
220 Experimental Job Rotation in Accounting Department
etc.

Facilities (300 Series)

310 Space Rental
320 Utilities
330 Equipment Rental
340 Maintenance
etc.

Materials (400 Series)

410 Teaching Supplies
420 A-V Materials
etc.

Equipment (500 Series)

510 Audio Equipment Rentals
etc.

Professional Services (600 Series)

610 Professional Memberships
620 Journals, Books, etc.
630 Seminars, Workshops, etc.
640 Professional Travel
650 Outside Consultants
660 Honorariums
etc.

Staff Salaries (700 Series)

710 Training Director
720 Instructors
730 Clerical Support
etc.

Capital Outlay (800 Series)

810 Tape Recorders
etc.

All of the above items except those in the 800 series reflect expenses for expendable items. The 800 series, Capital Outlay, refers to expenditures which result in the acquisition of fixed assets or additions to fixed assets. Using this or a similar coding system will help you to quickly assign expenses to various groups. This will be helpful for analytical reasons or preparation of the next budget.

SETTING UP CRITERIA TO CHECK YOUR RESULTS

The last of the seven steps is probably the most neglected but most important of the whole exercise of developing a training forecast. You should be checking your results as you go forward through the budgetary period and formally at the end of the period before you begin the next. This simply means that you will want to determine how well the organization's investment in your improvement activities is paying off. Any good businessman wants to know this. Have you reduced inventory shortages as you had planned? Have you shortened the time it takes a man to become a qualified supervisor? Have you reduced the scrap rate? Are there fewer grievances in your warehouse because supervisors know how to handle employee complaints before they become grievances? What criteria will you set up so that your department's performance can be measured? Unless these checkpoints are set up and used, you will have a difficult time defending next year's plans and budget.

These, then, are the seven important steps to developing a training forecast. This is a crucial document. Without it you will find yourself nibbling at one problem after another, never sure whether it is the one management feels is critical. Without it you will have a rough time getting your department to understand their overall direction. And finally, without it you will always be in the position of having your budget cut. Why not, if all you ever tell management is how much you need instead of how much you are giving?

3

Selecting and Developing an Instructional Staff

At a recent training workshop, we met a man who related the following experience to us about his first day at work as a new training director.

It seems that he had been previously employed as an educational writer in a training department staffed by 23 people. He changed jobs to become a training director and after being duly shown his new office, turned to his boss and asked to meet his staff. His boss looked quizzically at him for a moment and then replied, "You're it, fella!"

"But you have more than 5000 people to be trained," the subordinate stammered.

As the boss moved toward the door, he replied, "You'll find a way, I'm sure."

Training departments come in all shapes and sizes. In small companies, training is often only one of the personnel administrator's duties. In larger companies, the training function may be staffed by dozens of people whose sole responsibilities are to help others improve the organization's output.

HOW LARGE SHOULD A TRAINING STAFF BE?

Unfortunately, no rule of thumb is available to help the training director accurately calculate the size of his training staff. The training requirements of each organization vary so widely that any attempt to relate overall manpower staffing to the number needed for a *typical* training department is meaningless. Here are a few considerations which may be useful, however.

1. Consider the present population of your organization. Someone in it is responsible for manpower forecasting, however informal this may be. Will increases, decreases or changes in its manpower composition require an added training effort by your staff?

2. The product produced or service rendered by your organization will influence the size of your staff. Such factors as diversity of product or service, complexity, frequency of change of model or system, new products and services, and other factors related to the purpose of your organization all serve to increase or decrease the number of people required for the training effort.

3. The long- and short-term operational goals of the management and various staff departments will have a bearing on training staff size.

4. If the level of need for training of the organization's members is high, then obviously more training will be required and hence a larger staff.

5. The geographic location of training problems may influence staff size. A multiple-unit retail organization, for example, will probably require a larger staff because of travel to and from the location for training.

6. The extent to which staff members must develop custom training materials is an important consideration. Will commercially available materials be used in the main, or will it be necessary to start from scratch and create each program? Will outside consultants be used to develop some of the materials?

7. The availability of already trained workers in any given labor market will play a part. If many skilled workers are available for hire, the need for extensive orientation and job skill training, will, of course, be reduced.

8. The availability of training facilities and program schedules affects staff size. No one can be in two places at once. If you must offer several classes simultaneously, then obviously you must have more than one instructor. On the other hand, if the classes can be combined, it will be possible to save instruction time. If, for example, you were giving training in automotive mechanics to 60 men, you might consider the alternatives of holding a lecture and demonstration for all 60; dividing into three groups of 20 students each in simultaneous group discussions; or meeting in groups of 20 for lab work. Imaginative scheduling can save instructor time.

Naturally you cannot schedule all classes to meet your departmental needs. Often trainees are available only at certain times or places. If this is the case, then you must adapt your training staff to these circumstances.

Of equal importance to the number of classes required is the frequency of their presentation. Will they be scheduled once or repeated periodically? Will they involve meeting daily, weekly, monthly, or on some other periodic basis? The greater the frequency of classes and courses, the greater the probable need for trainers to handle these various class sections.

9. If a variety of courses is offered, your training staff must be either versatile or large. This will be an important consideration in the selection and building of a staff because in all likelihood you will be limited in the number of trainers you can hire. Too often a department will develop a training staff without giving consideration to this requirement, only to find that the internal needs of the organization cannot be serviced without hiring extra trainers while members of the present staff are not fully active.

WHAT KIND OF PERSON MAKES AN EFFECTIVE TRAINER?

The selection of a trainer for your staff requires the same degree of care and skill as the selection of any other staff employee – perhaps a little more because of this individual's potential for good or harm to an organization. In no case should the position be considered like the railroad crossing guard's job, a place where people are often put to pasture because they are no longer useful to the company in any other capacity.

Before starting a search for the right man, take whatever time is necessary to fully define the responsibilities of the job. You will not be able to effectively evaluate the qualifications of any individual until you have some sort of yardstick to measure him or her against. A typical job description for a trainer might look like this:

POSITION DESCRIPTION: Trainer
REPORTS TO: Training Director
MAJOR DUTIES:

1. Teaches training classes as scheduled.
2. Evaluates employees trained and reports results to supervisors.
3. Keeps training records on employees trained.
4. Develops training materials, including overhead transparencies, flip charts, and manuals.
5. Assists line managers to develop training objectives and programs as directed by the training director.
6. Assists line managers to improve their skill in training their subordinates.
7. Assists in the evaluation of current training programs.
8. Handles other projects as assigned by the training director.

Status is important to everyone. If the trainer is to be given a title, it should be conferred only after careful consideration of its implications and relationship to other department titles. A trainer's title may be any one of the following: trainer, staff assistant, instructor, course instructor. The title "instructor" is most frequently selected for entry jobs. After the man has gained experience and qualifies, he may be advanced to "senior instructor" or "course chief," depending on your preference. In a group of three or more instructors, trainers should be classified according to their seniority and ability. Avoid the problem, however, of all chiefs and no Indians. Use the titles discreetly and only when they are honestly merited.

Following the development and adoption of a job description, focus should be turned on the specific characteristics and qualifications of the individual required to fill that job description. Consideration should be given to personality factors relevant to success in this job; educational background; work experience; age and other physical requirements; and professional stature in the field.

1. *Personality factors.* A man or woman should, of course, be temperamentally suited to his or her work. The first step, then, in developing specifications for your candidate is to consider the personality characteristics you believe are related to success on the job. A personality test can be of assistance when you begin to screen your applicants. *The Predictive Index,* developed by Arnold S. Daniels Associates, is a useful example.*

The Predictive Index is a projective technique like the *Rorschach Inkblot Test* or *The Thematic Apperception Test.* Instead of using inkblots or ambiguous pictures, *The Predictive Index* offers lists of adjectives to which the subject responds. A highly reliable and valid statistical correlation has been developed, showing a relationship between the adjectives a man chooses to describe himself (both as he sees himself and as he believes others see him) and the way he actually behaves in real life.

Evidence based on *The Predictive Index* reveals that the best trainers are people who have a strong interest in other people. They cooperate rather than compete with others. They are usually unselfish and friendly. The best trainer is capable of following detailed instructions. He is patient. He enjoys communicating with others and is generally service-oriented in his ambitions.

---

*Arnold S. Daniels, Management Consultants, 131 Mount Auburn Street, Cambridge, Massachusetts 02138.

There are other characteristics, of course, but these are a few it would be well to consider. Jobs vary in their requirements. It would be a good idea to try to make some assessment of a candidate's personality before making the final offer of a job. A test like *The Predictive Index* can be a great help in avoiding a costly hiring error or at least gaining an awareness of the potential strengths and weaknesses of a candidate.

2. *Educational factors.* It is almost impossible to generalize about the importance of a college degree to a trainer. Here are some considerations to help you make your decision:

a) A degree in a specialty which the trainer will teach is desirable.

b) If the trainer will be teaching all nondegreed people, then a degree may not be essential.

c) A degree from an education school or teachers' college, with or without practical teaching experience, is helpful, but not critical. Course work in the field of adult education is highly desirable.

d) Do not select a trainer solely on the merits of a college degree.

3. *Age and physical requirements.* A trainer's age probably has little consistent bearing on his ability to train. His physical features have even less. Therefore, you should avoid picking a trainer on the basis of either his physical attractiveness or his age.

4. *Work experience.* The most important qualification a trainer should possess is a good track record in past jobs. A successful teacher often is a good choice. Teachers have had the experience of dealing with students and will already know many of the techniques useful in the training situation.

If training is to be provided in a technical subject, expertise in that line of work will be helpful. You will then need to look for or develop the other qualifications that make a man willing and able to communicate this expertise to others.

Other work requiring a high degree of personal contact and ability to verbalize instructions will be useful. The further removed from actual experience in teaching or training the candidate's background, the greater will be his need for guidance from you and others on your staff.

5. *Professional stature.* Professional stature is defined as recognition accorded by members of a profession to the work and writing of an individual. In the case of a training person, professional stature may be judged by such items as opinions of the candidate's work held by other

recognized professionals, governmental recognition, number and quality of professional journal articles and books, honorary degrees, prizes and awards for programs, and influence of ideas on the work and writing of others.

RECRUITING TRAINERS

There are a number of standard channels through which trainers may be recruited. Whichever ones you choose, the process will probably be slow and you may have to review the credentials of as many as 50 or more applicants to find five or ten people who are well enough qualified to rate an interview. From these five or ten individuals you can probably select one or two suitable trainers.

One source of trainers is found among present company employees. The selection of an internal employee as a trainer, however, often presents a problem. Politics is a force in any organization. The larger the organization, the greater the scope of the politics. A good man may not be available to you simply because his boss will not let him go, even though policy condones his transfer or promotion.

The best approach to hiring trainers from within is to obtain approval from management before canvassing the company for interested and qualified individuals. Given this permission, the next task is to receive similar consent from the line managers whose groups you wish to canvass.

If an internal search fails to produce satisfactory candidates, you will need to search outside the organization. There are a number of approaches to this task.

Employees' friends and relatives. This avenue can produce some excellent results because present employees already know the firm's strong and weak points and therefore do not oversell their friends or relatives. However, some organizations do not permit the hiring of employees' friends or relatives; others encourage the practice. Be certain you are permitted to pursue this approach before you start.

If you choose this avenue, prepare a bulletin, or if your company is small, write a memo to each employee stating what type of person you are seeking and giving pertinent data on the job.

Newspaper recruitment advertising. Advertising placed in newspapers produces the greatest response. It also produces the greatest number of undesirable applicants. People with minimal qualifications or a passing interest in the field will apply. Your ad, therefore, should be designed to

POSITIONS OPEN

TRAINING SPECIALIST
Morse Shoe Company in Canton, Massachusetts has an opening for a Training Specialist. Morse is the world's largest operator of discount shoe departments with more than 600 outlets in the United States and Canada. An opening has been created for a training specialist. The major responsibilities of this individual would be to develop training materials, train line managers to use these materials and do some direct classroom type teaching. Training will be directed toward rank and file, frontline supervisors and junior executives. This is an opportunity for a person with limited experience to develop his own training function.

The individual we seek must have a college degree, with preferably a master's in business administration, education or psychology. He must have at least 2 years experience as a teacher or industrial trainer. He must know how to organize and prepare training materials including audio-visual materials.

Please submit resume and salary requirements to:

R.O. GLASER
MORSE SHOE, INC.
555 TURNPIKE STREET
CANTON, MASSACHUSETTS
02021

All resumes will be acknowledged and held in confidence.

Fig. 3-1. Model ad for employment.

save you later time in screening. Spell out in detail the qualifications you want in your applicants and fully describe the work they will be doing. It's not the quantity of responses that counts. Important jobs have been filled by a single good applicant.

If you want to maintain the confidentiality of your organization, use a box number for replies instead of a name. "Blind ads" make it possible to describe a position in more detail and give salary information, if that is desirable. When using a "blind ad," it is a courtesy to the members of your own organization to inform them of the ad in advance (otherwise one of your own staff members might send his resume to you!) and state in the ad itself that "our employees know of this ad."

Consider using newspapers in other cities and nationally distributed papers such as *The Wall Street Journal.* You will have the additional expense of bringing in applicants from a long distance; however, your recruitment base will be greatly broadened.

Magazines and journals. Magazines and professional journals offer another good recruiting tool. The ad in Fig. 3-1 was placed in two professional training periodicals and drew a large response. Other examples can be found by simply turning to the back pages of *The Training and Development Journal.*

There are two drawbacks to using periodicals for recruitment. First, you will incur extra expense in bringing in applicants for consideration and later relocation expense for the successful candidate. Second, depending how close to the publication date you place the ad, there could be a significant delay in receiving letters of interest from applicants.

Employment agencies. There are many types of employment agencies. Look for those that specialize in specific careers. Be certain that the agency has a clear picture of your needs or you will waste time interviewing marginal applicants. After each interview let the agency know how close to or how wide of the mark they came.

If your job is highly specialized, you will probably want to go to a "search" organization. This kind of agency charges a higher fee, but is often capable of producing better results. A search agency starts from scratch. It does not maintain a file of interested applicants. Instead it proceeds to look for a candidate after it has had one or more comprehensive interviews with you about the exact specifications of the job. It then does research, contacts a large number of people that meet your specifications, screens these potential candidates, and returns to you with two or three of the best qualified individuals. The appendices contain the name of an organization of the type described.

Professional societies. Professional training societies offer an excellent recruiting resource. Some local chapters even maintain a placement service for their members. Simply spreading the word that you have an opening is usually enough to bring some referrals.

Meetings of professional people are also productive of candidates. If the meetings are longer than one day, you can usually post notices around the meeting rooms. Some members attending these meetings are really job-hunting and will respond to your notice or refer a friend.

To capitalize on the meeting notices, rent a room in the hotel where the meetings are held and where your notices are posted. Publicize a time and room number where you will interview candidates or where they can reach you by phone.

Other sources. The above list of recruiting sources is by no means exhaustive. University placement offices maintain files on recent graduates. Public school and university teachers are sometimes dissatisfied with pay and lack of opportunity. In the spring of the year, after the receipt of a disappointing contract, they are more interested in making a change. The list of sources is limited only by your imagination.

Effective recruiting, incidentally, is usually the result of using more than one of the above methods. Your approach should be a buckshot approach rather than a rifle shot. Try newspaper advertising at the same time you are circulating your interest in finding a job applicant at a cocktail hour of a local professional society meeting.

TOOLS FOR SELECTING TRAINERS

No single selection method will prove adequate in your attempt to evaluate potential trainers. You are best advised to use a variety of selection methods which will help you view a candidate from a number of angles.

1. *Resumes.* The typical resume provides information about personal characteristics, work experience, and educational qualifications. It is an excellent tool for initial screening.

In reviewing resumes look for key items which match your job description. Also look beyond this minimum to ascertain the potential growth of the applicant. At its best, however, the resume is limited, since it will not answer the many questions about personality or depth of experience, and because it is usually slanted by the applicant to show his qualifications in the best possible light. If the resume does not adequately answer your basic questions about the candidate, you can send back a standard application blank and ask that it be completed. Application forms are usually organized around the key information you need for deciding whether you will investigate an applicant further.

2. *Telephone screening.* After sorting out the resumes of candidates that could conceivably fill the job, contact each by telephone and probe his qualifications further. If you are satisfied that the applicant is still a good candidate, invite him for an interview. The telephone screening of applicants can save time and money, especially if an applicant is from out of town.

3. *Interviews.* While these few lines are not meant to be a complete course in depth interviewing, here are a few sound principles to bear in mind in any interview:

a) Let the applicant do most of the talking. You can learn little about a man when you are speaking.

b) Describe some of the typical problems he'll encounter while working for you. Then sit back and let him tell you how he would go about solving them. The quality of his logic and perceptions will be a valuable selection guide.

c) Have more than one person interview a candidate. A single opinion is usually risky.

d) Allow at least an hour or two for an interview. Depending on the exact nature of the job, you may need longer.

4. *Placement tests.* Tests should be used as a supplement to other standard selection techniques, not as the sole criterion for preferring one candidate to another.

Both standardized and custom-built tests are useful. *The Wonderlic,* for example, is a test typically used by business and industry as a quick measure of mental ability. On the *Wonderlic* the minimum cutoff score for people being considered for personnel administration, including trainers, is 28.* This score reflects the number of questions answered correctly in 12 minutes. The score, of course, must be considered in light of the complexity of the job you are offering and other factors.

Earlier in this chapter, *The Predictive Index* was described as a useful tool for measuring personality factors in relation to job requirements. *The*

---

*E. F. Wonderlic, *A Cooperative Research Study of Minimum Occupational Scores* for *the Wonderlic Personnel Test,* Northfield, Illinois, 1966, p. 23.

Predictive Index and other personality tests must usually be administered and interpreted by a trained analyst.

Not all testing is standardized. If you wish to glimpse a candidate's ability to organize and communicate material, for example, devise a test with two or three problems such as the teaching of a simple card game, or the rewriting of a disorganized paragraph that is difficult to interpret. The results of this brief test will give you some insight into the applicant's thought processes. Simply posing a typical training problem and asking an applicant to prepare a written analysis and solution will provide you with some useful revelations of a man's ability.

5. *Review of previous work.* Often it is possible to review a potential trainer's previously prepared manuals, lesson plans, filmstrips, etc. Be certain, however, to relate this work to the quality standards you have established. You should also ascertain how much of the project was performed by the applicant and how much was performed by other staff members working on the same project.

6. *References.* It is fundamental employment principle that no candidate should be hired before you have investigated the statements he has made about himself. Most application forms provide space for several references, both personal and business; check these out thoroughly. You should have someone else's opinion on your candidate's work and personal habits to determine how he will mix with your present group.

References may be checked by telephone, letter, or personal visit. It is preferable to check references on staff people by telephone or personal visit, if possible. You will want to probe responses, try to sense shades of meaning in facial expressions and voice intonations, and assess the quality of the reference in terms of the individual giving it.

DEVELOPING COMPETENT TRAINERS

All trainers, newly hired or experienced, should have a plan for their personal, professional development. The following discussion offers some methods for working out this plan.

Developing a Plan for Professional Growth.

Developing a plan for training staff members is similar to developing a plan for any employee. It involves the following general steps.

Step 1. Decide what the requirements of the job are. Use the written job description as the basis for the answer to this question.

Step 2. Decide what qualifications the employee who will fill this job must possess. The employee and the training director should jointly make this assessment.

Step 3. Estimate what the foreseeable future requirements of the job may be, and decide how the employee's present qualifications stack up against these future requirements.

Step 4. Jointly prepare a written plan of professional development to bridge the gap between the employee's present credentials and present and future job requirements.

Step 5. Establish a timetable for this plan.

Step 6. Establish periodic checkpoints along the way to jointly assess progress or lack of it. Adjust the plan accordingly.

Methods of Implementing the Plan

The following discussion covers some of the typical methods for implementing a plan for a trainer's professional growth. The extent to which you use any one or all of these methods will naturally depend on the individual trainer's developmental needs, which you jointly assessed prior to putting together the plan.

1. *Professional reading materials.* Happily, the quantity and quality of professional journals and books on the subject of training are rapidly increasing. The appendices contain a list of books for the training director's bookshelf and a list of professional journals. The journals provide basic reading on current training problems. The books should be assigned as required.

2. *Seminars, workshops and conventions.* The professional growth of trainers occurs through both internal and external stimuli. A trainer confined to the four walls of his classroom and office, without breaks in his schedule, will soon become mentally dry and boring to his students.

You can provide outside opportunities for growth and motivation through seminars, workshops, and conventions. These outlets serve many purposes. Specifically they offer the trainer an opportunity to meet fellow professionals and exchange ideas, to be exposed to new ideas, and to see and discuss new training equipment with manufacturers.

Deciding when and to which seminar, workshop, or convention to send an employee is not an easy task. Every training director is subjected each day to tons of circulars from organizations hawking their wares. Here are a few common sense suggestions to help you in making a decision:

a) Workshops and seminars tend to be less social and more serious than conventions. If your purpose is to have a trainer actually learn a skill or acquire knowledge of significant depth, send him to either a seminar or a workshop.

b) Again, if you are concerned with the learning value of the experience, choose your seminar or workshop on the basis of the experience of past attendees or the credentials and known ability of those who will lead the seminar or workshop.

c) If you want the trainer to have maximum opportunity to exchange ideas with his counterparts in other organizations and to personally confront and solve problems, send him to a workshop. If you want him to be exposed to the thinking of experts, send him to a seminar where he will listen to lectures from outstanding people.

d) Require a written report on the seminar, workshop, or convention. This will force some examination of the content of the event.

e) Before the trainer goes, instruct him to engage his peers in conversation, visit nearby training installations, talk privately with the attending experts, etc. In short, tell him that you expect him to drain the most he can from the experience to justify the expense to the organization.

3. *Professional societies.* Professional societies such as the National Society for Programmed Instruction are useful developmental tools for trainers because they have local chapters which hold meetings and provide contact with other professionals, publish journals which afford the opportunity to read and write articles of current interest, and hold national seminars, workshops, and conventions.

4. *Training consultants.* Outside consultants are useful for providing specialized training or periodic stimulation to a training staff. Their assessments of your staff's abilities are often helpful for charting the future developmental plans.

5. *University courses.* Local universities may offer degree programs or individual course useful for a trainer. A semester course in instructional

television, for example, might serve as an excellent introduction to teaching with television if you are planning to install a videotape capability in your department. The advantage of university courses, assuming the quality to be high, is that greater depth of subject matter treatment is provided at a lower cost than is charged by commercial seminars, workshops, or conventions. State universities, of course, will be less expensive than private ones.

6. *Writing for professional books and journals.* Writing for professional books and journals affords a useful learning experience for the trainer. It forces him to research the materials already available, design learning experiments, crystallize his thinking, and sharpen his ability to handle the written word. All trainers should be encouraged to contribute at least an occasional article for publication.

7. *Special development tasks.* Every trainer should have built into his personal plan of development one or more special developmental tasks. These tasks should afford an opportunity to wrestle with training problems that are presently beyond the abilities of the trainer. They should be assigned and carefully monitored for their value as teaching devices. Suppose, for example, that a trainer has never had the opportunity to work with first-line supervision. He might be assigned the task of analyzing the training needs for a specific group of foremen.

8. *Informal on-the-job development.* Many of the trainer's routine assignments offer opportunities for informal on-the-job development. This can be built into conversations about training experiences, evaluations of training materials, discussion of articles and books, and countless other training situations.

9. *Videotape feedback for trainers.* One of the most useful applications of videotape is that which provides feedback to an instructor, showing him how he comes across to his trainees. The use of videotape is discussed in greater detail in Chapter 17.

10. *In-house train-the-trainer course.* The nine methods for developing trainers discussed above are not in every respect geared to the specific needs of your trainers. In order to get closer to the mark, you will need to develop and present your own course. Assuming you have the resources to present an in-house course, the following description offers some ideas on how you might go about it.

A train-the-trainer course has several objectives. Its primary intent should be to teach basic skills in analyzing and organizing a course, setting objectives, selecting and preparing media, and applying learning theory to training. While learning these basic skills, a trainer must also acquire the necessary platform technique.

More specifically, the objectives of a train-the-trainer course should include the following:

a) To improve the trainer's ability to motivate students in their studies.

b) To develop control of the language necessary to teach a given subject and communicate with a given level of student.

c) To help the trainer to organize lesson plans.

d) To expand a trainer's understanding of his role. The trainer must create learning experiences for the students and not stand by hoping learning will occur just because he lectures to them endlessly. A good trainer is an *arranger* of *learning experiences.*

e) To improve the trainer's understanding of learning principles. It is learning – not the lesson plan – that is the purpose of any training situation. Many trainers focus their whole attention on following the lesson plan and refuse to be shaken from this course regardless of the

Fig. 3-2. Train the trainer course schedule, first week.

First Day

Principles of learning as applied to training.

Second Day

How to analyze training problems.
How to develop learning objectives.
How to translate learning objectives into learning experiences.

Third Day

Basic verbal training techniques: lectures group discussions, conference method, simulation devices.

Fourth Day

Basic audio-visual techniques.
Preparation of flip charts, overhead transparences, and use of the opaque projector.

Fifth Day

Preparation and delivery of mini-lesson. Sample lesson to be videotaped and evaluated.

student's needs. A good instructor meets the needs of his students regardless of the variations from his predetermined plan.

f) To improve an instructor's platform habits. To many trainees the most distracting aspect of a learning situation is the manner in which an instructor conducts himself in front of the class. Some dress poorly, smoke cigarettes, mumble their words, and so on.

The format for a course embodying the above objectives will depend on the level of experience of the participants and your own resources. If you are starting from scratch with an inexperienced trainer or group of trainees, your comprehensive program should last a minimum of six months. In this period there would be sufficient opportunity to teach basic teaching skills, and their application, and to follow up on progress.

During the first two weeks of the course, training should be full time, eight hours a day, five days a week. In this period all of the basic training theories and techniques are taught. Topics for the first week of this course are listed in Fig. 3-2.

Fig. 3-3. Train the trainer course schedule, second week.

First Day

Basic techniques for motivating people to learn.
Application of these techniques to example learning situation problems.

Second Day

Test construction and other methods for evaluating learning.
Application of evaluation methods to typical learning problems.

Third Day

Policies and procedures governing classroom and equipment usage.
Training record keeping.

Fourth Day

Preparation of mini-lesson including methods for evaluating results, scheduling classroom and equipment, and completion of related records.

Fifth Day

Presentation of mini-lesson to sample student group. Later evaluation of results of trainer's efforts.

The second week of training should be a combination of classroom work and practice teaching. The objective of this phase is to monitor the new trainer's teaching efforts under actual classroom conditions, and to use the feedback from these experiences to improve and polish the trainer before he assumes his full-time classroom duties (Fig. 3-3).

At the completion of the two-week classroom training period, the trainer is ready for a classroom assignment on a provisional basis. To ensure proper professional growth, an on-the-job, six-month apprentice cycle should be constructed.

The six-month cycle is an arbitrary period designed to allow the new trainer an opportunity for full-time teaching under guidance, punctuated each month by one-day group meetings to discuss and reinforce what he has learned and how well he has applied this knowledge to his classroom work. Each month the apprentice trainer should be expected to show improvement in his teaching skills, platform habits, planning, and ability to handle individual student problems. If he fails to show improvement from month to month, it may be necessary to withdraw the trainer from the assignment and retrain him in fundamentals where his weakness has persisted, much as a baseball manager will remove a player from his lineup if he hits or fields poorly. Figure 3-4 shows a sample schedule for this six-month cycle.

Evaluating the Quality of a Trainer's Work

Evaluating the quality of human effort is always a difficult and uncertain process. The trainer's work is especially hard to evaluate because so much of it takes place out of the sight of the supervisor and because the results of these efforts are affected by so many intervening variables. Here are some guideposts to follow when evaluating your instructors:

1. Develop a formal program of evaluation. Carry it out periodically, preferably every six months.

2. Develop standards of performance for each element on the written job description. Measure a trainer's performance against these standards.

3. Communicate your evaluation program to your trainers. Be certain that they understand when and how they will be judged.

4. In general, you will attempt to judge an individual trainer's contribution to the organization's overall mission. Depending on the

Fig. 3-4. Train the trainer course schedule, six-month apprentice plan.

First Month

A new trainer is apprenticed to an experienced trainer. All training plans and materials are reviewed by the experienced trainer before being implemented by the apprentice trainer. Most of the apprentice trainer's classroom work is monitored by the experienced trainer. The apprentice trainer in turn observes many of the sessions conducted by the experienced trainer. Informal evaluations are held each day. At the end of the first month, the new trainer returns to the classroom for a full day of evaluation and review of the basic materials presented during the first weeks of his training.

Second Month

The support of the experienced trainer is gradually withdrawn during the second month. Most plans and materials, however, continue to be reviewed with the experienced trainer. At the close of the second month, a full day is spent in the classroom, but the time is divided between evaluating past efforts and learning/practicing new training techniques.

Third Month Through Fifth Month

The relationship between the new trainer and the experienced trainer should continue to weaken. Evaluations should be reduced to once a week. Monthly classroom critiques for the new trainer should continue but should emphasize new techniques rather than reviewing old. The new trainer should become increasingly more involved in the current work of the department.

Sixth Month

In the final month of the apprenticeship arrangement, the experienced trainer and and department head should make every effort to thoroughly evaluate the new trainer's strengths and weaknesses. A judgment should be made during this month to prorate the trainer to permanent status, continue apprentice training for a specified period of additional time, transfer the employee to another department, or sever the employment relationship.

mission of the organization, this may be calculated in terms of number of tellers trained, merchandise shrinkage reduced as a direct result of improved knowledge of procedures, number of district managers prepared to take over territories, and so on. Your judgment of an individual's overall contribution to an organization's mission is bound to be imprecise, but it is obviously an important exercise. The following approaches are less satisfactory, but useful, ways of getting some feel for the trainer's contribution to the organization's objectives.

a) Robert Mager has written an excellent little book called *Developing Attitude Toward Learning.** Mager explains that a teacher's ability to influence his students' future performance is in part a function of his success at sending students away from the learning situation with tendencies to approach rather than to avoid the subject matter of the instruction. Mager identifies many of the aversives and positives of the learning situation and the instructor's role in controlling them. One way of judging your instructors, then, is to assess the strength of their ability in developing in their students positive attitudes toward the learning of required training material.

b) While not specifically a measurable trait by so-called test standards, the ability and desire of an instructor to take a personal interest in the trainees' work, and his willingness to spend whatever time is necessary to teach or improve the trainees' effectiveness, will provide you with some insight into the trainer's competence.

Do not be deceived by the over-friendly "nice guy" whose motives in mingling with the trainees are purely social. The instructor's only role in the classroom is that of fostering learning. His personal involvements with the students beyond this should be kept to a minimum.

c) An outside consultant's opinion of a trainer's work is a valuable third-party opinion. The consultant has probably had experience in judging the work of a large number of trainers in similar situations.

d) Encourage a trainer to prepare a written evaluation of his work. He will probably be much more demanding of himself than you are. The self-evaluation affords the training director one more tool for arriving at a fair judgment of the trainer's work.

e) The students should be asked to evaluate their trainer during or at the close of each course.

f) If adequate preparation is made, peer evaluation, i.e., the evaluation of a trainer by his colleagues, can provide another dimension to a program of evaluation.

g) Chapter 2 discussed the training forecast as a program/budget planning tool. Individual trainers may be judged in relation to their role and contribution to the department's forecast.

---

*Robert F. Mager, *Developing Attitude Toward Learning,* Palo Alto, California: Fearon Publishers, 1968.

h) Figure 3-5 is an example of useful trainer evaluation form. This form can serve as a guide during the evaluation and later record to be used for developing a program for improvement.

The selection and development of a competent instructional staff will occupy a major portion of the training director's time. But as in any well-run and professional department, the benefits to the organization as a whole are incalcuable.

Fig. 3-5. Trainer evaluation form.

COURSE__________ OBSERVER__________

UNIT__________ TOTAL SCORE__________

INSTRUCTOR__________ DATE__________

TIME OBSERVED__________ ROOM #______ BLDG.______

NO. TRAINEES__________ KIND OF TRAINEES__________

Area	*Rating Scale* High 4	3	2	Low 1	*Remarks*
A. *Technical Analysis*					
1. Knowledge of Subject					
a) Theory					
b) Practical					
2. Knowledge of Lesson					
a) System					
b) Tools and equipment					
c) Latest technical changes					
B. *Communicative Competence*					
1. Use of Lesson Plan					
a) Sequence					
b) Continuity					
c) Variance from plan					
d) Need to refer					

(cont.)

Fig. 3-5 (Continued)

Area	*Rating Scale* High 4	3	2	Low 1	*Remarks*
2. Use of Materials					
a) Assignments					
1) Class problems					
2) Homework					
3) Textbook					
3. Student Involvement					
a) Motivational techniques					
b) Control of discussion					
c) Encourages individual					
d) Channels discussion					
4. Communication					
a) Empathy					
b) Simplifies complex concepts					
c) Use of correct technical terms					
d) Defines all new terms					
5. Use of Training Aids					
a) Techniques					
b) Effectiveness					
c) Variety					
d) Appropriateness					
C. *Managerial Competence*					
1. Control of Trainees					
a) Security					
b) Group control					
c) Individual student's control					
2. Environmental Control					
a) Ventilation					
b) Lighting					
c) Physical condition in room					
3. Testing Procedure					
a) Test qualities					
b) Test administration					
c) Use of test results					

Fig. 3-5 (Continued)

Area	*Rating Scale* High 4	3	2	Low 1	*Remarks*
D. *Personal Characteristics*					
1. Speech					
a) Audibility					
b) Clarity					
c) Pronunciation					
d) Mannerisms					
e) Vocabulary					
f) Voice inflection (pitch)					
2. Appearance					
a) Attire					
b) Grooming					
c) Bearing					
3. Behavior					
a) Relation with trainees					
b) Composure					
c) Punctuality					
d) Mannerisms					
4. Attitude					
a) Sincerity					
b) Tact					
c) Confidence					
d) Objectivity					
e) Enthusiasm					
f) Humor					
g) Humility					
h) Patience					

E. *Notes:* ____

____

____

____

____

4

Equipping the Training Department

Not long ago we heard about a new training director who took a tour of his facilities and came across a storeroom which he was told contained training equipment. Upon entering the room he was faced with several large cartons containing hundreds of penlight batteries. On the opposite side of the room was shelving containing more than a thousand cartons of teaching machines. Except for a few manuals the storeroom was otherwise empty. When he asked where the other equipment was, he was told that that was it. What the organization believed in and had invested in was clear in an instant. What, then, would be his course of action? Would he hurriedly write programs to fill the machines he already had? Would he damn the machines and go full speed ahead to the purchase of other equipment? Or would he make use of the machines where it made sense to use them and ignore them where it did not? Training directors often find themselves faced with this kind of equipment dilemma. The purpose of this chapter is to help the training director chart a realistic and effective equipment program. Like our training director in Chapter 2, your initial task is to survey existing equipment within the department and potential sources of equipment within the company. Quite often other departments such as public relations, advertising, or sales promotion have more equipment than the training department. In conducting this survey keep in mind that equipment as we refer to it in this chapter includes more than just audiovisual devices. All learning materials including printed media should be inventoried.

The inventory of equipment should be taken and recorded. The records should indicate the item by name, size, specifications, location in storage, and any constraints regarding its use, such as need to requisition

Fig. 4-1. Equipment inventory form.

Quantity	Item Description	Storage Location	Lamp Size	Lens Size	Weight	Comments

from a storeroom or to schedule use from another department. (See Fig. 4-1.)

All equipment available should be recorded in your inventory, but caution should be taken to ensure that only equipment which is usable is included in a working inventory. For example, your 16mm projector may in reality be a worthless machine, as old as electricity itself.

With an inventory in hand, you at least are in control of the existing situation. Your next step is to note where equipment may be purchased or rented locally. The best source of this information is the local telephone directory. For larger, more complex equipment you may have to turn to national dealers, but most local audiovisual distributors can tell you how to get in touch with these people if their services are required.

GUIDELINES

Equipment purchases, like all purchases, should be based on plan, not chance. The requisition of any device, whether it be a book, teaching machine, or 16mm projector, must serve an established need or it should not be purchased.

Course objectives and lesson plans, which will be dealt with in detail in Chapters 6 through 9, are, in effect, the "scripts" for the courses to be presented. These scripts can be used to help determine which medium is the most appropriate for the problem at hand. In such planning you will note that efficiency and effectiveness are often at odds because you normally have a limited training budget to accomplish your goals.

In considering equipment for training, it is interesting to note that most hardware has been designed and built for another purpose and later adapted to training uses. Most manufacturers have treated the design of equipment in this manner simply because the educational market has not been sufficient to support specially built equipment. As a consequence, the human factors aspects of equipment for training has often been neglected.

The prime emphasis should be on the needs of the student and not on the equipment. This is especially so when the equipment will be used in remote locations by laymen. For example, in a recent training problem associated with a fast-service food operation with over 500 locations, a rather elaborate filmstrip program was devised to teach basic work-station fundamentals. While academically sound, the project was a failure. Why? Because those responsible for training neglected to consider the reaction of the learner who worked in a remote location where the supervisor of the local restaurant was the instructor. No one wanted to take the time and trouble to set up and view the material in the busy work environment. The real solution was found in a completely different equipment format, which presented programed materials in small, compact, battery-operated teaching machines. Nothing had to be set up. The equipment could be used by individuals with no mechanical aptitude.

Keep in mind that you do not plan equipment for a single course, but for an entire organization's training needs. It is wise to consider developing a five-year equipment plan. In this way you can allow for the phasing out of obsolete equipment and the acquisition of new equipment as need and budget permit. Because improved models may be available at a later date, you should be sure to purchase only the equipment you require for immediate use.

Another factor to remember is that often we are swayed by glamorous new media like television, and are therefore induced to purchase a system when no educational or training need exists. Popularity or newness as such have no place in the wise planning and selecting of equipment.

Renting or leasing should be considered when the use of equipment is spasmodic or limited to one program. If you rent, you are usually given up-to-date models and relieved of maintenance responsibilities.

Equipment should be selected that is easily used by an average instructor. This equipment should have a minimum of adjustment devices and controls. You can build to more complex systems as both your program and your instructors grow in sophistication.

Component compatibility is another key factor. All components should be capable of being matched with other components to form a system. Mismatching can be costly. There are, for example, several low-priced, closed-circuit television units on the market today. While they perform as systems when all components are from the same manufacturer, the components of different manufacturers (i.e., cameras, recorders) are not interchangeable.

Other factors to consider in equipment purchasing are as follows:

1. Mobility.
2. Noise.
3. Heat problems, if used in confined areas.
4. Maintenance requirements.
5. Storage problems posed by sensitivity or size of equipment.
6. Complexity of operation (whether an expert is needed to operate).
7. Ease of repair.

Age per se is no more a factor in obsolescence in equipment than it is in human beings. Obsolescence occurs when the equipment can no longer perform the functions your program requires. There will be times when new equipment will be obsolete by your standards, whereas an old piece of equipment will work well. Be sure, however, to anticipate obsolescence in your five-year plan, and to ensure that budget funds will be available for replacement.

When considering equipment for purchase, look for the basic points outlined below. These points will help you to form a sound basis for your purchasing action.

SIX FACTORS TO CONSIDER BEFORE PURCHASING EQUIPMENT

1. *Obsolescence is inevitable,* but the fear of obsolescence should not prevent you from buying the equipment you need. The danger of obsolescence can be reduced if care is taken to purchase conventional equipment, leaving the more experimental equipment to be rented or purchased in a minimal quantity on a trial basis.

2. *Standardization and compatibility* are critical for the system's work and for interchangeability of the software. If you use different 35mm slide projectors, for example, you will need different cartridges. The loading of different slide cartridges can be time-consuming.

3. *Functional design* is important to all equipment. Proper placement of controls such as on/off switches is important for ease of operation. The mechanics for threading film and adjustment devices should be simple, especially if the equipment, such as videotape recorder, is new to your staff or will be operated by line supervisors. Start with simplicity; grow into complexity.

4. *Equipment change or expansion* of the system must be considered where more than one component is involved. Will you have space to accommodate future growth?

5. *Preparation of the facilities* is important. Do you have the necessary power to operate the lights or equipment you are considering? How about the acoustical properties of the room? Is the ductwork for cables adequate? Will it be in the future?

6. *Storage of equipment* is critical. Failure to provide a clean, humidity-controlled environment for equipment is like throwing money away. If you can afford the equipment, you should be able to find space to store it properly. Look for the space before you acquire the equipment.

TECHNICAL FEATURES OF EQUIPMENT

Buying equipment today is much like buying a car. We look for certain minimum mechanical standards, but we do not expect to dig too deeply into the pile of technical data available simply because we do not know exactly what to do with it. The training director, however, should consider the following basic technical features of a piece of equipment he intends to purchase:

Lamp size. Lamps vary both in size and quality. Different projectors require different lamps. Check the wattage as well as the cooling system. Is it adequate for your needs? Remember that sound projectors also have a second lamp in the exciter circuit of the sound system. Will it be easy to replace?

Lenses. The characteristics to consider are size, clarity of image, ease of focus, ease of changing the lens if necessary, focal length, and *f* stop. These last two require further explanation.

All lenses can be grouped into short lenses (wide angle) and long lenses (narrow angle). Long lenses are also called close-up lenses. The terms "short" and "long" refer to the *focal length.* A short wide-angle lens projects a larger, wider image by exaggerating depth and speed of movement toward or away from the camera. The long narrow-angle lens squeezes close objects up against distant ones, increasing the depth of field, but giving the illusion of less width.

Consult the table in Fig. 4-2 before buying a piece of equipment with a lens.

Fig. 4-2. Lens conversion chart.

Lens Size 35mm camera	16mm camera	Other	Purpose
35mm	12mm	1/2 in.	Extreme Wide Angle
50mm	25mm	1 in.	Wide Angle
75mm	—	—	Medium Lens
90mm	50mm	2 in.	Normal Lens
135mm	75mm	3 in.	Close-Up Lens

The lens diaphragm is used to control the amount of light that enters the lens. The *f stop* indicates the size of this opening. The lower the *f* stop, the wider the lens opening. Conversely, the higher the *f* stop, the narrower the opening. The *f* stop is set to control the light level entering the camera and to achieve a desired depth of field.

Controls. Common sense will tell you whether the equipment is easy to operate. Look for equipment that can be operated with a minimum of instruction. Most users ignore printed directions anyway. If the instructions are printed on the case of the equipment, all the better.

Check to see where the controls are placed. Are they easily accessible? Are they clearly labeled? Are they of sufficient quality so that they will not break with repeated use? Are the controls strong enough to withstand the day-to-day combat of the training situation?

Durability. What kind of wear will this piece of equipment receive? Are the case and the mechanism sturdy enough to withstand shipping? What will happen if the equipment is bumped or dropped?

To aid in forming your judgment of equipment, let us look at some of the salient features to consider in certain types of equipment you are likely to need.

Still Projectors (Filmstrips/Slides)

1. *Power of lamp.* Select a projector with the most powerful lamp you will need for your own projection room. Check to be certain that the projector has a fan if the lamp wattage is 500 or more.

2. *Picture brilliance.* Check the efficiency of the optical system by comparing the picture brilliance with that of other makes of similar wattage.

3. *Size of lenses.* Make sure lenses of different sizes are available and can be fitted. If you do not, you might find later that the projector is usable at only one distance.

4. *Slide size.* Make sure the projector can project the slides or filmstrips you own. Slide sizes are 2 X 2 (35mm), 2-1/4 X 2-1/4 (120 film), and 3-1/4 X 4 (lantern slide). Filmstrip size is 35mm.

5. *Protection of slides.* Check the mechanism which feeds the filmstrips or slides to be certain it will not scratch the material.

16mm Movie Projector

1. *Power of lamp.* One thousand watts is normal, 750 will do, but no less.

2. *Silence of operation.* Remember that the noise of most machines is distracting. Test the noise level before you buy.

3. *Portability.* Be certain the machine is designed to take the beating of being frequently moved if this is a requirement of your training situation.

4. *Sound quality.* Output is measured in watts; 10-15 watts is adequate for most tasks. You should be certain, however, that the volume is adequate for your rooms. For example, a large hall in a noisy area will require 15 watts.

5. *Lens.* A 1-1/2″ to 2″ lens is adequate for a room for 20 to 40 students. Large rooms require 3″ lenses.

6. *Magnetically striped film capability.* This feature is a great advantage as more and more commercial films are being produced in this format, to say nothing of the sound movies you can make with magnetic striping right in your own shop.

7. *Tone controls.* Separate bass and treble controls are desirable. Speech becomes clearer through a loudspeaker when the treble is high and the bass low.

8. *Other points.* It is a good idea to buy a projector that runs at 16 frames per second for silent projection and 24 frames per second for sound projection. To be able to reverse film is sometimes important. An extra microphone jack is useful. Self-threading is also helpful.

Tape Recorder

1. *Quality.* Unless you have a technical background, the quality of a tape recorder is hard to judge from the complex "facts" sheets most manufacturers publish. How it sounds to *you* provides the best guide.

2. *Repairs and maintenance.* The machine should be easy to service, and a good manufacturer's service organization should be available in your locale.

3. *Frequency response.* This means the "high" and "low" at which the machine will reproduce sounds more or less faithfully. The best nontechnical test is simply to record the various kinds of sounds you are likely to want, play them back, and judge for yourself.

4. *Ease of operation.* Most machines today have simplified their controls. But check to be certain.

5. *Speeds available.* The standard speeds of 7-1/2 and 3-3/4 inches per second (ips) are essential. Speeds of 1-7/8 ips and 15 ips are useful extras.

6. *Tape loading.* Check for ease of loading. Can you see the track? Does it use a cassette which is large enough for your needs?

7. *Braking system.* This is especially useful in a fast forward and rewind speed. It should stop the tape without breaking it.

8. *Inputs and outputs.* Microphone and amplifier inputs are essentials. Outputs for external speakers and amplifiers are also useful. Do you need a machine with multiple outputs?

9. *Tape reels and cassettes.* For most situations it is best to have a machine that has the capacity for at least a 7″ reel. This will give you about one to two hours of recording without changing tape reels. For cassette recorders it is essential that the size be compatible among all machines.

Overhead Projector

1. *Typical sizes.* 8-1/2″ × 11″ light table; 10″ × 10″; 7″ × 7″.

2. *Other points.* Look for ease of focus. How clear is the projected image? Check for a quiet cooling fan and easy access to the off and on switches so you do not fumble with this in use. You will find more information on what to expect from your machine in Chapter 14 "Overhead and Opaque Projection."

Opaque Projector

1. *Size.* It is best to buy a 10″ × 10″ size stage.

2. *Other points.* Is the projector overly bulky or heavy? How efficient and quiet is the cooling system? Ease of changing the lamp?

Record Players

1. *Quality in recordings.* Quality is measured in the reproduced sounds as we normally hear them. The more life-like the sound, the better the quality. For the human ear the range is 50 to 15,000 cycles per second. The best is 20 to 20,000 cycles per second.

2. *Formats.* Records are made in several speeds – 16, 33-1/3, 45, and 78 revolutions per minute (rpm), also in sizes from the 7″ 45 rpm disc to the 16″ 33-1/3 rpm disc. The player should be able to handle all of these formats.

3. *Controls.* For quality reproduction the system needs both treble and bass controls as well as a volume control. Easy access is necessary. A scratch filter is useful because it reduces the problem of surface noise.

4. *Tone arm.* It should have a variety of needle selections and tension control. Needle selection allows you to play the records at various recording speeds.

5. *Needle.* This is one of the most critical parts. All sound is reproduced through this point. Diamond is best; sapphire is next.

6. *Components.* Overall quality is a function of all components in the system. The amplifier should be capable of producing a strong high quality tone. The turntable drive motor should be quiet but of constant speed.

7. *Housing.* Most training functions require portability in record players. Be sure yours is in a strong case designed to take a beating. Unless you have a fixed installation it is not advisable to use separate components. Buy self-contained units.

Microphones

1. *Types.* Unidirectional is good for single person speaking; reduces extraneous sound pick-up. Bidirectional picks up two or more people, but also picks up noise in areas. Omnidirectional is good for group pick-up work, but has high noise pick-up.

2. *Plugs.* Match the plug type to your recorder or amplifier socket. Most new microphones do not come with a plug on the cord. This is a separate item.

Television

1. *Quality.* This is an extremely difficult problem in TV. The quality is often directly proportional to cost because price normally governs the quality of the components. Your best bet is to see the output of the TV system yourself. Is it suitable to your needs? How "grainy" is the picture? The higher the quality, the sharper the picture. A poor quality image, however, might not make a significant difference in your training results.

2. *Compatibility.* This is an important consideration if the components in the system must be interchangeable with equipment designed by other manufacturers. If components lack compatibility, then you must be prepared to live with a single, inflexible system.

3. *Camera.* How portable is it? How much light is required to shoot a picture? What is its adaptability to other equipment?

4. *Recorder.* Alignment problems are critical. Are the tapes interchangeable with another manufacturer's recorder or even with another recorder of the same brand? Many are not. Check the ease of

control. Adjustments should not be critical or complex. Weight should not be excessive.

5. *Tape size.* Some recorders are 1/4″-tape formats. Most are 1″ formats.

Screens

1. *Quality.* This is reflected primarily in the screen's surface and its housing.

2. *Types.* Several types of surfaces are available to serve different purposes:

a) Matte white screen – Useful when audience must be seated close to the screen. Here maximum resolution at a short viewing distance is important.
b) Glass beaded screen – Most economical type of screen. Projected image is bright, but grainy if viewed at a distance of less than 7 feet.
c) Lenticular silver screen – "Lenticulation" refers to the breaking up of the screen surface into many reflection surfaces to increase the effective viewing area on each side of the projection axis. Screen surface is silver-colored. Room requires less darkening. Color fidelity, contrast, and brightness of image are improved with this type of screen.

3. *Screen size.* There should be one foot of screen width for each five feet of viewing distance. For example a 60-foot classroom would require a 12-foot screen. Rear projection screen needs are 40% less than front projection needs. The type of screen surface will modify this formula slightly.

4. *Screen stands.* Ease of erection and dismantling is important. Screen reel holder should be of sufficient quality so that the mechanism will not fail when pulled.

Flip Charts

1. *Size.* The size of the chart should be directly related to the number of people who will typically view it and the distance this group will normally be away from it.

2. *Portability.* This is an important consideration if you expect to move the chart from place to place. If the legs are collapsible, it will be easier to store.

Demonstration Boards

1. *Size.* The size of the board should be related to the average audience size and typical distance this audience will be from the board.

2. *Portability.* This is relatively unimportant as they are normally in a fixed location. If you intend to travel with your board, you will need to consider its weight and size.

3. *Nature of the display.* This will determine the type of board construction you purchase. Hook and loop is used for three-dimensional objects. Flannel boards are preferred for light paper objects. Magnetic boards are used when you wish to be able to move an object across the board without having it fall off.

WHAT IS BASIC TRAINING EQUIPMENT?

Any answer to this question must be based on your department's training plans. Anything else is merely an educated guess. If we had to make such a guess and list basic equipment without regard to need, we would recommend the following items:

16mm sound projector
filmstrip projector
35mm slide projector
tape recorder
overhead projector
flip chart
projection screen

Quality and cost will be determined by your training needs and budgets, but we do not suggest that you buy low-priced equipment. You will not save money in the long run.

SOURCES OF INFORMATION

We have not listed the many and varied resources for equipment because they are too numerous. Rather, we suggest you consult the appendices for this information. Most training periodicals have extensive advertisements which are useful for locating sources of supply.

TESTING OF EQUIPMENT AGAINST CLAIMS

Testing of equipment is difficult to perform because most manufacturers fail to discuss the weaknesses of their products. To truly perform an analysis of the equipment's capabilities, you must start with the known facts presented in the manufacturer's literature. If you are lucky, you may find a chart in one of the magazines which lists all competitive models in a given equipment category. If not, make your own chart similar to the one illustrated in Fig. 4-3. With this you can record all the data and then make comparisons against your requirements.

Fig. 4-3. Audiovisual equipment comparison chart.

Item	Lamp	Lens	Audio	Weight	Size	Price	Comments

After you have narrowed your selection to two or three brands, it would be helpful if you could borrow these machines and actually test them against their specifications and your needs. As you know, you cannot always rely on the descriptions of a product. The actual item may be considerably better or worse than the claims for it.

Unfortunately, trainers often accept without question the advertising claims of a manufacturer as the true specifications for a piece of equipment. While manufacturers usually do not falsely represent their equipment, it is equally true that they may not thoroughly represent it. A television manufacturer, for example, may speak in glowing terms of the picture quality of his closed-circuit camera and include significant technical data to allow his camera to measure up to standards, yet never speak about the fact that the camera is usable only with his own receiver. As a consequence you will be led by the advertising to buy XYZ equipment simply because its specifications appear to be good. Your purchase should be the result of comparing equipment standards and specifications with your own training needs.

MANAGEMENT OF EQUIPMENT

Too often the function of equipment management is either ignored or given to an individual who "manages" the goods simply by locking them up when not in use. Neither is a solution to an important aspect of the training department's function.

First, you must recognize that the equipment in your department is often very expensive to acquire and not readily replaced when it fails to function because of maintenance problems. Perhaps more important is that failure to function when needed will cause considerable harm to a training program. Because most equipment is not tested or used except at the point of need, failures are not detected until the instant of need. The managing of equipment use, storage, and maintenance is therefore an important function.

Many times the control of all equipment is entrusted to an individual or system which is so strict that the potential users either shy away or are so frustrated that they use it only when it is mandatory. Control is important, but over-control is deadly to your primary objective of appropriate media usage in training programs.

Some points for effective equipment management are as follows:

1. One person should have the responsibility for the administration of the control function.
2. A system should be developed by the training director for the administrative control. Do not leave this function to a subordinate.
3. All equipment should (if practical) be stored in a single central storeroom area which can be locked.
4. All equipment checked out should be in working order and complete; all returned equipment should be checked in to be certain it is still in working order and complete.
5. The person in charge should know the whereabouts of all equipment after it is checked out.

6. Maintenance should be performed on a regular schedule, not at random or when a breakdown occurs.
7. Proper dust covers should be provided for all equipment.
8. Proper carts for equipment should be provided.
9. Adequate conditions for storage of all equipment should be provided. This is particularly important when humidity and air control factors may affect the condition of the equipment.

5

Managing the Learning Environment

One of the primary functions of the training director is to create and manage the environment in which teaching/learning activities take place. We have deliberately selected the term "environment" instead of classroom or meeting area because it carries a broader, more diversified meaning. Most people conceive of instruction as taking place within four walls in something called a school. We all know, of course, that learning may or may not take place in school, and certainly does take place outside of it.

Learning takes place in large public auditoriums, at home while watching TV with the family, at practice fairways, while reading a journal article, and so on. Salesmen for one company are trained in lavishly furnished railroad commuter cars; stitchers are trained amid the noise and confusion of a shoe factory. An IBM service representative receives training as he works alone on a programed textbook. The training director has the responsibility for arranging and managing whatever environment is appropriate for the teaching/learning activities required to perform a given organizational task.

The notion that learning must take place in a conventional classroom is deeply embedded in our thinking. Historically the teacher was one of the few people in the American villages who owned books. He needed a place – a schoolroom – where he could stand before a group and read these books aloud. This was a very practical consideration, but one that can no longer be supported. Yet the concept of the teacher-oriented classroom with pupils in rows is still the departure point when the locus of training activities is considered. We always begin any planning of a learning environment by projecting a classroom situation and working away from it, or at best, adapting it to a few audiovisual aids.

The training director himself is often guilty of thinking in terms of the public school or college instructional setup. He sometimes aspires to become a principal or a dean like his academic counterpart, presiding over a group of cubes and the staff members who teach in these cubes.

Management is also guilty. It thinks of training in terms of traditional classrooms and caps and gowns. When members of the management team think of places where management development takes place, they think of a cube with walnut paneling and upholstered chairs. The trappings may change but the cubes always remain. A training director who tries to arrange things differently has some hard selling ahead of him. Furthermore, the classrooms frequently become corporate showplaces.

And, finally, the students have been conditioned over the years to expect the four-walled classroom as the place where they will be taught. If an organization does not have a classroom in the traditional form, it doesn't really do any training that is worth talking about, or so the thinking goes.

But if we discard the notion of the traditional classroom as the only place where training/learning activities can take place, what then is the training director's responsibility? Very simply stated, the training director's job is to create an optimal climate for learning. This will not happen by accident, and it may not happen by recreating the traditional classroom. The trap most training personnel fall into is that they accept the classroom as they accept the 16mm movie projector. They build their programs around existing facilities and equipment rather than arranging the facilities and equipment to fit the particular learning task. The usual result is too little learning for the organization's investment.

We have already looked at training from an economic point of view. Let us zero in a bit more and look at meetings (a vehicle for training) from an economic point of view. Take for example the $30,000-a-year executive who spends 60 percent of his time at meetings. He is an $18,000-a-year meeting man, according to an article in a journal called *More Effective Meetings* by Minnesota Mining and Manufacturing Company.* A top management meeting that runs six hours may represent in terms of salaries alone an investment of about $6000. A single national sales meeting may run up costs in excess of $75,000, not counting time lost from the job. Clearly the cost of meetings – of training time – is an important factor to consider. The training director has a considerable responsibility to create the most effective environment for meetings that he can.

---

*B. Y. Auger, "Meetings: an essential management tool," *More Effective Meetings*, Winter, 1968, pp. 2-4.

Recent designs for improving learning environments have begun to move away from the four-wall concept. Even the names of these places have changed – learning centers, educational centers, communications centers, multimedia classrooms, learning resource centers, etc. In many cases, however, the space has simply been redesigned to accommodate built-in audiovisual equipment. And while this may be a step away from the four-wall concept, it still misses the key consideration of developing the space to mesh with the educational philosophy and objectives of the people and programs using it.

THEORETICAL CONSIDERATIONS IN THE DESIGN OF LEARNING SPACE

The training director should give the following points general consideration in creating optimal training environments. Many of these considerations were suggested in "The Summary Report Working Papers" of the 10th Annual Lake Okoboji Audiovisual Leadership Conference, 1964.*

1. The determination of educational philosophy and objectives must precede a design for learning space.
2. For efficient learning it is necessary to provide for rapid reinforcement of desired behavior when it occurs. An example of one kind of reinforcement is provided in programed instructional materials which verify or correct a response immediately.
3. Space should be flexible so that it can be used by an individual learner or by groups of learners of varying sizes.
4. Space must be designed so that it provides for a choice of materials, media, subjects, or achievement levels.
5. Space should be designed so that supplementary information is easily and quickly accessible. For example, it should be close to library facilities.
6. Learning spaces should provide for the control of the significant physical comfort variables, both for comfort reasons and to enhance specific learning situations.
7. Learning environments should provide for social interaction.
8. Learning spaces should not be geared solely to audiovisual equipment needs.

*Sponsored by the Department of Audiovisual Instruction, NEA and The University of Iowa.

9. Learning environments should be only as complex as necessary to handle predetermined learning tasks. They should, in other words, be constructed as simply as possible.
10. Learning space should be designed with future needs and equipment changes in mind insofar as possible and in keeping with present objectives.
11. Architectural design must follow function. The general design of training facilities must be geared to the known communications problems.
12. Select or design a learning environment to handle its greatest potential problems, numbers of users, etc.
13. Use folding units for as many purposes as possible, including folding partitions, tables, and chairs. Store these items on hand trucks for maximum portability.

PRACTICAL CONSIDERATIONS FOR PERMANENT FACILITIES

The following items must be considered by the training director whether he is simply managing his present space or planning for remodeling or new space.

1. *Room shape.* Room shape need not be square or rectangular. Triangular rooms have been found to be superior acoustically and less expensive to construct. Room shape should be dictated by the purpose to which a particular space will be put.

2. *Placement of doors.* Rooms should have more than one exit. Doors should be on noiseless hinges to prevent disruption of learning activities. Openings should be wide enough to accommodate large pieces of equipment. A double door may be in order if the room is frequently used for projection purposes.

3. *Concealment of audiovisual equipment.* Concealing audiovisual equipment keeps it safe from dust, damage, and theft. Built-ins always give the room a better appearance.

4. *Storage space.* Plan double what you think you will need. It will be used for tables, chairs, equipment, and materials.

5. *Security.* Design the room so that it can be locked to safeguard equipment and supplies. We once heard about a retail store training department that had registers for training purposes in the classroom. These registers had to be kept locked to prevent the theft of registered sales checks which could be later used to get stolen merchandise out of the store.

6. *General decorating.* The decorating scheme should neither add nor subtract anything from the general atmosphere. The trainee's attention should not be distracted by decorative additions to the room.

7. *Floor covering.* Carpeting should be investigated for its noise, cost, and decorative factors. It may cost far less, for example, to maintain than tile.

8. *Acoustics.* Noise is a relative factor. Noise that is disturbing should be eliminated. The sound of a projector, for example, may be disturbing. This may be eliminated or reduced by constructing a projection booth, buying or building a blimp, or buying better equipment.

a) Noise from projection booths will be best reduced if the port is covered with a plate glass window. The glass will have no effect on image quality as long as the angle of the projection beam is not more than 15 to 20 degrees off the perpendicular.

b) Some projector noise can be reduced by using a lens of longer focal length and setting up the projector behind the viewers rather than in their midst. (See Fig. 5-1.)

c) A blimp is an open-bottomed box that is set over a projector to reduce the noise. Directions for constructing an inexpensive one can be obtained from Kodak Corporation.

9. *Ventilation.* A ventilating system should be capable of changing the air in a training room once every one to one-and-a-half minutes, depending on the latitude of the locality. Your building engineer will be able to tell you what the system is equipped to handle.

10. *Room blackout facilities.* Complete blackout is no longer required because of the improvements in projection equipment; nonetheless you will need some way of reducing the light. Occasionally light switches are left out of the room and located elsewhere so that it is inconvenient to even turn off the lights, let alone darken windows.

11. *Utilities.* Be certain to plan for future equipment outlets and other facilities.

12. *Telephone service.* Avoid having telephone service if at all possible. Rest assured that people in the organization will not hesitate to call the instructor or members of the class during training, even for foolish reasons. If you must have a telephone, it should be equipped with a beehive light and a bell cutout. In that way you will be able to ignore it if you choose.

13. *Sound systems.* You may need a public address system or an amplified speaker's lectern if your room is too large for normal speech to be heard by everyone. Extension speakers should be placed high enough to be seen by everyone. If the speaker can be seen, it can probably be heard. If there are two speakers, one can be placed at the front and the other part-way toward the back of the room.

14. *Cork boards, chalk boards, and flannel boards.* Display boards can be used for walls or portions of walls. A sliding panel arrangement can be created so that more than one material can be used on a given wall area at a time.

15. *Lighting.* Most lighting systems will be fluorescent because of cost. Care should be taken to replace flickering or dim tubes because of the distraction they cause. Lighting intensity is expressed in foot-candles and varies, depending on the illumination required for certain kinds of work. An engineer will be required to help you work out these values. Dimmers should be available. Lighting controls should be easily accessible to the speaker or trainer so that he can manipulate lighting changes with a minimum of distraction from his teaching task.

16. *Communication between trainer and assistants.* There should be a simple electronic communications system between the trainer and others assisting him in the training room.

17. *Tables, desks, or writing pallets.* Consideration must be given to work space. Most meetings require tables. Usually a table 30 inches wide is best. Widths of 18 and 24 inches are also standard. Lengths vary from 60 to 96 inches.

18. *Chairs.* Folding chairs embodying the following ten features are recommended by *Training in Business and Industry**:

a) Ash receivers with removable interiors for washing.
b) Comfortable curved backs and padded seats.
c) Seat locks to keep chairs from folding accidentally.
d) Quick gang clamp so you can couple chairs in a row.
e) Nonskid feet.
f) Washable upholstery.
g) Stacking for easy storage.
h) Detachable tablet arms.
i) Correct seat heights for every use.
j) Protective surface treatment against abrasion and corrosion.

19. *Name-card holders.* Simple name-card holders should be available if the group contains more than five members.

Fig. 5-1. Projector lens focal length chart.

	Width of screen (inches)					
Lens focal length (inches)	40	50	60	70	84	96
1-1/2	13 ft.	17	21	24	30	34
2	18	23	27	32	39	44
2-1/2	22	27	33	38	46	53
3	26	33	40	46	55	63
3-1/2	30	37	45	54	62	72

20. *Location of projectors.* Lens focal length was explained in Chapter 4. The focal length of your projector's lens determines where the projector must be placed in relation to the screen. By choosing the correct lens focal length, you can control where you place your projector. The tables presented in Figs. 5-1, 5-2 and 5-3 will help you decide what focal

*Reprinted with permission from the article "A good chair," which appeared in the issue of *Training in Business and Industry,* April, 1967, © MCMLXVII Gellert Publishing Corp.

Fig. 5-2. 2 × 2 slide projector lens focal length chart.

	Width of screen (inches)				
Lens focal length (inches)	40	50	60	70	84
3	11 ft.	14	17	19	23
4	15	19	22	26	31
5	19	23	28	32	39
6	22	28	33	39	47
7	26	32	39	45	55
8	29	37	45	52	62

Fig. 5-3. Overhead projector lens focal length chart.

Distance from screen (feet)	Width of image (inches)
6	33
12	66
18	100

length to choose based on the size of your screen and where you want to locate your projector.

The lens on an overhead projector is fixed. The image is increased or decreased in size by moving the projector toward or away from the screen. One recent model has an electric focusing mechanism, making it unnecessary to move the entire projector.

21. *Eliminating the keystone effect.* The keystone effect occurs when the image projected on the screen is wider at the top than it is at the bottom. This can be eliminated by leaning the screen forward at the top or backward from the bottom or a combination of the two. To be completely free of distortion, the plane of the screen must be perpendicular to the beam of light from the projector. A metal extension screen hanger can be used to lean the screen forward.

22. *Selecting the correct screen size.* Most of the time a projector is simply wheeled into a room and an image is thrown up on the screen. Little if any concern is given to the projector's distance from the screen, the focal length of the lens, the type of projector, or the type of screen. Yet to achieve the best results – everything that has gone into the film has been done for the moment of projection – care must be taken to coordinate each of the above variables. In Chapter 4 the three basic types of screen surfaces were identified. Radiant Manufacturing Corporation has published a very helpful booklet on selecting screens. The title of it is *Audio-Visual Guide to Better Projection.* Whether you are considering a permanent installation or not, the sections dealing with screen type and size selection are worth reading.

23. *Rear screen projection.* Rear projection can often be used to solve viewing problems that could otherwise not be solved by ordinary screen projection. Rear screen projection is accomplished by placing the projector in front of the audience with a translucent screen in between. The advantages of rear projection are that any size room can be used and a picture of maximum size can be projected. The viewing room need not be darkened. Running the machinery is a noiseless operation. Figure 5-4 shows a diagram of rear screen projection setup.

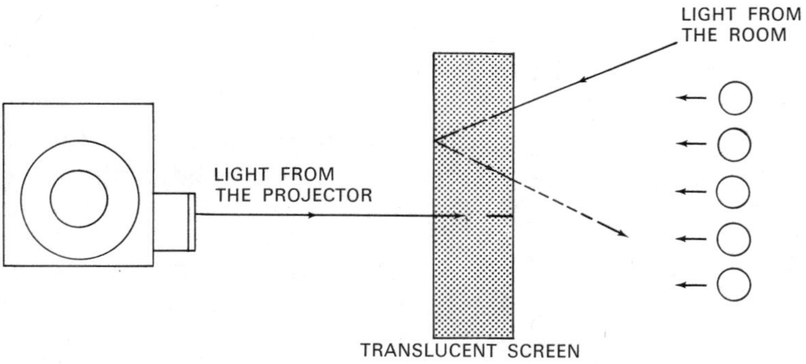

Fig. 5-4. Set-up for rear screen projection.

Compact rear screen setups which use mirrors and do not require projection rooms behind the screen are also available (Fig. 5-5). These screens are highly portable.

In large corporations there is the danger that you may not be consulted when training areas are planned or remodeled. You will want to have a strong voice in anything that affects the learning environment

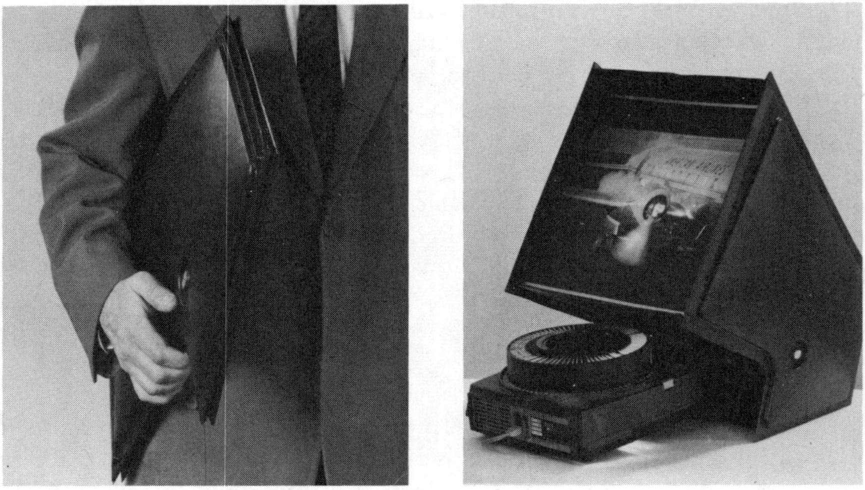

Fig. 5-5. Caritel ® portable rear screen projection cabinet. (Courtesy Hudson Photographic Industries.)

inasmuch as its construction directly affects the success of your training program. The above items offer some guidance as to what to consider and perhaps study further.

HOW TO DESIGN ROOM ARRANGEMENTS

The following are five basic room arrangements that will help you get the most out of your environment.* Obviously these arrangements can be modified to suit your specific requirements.

Arrangement A. Auditorium style arrangement for 20 or more people at 12 or more tables (Fig. 5-6). This is useful for a lecture or similar presentation when a projector is used.

Arrangement B. A U-shaped arrangement for 12 to 20 people using six tables (Fig. 5-7). This arrangement is useful for guided discussion meetings because no one has his back turned on anyone else. There is plenty of work space for the participants. Quick delivery of handout materials by the leader can be accomplished by merely walking around the inside of the U.

*Arrangements A, B, and C are reproduced from "The effective meeting," pp. 6-7 with permission of Automatic Retailers of America Services, Inc., Philadelphia.

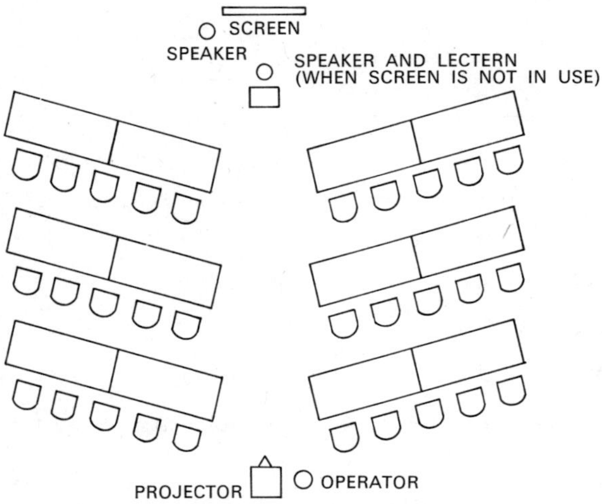

Fig. 5-6. Auditorium-style seating arrangement. (Courtesy ARA Services, Inc.)

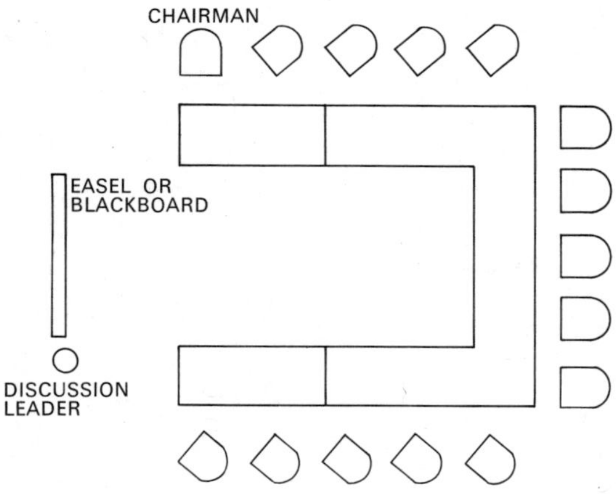

Fig. 5-7. U-Shaped seating arrangement. (Courtesy ARA Services, Inc.)

Arrangement C. This is a conference table arrangement (Fig. 5-8). It is useful for both guided discussion and straight lecture presentations. It is good for small groups. If the projector is used, it will have to be of the rear screen variety.

Arrangement D. This is a room utilizing individual learning carrels (Fig. 5-9). Each man has in effect his own classroom where he works with self-pacing materials.

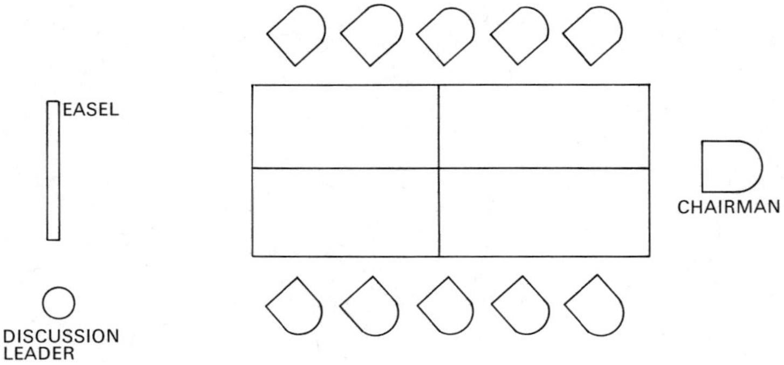

Fig. 5-8. Conference seating arrangement. (Courtesy ARA Services, Inc.)

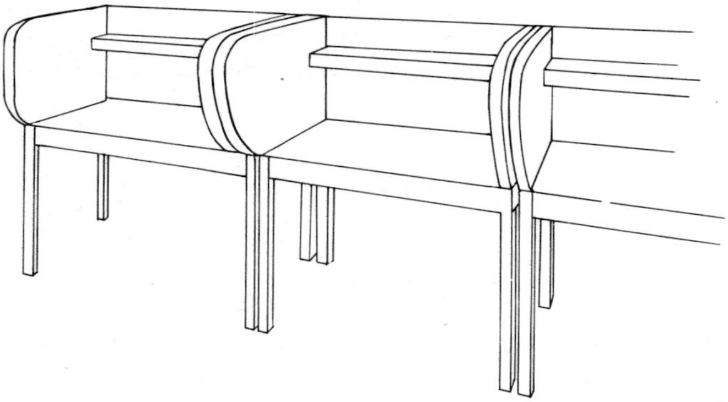

Fig. 5-9. Seating arrangement using individual learning carrels.

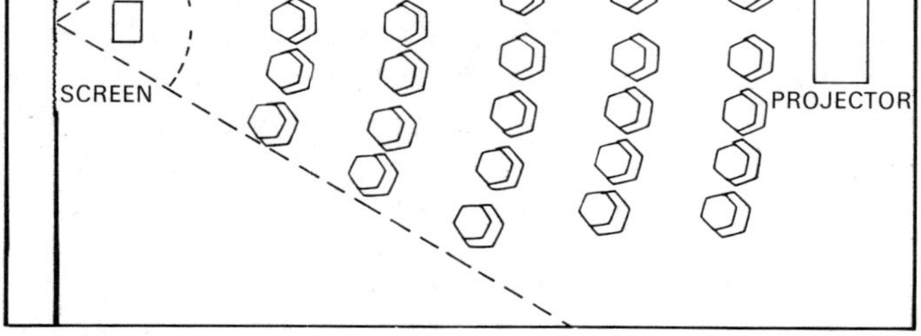

Fig. 5-10. Auditorium seating for viewing screen.

Arrangement E. This is a typical auditorium seating arrangement which offers good viewing from any chair position (Fig. 5-10). Note that the type and size of the screen will add or subtract seats.

Brunswick Corporation has published a useful free booklet called "How to Set Up An Effective Training Room." It may be obtained by writing to Brunswick, 2605 E. Kilgore Road, Kalamazoo, Michigan 49003. The booklet briefly discusses the elements of a good training room, ending with a checklist and a graph for you to use in laying out a room to meet your organization's training/learning requirements.

THE TRAINING CENTER

So far we have discussed the characteristics of a satisfactory training room. A learning environment, however, is much more than a meeting room or a group of meeting rooms. The following is a partial list of the kinds of teaching/learning activities that take place in training space and must be taken into account in the design of the learning environment. This list was compiled by members of the 1964 Iowa Lakeside Laboratory.

Production activities. This includes the production of photographic products, graphics, three-dimensional materials, radio and television, instructional systems, and printing and duplicating.

Distribution activities. Storage of books and printed materials, nonprojected visual materials, cartographs, projected materials, programed materials, supplies, equipment. Utilization areas including listening stations, viewing areas, inquiry stations. Work areas including library workroom, shipping, materials inspection and maintenance. Service areas including checking in and out, and operator instruction.

Consultation and instruction. Individual, small group, and large group.

Demonstration and display. Individual, small group, and large group.

Information processing and control. Data processing, information storage and retrieval, and research.

Evaluation. Developmental testing of methods, materials, and facilities.

Administration. Staffing, budgeting, records, etc.

All of these activities and many others take place in the learning environment. The job of the training director is to take them into consideration when he plans the utilization of his learning space. As can be easily seen, these activities require more than a single room or group of rooms with similar characteristics. The trend now is to the construction of learning or training centers. The examples shown in Figs. 5-11 through 5-14 illustrate the conglomerate of teaching/learning activities translated into architectural design.*

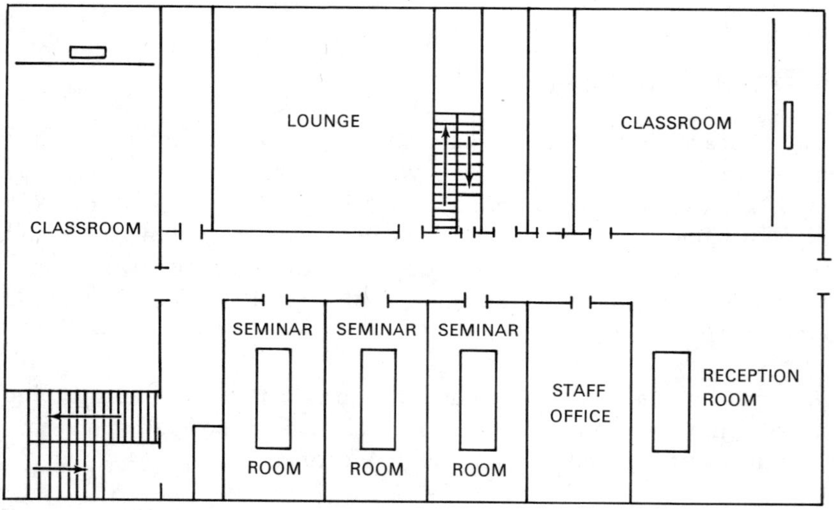

Fig. 5-11. Multipurpose training facility.

These illustrations of sophisticated learning environments will probably cause you to wonder about and envy those corporations that have committed enormous resources to their construction and maintenance. Such environments of course did not happen overnight. They grew out of management's interest and understanding of the need for optimum learning from the training it felt necessary to provide its employees. Their purpose has not been to create a flashy way to display corporate sophistication, but rather a recognition of the complexity of the

*Figures 5-11, 5-12, and 5-13 were presented in an issue of *Audiovisual Instruction* devoted entirely to the "Instructional materials center: philosophy, facilities and design." Vol. 12, No. 8, Oct. 1967, pp. 788, 789 and 809. (Used with permission of *Audiovisual Instruction*)

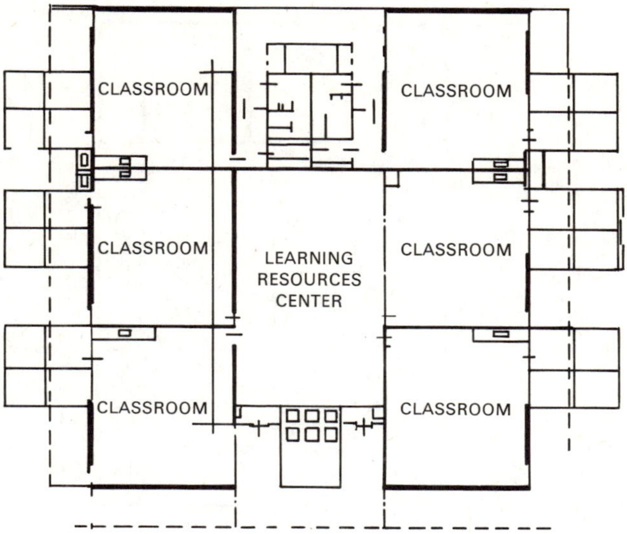

Fig. 5-12. H-plan. Learning resources center with three classrooms on each side. (Courtesy *Audiovisual Instruction.*)

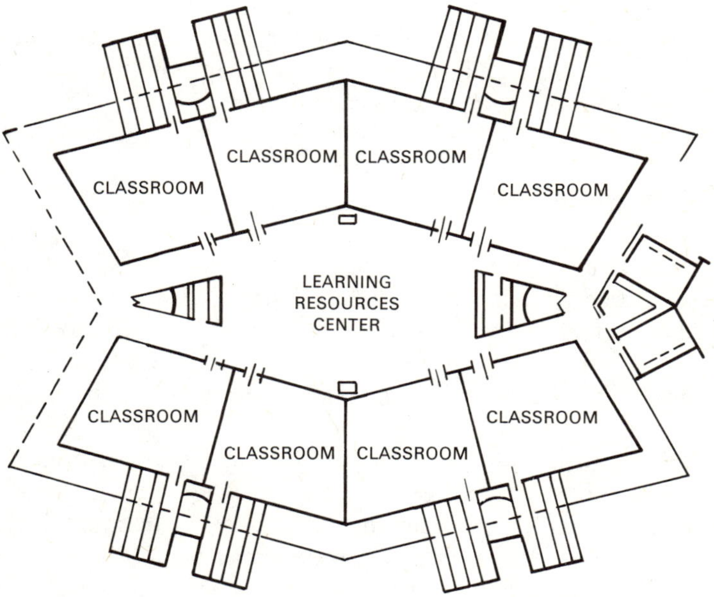

Fig. 5-13. Lantern plan. Learning center surrounded by eight classrooms. The center itself may be divided into two units, depending on the program. (Courtesy *Audiovisual Instruction.*)

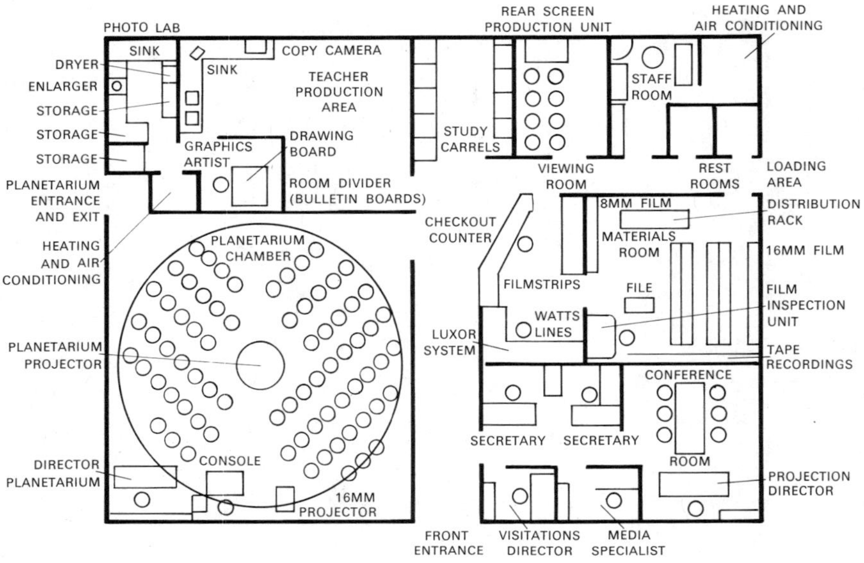

Fig. 5-14. Southwest Iowa Learning Resources Center. (Courtesy *Audiovisual Instruction.*)

requirements of the effective training environment. The appendices contain a list of architects and companies who can assist you in the planning of a single room or complete learning center.

RENTING TRAINING SPACE

The creation of permanent training quarters must be considered and justified like any other important and costly business decision. Suppose you do not have enough use for space or it is too costly to bring employees in from other parts of the country for training. It is always possible to rent space in a hotel or motel or other places with training accommodations.

The advantages to using outside facilities include isolation from the office, ample parking, food services, and so on. There are also some disadvantages; for example, the meeting rooms themselves are often poorly designed for training. The sleeping rooms may be poorly arranged for evening study. The meeting room may need to be cleared of furniture or equipment at the close of each day if other meetings are scheduled for the evening. Chairs and tables may not be of good quality.

If you are planning to use hotel or motel facilities you will need to check the following before committing yourself to a location.*

1. How many students must be registered to get a special rate if there is one?
2. How quiet are the living quarters if it is intended that they will be used for study?
3. Do the rooms have suitable desk space, a chair, and lighting?
4. Is the air conditioning or heating adequate for the weather expected?
5. Are adequate eating facilities available?
6. Are there adequate outlets and extension cords for your audiovisual equipment?
7. Can the hotel/motel supply you with easels, projectors, or other audiovisual equipment?
8. Is a public address system available and in working order?
9. Will a rigid lease or contract be required?

The Butler Training Center in Kansas City has brought together the best of two worlds.† Its personnel has persuaded a motel in the city to build a wing onto its facility and lease it back to the company for a training center. In this way employees have the use of the living facilities of the motel and use of an adjoining training center which meets their special requirements. When the center is not in use, it is rented to other companies to help defray the expenses of operation and maintenance.

GENERAL MEETING-ROOM CHECKLIST

Before any training session you or someone on your staff should check the area to be certain that the minimum requirements have been met and that the room is in fact ready for the participants. The following checklist could be duplicated and used as a guide for whoever conducts the inspection.‡

*Martin M. Broadwell, "Bed and Board for Training," *Training in Business & Industry*, Vol. 3, No. 7, July, 1966, pp. 36-39.

†"Butler Training Center," *Training in Business and Industry* Vol. 5, No. 3, March 1968, pp. 32-33.

‡George Gill, "Elements of a successful meeting area," *Film and A-V Annual*, 1966. (Used with permission *Film and A-V Annual*)

Meeting-Room Checklist

1. Physical Environment
   a) Air-conditioning in operation?
   b) Seats cleaned and operating?
   c) Room cleaned?
   d) Ash trays, water glasses and pitchers?
2. Display Media
   a) Blackboard. Is it clean with chalk and erasers?
   b) Are easels set up and in good order?
      Crayons or other markers ready?
   c) Flashlights or pointers ready for speaker?
   d) Exhibit and display materials on hand with sequences checked?
3. Projection Equipment
   a) Plugged in and tested?
   b) Focused, framed and leveled, using actual materials?
   c) Spare lamps and fuses on hand?
   d) Lenses clean?
   e) Sound system tested with loudspeakers in place?
   f) Communication system with projection room tested?
4. Power Requirements
   a) Provision for room or area darkening?
   b) All equipment tested on existing outlets?
   c) Extension cords in place so no one will trip over them?
5. Lighting
   a) Can audience take notes during projection?
   b) Has glare been eliminated?
   c) Provision for additional illumination if necessary?

Your inspection of training facilities will become more detailed and more thorough depending upon the elaborateness of the preparation that has gone into a given meeting. The Gellert Publishing Company publishes a bimonthly magazine, *Meetings and Conventions,* devoted entirely to helping the meeting and convention planner run a successful show.* The following checklist prepared by a major motor lodge corporation will help you keep track of hundreds of important details if you are charged with the responsibility of running a convention or other large meeting which will be attended by people from distant locations.

*For more information, contact 3M Company, St. Paul, Minnesota, 55101.

Checklist for Convention Preparations

I Preliminary Planning

1. Meeting objectives defined?_____
2. Subjects to be discussed?_____
3. Who will attend?_____
4. Size of group?_____
5. Type of presentation?_____
   Assigned speakers only_____
   Seminar_____ Panel Discussion_____ Group Discussion_____
   Workshops_____ Multiple-location (videotape, closed circuit TV)_____
   Question-and-answer period_____
6. Arrival date?_____ Time?_____
7. Departure date?_____ Time?_____
8. Meeting agenda developed?_____
9. Social agenda developed?_____

II Selection of Meeting Facility

A. General

1. Clean and appealing?_____
2. Conveniently located?_____
3. Good transportation?_____
   Bus, taxi or limousine service from airport to facility?_____
4. Checkout time?_____
   Can special checkout arrangements be made?_____
5. Easy, free parking?_____
6. Billing arrangements understood?_____
7. What items may guest charge?_____

B. Meeting Room Facilities

1. Number of rooms needed?_____
   For general sessions?_____
   Smaller sessions?_____
2. Individual room controls?_____ Air conditioning?_____
   Heat?_____
3. Floor plan furnished?_____ L._____ W._____ H._____
   Door sizes?_____ Obstructions?_____
4. Seating arrangements desired:
   Conference_____ Theatre (auditorium)_____ School room _____
   "U" shape_____ Head table?_____ Number of persons?_____

5. When can room be set up?_____
   For morning meeting_____ For afternoon meeting_____
   Will lodge staff be available to assist?_____
6. Schedule of all meetings provided to motor lodge?_____
7. Room rental?_____
8. Display area?_____
9. Restroom availability?_____
10. Checkroom facilities?_____

C. Equipment Needed

1. Projection equipment?_____
   35mm_____ 16mm_____8mm_____ Super 8mm_____
   Slide_____ Filmstrip_____ Overhead_____
2. Tape recorder?_____
3. Blackboards?_____
   Chalk_____ Flannel_____ Magnetic_____
4. Chart stand?_____
5. Public address system?_____
6. Lectern?_____
7. Screens?_____
8. Easels?_____
9. Other: Chalk_____ Erasers_____ Masking tape_____
   Scissors_____ Pointer_____ Blackout drapes_____
   Extra cords_____ Name badges_____ Place cards_____
10. Special lighting?_____
11. Platform?_____

D. Visual Aids Needed

1. Film_____ Slides_____ Transparencies_____
2. Tape?_____
3. Material for board presentation?_____
4. Chart pad?_____
5. Charts?_____
6. Display cards?_____
7. Work books? _____
8. Meeting kits?_____
9. Product samples?_____

E. Sleeping Room Accommodations

1. Number of rooms needed?_____
   Single_____Doubles_____ Suites_____
2. Room rates?_____

3. Clean, comfortable rooms?_____
4. Individual controls_____ Heat_____ Air Cond._____
5. Written confirmation received?_____
6. Date uncommitted rooms are to be released?_____
7. Hospitality rooms needed?_____
8. Preregistration of delegates?_____

F. Meal Service

1. Dates and times?_____
2. Breakfast?_____ Luncheon?_____ Dinner?_____
   Receptions?_____ Coffee breaks?_____
3. Menu selections?_____
4. Price per plate (Including tips and taxes)_____
5. Total number to be served?_____
6. Head table?_____How many persons?_____
7. Place cards for head table?_____
8. Minimum guarantee?_____
9. Liquor policy?_____ "By the drink"?_____
   "By the bottle"?_____ "Selected liquors"?_____
   Complete bar?_____
10. Reception: Appetizers to be served?_____
11. Coffee breaks? A.M._____ P.M._____

III Speaker and Other Guests

Invitations sent?_____
Reservations confirmed?_____
Arrangements made to greet them on arrival?_____
Transportation provided?_____

A. Speaker

1. Has speaker been notified of his allotted time?_____
2. Are financial arrangements clear?_____
3. Photos and biographical information available for publicity and introduction?_____
4. Will speaker require special equipment?_____

IV Publicity

1. Newsworthy releases prepared? _____
   Advance releases_____ On-spot releases_____
   Follow-up releases_____
2. Photographer needed?_____

3. If appropriate, have newspaper, radio and TV people been contacted?_____
4. Introductions prepared for head table?_____
5. Introduction list for other than head table?_____

V General Items

1. First notice of meeting mailed? Date_____
2. Follow-up notice sent? Date_____
3. Registration desk needed?_____
4. Special announcement sign in lobby?_____
5. Directional signs elsewhere? _______
6. Credit card and check cashing facilities?_____
7. Special union requirements (if any)?_____
8. Florist – special decorations?_____
9. Will minutes of meeting be taken?_____

VI Checklist – Prior to Meeting

Checkroom facilities opened?_____
Check operation of lights_____
Proper seating arrangements?_____
Enough seats?_____
Cooling/heating system operating?_____

A. Equipment Set Up and Operating Properly

Projectors_____ P. A. system_____
Recording equipment_____
Lectern (check light)_____
Special lighting (if any)_____
Chart stands_____ Easels_____
Blackboards_____ Pointer_____

B. Material Properly Distributed

Water and glasses_____
Ash trays_____ Matches_____
Pencils_____ Note pads_____
Flowers_____

Arrangements made to take telephone messages?_____
Special decorations properly set up?_____

A new wrinkle has been developed by 3M Company called the Jet-ference. The Jet-ference is a meeting center a few minutes from the airport, designed to eliminate the waste of time executives normally experience when they attend conferences. The 3M airport meeting center has special meeting rooms complete with all types of communication equipment and secretarial services. The Jet-ference makes the one-day fly-in /hold meeting/ fly-out schedule more convenient.*

A COMPLEX TASK

The managing of the learning environment is a complex task involving many variables. It goes far beyond the checking of housekeeping and ventilation. An old college professor from the education school used to talk to prospective student teachers about "managerial manipulation." He illustrated his remarks by adjusting the shades or raising and lowering the window. Management of the space where people learn is a far more demanding task than that. We recently talked with an employee of a famous round building in Hollywood where the rooms are all pie-shaped. He complained of a chronic disorientation because of the unorthodox room shape, a disorientation which kept him confused every evening for the first few moments after leaving the office. The rest of his world was rectilinear except for the nine-to-five world he lived in five days a week. Effective as the triangular classrooms are from the audiovisual standpoint, the designers may well need to consider the ultimate effect of the triangular shape on the psyche of a student living in a generally rectilinear world. The point again is that learning space problems are not simple and, in fact, offer the training director one of his more significant challenges.

*See Appendix.

Part 2

Developing a Strategy for Training

Part II is devoted to an identification of some of the basic conceptual skills needed by training personnel in their day-to-day work. These skills range from a knowledge of learning theory to an understanding of the techniques used to evaluate the diverse and complex outcomes of training programs.

6

Learning Theory Applied to Training

The relationship between the scientific study of learning and the practical problems of training is often a matter of debate. There are those who argue that "theorists" are not much help when it comes to solving the real problems connected with training, and there are those who take a different position by insisting that good training ultimately depends upon a knowledge of learning. Both positions in the debate are partially correct, but neither side is sufficiently correct to settle the matter. Theories of learning seldom, if ever, provide direct answers to the kinds of questions asked by instructors, and laboratory studies of learning do not usually apply directly to the classroom or to the shop. However, training is a set of procedures to facilitate learning, and any serious consideration of the techniques of training cannot ignore the study of learning.

The debate and the dilemma arising from it can be avoided if we seek to recognize the limited role of theories of learning and the potential contribution that principles of learning can make to the problems of training.

The discussion that follows comes from the view that the processes of learning and training depend on each other. The discussion is organized around four topics: (1) the fundamental processes of training, (2) theories of learning and their relationship to training, (3) the principles of learning produced by theories and research, and (4) principles of learning and techniques of training.

---

*This chapter was prepared by Dr. Robert E. Silverman, Chairman, Department of Psychology, New York University, College of Arts and Sciences.

THE FUNDAMENTAL PROCESSES OF TRAINING

It should be noted that processes are not techniques; process refers to something more general and technique refers to something quite specific. For example, guiding behavior is a process; guiding refers to a general set of procedures, not to a specific procedure. On the other hand, the use of animated transparencies or the use of role playing is a specific technique. Ultimately the trainer wants to know about techniques, for these are his basic tools, his bread and butter. But to concentrate on techniques without understanding something about the underlying processes is to drive the car without knowing it has a motor. Techniques of training are more useful and more flexible when the user understands processes of training. It is true that common sense and experience are the basis for some successful techniques, but usually the application of these techniques is limited. If these same techniques are related to processes of training, there is a good chance their application can be extended to a wider variety of problems.

The training technique of role playing is a case in point. Role playing was originally devised as a therapeutic technique to enable emotionally disturbed patients to "act out" their problems. This application was followed by a similar application to leadership training, where it was used to help potential leaders confront different types of situations. As people began to recognize the relationship of role playing to a fundamental principle of learning, the principle of learning by doing, role playing became an increasingly useful tool in a wide variety of training situations.

The processes of training are classified here into four groups, with three groups dealing primarily with the task of getting learning to occur and the fourth dealing with maintaining learning once it has occurred.

Guiding and Reinforcing

All learning requires activity on the part of the learner; the learner must ultimately make the responses he is being trained to make. A better way to say that is – the learner learns what he does. Therefore a basic condition of training is seeing to it the learner can make and does make the appropriate responses.

There are a number of ways to get the learner to make the appropriate responses, but very often it is done by direct guidance or prompting. For example, the learner is shown the appropriate response and told to copy or to imitate it. He is then given informative feedback, indicating to him whether his response was correct. A less direct and sometimes more effective form of guidance involves arranging the conditions of learning so as to make the appropriate responses likely and then to reward the responses when they occur. For example, in teaching someone to operate a piece of machinery, the conditions might be arranged so that the machine remains locked until the trainee makes the appropriate response or series of responses. When he responds correctly, perhaps to a signal of some sort, the machine goes through the first stage or cycle of operation; when he again responds correctly, perhaps to a second signal, the machine goes through the second stage and so on. A correct response results in something happening; when the machine operates, the trainee's responses that led to this are strengthened. Seeing the machine operate successfully is for most trainees, a form of feedback that also serves as a reward. This reward tends to strengthen the correct responses. This strengthening process is known as reinforcement.

In practice both informative feedback and reward feedback are used because both are involved in the process of reinforcement. The role played by feedback depends on how it is provided. If a trainer provides feedback by saying, "Good; you did that one very well," he is probably giving information and a reward. If he merely says, "That's right. Notice the manner in which the gear moved when you gently pressed the lever," he is providing information but much less in the way of reward. However, there is probably still some reward here for trainees who delight in being correct and who do not need to be told regularly that they are "doing well."

Telling or showing a trainee that he is wrong is also an informative type of feedback. However, this type of feedback contains no reward function, and its information depends on how much direct guidance is given to show the trainee why he was wrong and how to correct it.

An analysis of the process of guiding and reinforcing leads to the conclusion that informative feedback is crucial. Another way to put this is to say that all training requires that the learner receive feedback regarding the correctness or incorrectness of his responses; learning cannot proceed unless the learner has knowledge of results. This applies whether the training concerns the operation of a machine, the acquisition of a vocabulary, or the making of management-level decisions. A furthur analysis leads to the conclusion that reward feedback may or may not be crucial, depending on the motivation of the learner. In most cases reward feedback keeps the learner interested in learning, and therefore it is a basic consideration in training.

Association

All the processes of training involve finding ways to ensure that the appropriate responses are made at specified times on specific occasions. In other words, we want the learner to make the correct responses at the right time and in the right place. It is of little value if a trainee has learned to define "margin" but does not use the term properly when talking to a brokerage client.

Getting the correct responses to occur at the right time and place involves the process of association. Through the process of association a learner comes to link the appropriate responses with the appropriate environmental situations. These situations are usually referred to as stimuli, and many writers (see S-R theories below) refer to stimulus-response associations. By means of association, a trainee is taught to say or write "oscilloscope" when he sees an oscilloscope. The piece of equipment – the stimulus – cues the response of saying "oscilloscope." It is the process of association that enables the student to recognize the word "arduous" as a synonym for the word "hard," or the word "chien" as the French equivalent for the word "dog."

Most training situations require that trainee make discriminations among stimuli. This is done by means of controlled associations in which particular stimuli and responses are associated with each other in the presence of some form of reinforcement. For example, the technician trainee learns that when the red light is on he should move lever "A," and when the green light is on he should move lever "B," because a movement of lever "A" to the green light produces no result and a movement of lever "B" to the red light produces no result. The correct association, however, produces the desired result, thus reinforcing that association. In this same way, the sailor learns the difference between "port" and "starboard," the golfer between a wood and an iron, the driver between the red traffic light and the green traffic light, the broker between a "put" and a "call." These and much more complex discriminations are developed through the process of association and differential reinforcement in which a particular stimulus is associated with a particular response, and the response is reinforced and another stimulus is associated with another response and that response reinforced.

Discovery

The processes of guiding and reinforcing and of association are often controlled by the trainer; the learner is a receiver and plays a less active role than would be the case if he were encouraged to discover the correct responses himself. Discovery training differs from guiding because the learner is encouraged to come up with responses without being shown or told. Actually the process of discovery training is on a continuum with guiding. The process of guiding sees to it that the learner makes the correct responses initially. In discovery training the learner is relatively free to find solutions to the problems presented, but the discovery process does not preclude guiding. This process is almost always used in some combination with discovery. This is especially true in training students to solve problems. If a trainee is learning to trouble-shoot malfunctions in TV sets using the discovery process instead of being given rules, he would be asked to find them for himself. He may be given hints or prompts if he needs them; the more of these he is given, the more the process becomes one of guiding.

The process of discovery training is an important one in any consideration of retention. Material learned by means of discovery is more meaningful to the learner, for it fits into his own knowledge structure and is better retained. A good example of this is found in learning a formula such as the Pythagorean theorem (the square of the hypotenuse of a right triangle is equal to the sum of the squares of the two legs of the triangle). The student who discovers this formula after he has been given a number of examples retains it better than one who is merely given the formula to use.

Practice and Application

The acquisition of knowledge does not guarantee the retention of the knowledge, nor does it ensure the effective use of the knowledge. Retention and transferability (availability for use) depend on the amount and kind of practice the learner engages in. Retention also depends on the degree of meaningfulness of the material learned.

To ensure retention and transferability, the material must be practiced in a wide variety of situations with particular emphasis placed on situations likely to recur. The more varied the situations the more useful and transferable the learning will become and the better it will be retained.

Overpractice, that is, practice that goes beyond the normal practice requirements, is important in novel tasks. When a task is very novel and unfamiliar, extensive practice is usually an effective means of establishing the learning and insuring that it is retained.

THEORIES OF LEARNING AND THEIR RELATIONSHIP TO TRAINING

Theories of learning are concerned with the "how" of learning. The learning theorist seeks principles to explain how learning occurs. In constructing a theory the theorist goes beyond the facts and creates an organization of principles to bridge gaps in our knowledge and to generate new knowledge.

A theory of learning is a systematic set of guesses about the nature of learning. These guesses are based on observations and on laws of learning linked to each other by the theorist to produce a coherent picture of learning. We say the theory is a good one if it is useful, if it gives rise to predictions that are found to be correct.

Learning theories can be classified into two groups, the stimulus-response (S-R) theories and the cognitive theories. The two groups overlap at points, but it is easy to distinguish one from the other because they emphasize different features of learning.

S-R Theories

The S-R theories are derived from the work of Pavlov in Russia and E. L. Thorndike in the United States. They are referred to as S-R theories because they typically represent learning in terms of changes in association between stimuli and responses.

The simplest of the S-R theories, although the simplicity may be illusory (Hilgard and Bower, 1966), is that of E. R. Guthrie. Guthrie's contiguity theory is based on a single principle stated as follows: "A combination of stimuli which has accompanied a movement will on its recurrence tend to be followed by that movement." (Guthrie, 1935, p. 26) This is the basic principle of learning by contiguous association between stimuli and responses. According to Guthrie, once a stimulus has been associated with a response, the stimulus will thereafter elicit that response. The key to teaching is seeing to it that the proper stimulus is associated with the proper response without any interference from competing responses.

Guthrie paid little or no attention to the problem of rewards. He held the position that we learn not as a consequence of reward but as a consequence of making responses in the presence of stimuli. We learn what we do and we learn by doing. If you want to know what a person is learning, look at what he does. This is certainly not an elegant theoretical principle, but it is good advice and Guthrie's writings are filled with other homilies and maxims that are well worth reading.

The most elaborate and highly developed of the S-R theories of learning is Hull's theory (Hull, 1943). This theory makes use of the work of Pavlov in conditioning and Thorndike in "trial and error" learning.

Two of the key concepts in Hull's theory are habit strength and drive.* A habit is a permanent connection that develops and is strengthened each time a stimulus and response are associated, if their association is accompanied by the reduction of some drive. For example, a child learns to find candy under a round box because the stimulus, the round box, is associated with the response, lifting the box, and this is accompanied by a reduction of the hunger drive that takes place when the candy is eaten.

This theoretical postulate dealing with the strength of habits contains the basic associational doctrine of Guthrie and it stems in part from Thorndike's theoretical principle referred to as the "law of effect." The "law of effect" states that a modifiable connection between a stimulus and a response is strengthened when the association between them is accompanied by a state of affairs satisfactory to the organism. Hull did not talk about "satisfaction." He spoke instead about the reduction of bodily needs and the consequent reduction in drives. For Hull, learning depends on association and drive reduction, with drive reduction being the basis of reinforcement. Hull's theory is a reinforcement theory, and when a Hullian refers to reinforcement, he is usually thinking about drive reduction. Contrast this position to Guthrie's, where no reference is made to reinforcement.

B. F. Skinner (1953) represents a major school of thought within S-R psychology. It is more appropriate to refer to Skinner as a systematist rather than a theorist because he has really founded a system rather than a theory. His system relies on descriptive behaviorism and the concepts of stimulus, response, and reinforcement. However, the reinforcement concept is defined in nontheoretical language: A reinforcer is any stimulus that strengthens responses that lead to it. Anything that increases the likelihood that responses will occur may be regarded as a reinforcement. Food, praise, money, a nod of the head, a smile are all examples of possible reinforcers. No mention is made of such theoretical notions as drive reduction.

Skinner distinguishes between two types of learning, respondent and operant. The respondent type is classical conditioning, described originally by Pavlov. The key feature of this type of learning is the pairing of two stimuli, the conditioned stimulus and the unconditioned stimulus, in such

*Drive has two functions in Hullian theory. It participates in the development of habit strength each time it is reduced, and it operates to energize existing habits. A hungry person is more active (up to a certain point) than a satiated one, and his hunger will serve to energize everything he does.

a way that the conditioned stimulus comes to evoke a response similar to that evoked by the unconditioned stimulus. Pavlov demonstrated that a dog could be conditioned to evoke the response of salivating by pairing the sound of a bell (conditioned stimulus) many times with food (unconditioned stimulus). Food naturally evokes salivation and the bell came to do so as a result of conditioning.

The operant type of learning is, for Skinner, the more important type, insofar as it bears on complex forms of learning. This type of learning requires that a response lead to a reinforcement. An *operant* is a response that *operates* on the environment to produce reinforcement. In operant learning (often referred to by others as instrumental learning), the emphasis is on arranging situations so that the response to be conditioned is appropriately correlated with reinforcement. This is a basic feature of the system of programed instruction developed by Skinner in terms of the operant learning model.

Skinner's system lends itself well to application. In fact, his system has been developed with an eye to application. It is a kind of behavioral engineering in that it constantly seeks ways to control and modify behavior. Because it is application-oriented, the system is attracting the interest of many persons engaged in teaching and training.

Cognitive Theories

The cognitive theories include those derived from Gestalt psychology. Theories in this group are closely related to each other with each of them emphasizing perception and perceptual processes. Cognitive theorists take the position that learning is a change in perception. Their basic question is, "How has the learner's perception of a situation changed?" While S-R theorists emphasize response and stimulus-response association, cognitive theorists emphasize the processes whereby the stimuli are differently perceived.

The foremost Gestalt psychologists, Wertheimer, Kohler, and Koffka, were less directly interested in learning than in perception, but these men exerted strong influence on Kurt Lewin and E. C. Tolman, who were interested in learning. Lewin's theory (1942) makes use of the Gestalt concept of "field." The "field" is likened to a magnetic field or an electric field in which the key property is the dynamic one: every part is dependent on every other part. As learning occurs, the "field" changes and the learner behaves differently because he perceives the stimulus situation in a different way. This change in the "field" comes about quite suddenly, and when it does, the new behavior emerges quickly in an "insightful" manner. A favorite field-theory example is found in motor skill learning, where the act cannot be done properly until the learner "gets the hang of it," that is, until he perceives what it is he has to do. A person may work at learning to swing a golf club and seem to be making no progress when quite suddenly he finds (perceives) the correct muscular relationships and does it correctly.

Another cognitive theorist, E. C. Tolman (1932), attempted to combine parts of cognitive theory with aspects of S-R theory. Tolman's theory is often referred to as purposive behaviorism, following his own emphasis on goal-directed behavior and his attention to the details of stimulus and response. According to Tolman the learner's activity is always directed toward some goal. When he learns, he does so by finding what leads to what. He develops a "cognitive map" of his environment. If a response is followed by a reinforcement, a cognition is produced, that is, the learner perceives that making the response will lead to reinforcement.

On the surface Tolman's theory appears to be a useful compromise between S-R and cognitive approaches. Furthermore, many are attracted to the theory because it makes use of language and ideas that are familiar to the layman. However, the theory has not lived up to its advance notices, and it would be a mistake to conclude at this time that the theory is a good one. Theories are good if they are useful, if they explain existing facts and give rise to answerable questions. It would seem that Tolman's writings fall short of both goals, in spite of the fact that his ideas are promising.

The foregoing account of theories of learning indicates areas of disagreement among theories and groups of theories. These disagreements are often a source of confusion and misunderstanding for persons whose primary concern is the practical problem of training. They ask, "Who is correct?" and "What theory shall I accept?" These questions should not be ignored, but they cannot be satisfactorily answered in the form in which they are asked because many of the disagreements among the various theories are not relevant to the problem of training. Most of the disagreements concern matters that are not related to the everyday problems of training and teaching, and where the disagreements are related to training the difference is one of emphasis rather than kind. For example, Guthrie emphasizes the stimuli that evoke responses, and Skinner emphasizes the reinforcers that strengthen responses. Hull emphasizes reinforcement, but his concern is with how reinforcers operate. Lewin's emphasis is on relationship among stimuli. He and Tolman want to know what the learner perceives and what he comes to understand. These differences in emphasis may lead to different methods in the study of learning, but they need not and generally do not lead to different methods of teaching and training because there are many principles on which the various theorists agree; and these principles can provide useful guidelines for the teacher and trainer.

USEFUL PRINCIPLES OF LEARNING

The nine principles discussed below are useful generalizations, and while there may be an occasional dispute, most of these principles are acceptable to representatives of the theories described above.

1. *The learner learns what he does.* This principle comes directly from Guthrie and is endorsed by most investigators of the psychology of learning. In use this principle directs the trainer to arrange the conditions of learning in a way that will enable the learner to make the correct responses early in the learning situation. The first impressions are often the most lasting. Therefore, it is important to see to it that the learner does not mistakenly learn the wrong responses.

This principle is easy to follow in practice when the processes of guiding and reinforcing are used, but it is more difficult to follow under conditions of discovery learning. The learner who is encouraged to discover solutions will frequently make mistakes, and it is the trainer's job to ensure that mistakes do not persist. This advice is more easily given than acted upon. Training by means of the process of discovery runs the risk of perpetuating mistakes, but it also allows the learner the opportunity to gain reward by solving something himself. The decision as to whether to take the chance that learner mistakes will interfere can only be made when the trainer is in a position to determine how well the learner can overcome his errors and how rewarding the process of discovery is to him.

2. *Learning proceeds most effectively when the learner's correct responses are immediately reinforced.* This is the principle of reinforcement without the theoretical trappings of Hull's drive reduction concept. This principle directs the trainer to arrange the conditions of learning so as to provide the learner with immediate feedback each time he responds. In line with the discussion of the process of guiding and reinforcing presented above, the feedback should always be informative and should be rewarding where possible. For example, a trainee learning to read a stock exchange ticker tape might be given a set of 15 symbols to learn by having the symbols presented to him one at a time. Each time he responds correctly by identifying what the symbol means, he is told he is

correct. If he makes an error, he is told the correct identification. When he has identified five successive symbols correctly, he is told he is doing well. Telling him that he is correct or showing him the correct identification provides information; telling him he is doing well provides reward. In this example, the reward is a comparatively minor one. The stronger reward will be his finding that he is learning and is on his way to taking his place in the brokerage office. However, minor rewards can play a useful role in applying immediate reinforcement, for they serve as a kind of subgoal in place of later and larger goals that cannot be represented in the immediate learning situation.

The principle of reinforcement suggests questions about the use of punishment in training. It is generally held that learning proceeds best when the consequences of the learner's actions are positive rather than negative. The direct use of punishment or the threat of punishment is often a tempting technique, but on close analysis it appears the technique is inefficient and in the long run undesirable. Punishment may help to suppress incorrect responses, but the suppression is often temporary and the emotional consequences of punishment can be disruptive to learning. No learner, whether he is an adult or a child, an executive or a trainee, likes to be told he did poorly or that he should be doing better. Even such mild rebukes can be detrimental because they may focus the learner's attention on what he should not do rather than what he should do, and they can lead to a desire to get out of the learning situation entirely. Learning is work, often hard work, and learners of all types seek rewards for their efforts. The evidence indicates that the use of reward for correct responses and nonreward for incorrect responses is more effective than the use of punishment.

3. *The frequency with which a response is reinforced will determine how well the response will be learned.* Practice does not make perfect, but reinforced practice helps in that direction. This principle needs to be qualified because the number of reinforcements (informative and/or reward) does not infinitely increase the strength of a learned response. In practice this principle directs our attention to the schedule or pattern of reinforcements as well as to the number of reinforcements. With a continuous reinforcement schedule a reinforcer is given for every correct response and with intermittent schedules only some of the correct responses are reinforced. The intermittent schedules generally lead to the learner's making responses for each reinforcing event. Furthermore, once reinforcement stops altogether, responses that were intermittently reinforced tend to persist longer than those that were continuously reinforced.

The relationship of reinforcement schedules to training is an interesting and an important one because questions about the permanence or maintenance of training are related to schedules. The evidence indicates that in general it is best to use a continuous schedule early in training and then to shift gradually to one or another form of intermittent schedule in order to maintain the response at a high strength. To illustrates the use of this principle, consider the example of an assembly line worker learning to use a gauge to make precise measurements. In the beginning each of his measurements is checked, and he is given feedback as to the accuracy of this measurement. Gradually the feedback is changed from continuous to intermittent, and finally his measurements are merely spot-checked. This procedure tends to maintain his accuracy at a high level, whereas a procedure in which he was trained with continuous checking and then not given further checking may well result in a reduction in the measuring skill because he had learned to rely on continuous feedback and had not been prepared to work without it.

4. *Practice in a variety of settings will increase the range of situations in which the learning can be applied.* Furthermore, such varied practice will make the trainee more resistant to forgetting.

Systematic research has shown that knowledge is generalized if it has been learned and used in a variety of situations. Material learned in one situation is often limited to that situation, but learning that has been associated with many situations is more easily transferred from one situation to another.

Psychologists distinguish between positive transfer, in which training in one situation benefits training in another situation, and negative transfer, in which training in one situation interferes with training in another. The trainer should be aware of the conditions promoting each type of transfer and be able to ensure positive transfer when it is desirable and guard against negative transfer where it may occur.

Positive transfer occurs when the responses learned in one situation are the same ones to be used in a different situation. For example, the transfer of training would be positive in going from driving an automatic transmission automobile to learning to drive a nonautomatic transmission truck. Many of the responses in the two situations are the same.

Negative transfer occurs when the stimuli in situations are the same, but the responses called for are different. For example, there is negative transfer in learning to drive an automobile in the U.S.A. and then trying to drive an automobile in England, where traffic moves on the left rather than the right side of the road. Many of the stimuli that the driver sees are the same in the two situations, but certain fundamental responses are different. Each time he turns a corner he must keep to the right in the U.S.A., but in England he must make the opposite response of keeping to the left. In this case, old learning interferes with new learning, giving rise to negative transfer.

5. *Motivational conditions influence the effectiveness of rewards and play a key role in determining the performance of learned behavior.* There is much controversy at the theoretical level about the role of motivation in learning and performance, but these controversies are confined to theoretical issues. In the realm of training, it is safe to say that the motivated trainee is more likely to learn and to use what he learns than is the unmotivated trainee. However, merely saying this does not make the principle useful; we need to turn our attention to rewards and motivation and to deal with the question of what kinds of reward are involved in learning. A useful classification of motivation-reward factors is presented below.

a) *Achievement motivation,* for which the reward is success.
b) *Anxiety,* for which the reward is the avoidance of failure.
c) *Approval motivation,* for which the reward is approval in its many forms.
d) *Curiosity,* for which the reward is increased opportunity to explore the environment and be exposed to novel stimuli.
e) *Acquisitiveness,* for which the reward is something tangible such as money or material benefits.

Generally speaking, the motivation-reward factors classified above are products of learning and at any given moment in time are influenced by the immediate experience of the learner. Achievement motivation is found in persons whose parents established goals for them and rewarded them as they obtained certain goals. Anxiety is fostered when punishment is a frequent consequence of failure to obtain goals. The achievement and anxiety groupings are often found among middle class persons, particularly where the parents aspired to see their children move up the social and economic ladder.

Both achievement and anxiety motivation are possible in the same person. In fact, none of the above classification groups should be regarded as excluding the other. There can be considerable overlap, and there usually is.

Approval motivation cuts across many experiential, familial, and cultural conditions. Most persons seek approval in some form.

Curiosity is a motivation-reward factor that is not particularly influenced by experiential, familial, and cultural factors. Persons from disadvantaged backgrounds are just as curious (perhaps more so at times) as persons from middle and upper class settings. Provide any healthy child with a device whose characteristics change as he performs certain acts and that child will spend considerable time manipulating the device and exploring the new or novel conditions it produces. This is less true for older children and for adults, but exploratory-curiosity motivation can be used effectively with adults if sufficiently rewarding opportunities for exploration are provided.

Acquisitiveness depends directly on the experience of the person. The desire to acquire money or material objects is related to the degree to which such rewards have been experienced in the past and then withdrawn. In most instances the key factor is the withdrawal or the deprivation of the material object. A rich man will work hard for money if he knows what it means to have been deprived of money. A child will seek to acquire toys if he has been deprived of toys. These tangible rewards acquire their reward effectiveness through learning and maintain their effectiveness through deprivation.

The acquisitiveness motive, as any personnel director knows, cuts across all classifications. It is found in persons from all walks of life and from all income levels. However, a safe and useful assumption is that people who have experienced poverty or who know what it is to be without adequate funds will be more responsive to tangible material rewards than those who have never had these experiences. Money or goods will reward most people but for some these are the critical rewards. After all, you cannot pay the rent with praise.

6. *Meaningful learning, that is, learning with understanding, is more permanent and more transferable than rote learning or learning by some memorized formula.* This principle suggests that the trainee should be encouraged or helped to find summarizing or governing principles to enable him to organize what he is learning. In cognitive terms we can say that material that is understood is better retained and is more available for use than material learned without understanding. The student who understands what an exponent is can learn to understand logarithms and is in a much better position to learn to use a logarithm table and to remember how to use it than one who merely is taught to use such a table without the basic understanding.

7. *The learner's perception of what he is learning determines how well and how quickly he will learn.* The way in which material is displayed can be a critical factor in determining the course of learning. The learner should be able to discriminate the important stimuli in the situation so

that these stimuli can be associated with the appropriate responses. Witness the class of second graders, all of whom erroneously learned that you put a period at the end of the line. They identified line with sentence because all the examples they were shown had sentences one line long. They learned what they perceived, and in this case the display led them astray.

There are many ways to attract the learner's attention to important stimuli. The problem is usually not one of finding a way; the problem is usually one of recognizing that the important stimuli must be perceived correctly if learning is to proceed.

8. *People learn more effectively when they learn at their own pace.* Self-pacing is effective because it enables different individuals to respond at a tempo that enables them to assimilate information. Individuals differ in the way they perceive and the amount they perceive at one time. Some can take in a wide range of stimuli at once, while for others the range is narrow. Some people make responses rapidly, others slowly. Some form associations quickly, others slowly. Self-pacing allows some people to learn rapidly and others to learn slowly, but properly administered, it provides the opportunity for all the learners to acquire the information if there is enough time to do so.

9. *There are different kinds of learning and they may require different training processes.* Learning to repair a piece of equipment is different from learning to identify the components of the equipment. The task of identifying components involves the processes of guiding and reinforcing. The trainee is shown the components, is given their names, and then is given time to form the correct associations. The task of troubleshooting involves the process of discovery, probably guided discovery in which the trainee is given hints as he is guided to discover the solution to the problem.

Learning to spell a list of words is different from learning to typewrite. Both of these tasks involve the process of association, but the associations include different types of stimuli. In the spelling task the learner must associate the sound of the words with their correct spelling. In the typing task the learner must associate the sight of a word with the proper keys. A person who is quick to learn spelling may not be quick to learn typing. Different kinds of stimulus sensitivity are required.

The fact that there are different kinds of learning calls attention to differences among learners. Just as different learning tasks make different demands, so are learners different in their ability to meet these demands. However, the statement that there are individual differences among learners says very little. It is more a warning than a prescription. A more complete statement would call attention to specific differences among learners. Such a statement should deal with such factors as aptitudes and intelligence as well as differences in backgrounds among learners. Space does not permit an extended coverage of the possible sources of differences here. However the reader is referred to Gagné (1967) for a thorough discussion of the topic of individual differences in learning.

PRINCIPLES AND TECHNIQUES

The principles of learning described above may be applied to all types of training situations, but these principles do not specify training techniques. A principle of learning identifies certain conditions affecting learning. Once we have the principle, the next step is to translate the principle into techniques that match the objectives of the training task and that fit the available resources.

The relationship between principles of learning and training techniques is illustrated in the following example of a training problem. Company XYZ noted that in training its salesmen there was often a wide gap between knowing the product and cost figures and applying this knowledge to the actual selling situation. The members of the training staff recognized the principle that the learner learns what he does, and they realized that some form of on-the-job training was required. But this was almost impossible to do because of the nature of the product and because much of the company's business was scattered over the globe in locations ranging from the Far East to South America. They decided to face this problem by devising techniques to simulate the actual selling situation so that the trainee could learn by doing. The decision to use the technique of simulation was only a first step. This step had to be followed by an analysis of just what should be simulated. Should they try to simulate the customer attitudes and different points of view found in the countries where they did business? Could they simulate the kind of "culture shock" one experiences when he visits an unfamiliar foreign country? Questions of this nature really concern the stimulus situation and how it is to be used in simulation.

The company decided to use a number of different situations. This decision was suggested by Principle 4: Practice in a variety of settings will increase the range of situations in which the learning can be applied. Each of the settings required the trainee to perform the actual function of a salesman. This is a form of role playing and is derived from Principle 1: The learner learns what he does. In order to increase the trainee's motivation and to have him perceive the situation as being close to the real one (Principle 7), the simulation included having the trainee receive commissions for his simulated sales. The giving of commissions also served to provide reinforcement in the form of reward feedback (Principle 2). In simulated situations like the one described above, the danger exists that the situation is perceived as a game and the trainee becomes preoccupied with winning the game rather than with learning. This danger was lessened by including frequent opportunities for trainees to discuss their experiences in "bull sessions" or seminars (often the same things) and to summarize what they learned. These sessions were designed to encourage the trainees to find general principles that they could apply (Principle 6).

This example shows how certain principles may be translated into techniques, but the example does not provide rules as to how to do this. *There are no specific rules.* There are the principles that serve as guidelines just as a blueprint provides guidelines, but neither principles nor blueprint produce specific techniques. These still remain the product of experience.

BIBLIOGRAPHY

Gagné, R. M. (Ed.), *Learning and Individual Differences.* Columbus, Ohio: Charles E. Merrill, 1967.

Guthrie, E. R., *The Psychology of Learning.* New York: Harper and Row, 1935.

Hilgard, E. R. and G. H. Bower, *Theories of Learning.* New York: Appleton-Century-Crofts, 1966.

Hull, C. L., *Principles of Behavior.* New York: Appleton-Century-Crofts, 1943.

Lewin, K., "Field theory and learning." Chapter 4 in *The Psychology of Learning.* Natl. Soc. Stud. Educ., 41st Yearbook, Part II, 215-242, 1942.

Skinner, B. F., *Science and Human Behavior.* New York: Macmillan, 1953.

Tolman, E. C., *Purposive Behavior in Animals and Men.* New York: Appleton-Century-Crofts, 1932. (Reprinted, Univ. of California Press, 1949.)

7

How to Analyze Training Problems and Develop Training Objectives

Requests for training usually come in this form: "We need to train a group of new salesmen." The training director could respond, "Great; I've got just the film to do the job." Or he might say, "I'll be glad to help, but first let me ask you a few questions."

Before a training program can be developed, a preliminary project analysis must be undertaken. The training director should probably start by asking questions like these:

1. What do you want these people to do after they are trained?
2. How large will this group be?
3. What product or service will these men sell?
4. What is meant by new? Have they ever sold before?
5. Is there a formal job description available?
6. How much time is available for training?
7. How will you measure results?
8. Where will they be trained?

These are but a few of the questions that could be asked. The important point is that a thorough analysis of the need for training must precede any decision by the training director regarding method or material. He could find that training will not be able to accomplish the particular change desired. A system may require updating; the supervision may need replacing; the original hiring and placement may have been incorrect. An initial analysis increases the probability that the training director will know the real need before he begins to seriously invest his time and that of his staff.

A second step in the initial analysis process is the investigation of the needs of the learners as they express them or as revealed in the records of their past work. This investigation could take the form of an opinion poll, a depth interview, or an analysis of the personnel records or any other source which provides insights into the experience, education, and personality of the men to be trained.

Armed with this information, the training man has a preliminary understanding of what everyone thinks he wants in this new training program. The question is whether they really want the program as you understand it. To find out you must first develop broad course objectives; compile a simple course outline of topics you propose to teach; determine the amount of time you plan to use in teaching this proposed course; and make a decision on other constraints such as location, equipment, and instructor needs. Having accomplished this, you are ready to talk once again with the manager who first requested the training to determine if you have met his needs.

It is always easier to edit a work than to create one. You can be sure that your interpretation of the new course will undergo several "comments and changes" from the manager. You must expect this, however, since this is exactly why you performed the analysis in the first place.

Comments and changes presented at this time prevent the more complex and time-consuming task analysis from being wasted. When you accept these changes, be sure you can see why the changes are proposed and how they will affect the final output of the course. Several revisions may be required before you achieve an acceptable outline.

The need problem must be reviewed in depth before the second step is taken. As training director you must be capable of supporting or rejecting this need for training with facts, not simply with a response that it was requested by someone in the organization.

After you have established the need for training and cleared the broad goals and outline with the intended consumer of the training, you are ready to perform a task analysis and the writing of specific course objectives.

TASK ANALYSIS

It is difficult to properly assess a problem if you have no idea of your objectives. The next step, therefore, is to define in broad terms what your course objectives are. What behavioral or performance change do you expect this course to produce in the learner? How will you know when you have reached this goal? How will you measure success?

Statements of goals or objectives need not be elaborate or complex at this point. In fact there is no rule which states they need be in any particular form at all. All we are indicating is the need for some broad organizational statements to clarify the goals you are reaching for in your analysis. The specific behavioral objectives will be derived from your analysis, a concept we will discuss later in this chapter.

Basically the task analysis problem is to determine what data, skills, and information must be taught to reach an acceptable job performance goal. A task analysis has been described as a specialized method for writing up a procedural job as a basis for preparing instructional materials, so that an instructor or teaching device can successfully teach the task to another person.

Many job performance goals are in writing; most are not. If you can easily determine the job criteria from existing written forms, your starting point is in hand. If no written standards exist, your problem is one of developing them with the supervisor who requested the training.

Subdivide the analysis problem into several categories as noted below.

1. Action such as processes, jobs, operations, or similar activity.
2. Objects such as parts of a system and its subparts.
3. Data regarding the system to be taught which is necessary to an understanding of the task.
4. Behavior of the individuals to be trained.

Analysis problems are not easily resolved by a pre-established set of rules. Nor are the four categories listed above necessarily analyzed separately, since many aspects are overlapping. Where possible, however, it is best to treat the topics as separate groups.

To start your analysis, gather a few basic tools to make your work easier. Start with a pack of 4 X 6-inch index cards. Use these large cards to record the steps in each part you are analyzing. A large card is more effective because it allows room for illustrations or drawings to be included with each step. In some instances the actual recording of steps is not physically possible because the object in question may be remote or for other reasons impossible to set down in writing. In these instances, use a portable tape recorder and dictate your notes as they come to mind. When you transcribe this material, you will be surprised at the amount of information you can collect in this way. Record everything you see, hear, do, or even suspect is meaningful. Remember that it is the thoroughness of this effort that is important. With this as background, you are ready to attack the actual problem of analysis.

Stage 1: Analysis Background. Review the need analysis which led you to this point. In doing so, be sure to review thoroughly your assumed objectives. Keep them in mind as you work your way through the problem which will lead you to your specific course objectives. The earlier objectives derived from the need analysis are simply working goals.

Stage 2: Points to Remember in Performing the Analysis.

a) Start your analysis at the beginning of the process under review and do not avoid any steps no matter how simple they may seem. Record all alternative steps which may occur in the step-by-step teaching of the course.

b) In writing each element of the analysis on the 4 X 6-inch index cards, show the two key elements: *stimulus* and *response.* (See Fig. 7-1.)

A stimulus is defined as something that incites the learner to action or thought. It may be a word or a physical action. The response to a stimulus is the answer or reply, whether in verbal or nonverbal form.

Fig. 7-1. Analysis card (front)

Topic:	Telephone usage	Step 1
Stimulus:	The telephone is the black instrument on the desk.	
Response:	It is used for calling people.	

c) The responses are always expressed by action verbs. In other words, the student is required to *do* something.

d) Explain all technical terms when they occur; do not assume that a definition is understood.

e) Each 4 X 6 card should also contain the information you expect each learner to absorb at that point. Too much information on a given card may indicate that you have more than one major point per card.

f) Each point must have a rationale for why it must be taught and how it fits into the whole course. Look at each point as a part in a puzzle. Each piece should fit the total pattern. (Fig. 7-2).

Stage 3: Object Review. The first step in reviewing a problem begins with the tangible objects (if any). Start with the whole and work to the smallest subunit possible. If the task, for example, is to analyze the

Fig. 7.2 Analysis card (back)

Illustration 1		Step 1
	(Picture of telephone)	
Rationale for steps – need to know what phone looks like prior to study of its use.		

problem of teaching someone how to dial a telephone number on a standard telephone, the "whole" would be the telephone instrument. Let us see how this will break down into subparts.

Stage	Object
Whole	Telephone instrument.
1st	Handset (receiver/transmitter).
2nd	Dial assembly.
3rd	Numbers on dial.
4th	Letters on dial.
5th	Finger holes in dial.

If our object were more complex, we would have several subgroups in the picture and, of course, subunits. We would continue this breakdown until we reached a complete set of object profiles.

Stage 4: Action Review. The action portion of a problem involves the breakdown of components into stages similar to our object review. The "whole" is an action which occurs in the learning process and is listed as the main action followed by actions, steps, and substeps. All action analysis steps are preceded by an action verb such as those listed below.

Some action verbs		
open	remove	align
pull	place	adjust
lift	slide	push
turn	check	etc.

If we follow through on our telephone dialing problem, it will take the following form.

A. Main action – dialing telephone.

1. Action – dialing AB211.
a) Step – place finger in hole marked A.
b) Step – turn dial clockwise until finger hits a stopping point.
c) Step – release finger to allow dial to return.

Stage 5: Information Review. Information is used to explain the "why" of most problems. In analyzing information adhere to the same procedure employed in the object and action analyses. Again using the telephone problem as an illustration, we would have the following:

A. Information – instructions for dialing.

1. Main fact – use of index finger of right hand in dialing.
a) Fact – when dialing, finger is released when dial reaches finger stop.
(1) Point – watch for individual who returns dial with finger.

Stage 6: Analysis. We have now established a system for recording our observations and the methods for observing the three key elements (object, action, and information) of a problem. Using this analysis procedure, we will now apply it to an actual analysis exercise.

Our problem in this analysis is to devise a training program to teach the student how to dial a telephone. Our steps in the analysis are as follows:

1. The need analysis has been established.
2. The tentative objective is to train students in the proper methods of using the telephone dial system.
3. Using the card recording system noted in Figs. 7-1 and 7-2, record the first steps in your analysis activity. In this problem the first step will be the object (telephone) and its components. Your problem is to record the analysis in a stimulus-response (S-R) layout.

The analysis phase should continue until such time as you have successfully listed all steps in the analysis of object, action, and information. The real test of your effort is whether a person who knows nothing about the subject can sit down, read your analysis cards in their proper sequence, and then perform the operation you set out to teach. If he cannot, the analysis is probably incomplete. At the same time, have a knowledgeable instructor review the analysis. By using both sources you will be able to determine whether you have completed a valid analysis of the problem.

With the completed step-by-step analysis you can determine whether your post-analysis objectives are valid. Ask yourself whether these objectives are really what you expect of the student or whether you desire a different behavior. Assuming you agree that the post-analysis objectives are correct, you can then proceed to test the analysis procedure.

Select one or two untrained students and submit the analysis material for their review. In using trainees as test subjects, be certain not to provide any instructions beyond those contained in the task analysis they are actually reading. When the trainee stumbles or omits a step, you must assume your analysis was wrong and note the need to make adjustments. When this occurs, tell the trainee the missing part and let him go on. This method of testing will produce a valid critique of the analysis. Schedule this test with other untrained students until your analysis is complete and valid.

With your completed analysis you will have established all of the steps required to teach the problem or task. You will also have established the objectives of the program. But how do you know these are valid behavioral objectives? Can these objectives be measured to determine if the student has reached them?

Objectives

At one time or another most of us have purchased a large piece of equipment such as an automobile. When the salesman asks, "May I help you?" you can answer by simply stating, "I wish to buy a car," and leave the rest to chance; or you can respond by stating your objective, i.e., the type of car you desire. This objective might be, "I'm looking for a 4-door, 8-cylinder, 310 horsepower, medium-priced ($2500 to $3000) car with XYZ optional equipment." You could further define color combinations and other design features. You have stated your objective in such a form that the salesman can now show you cars which fit this description. If he fails to meet your preset objective, you probably will not buy from him. But at least you both knew what was expected and why or where the end result failed to meet the objectives. In other words, you could measure the results. Why then should we not expect training objectives to be at least this clear and well defined?

We have seen an everyday example of the use of objective setting to accomplish a goal in our car-buying illustration. This same approach will now be applied to the development of course objectives. If we review our car illustration, precisely what did we do when we decided upon the specific car we wished to purchase and the objectives that that car had to fulfill?

Our first step in this process was to perform an analysis of the possible automobile models available to us and the many options and constraints. We then set out to organize these data into coherent form. Next we superimposed our need over these organized data and zeroed in on the specific car or cars which could meet our need – a need, incidentally, which we measured by actually seeing, driving, and perhaps even kicking the tires of the car.

While we did not formally perform the act of writing objectives, we did establish them subconsciously. The act had three phases of development. The first was to identify the terminal behavior desired – to purchase a new car. From this goal we then set out to further refine the terminal behavior, buying a car, as "to purchase a 4-door, 8-cylinder, 310-horsepower car." But this was not really sufficient for our complete understanding of the terminal behavior, so we further refined our objective by stating the criteria of acceptance. In this case we stated that the car had to be "a medium priced ($2500 to $3000) 4-door, 8-cylinder, 310-horsepower car." We knew what we expected from the salesman when we stated our objective in purchasing the car. In developing objectives for training, the same logic should be employed, leaving no doubt in anyone's mind as to what is expected of the student (buyer) and what he may expect from you (salesman) in a course.

Developing Objectives

Dr. Robert Mager defines an objective as ". . . an *intent* communicated by a statement describing a proposed change in a learner – a statement of what the learner is to be like when he has successfully completed a learning experience."*

It is the responsibility of management to provide the training director with the behavioral objectives it wishes to achieve in any training course. In reality most management groups do not fulfill this obligation simply because time and/or their backgrounds do not make it possible. Consequently the development task of writing behavioral course objectives usually falls to the training director.

*Robert F. Mager, *Preparing Objectives for Programmed Instruction,* San Francisco: Fearon Publishers, 1962, p. 3.

A behavioral objective is a means of communicating to the learner the instructional intent (outcome) of the course. It states what a learner will be doing upon completion of the particular course. When objectives are missing, it is impossible either to test for results or to establish rational plans for the use of instructional media. An objective may be verbal or nonverbal. In preparing behavioral objectives, it is important that care be exercised to write clear and concise objectives which are understood by all readers.

Examples of unambiguous terms are as follows: to write, to identify, to solve, to list. Used in objective-writing they might appear, "To write a list of the ten largest countries in the world," "To identify the parts of an automobile engine by listing them on a cutaway diagram of the engine."

Conversely, objectives written in ambiguous terms are open to many interpretations by the reader. Examples of ambiguous terms are as follows: to understand, to learn how to, to appreciate, to enjoy, to believe. How, for example, could you test to determine whether a student had mastered a course if the objective was stated, "To understand American history"? You could not. For this reason all words chosen to express an objective must be clear, precise, unambiguous words. This does not mean that you have committed a sin if you use such words as "understand" or "know" in the writing of an objective, so long as the statement goes on to explain what you mean.

Could you, for example, explain in clear and precise behavioral objectives what you would be teaching if the objective provided by management was to "teach the students to understand the salesclerk's job"? We seriously doubt that anyone could measure whether the learner "understands" the salesclerk's job. If, however, you were instructed "to teach the students the five basic functions of the salesclerk's job," you could teach and measure whether the students actually learned the five basic functions.

The development of objectives is more easily said than done. A single course hour, for example, may require 25 behavioral objectives. If we project this figure to a full course, you will find that it could become a substantial job to establish behavioral objectives to teach a single course. While the task of developing behavioral objectives is not an easy one, it is a critical phase in course development.

Here are some pointers to keep in mind when developing behavioral objectives:

1. Is the objective clear to anyone who reads the statement? Will everyone interpret it in approximately the same way?

2. Can you measure (test) for the objective at the completion of the course and clearly demonstrate that it has been achieved?
3. If you gave the objective to another instructor, would he teach the same lesson or would he interpret the objective differently than you intended?

If you keep the word "doing" always in mind when you develop, criticize, or apply an objective, you are not likely to go wrong. If the student is going to do something which you can measure through verbal or nonverbal means, then you have probably clearly stated your course objectives.

The writing of objectives can be accomplished in three steps:

1. Identify the desired terminal behavior.
2. Further define the conditions under which this terminal behavior will occur.
3. State the criteria of acceptable performance.

By applying these steps to a simple problem we can get a better picture of how and why we need to clearly define the outcome of the course we are teaching. As an illustration, let us assume that our problem is to teach a course in automotive mechanics. One lesson covers the adjustment of an automobile spark plug.

Step 1. Identify the desired terminal behavior. Objective: To adjust spark plugs in automobiles.

The objective stated in Step 1 conveys our instructional intent. It does not, however, clearly state *how* we can measure "adjust" as it is used in this statement. We must therefore go to the next step and further refine our objective.

Step 2. Further define the conditions under which this behavioral objective will occur. Objective: With the aid of a feeler gauge adjust the spark plugs in an automobile.

Again we see that our objective has become much clearer. We have conveyed the fact that our intent is for the student to "adjust" the spark plugs, using a feeler gauge. But we still do not state what we will accept as a proof of the student's learning. How would we measure the results? We cannot at this point. The objective must be further developed.

Step 3. State the criteria of acceptable performance. Objective: With the aid of a feeler gauge, adjust the spark plugs to a setting of .003 inches.

Now our objective is complete. We can easily measure the results of the student's work. Our intent was to teach how to use a feeler gauge to adjust the spark plugs to a setting of .003. We can measure how well we taught by simply testing the student's adjusted plug with a .003 feeler gauge. Anything different from this adjustment would be a failure – a measurable failure on the instructor's part and on the student's part. By following this simple three-step method for developing an instructional objective, you will avoid the common error of developing a description rather than an objective.

Teaching Others to Write Objectives

It is one thing to be capable of writing objectives, but quite another to teach others how to do it. Experience has shown that most instructors who start on the task of objective-writing normally cannot see the difference between course descriptions and course objectives. Sometimes they cannot understand the reasons for writing objectives at all.

Occasionally you will also find instructors who object to writing in "educational jargon," as they put it. You will find it hard work to change this attitude.

There are many ways to teach objective writing; some of them you may already have been exposed to or taught. We will discuss one method which has proved successful in teaching new instructors how and why to write objectives for training programs.

Your first step must be to explain or teach the methods of task analysis. If the instructors do not understand how a course is structured, then they will not understand how or why objectives are necessary parts of this procedure. The teaching of analysis procedures should follow the example noted at the beginning of this chapter.

With this as background, the next step is to teach the concept of objectives and how they are prepared. A straight lecture presentation with examples and work problems is possible but often time-consuming and confusing. Overhead visuals can also be employed to visualize the concepts. We have found, however, that a successful method of teaching is to use programed instruction as the basic teaching method. The procedure used is as follows.

Step 1. Using Mager's programed book *Preparing Instructional Objectives,** allow each student to work through this program in class. Do not force the time; allow each person to pace his own learning. The group should finish in 40 to 60 minutes. Even those students who may have read this book (or any other similar book) in the past should work through the program again in class.

This program will provide the group with a common base of knowledge and terminology. They will now be capable of understanding the concepts of objective-writing but will not be capable of actually writing objectives.

Step 2. At this point you should present in a summary lecture the key facts covered in the book. Use the overhead projector or blackboard to list the key points and key words you want the student to retain. Work out an example in the three-step approach and solicit student participation and comments as you build up the objectives in your illustration. A good approach is to write out several examples on overhead transparencies and include some wrong or weak forms to see whether the students understand the concept. By using the overhead, you can produce visuals with a poor statement of the objective on one overlay and a correct statement on another overlay.

Step 3. Having completed the individual work and the group presentation, break the class into pairs of students. Have one student of each pair write an objective for any subject on the blackboard. The second student in the pair should then criticize this objective. The class should also have an opportunity to comment. Hopefully you will have enough board space so that three or four students can write at the same time. If an objective is poorly constructed, have the students work on it until it is modified and corrected. Let the students indicate where the statements are right or wrong. After the first student is finished, let the other student of the pair try constructing an objective. The students learn more quickly from doing than from watching or listening.

Step 4. Have each student write a series of specific objectives for a common problem. This test should show you where they need help and where they have grasped the process. Repeat as required until every student understands and can write correct objectives.

Another way of testing the ability to construct objectives is to provide a set of completed correct and incorrect objectives and require the

---

**Ibid.*

students to discriminate between the correct and incorrect constructions.

A training objective is a statement or collection of words and/or symbols conveying one or more training intents. The objective will communicate your intent in proportion to the degree that you have explained what the student will be doing when demonstrating his achievement. In writing these objectives use the three-step development method of (1) identifying the desired terminal behavior, (2) further defining the conditions under which this behavior will occur, and (3) stating the criteria of acceptable performance (testing). Remember that objective-writing is not intended as an educational exercise. It is a critical function in the development of any course.

8

Selecting the Media of Learning

The development of training needs, analyses, and objectives is the first major step in course design and planning. These efforts would be futile, however, if we failed to choose the most effective method for communicating the subject matter to the learner. Before we get to the stage of developing lesson plans and courses discussed in the next chapter, we need to review the criteria for selecting the media of learning.

The term media is not restricted to equipment or gadgets. It includes all forms of communication ranging from words to direct on-the-job experience. To many trainers the term audiovisual would be more meaningful than media. But it would also not be a complete description. The term media includes the broader human experience of learning through all of one's sensory facilities. These media and their potential use in training programs are discussed in this chapter.

Too often the trainer considers the lecture the only communication method available. While there is no denying that this method is effective for many training tasks, the trainer has a much wider variety of channels open to him. For an instructor to function in a creative fashion, he must be knowledgeable about various media, their advantages and disadvantages, as well as their costs.

Our intention in this chapter is not to explain how to use these media, but rather to explore their usefulness to the communication process. This discussion is designed to increase your understanding of these media and foster a more meaningful use of them in the training situations.

HUMAN SENSES

Human beings have many channels of learning available to them No single avenue should be excluded if it will aid in the teaching of a lesson. The human sense organs and their corresponding purposes are noted below.

Sense Organ	Purpose
Eyes	Seeing
Ears	Hearing
Nose	Smelling
Tastebuds	Tasting
Skin	Feeling

This discussion of basic human senses may seem elementary, but it is surprising how few instructors fully consider all of the senses when developing training materials. The learning process must employ as many of these sensory elements as possible. To rely upon hearing alone is much like assuming we are blind; to rely upon sight alone is like assuming we are deaf. In real life one sees and hears simultaneously, to say nothing of the senses of smell, touch, and taste which are also functioning at the same time. Knowing this, why do we persist in utilizing either one sensory medium at a time, or at best the two senses of sight and sound?

We must also recognize that these same sensory mechanisms which we use for learning can also become inhibitive factors in learning. For example, poorly constructed sight/sound presentations can fail to motivate or teach. The learning environment may adversely affect the student's senses if it is too hot, too cold, stuffy, noisy, or badly lighted. The problem is to devise training programs that adequately consider and use all of the human senses to advantage and neutralize the inhibiting factors affecting these senses.

MEDIA SELECTION

In general, training should be designed to simulate as closely as possible the actual work experience and/or the work environment. The task of selecting the most appropriate media is based on this principle.

In selecting the most appropriate medium, one must consider its level of abstractness in relating the lesson to the task. It would serve no purpose, for example, to lecture on how to tie a shoe and never allow the student to tie one, when the training objective is the performance of shoe-tying. In this instance, why not approximate or duplicate the real world by actually tying shoes? Although this example oversimplifies the problem, verbal instruction is normally the chief medium in training programs, while other media are overlooked.

Below we have listed the more common media and structured them in order from the most abstract of all forms – words or symbols – to the most concrete – direct experience.

Words (symbols)
Graphics
Still pictures
Motion pictures
Television
Field trips
Demonstrations
Simulation
Direct experience (on-the-job)

In the selection of media, we must consider both the problem of the learner's sensory perceptions and the training budget. When the ideal medium is too costly or impractical, we are forced to utilize a second or third choice for the training task. This choice ought to be consciously made, however. In addition to budget considerations, some of the other criteria to consider when selecting media are:

1. The learning group's and instructor's background, abilities, and motivation will help to determine what media would be most appealing to them.
2. Course objectives are the key to all instruction and must be considered in selecting media. How can the objective best be achieved?
3. The location of the classroom will indicate the various constraints of time, travel, and physical environment.
4. Media which are beyond your control to schedule (*e.g.* film rentals) must be checked for availability. The equipment to convey these media must be available and in good working order.

Always judge the medium on the basis of its ability to economically and effectively solve your training task. Do not let your personal bias for certain equipment or formats be the basis of your judgment. The training content should determine the media selection. Don't solve the problem by working the available media around the training task.

We all recognize that budget constraints on the selection and use of media is an everyday problem. Because of this we may find that the most appropriate media simply cannot be afforded. It is best, however, to start your planning with the assumption that the sky is the limit and any medium needed will be available. With this approach you will find that you can establish an ideal lesson plan and then lower your sights to the second or third media choice, if necessary, for the solution to the task. This approach will provide you with the opportunity to (1) see where new media may be needed so that, hopefully, in your five-year projection you can procure the new media for the organization; and (2) aid your adaptation of the available media to your training needs.

ADVANTAGES AND LIMITATIONS OF MEDIA

To properly select media for training objectives, you must understand the advantages and disadvantages of each. Each major medium is discussed below, starting with words (symbols) as the most abstract and, therefore, most difficult form to use.

Words (Symbols)

The most commonly used and misused medium of teaching is the spoken or written word. Some studies indicate that we retain only 20% of what we hear. If this is true, then it raises a serious question as to why we place such great emphasis upon the lecture method when we achieve so little learning from it in relation to the time spent.

The written word is also open to question. Words alone will be interpreted by the learner in relation to his personal background and experience. How often, for example, have you faced a classroom situation where the learner had read the textbook the night before as his homework assignment and orally repeated an interpretation of the printed lesson which was the opposite of its intent? The problem lies as much with the learner's perception of what he has read as it does with the medium's ability to communicate.

We must also recognize that the average learner is likely to possess a reading ability of eighth grade or lower. His vocabulary and comprehension as a reader are probably at this level. All too often the student will read extensively and comprehend little of what he has read.

Use the spoken or printed word wisely and sparingly. Plan the use of lectures and printed media just as you would films or other media. Do not take them for granted. Some students are highly verbal, others nonverbal. Know your learner and adjust your communications methods accordingly.

Graphics

Our ladder of abstraction in the media of learning progresses from the purely verbal presentation, as the most difficult to use effectively, to the direct experience as the most concrete medium of learning. In this progression one realizes that no single medium is employed in isolation, except perhaps the spoken word. Most training should be designed to employ a mixture of media. Graphics, for example, are often used to support lectures. If we believe statistics and studies on learning, we can assume that we retain 80% of what we hear, and as much as 95% of what we see. A verbal presentation supported by graphics or visuals relies upon several principles of learning:

a) They make use of two or more senses.
b) They can create a sense of participation and involvement in the learning task.
c) They can establish association from the unknown to the known.
d) They can arouse and hold interest.

In many cases visuals can actually save teaching time because they add to the student's ability to remain interested in the subject and prevent mental wandering. They also provide a means of improving upon the verbal presentation because the average learner can comprehend more words than the average lecturer can speak in a given period of time. In fact, our listening speed is four times greater than the speed of speaking.

Like words used alone, visuals used alone are marginal in their teaching value. We must remember that the quality and appropriateness of the visual are equally important to the effectiveness of learning. A recent experiment on the use of visuals in an entertainment sequence on national television employed the technique of flashing a series of still shots of old masters oil paintings on the screen. The visuals were flashed on the screen for 1/12 of a second each, which is equal to 720 visuals a minute. In spite of this extremely rapid presentation, it was possible for the viewers to recall a substantial portion of what they saw in those brief flashes. Why was this possible? For one thing the viewers were motivated to watch since they had tuned in on this sequence of their own free will. Secondly, the brief 1/12 of a second sequences were repeated several times to allow repetition of the viewing, and third, the entire sequence was arranged as an integrated portion of an aural message. The visuals were used to reinforce the aural portions. Certainly the intent of the producer in this case was not to teach the visual message, but to improve and reinforce the audience's retention of his musical presentation.

Visuals can and should be used for similar purposes in teaching. They may not be as brief as 1/12 of a second, but they certainly do not necessarily need to be one-hour films either. Appropriateness of size, type, quality, and duration of presentation should be carefully considered in developing the course in which visuals will be employed.

Types of graphics. When considering the use of graphics in lessons we must also consider the types of visuals available to the instructor, and their potential as learning devices. In doing so we will not cover the "how to" aspect in this chapter but will restrict ourselves to the theory of why we should or could use a certain format. The "how-to" will be covered in later chapters of this book.

Graphics can be divided into two categories: apparatus and aids. The apparatus category includes such items as the chalkboard, easel pads, bulletin board, flannel board and magnetic board. The aids category includes illustrations, charts, posters, graphs, and diagrams.

The prime use of graphics is to distill the vast amount of data, figures, and abstract information into visual symbols so that they can be readily understood by a student. Graphics in support of words help gain and hold attention, and make words that might be misunderstood precise.

Of all graphic forms available, the chalkboard (blackboard) is perhaps the most familiar. It is one of the oldest pieces of training apparatus. Because of this, it is probably one of the most misused tools. Unlike the newer easel pads, flannel boards, and charts, which the instructor takes time to prepare and relate to his teaching, the chalkboard is old reliable, to be used on the spot for spontaneous, and sometimes unorganized ideas.

This does not mean that all graphic presentations must be well organized. In fact, one of the great assets of the chalkboard is its flexibility. The point here is that the best use of any graphic tool is achieved by planning in advance to maximize its effectiveness, and minimize the classroom time spent in creating the graphic.

Still Pictures

The term "still" denotes a motionless state. The still picture category includes photographs, illustrations, transparencies, slidefilms, and slides.

These are used to portray people, places, events, actions; in other words, they illustrate what might not otherwise be seen within the classroom. Stills can be used to focus attention, arouse emotions, and create curiosity in the learner.

The mere viewing of a still picture will not necessarily be any more effective than the viewing of any other graphic in isolation. For best results a relationship between the still visual you are using and the point you are making in that particular segment of the lesson must be created. Unless pictures actually contribute to learning, they should not be used.

The most commonly used still picture format is the 35mm slide. This can be found in many adaptations from single slides to coordinated sound-slide presentations. The slide is also the basis for the filmstrip, which is basically a series of slides bound into a fixed sequence. There are limitations on both the individual slide and the filmstrip that affect their use.

The slide, for example, is readily produced by the amateur or professional, and can be photographed and developed quickly and easily. It can be in color, black and white, indoors, outdoors, and in sizes ranging from the standard 2-inch to 2-1/4-inch size to the 4-inch lantern size. Its flexibility in changing sequence is obvious. Cost is minimal. Its shortcoming is primarily the logistical problem of storage and classification necessary to prepare it for use.

Filmstrips are really a series of slides tied together in lengths of 35mm film; the length of the filmstrip can vary according to the topic and is limited only by the capacity of the filmstrip projector. Filmstrips are also called stripfilms and filmslides, but most often filmstrips. They are compact, easy to store and handle, simple to project, and inexpensive to buy and maintain. Commercial film people have produced a vast array of subjects that are available in this format. Its prime weakness is its fixed sequence of pictures, making the use of single frames impractical in a classroom.

Motion Pictures

To most of us, the motion picture format is the most familiar form of visual communication, aside from the printed book. Even though television has made inroads into its popularity, it is still a popular visual entertainment medium.

As a training medium it has for the most part been neglected or misused. Part of the difficulty may lie in the fact that the motion picture, whether it be the 16mm, 8mm, super 8mm, or 35mm commercial format, has been expensive to produce, difficult to project, and inflexible in adapting to subject change. Few institutions produce their own 16mm films. Most are purchased readymade or are contracted for outside. Today, however, an increasing number of organizations have begun to produce their own films because of the easily used and inexpensive cameras now available.

Aside from the film size, the user has many other features to consider in selecting the appropriate film form. These include the questions of whether to use standard reel-to-reel, cartridge load, or continuous loop film. Even the choice of a cartridge format poses a problem.

There are many advantages and disadvantages to using film in a training program. As a medium, film provides an effective means of communication with large, geographically distant groups. It is also capable of visualizing ideas that might not be seen in their concrete form. For example, the interworkings of a combustion engine during its four stages of compression, ignition, power, and exhaust can be easily animated. Many other effects such as the blending of live action with animation and trick photos designed to create sensory illusions, can be obtained.

But there are disadvantages too. Film is a highly inflexible tool. Only a small percentage of the total available commercial films is really applicable to your specific needs. In any given film you may have to show 20-minutes or more to reach a 2-minute segment that is pertinent. You can overcome this by selective previewing to determine what segment of the film will serve your specific need; then you can use only that specific segment of the film. Too often instructors show an entire film when most of the footage is extraneous or even inhibitive to the learning objective.

Do not use films to kill time when they are unrelated to the subject being taught. Select only appropriate films. Don't be afraid to show the same film more than once if it will strengthen the concept being taught. There is no rule that says "one time only" for viewing films. Encourage student participation in discussions of the film, its content, and even its degree of effectiveness in teaching the point of the lesson. Film content quality will vary just as book content quality will.

Single-concept films, open-ended films, and small cartridge films are far more flexible for teaching purposes because they deal with small portions of a subject. Film segments can be easily integrated into a lesson plan. For example, if you are teaching a course on the automobile engine and your current lesson is the action and reaction of the ignition stroke of the engine, a short two-to-three-minute film loop shown several times, possibly once in slow motion, will illustrate this cycle without distracting the student by presenting too much of the extraneous material normally found in a full length film. By focusing the student's interest on a small but significant point your training objective will be more efficiently achieved.

Mechanical problems of projectors, seating, lighting, and other physical environment factors clearly affect not only the instructor's motivation to use films, but also the student's ability to learn from them. Nothing succeeds in destroying the student's interest and attention span more than viewing a film under poor conditions. You must be certain when making arrangements for a lesson that when the time arrives to show a film the room does not turn into a circus of people setting up equipment and lights, pulling shades, arranging seats, and so on. If you prepare in advance to avoid these problems, your learner will benefit.

In most cases the follow-up on the film is overlooked in lesson planning. Yet little educational benefit will be derived from this medium if a student is simply informed that "we are going to have a movie on automobile engines," and is then shown the movie with no further preparation or discussion. To derive full benefit, explain in detail what he will see, and why and how it will help him in the lesson he is studying. Prepare follow-up materials to be certain the student has learned the important points you sought to impart through the film. This preparation will also serve to show you whether or not the film you selected does in fact teach or reinforce the particular objective you are seeking. If you cannot develop proper follow up materials from the selected film, you should question the validity of its use.

Aside from using off-the-shelf films produced by a number of companies, the instructor may elect to produce his own film or contract outside for its production. Internal productions are often practical and effective for showing job functions such as salesclerk behavior and other broad subjects. They are seldom practical for photographing detailed studies because most instructors lack the talent, time, or equipment for professional production.

Externally produced films are expensive. The cost can vary considerably from $1000 a running minute and up. While at first this may not seem too expensive, remember that you cannot buy a couple of minutes any more than you can buy 100 square feet of house when the house is quoted at $20 a square foot. Custom productions have their place in a well-designed instructional system when the size and quality of the student group warrant the investment. In deciding whether to pay for a custom production, be certain that all alternative approaches to teaching the specific material have been carefully explored and reviewed for both effectiveness and economics.

Like all training media, the motion picture has its place in the curriculum, but it must be wisely selected with learning objectives and economic factors in mind.

Television

Much of what is said about the use of films in training programs is also applicable to television. Television, like film, comes in many forms, including off-the-air, closed circuit programs and video tape. Unlike film, television is less flexible in terms of when you can view off-the-air and closed circuit programs. Video tape overcomes this problem.

The cost and complexity of television are the greatest drawbacks to its widespread use. When only TV receivers are employed to receive off-the-air programs, these factors are not important. But few formal training programs can use off-the-air programs for training. In industry closed circuit or video tape systems are more important.

Closed circuit television can be connected via cable to any number of locations. This allows simultaneous viewing of presentations by a large number of students. Films may also be shown on closed circuit TV.

The greatest deterrent to widespread use of closed circuit TV is the technical problems of production and broadcasting. To do an adequate job requires considerable planning and preparation as well as technicians to handle the equipment. There are few training installations where these costs are warranted. Again you must assess the question of whether to use closed circuit TV against a backdrop of training effectiveness and cost.

Perhaps the most widely used form of television in industry is video tape. Recent engineering advances have brought the cost of video tape recording and playback systems down to less than $1000 a unit. With this economic breakthrough we shall see even greater use of this medium.

The instant playback feature of video tape is its chief asset. Because of this the medium can readily be employed in a training program to record an event, action, reaction, or even instructors in the act of teaching. The ability to replay this material immediately affords the instructor an opportunity to involve the student in the learning process on a more intimate basis.

The coordination of a closed circuit TV system with video tape can be effective in recording material off the air and then blending it with live performances and locally recorded material to provide an effective television presentation. As with all media, however, the cost question must always be carefully considered.

Field Trips and Exhibits

While some people may debate whether one can classify field trips and exhibits as media of learning, we doubt that anyone can argue against the value of these as teaching methods. Both forms are often overlooked as training tools, mainly because they require considerable advance planning.

Field trips in particular require the coordination of the necessary transportation and the use of field facilities for learning. The trips make use of the actual environment as a learning laboratory and can add realism to an otherwise abstract subject. Planning is the essential key to the effective use of the field trip as a training device. The need to plan what is to be accomplished is of utmost importance.

Exhibits are still another method for providing concrete knowledge of the subject being taught. They are used when it is difficult or impossible to present the actual object or action due to its size or its remoteness from the training site. They are also employed to make three-dimensional presentation. The exhibit can be a static or active model, a reduced or enlarged cutaway, or an exact replica of the equipment or process involved. Another interesting aspect of models is their ability to incorporate the senses of smell, feeling, and touch in the learning process. This is not possible with visuals alone.

Demonstrations

In a demonstration the instructor shows how to perform an operation. The learner normally observes this action, but he may participate. The demonstration is effective in illustrating the desired student behavior in the work environment.

Demonstrations can take many forms. They may include the use of cutaways, full-scale mockups, laboratory experiments, performance skills, or man-machine relationships. Like all such presentations, however, the demonstration method requires extensive rehearsal by the instructor for the most effective presentation.

This method of teaching is especially effective for skill training in the use of machines, weapons, and other equipment. It is also effective for training a man in selling skills or other verbal patterns where exact duplication is desired.

Simulation and Direct Experience

Simulation provides the student with an experience approximating that found in the real job situation. The closer the simulation comes to the actual job, the greater the probability of transfer. Simulation exercises can be either mockups or game problems. Mockups are effective for training skills such as flying, driving, machinery operation, etc. A good example is the simulation training of pilots on link trainers which approximate actual flight conditions. In pilot training this mockup is a replica of the plane's cabin with all of its instruments. The pilot is also faced with a simulated visual problem via film and readings on his instruments. He must then react as though he were actually in flight under the same conditions. Clearly such simulations are safer than actual flights for developing proper pilot reactions.

Gaming is employed primarily to simulate a real-life problem or situation in decision making. The problems may range from management decisions regarding schedules to training military officers in combat problems.

A mockup or a game cannot always be substituted for the "real thing." Sometimes it is more desirable to train by on-the-job instruction or direct experience. In this form of learning, however, proper student preparation is essential. The direct experience approach is another name for apprentice training. As a training device, the method is old yet highly effective. In using the direct experience approach, the instructor must structure the program to provide guidance in the student's performance of each step so that the course objectives can be achieved.

The on-the-job approach to training can be disruptive to the normal flow of work in an organization. In scheduling this kind of training, care must be taken not to interfere with the flow of work. Interference with the routine will only frustrate the student, upset the output of the organization, and result in future difficulties in arranging similar exercises. It is best, if possible, to establish a separate work area for on-the-job training so that the trainees will have a chance to become proficient at their task before being put on the line. If this is not practical, the instructor should schedule the use of equipment and facilities during slow periods or off hours.

In summary, when selecting the media for communicating training content, consider the following:

1. Determine your training objectives first; then choose the means with which you will convey them to the learner. Do not reverse the process and develop objectives after choosing the media.
2. Consider the physical conditions of learning. How will they affect the learning media you have selected? How many students will there be at one time? Where will they be trained?
3. Consider the collective abilities and backgrounds of the students who will receive training. Which media have greatest appeal and teaching effectiveness for them?

4. Consider learning efficiency. Which media will produce the greatest learning in the shortest time with the greatest retention?
5. Work out the economics of the ideal media to achieve your objectives. Look carefully at the costs of alternatives.

9

Building Programs, Units, Courses, and Lessons

The chapters in Part II, "Developing a Strategy for Training," have been arranged in a particular sequence because the process of creating training materials generally follows a similar pattern. The various theories of learning, for example, supply the training director with a conceptual framework for his ultimate training design. A painstaking task analysis must precede the development of training objectives. Consideration must be given to the choice of one or more of the communications media for accomplishing these objectives. All of this work is preliminary to blueprinting the programs, units, courses, and lessons which are the information increments of any teaching/learning system. Subsequent chapters in this section will deal with the principal methods of instruction and production of the basic learning media to be used in programs, units, courses, or lessons.

WHAT IS A PROGRAM?

To understand the role of course and lesson plans in teaching, we must first consider the training program as a whole. A program is defined as the entire training effort given to solve a training problem, and may include any number of subunits. The precise length and scope of any program will be determined by the subject matter and the depth of teaching required to reach the objectives.

In establishing a training program the scope of the organization's operations, its budget, limitations, and philosophy must be considered. The starting point is the training forecast (Chapter 3). We use the term "forecast" to refer to the result of the training director's efforts to assess

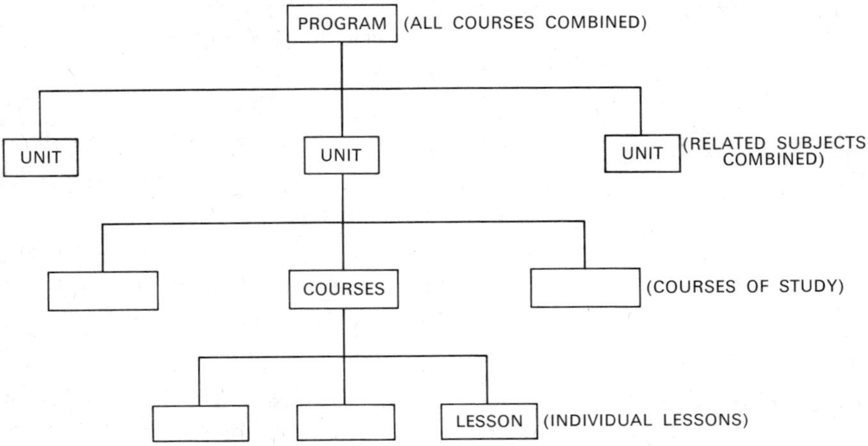

Fig. 9-1. Diagram of program organization.

the training needs of the organization, and the general approval required to set prescribed programs in motion. The forecast is the source document authorizing all program, unit, course, and lesson plan development.

Individual programs must be divided into units of instruction. Suppose a program must be designed to teach automobile mechanics methods of repairing and servicing the XY automobile. A typical unit of instruction might be "automobile functions." This unit would then be further divided into subunits (courses) and then into specific lessons. The diagram in Fig. 9-1 is a graphic representation of this concept.

The cornerstone of sound program planning is objective-setting, as discussed in Chapter 7. The sum of individual objectives of units and lessons must equal the overall program's objectives. Each objective is like a block in a pyramid. One fits into the other so that none can be omitted without causing the pyramid to collapse.

If we continue our automotive example, we can follow the development of a program from its conception in the training forecast.

Training Program

Curriculum	Automotive mechanics training for XY dealers.
Program objective	To provide trained XY mechanics with the necessary skills and attitudes to perform maintenance and repairs of XY automobiles.

Scope of program	1. To provide a comprehensive knowledge of theory of the XY automobile and its components. 2. To develop competence in the maintenance and repair of the XY automobile. 3. To provide direct experience in the XY work environment. 4. To develop positive attitudes toward mechanic's role within the corporation's objective of good customer service.
Units of instruction	(Here would be inserted a detailed list of the many units of instruction necessary to train mechanics on the XY, including units on the engine, body, and so on.)

The training program represents the overall strategy for training. It contains the comprehensive plan which all instructors are expected to follow in their course and lesson planning. The task analyses with objectives form the basis for each instructional unit, course, and lesson.

WHAT IS A UNIT?

A unit is the next subdivision of a program and represents a major block of instructional information as noted in Fig. 9-1. A typical unit plan is illustrated below.

Unit Plan

Curriculum	Automotive mechanics training for XY dealers.
Unit of instruction	Engine and subsystems.
Unit objective	XY personnel will be capable of performing all necessary engine maintenance and repairs as specified by policy on all current XY models.
Specific objectives	(All unit objectives should be detailed here.)

Unit courses (Here would be inserted a list of all courses or subunits which are necessary to reach the overall unit objectives. The list should include course content and the length of time necessary to teach each course. The course on "Electrical Components of the XY Engine." for example, may require five one-hour lessons.)

Having developed the program plan to this stage, we now have a master plan and the more specific unit plans which represent blocks or subtopics necessary to accomplish our overall objective of training XY mechanics. In practice, the program plan and unit plans will be highly detailed and may require many pages. These plans will be used by you and others who must work with the curriculum, to ensure that everyone follows the same plan at all times and at all levels.

COURSE PLANS

Course plans represent the heart of the training effort and the point at which the individual instructors are normally brought into the picture. The training director should provide the instructor who is responsible for developing lesson plans with sufficient data so that he has a grasp of his role within the overall training program. The instructor's data form (below) should contain enough information to permit the assigned instructor to use this form as his blueprint for lesson planning.

Instructor Data Form

Instructor Name.

Curriculum Automotive mechanics – XY type.

Unit XY engines.

Course Electrical systems.

Course objective Students will be able to maintain and repair, using the current XY shop manuals, tools, and data, XY electrical systems.

Specific objectives (List all objectives which pertain to the course.)

Specific topics	(Topics to be taught should be derived from the objectives and task analysis.)
Task analysis	(Include as much of these data as practical from the program information.)

The prime purpose of the instructor data form is to ensure that each course fits into the overall program plan, and that no facet of the subject is left untaught. This document will help instructors to develop lesson plans, to select the appropriate strategy for teaching, and to coordinate their individual goals with those of the larger program.

DEVELOPING THE LESSON PLAN

There is no magic formula which will provide an instructor with a foolproof approach to lesson preparation. It takes hard work and organizational ability. There are a few pointers, however, which will help him in his task.

Experience. Ideas, approaches, data, or other background information derived from the instructor's personal experience are probably the most useful tools. This is especially valuable for the development of case histories, anecdotes, and critical incidents related to the subject.

Observation. The instructor should have personally observed the job, operation, or skill to be taught. He should verify any task analysis he is given by reviewing the operation, using the task analysis as his guide.

Interview. While the instructor may be an expert in his subject, he can still gain insights into the tricks of the trade from fellow instructors or employees currently working on the job. He will always find new and interesting ways of teaching from the "pros." Interviewing these people is imperative if the instructor has never actually performed the skill himself.

Literature. A search of literature which pertains to the subject may help the instructor to prepare a lesson plan. This should not be a substitute for experience, but should function as reinforcement for experience.

Lesson Plan Format

The actual lesson plan form should be developed and supplied by the training director. Standardization is helpful so that the lesson plan can serve as a guide when an instructor must be absent and it would be impossible for a substitute to develop a new lesson plan in time to conduct the course.

For illustrative purposes a simple form (Fig. 9-2) has been devised which contains the important data needed for lesson planning.

Fig. 9-2. Lesson plan format.

LESSON PLAN

PROGRAM: INSTRUCTOR:

UNIT: CLASS PERIOD:

COURSE: DATE:

LESSON: LOCATION:

LESSON OBJECTIVES:

MAIN FACTS	TEACHING POINTS	MEDIA SELECTED

Instructors should be expected to prepare relatively standardized lesson plans to ensure the interchangeability of all plans within the total program. Copies of all lesson plans are filed with the training director and become part of the master plan, which is used to be certain that all parts of the program, units, and courses are integrated.

How to Prepare a Lesson

It is a well-known fact that writing lesson plans can be painstaking and monotonous work. Instructors, therefore, need to exert considerable self-discipline in this task. The instructor should follow these basic steps in developing his lesson plan.

1. Gather all data and information necessary at one location.
2. Select a quiet spot where work can be done without interruption.
3. Allocate a block of time for the task; time blocks of at least two to four hours are necessary.
4. Lay out the entire lesson in block (objective) form so that the basic steps that must be taken to reach the goals can be easily visualized.
5. Break the subject blocks into time blocks of 15 minutes each.
6. List all topics within each subject block.
7. Select the media of presentation for these subject blocks.
8. Interlock these subject blocks to ensure continuity of thoughts.
9. Tie all of these subject blocks together with summary points and a final lesson summary.
10. Establish backward and forward bonds with previous lessons and indicate the scope of the present lesson.
11. List all tools, media, and special equipment needed for the lesson.
12. Review your work for completeness and accuracy of the lesson to meet stated objectives.

Fig. 9-3. Completed heading of lesson plan.

LESSON PLAN

PROGRAM: Electronics I INSTRUCTOR: C. Otto

UNIT: Math. of Electronics CLASS PERIOD: 9:30 - 10:30

COURSE: Fund. of Radio DATE: March 26

LESSON: Ohm's Law LOCATION: Classroom A

LESSON OBJECTIVES: Solve Ohm's Law problems

MAIN FACTS	TEACHING POINTS	MEDIA SELECTED

13. Let a fellow instructor and the training director read the lesson plan draft to verify that the approach has been made clear.
14. Revise as required.
15. Prepare final draft from all comments.

The initial step in completing the lesson plan form is to fill in the heading. The heading should contain all the necessary background information on the lesson to be taught – program, unit, and course and lesson titles, lesson objective, instructor's name, time of class, and classroom location. An example of a completed form heading is shown in Fig. 9-3.

The body of the lesson plan form is divided vertically into three columns entitled "Main Facts," "Teaching Points," and "Media Selected."

Fig. 9-4. Lesson plan form with teaching points.

LESSON PLAN

PROGRAM: Electronics I	INSTRUCTOR: C. Otto
UNIT: Math of Electronics	CLASS PERIOD: 9:30 - 10:30
COURSE: Fund. of Radio	DATE: March 26
LESSON: Ohm's Law	LOCATION: Classroom A

LESSON OBJECTIVES: Solve Ohm's Law problems

MAIN FACTS	TEACHING POINTS	MEDIA SELECTED
A. Ohm's Law	$E = IR$ or $R = \frac{E}{I}$ E = volts I = amperes R = ohms	

Main Facts. The first column of the lesson plan form should contain a listing in proper sequence of all facts that must be taught in the lesson. The instructor will derive these main facts from the task analysis portion of his data form. Usually the first main fact will be the introduction and the last, the summary. The number of main facts listed will depend on the length and nature of the lesson. It is difficult to determine precisely how many facts can be taught in a given period of time.

Teaching Points. The main facts must be amplified and broken into logical small steps or teaching points which form the backbone of the lesson plan. These teaching points may be objects, actions, or information, depending

Fig. 9-5. Instructional media stimulus relationships to learning objectives.

Key: L = Low, M = Medium, H = High

Learning objectives	Instructional media type								
	Still pictures	Motion pictures	Television	3-D objects	Audio recordings	Programed instruction	Demonstrations	Printed textbooks	Oral presentations
Learning factual information	M	M	M	L	M	M	L	M	M
Learning visual identifications	H	H	M	H	L	M	M	L	L
Learning principles, concepts, and rules	M	H	H	L	L	M	L	M	M
Learning procedures	M	H	M	L	M	H	H	M	M
Performing skilled perceptual-motor acts	L	M	L	L	L	L	M	L	L
Developing desirable attitudes, opinions, and motivations	L	M	M	L	M	M	M	M	M

Adapted from William H. Allen, "Media Stimulus and Type of Learning." *Audiovisual Instruction,* Vol. 12, No. 1, January 1967. Reproduced with permission of the Editor, Audiovisual Instruction, Department of Audiovisual Instruction, National Education Association.

on your objective. In developing these teaching points, do not leave large gaps in the lesson plan because you "know all about that." Commit all points and every step to writing. A completed "Teaching Points" column for one main fact is illustrated in Fig. 9-4.

Media Selected. The third column in the lesson plan form is as important as the first two. The instructor should list the medium of communication

Fig. 9-6. Completed page of lesson plan.

LESSON PLAN

PROGRAM: Electronics I INSTRUCTOR: C. Otto

UNIT: Math. of Electronics CLASS PERIOD: 9:30 – 10:30

COURSE: Fund. of Radio DATE: March 26

LESSON: Ohm's Law LOCATION: Classroom A

LESSON OBJECTIVES: Solve Ohm's Law problems

MAIN FACTS	TEACHING POINTS	MEDIA SELECTED
A. Ohm's Law	$E = IR$ or $R = \frac{E}{I}$ E = volts I = amperes R = ohms	Blackboard Filmstrip on Theory
B. Current flow problem solving	1) If resistance remains same, increase in voltage produces more current	1) Students work at blackboard 2) Workbook problems

Fig. 9-7. Last page of lesson plan.

MAIN FACTS	TEACHING POINTS	MEDIA SELECTED
	Student assignment Lesson II: 1) Workbook	problems 2-4
	2) Read pp.	20-40 of text
	Instructor notes for Lesson II 1) Need filmstrip #2 on Ohm's	Law problem solving
	2) Arrange for special projector	April 2 class

he plans to employ in teaching each specific main fact. As an aid to media selection we recommend the use of the media-stimulus table in Fig. 9-5. This table will enable the instructor to make a preliminary determination of what medium or media are best suited for the teaching of a specific objective. If the problem, for example, is to teach how to perform a manual skill such as adjusting spark plugs, the media-stimulus table suggests demonstration via film as an effective teaching method.

Figure 9-6 is an example of a lesson plan as completed in all three columns for two main facts.

The last page of the lesson plan (Fig. 9-7) should include the following information:

1. Student assignment for next class.
2. Materials to be supplied to the students prior to their next lesson.

3. References used by the instructor in the preparation of the lesson plan.
4. Reminders of special arrangements which are necessary before using the training area, along with a list of items not normally found in the area.

One final attachment to the lesson plan is a detailed list of materials, aids, devices, etc., which are needed to give the lesson. This list should include the sources of these aids, even if they are located within the building. The list will serve as a reminder to the instructor.

The completed lesson plan should be reviewed by the training director to be sure that it fits in with the program and covers all of the assigned topics. If not, it must be revised until it meets the objectives set for the lesson.

10

Evaluating Training Outcomes: The Training Department's Bottom Line

When a woman makes a dress from a pattern, she is interested in one thing – the fit and look of that dress when it is finished. She tries it on many times during the production, taking a tuck here, cutting a piece of material there. If, after hours and perhaps days of making minor adjustments, the dress fails to meet her initial expectations, she may angrily throw it in a drawer, never to take it out again, or in a fit of temper she may rip it apart and start from scratch. Most of us have witnessed a scene or two like this.

The preparation and administration of training programs has a number of parallels to dressmaking. Developing the objectives and the training plan is like selecting a pattern. Choosing the best media of learning is similar to selecting the most appropriate fabric, buttons, thread, and so on. Taking a hard look at the results of your training efforts to make certain the organization got its money's worth is like checking the final fit.

In theory the parallels are pretty accurate. In practice the final step – checking the fit and look – is usually neglected.

This chapter is about evaluation. "Evaluation" is used in its broadest sense to include the full range of value judgments about training, from what trainees think of your program to what dollars and cents difference the whole effort has made to your organization. The purpose of evaluation activities is to find out whether the goals and content of training programs are compatible with the mission and current needs of the organization, and to find out whether the goals are being reached in the most effective and efficient manner so that any necessary adjustments may be made. Evaluation must include the training plan, methods, and materials of learning as well as the "before and after" performance of those who have received the training.

No right-thinking training director doubts the need to know whether his programs are actually accomplishing their goals. Evaluation is like mother and country – everyone wholeheartedly subscribes to the dogma. Nevertheless, few are willing to take the time or allocate the money to find out if the dress really fits the way the pattern said it would.

Occasionally a program comes under attack, often because someone up the line caught a glimpse of how much money was being spent. We usually respond to the attack with a few statistics or well-stated opinions to preserve our vested interests. Then, like the proverbial doctors, we bury our mistakes – deep under the hundreds of corporate variables that affect training outcomes. We blame the quality of the student, the supervision that follows training, vague company policy, the work load, or something else for our lack of the overwhelming success we had routinely predicted at the outset of the program. The bulk of our energies are channeled into hammering out the program's content and selling our ideas to others. Once the actual program is under way, we are off on another project, blithely assuming that our last piece of work was wholly successful.

The short shrift given the evaluation of training outcomes is readily explained. Evaluation requires people with time to dig out the facts, people with sophisticated measuring devices, and people who have the courage to admit that the last program was a bit of a bomb. Management itself often does not take the trouble to evaluate its own decisions, nor does it require a rigorous analysis of program outcomes from other departments. The training director lacks appropriate models to imitate. Like his peer department heads, he tends to concentrate on what is visible and obviously appealing to management. And, finally, evaluation is not a particularly glamorous training activity. Kicking off a new and glossy program is infinitely more attractive and ego building. Sifting through training records, interviewing old students, playing with the mean, median, and mode, and talking with supervisors who always put production first is plain and simple hard work!

Chapter 18 of this book describes one of the new and revolutionary training techniques of this century – programed instruction (PI). One of the reasons for the success of this method is its built-in mechanisms for evaluating the outcomes of learning. If we have learned anything from PI, it is the importance of evaluating our teaching through student feedback, criterion frames, pre- and post-tests, and many other procedures which are an integral part of the technique.

With this in mind, let us go on and talk about a concept we have chosen to call "total evaluation."

TOTAL EVALUATION

Donald L. Kirkpatrick, in a chapter entitled "Evaluation of Training" in the *Training and Development Handbook,* divides the evaluation of training programs into four categories – reaction, learning, behavior, and results.* Reaction evaluation refers to how well the trainees liked the program. Learning evaluation refers to how well they learned facts, principles, and techniques. Behavior evaluation asks the question, "What changes in on-the-job behavior have occurred as a result of the training?" Results evaluation requires concrete evidence that the training actually reduced costs or produced other improvements for the organization.

Our concept of total evaluation requires the use of all four categories of evaluation. Too often training directors are content with trainee reaction to the program, the least valuable type of evaluation. This is at best an indefinite method for assessing the effectiveness of training outcomes. While it may serve a purpose, it provides only a tentative answer to the question, "Did the training do its job?" The training director must continue with the other three forms of evaluation to fully answer the question.

Kirkpatrick's division of the evaluation of training into four categories provides a convenient way of looking at the process of total evaluation.

REACTION EVALUATION

Anyone who has participated in a training course has been subjected to reaction evaluation at one time or another. Reaction evaluation is simply an analysis of the trainees' feelings about a particular program. This type of evaluation tells you nothing about the effectiveness of the program in terms of the other three categories. It simply tells you the degree of apparent acceptance of the program. We say "apparent" because a trainee may be reluctant to tell the truth about his feelings for fear of what his opinion might do to his future chances with the organization.

---

*Donald L. Kirkpatrick, "Evaluation of training," *Training and Development Handbook,* Robert L. Craig and Lester R. Bittel (eds.), New York: McGraw-Hill, 1967, pp. 87-112.

Here are a few guideposts for the construction of a trainee reaction sheet.

1. Decide in advance what it is you want the trainees to react to and how you will use this information once you get it. Design your questions accordingly.
2. Design the form so that the responses can be easily tabulated and treated statistically.
3. Build in a few open-ended questions so that the trainees will have an opportunity to express all of their opinions about the program.
4. Do not require that the sheets be signed. This will improve the probability of an honest reaction.
5. Emphasize your desire to get the trainee's assistance in improving the program.
6. Word the items on the sheet so that they arouse as little emotional reaction as is consistent with what you are trying to measure.

LEARNING EVALUATION

A more complicated kind of evaluation is involved when the training director goes beyond the mere measurement of the trainee's attitude toward his training. Learning evaluation is simply an attempt to assess the amount and quality of learning which has taken place during a particular training session. Even though the trainee may not have liked the course, he still may have learned a great deal from it. The kind of learning we are identifying has nothing to do with how well the new information is applied to job problems or whether it initiates any behavior changes. Evaluation of the quality and quantity of a learning experience will simply reveal whether information has been transmitted as planned by the training staff.

The learning of information is generally evaluated with oral performance tests or paper and pencil tests. The following sections summarize basic information on test administration, types of tests typically used, means of describing the group's test performance, and ways of evaluating the classroom performance of both trainees and instructors.

How to Administer a Test

Use common sense in the administration of any test. This is probably enough instruction in how to administer a test for most requirements. The following points are summarized from David Payne's *The Specification and Measurement of Learning Outcomes* and bear repeating:

1. The directions for taking the test should be clear and complete.
2. If necessary, trainees should be given practice items so that the form of the test does not hinder optimal performance on the content of the test.
3. Tests should be announced in advance so that the student will obtain the benefits of preparation.
4. The testing room should be relatively free of distractions. Trainees should be permitted to move about or leave the room temporarily if necessary.
5. If speed of response is not an important variable in the test situation, adequate time should be given for all or nearly all students to complete the test.
6. Items on the test should probably be arranged in order of their difficulty with the easiest first. The trainee will probably gain some sense of success if he can succeed early in the test situation.
7. Students should be given detailed instructions on how to prepare for the test and what type of test will be given.
8. The test should contain instructions about guessing. Whether or not guessing should be permitted has not been resolved by research. You can probably safely give the following directions and expect a negligible effect from chance success: "Answer all questions. Select the alternative you feel is best even though you are not absolutely sure." If you have reason to believe that guessing may create problems for your test, simply request when the test is administered that the students not guess. This is generally sufficient to reduce the effects of guessing. No correction formula need then be applied. A comprehensive text on testing can provide you with formulas for correcting for guessing if this is necessary.*

Types of Tests

Oral tests. Oral tests have the following advantages:

1. An instructor may restate or reframe the question until he is certain that the student understands it well enough to give the best answer he is capable of giving.

---

*From David A. Payne, *The Specification and Measurement of Learning Outcomes*, Waltham, Mass.: Blaisdell Publishing Company (a division of Ginn and Company), 1966, pp. 40-45.

2. An instructor can probe the student's depth of understanding and not be left in doubt.
3. The oral test is more closely allied to the situation in which most trainees will need to regurgitate information back on the job. They will probably be forced to deal with problems verbally. The oral test provides the examiner with insight into how well a student is able to think through and articulate an answer.

Oral tests have the following disadvantages:

1. An instructor's judgment is subject to great variations.
2. Oral exams are time-consuming for trainers to give.
3. The trainer's presentation of the questions is subject to a wide variety of methods.

David Payne, in *The Specification and Measurement of Learning Outcomes,* quotes fourteen principles for administering an oral examination which are useful to the trainer giving an oral test.

1. Use oral examinations only for the purposes for which they are best suited, i.e., to obtain information as to the depth of students' knowledge where oral presentation is clearly a purpose of the course or program, or where other means are simply inappropriate.
2. Prepare in advance a detailed outline of materials to be sampled in the examination, even to the extent of writing questions which will be asked.
3. Determine in advance how records of student performance will be kept and what weights will be assigned various factors.
4. Keep the questioning relevant to the purposes of the course or program.
5. Word questions in such a way that the students can see the point of the question with minimum difficulty.
6. Where several examiners are involved, make each one responsible for questions on a specified part of the full examination.
7. Judge students on the basis of their performance precisely defined – not in terms of a generalized impression of their total appearance.
8. Pose questions which students with the training which has preceded a particular examination can reasonably be expected to know. An examination is not the place for an instructor to demonstrate his own erudition.
9. Use both general and specific questions but do so in some logical order.

10. Do not spend a disproportionate amount of time probing for the answer to one question. If the first several questions do not elicit the desired response move on to some other matter.
11. Develop some facility with several basic techniques for successful oral examining such as creating a friendly atmosphere, asking questions and recording responses.
12. Make a written record of the student's performance at the time it is given. However, do so without disturbing the student or disrupting the flow of the examination.
13. In most situations allow students ample time to think through and make responses to questions.
14. Avoid arguing with the student. It is his show – let him make the most of it.*

Performance tests. Unlike an oral or paper and pencil test, a performance test requires an actual demonstration of skill. A trainee is asked to demonstrate, for example, some maintenance skill of some electronic system. Rather than talking or writing about it the trainee must actually show that he has learned by performing the task(s) previously taught. The following suggestions may help in constructing a performance test.

1. The test should yield consistent results no matter who rates it.
2. The trainee should be permitted to use any reference material during the test that he would normally be able to use on the job.
3. The actual job should be the primary source for the test material.
4. A numerical rating scale from 0 to 100 should be used rather than letter grades or pass/fail ratings. Seventy can be arbitrarily adopted as the passing number with ratings from 71 to 100 indicating intermediate qualities of performance.
5. Construct a rating form to insure consistency of rating.

Paper and pencil tests. Paper and pencil tests are familiar to everyone. We will simply review the advantages and disadvantages of the basic types and provide a few checklists for constructing your own tests. The whole subject of testing, however, deserves further study. References are suggested in the appendices.

---

*These points are taken from *Michigan State Testing Bulletin No. 7*, published by the Office of Evaluation Services, Michigan State University, and are reproduced as quoted in Payne, *ibid.*, p. 34.

1. *Essay tests.* The advantages of essay tests are as follows:

a) Essay items provide an opportunity for the student to express himself in his own style of organization and presentation.

b) Essay items provide an opportunity for the instructor to see the student's mental processes.

c) Some learning outcomes such as cause and effect relationships, applications of principles, drawing conclusions, explaining methods, evaluating the worth of ideas and so on can be measured best in essay items.

The disadvantages of using essay items are as follows:

a) Scoring of essay items varies significantly with the instructor.

b) They are difficult to score.

c) It is possible to bluff.

d) The number of items may not be sufficient to fairly sample all of the content covered in the program.

The following considerations should be made when constructing essay test items:*

a) Before writing the question know specifically what points must be included in an acceptable answer. Write a detailed "ideal" answer. Use the list of points as a reference tool when reading the essays.

b) Write clear precise questions. Test the question for these qualities or have other staff members do so.

c) Do not mix essay and objective questions when time is limited. If mixing is necessary allot definite time limits for each item on the test.

d) Carefully determine the time required to write an answer to your essay item.

e) Have students number test booklets so that answers can be scored anonymously.

f) Score a particular item for all trainees at the same time.

---

*Many of the suggestions for constructing essay, multiple choice, true-false, matching, short answer, and completion questions have been taken from H. W. McNeese, "How to rate your tests," *Training in Business and Industry,* May-June 1965, © 1965 by Gellert Publishing Company.

g) Use essay questions for the purpose of measuring those behaviors such as analysis, judgment, and understanding, best assessed by essay items.

h) Do not offer a choice of essay questions.

i) Do not make a generalized estimate of the paper's worth.

j) Do not construct a test consisting of only one question.

k) Assign relative weights in points to each element in the expected answer in advance and use this method for scoring.

2. *Multiple choice tests.* As with the essay, most training people have had some experience with multiple choice tests. Multiple choice items possess the following advantages:

a) They can be used to evaluate a wide range of types of learning including facts, principles, and analysis.

b) Because alternatives are presented, the multiple choice item will be less ambiguous than some other objective forms.

c) The effect of guessing is reduced because of the number of alternatives presented.

d) Responses to a multiple choice item can provide good diagnostic information if the alternatives are carefully constructed.

The disadvantages of the multiple choice item are listed below:

a) Construction of good items is time-consuming and difficult.

b) Good fourth and fifth items are often difficult to find.

Here are some pracical hints for preparing multiple choice items:

a) A multiple choice item consists of a stem and three or more alternative answers. The stem should be a direct question.

b) Keep the reading difficulty of the items low.

c) Include in the stem any words that would need to be repeated in the alternatives.

d) Streamline the wording of the item to include only the minimum for clarity.

e) Be careful not to give away the answer to one item in the responses of another.

f) Avoid negative statements. Call attention to the negative by underlining it if it is necessary to use it.

g) Construct the correct responses so they follow a random pattern.

h) The stem should clearly present the problem.

i) Include as much of the item as possible in the stem.

j) Do not load the stem with irrelevant material.

k) Do not use a statement taken directly from a lecture or text.

l) Do not make the correct response obviously different from the other alternatives.

m) Alternatives should be mutually exclusive.

n) Construct alternatives so that they are grammatically parallel and consistent with the stem.

3. *True-false tests.* True-false tests require the trainee to select the correct response from two alternatives. Other forms of the true-false test include right-wrong, yes-no, same-opposite, and correct-incorrect. Sometimes a third alternative is included such as true-false-depends. True-false tests have the following advantages:

a) They can be constructed quickly.

b) A relatively large number of items can be presented because they can be answered quickly.

c) Scoring is easy and rapid.

d) They are useful for testing situations where only two logical responses are possible.

The disadvantages of this type of item are as follows:

a) They can be ambiguous if not carefully constructed.

b) Guessing can significantly affect the reliability of the test.

c) There is a tendency to respond "true" when in doubt about a particular item.

The following points will help you construct better true-false questions:

a) Items must be definitely true or definitely false.

b) Avoid building in specific determiners such as "all," "always," "no," "never," and other all-inclusive terms. A statement constructed in this way is usually interpreted as "false" by the student. Similarly, when "usually," "sometimes," "could," "generally," and others are used, the statement is normally interpreted as "true."

c) Avoid ambiguous and vague terms of degree or amount such as "frequently," "greatly," or "to a considerable degree."

d) Avoid items containing more than one statement, particularly when one is true and the other false.

e) Avoid constructing items where the correct answer depends on one insignificant word or phrase.

f) Avoid complex sentence structure.

g) Use about 60% false items to 40% true. False items tend to be better-discriminating items.*

4. *Matching tests.* Matching exercises are variations of multiple choice questions. The multiple choice item presents a problem in the stem and several possible answers. The matching item presents the same answers for different problems. Matching items can be used to check nuts-and-bolts type information or more complex information such as cause and effect relationships. Matching items are efficient in time and space because the same set of alternatives can be used for a group of stems.

The following rules should be observed in the construction of matching exercises:

a) The number of alternatives should be greater than the number of problems presented.

b) The entire set of problems and answers should be kept relatively short.

c) The directions should indicate whether an answer choice may be used more than once.

d) A matching exercise should be complete on one page.

e) The alternatives should be related but mutually exclusive.

f) The basis for matching should be explained in the directions.†

5. *Short answer and completion tests.* Short answer and completion items are useful for quickly checking on the possession of facts by a student. They have the following advantages:

a) The effect of guessing is minimized.

b) They are relatively easy to score.

---

*Payne, *Ibid.*, pp.56-63.

†*Ibid.*, pp. 72-75.

The chief disadvantage is that they are not always completely objective. The instructor must be prepared to accept plausible, unanticipated answers.

The following points will help in constructing short answer and completion items:

a) Omit only key words.
b) Do not leave too many blanks in a statement.
c) If a problem requires a numerical answer indicate the units in which it is to be expressed.
d) Require short, definite answers.
e) Blanks should come at the end of a completion statement.
f) Direct questions are preferable to incomplete declarative sentences.*

How to Describe the Test Performance of Groups

Statistics are used to summarize large amounts of data about an individual trainee or groups of trainees. The training director should have a basic understanding of frequency distribution, percentiles, the basic measures of central tendency, the basic measures of variability, and measures of relative position. He will need these to treat data derived from testing his own training groups, and to understand the articles he reads in the professional journals. It is beyond the scope of this handbook to provide a basic course in statistics. The appendices, however, list some useful texts to which the training director can refer.

Evaluating the Classroom Performance of Trainees

Tests alone will not give a sufficient appraisal of a trainee's progress. The instructor is in an excellent position to make observations about the work of trainees in a group training situation. The following questions are useful ways of evaluating trainee's learning behavior:

1. Is he industrious?
2. Does he keep up with training assignments?
3. Does he select proper tools and use correct procedures?
4. Does he have the manual dexterity to perform the work, if this is important?

**Ibid.*, pp. 53-56.

5. Does he require excessive supervision?
6. Does he cooperate with other members of the group?
7. Does he observe safety rules?
8. Does he handle tools and equipment with reasonable care?
9. Does he come to group meetings when they are scheduled and on time?
10. Does he contribute to class discussion?
11. Does he make a visible effort to learn by asking questions, taking notes, and so on?

Evaluation of the Instructor

Any evaluation of learning must include an evaluation of the instructor's proficiency. An evaluation of an instructor should take into account the following factors:

1. Knowledge of the subject matter.
2. Use of a lesson plan.
3. Participation of class.
4. Communication.
5. Knowledge of individual trainees.
6. Integration of the media of learning.
7. Ability to evaluate training.
8. Control of group and environment.
9. Record keeping.
10. Speech.
11. Appearance.
12. Relationship with trainees.
13. Attitude.

BEHAVIOR EVALUATION

Our concept of total evaluation requires that we not be satisfied with just classroom test results. Everyone can point to cases in which an individual has done well on a test, yet failed to demonstrate his achievements in real life situations. A man may be able to talk about how to motivate employees but be unable to stimulate his own subordinates. The goal of all training should be to change behavior patterns to fit a standard. If we accept this definition, then a passing score on a test only indicates that a trainee has received the information we have sent. Our objective, however, is to have him change his on-the-job behavior in terms of his new information.

Basically what is involved is finding ways to measure before and after job behavior. This can be accomplished in one or more of the following ways:

1. Interview or give a questionnaire to the trainee's subordinates before and after the training.
2. Have an impartial member of the training department observe the trainee's work at the job site before and after the training.
3. Interview or give a questionnaire to the trainee's boss before and after the training.
4. Interview or give a questionnaire to the trainee's peers before and after the training.

Some attempts have been made to perform this kind of evaluation. It is time-consuming and difficult. Standardized measuring instruments can be used, but the training director will need to spend a great deal of time and effort developing his own devices for observing, recording, and measuring the changes in behavior. Despite the difficulty of behavior evaluation it is one of the most important forms of evaluation. The training director cannot be content to say, "I can't understand why he is doing such a poor job; he was an outstanding student in my class."

RESULTS EVALUATION

Each of the types of evaluation has become progressively more difficult to perform. The fourth type is the most difficult because of the large number of variables the training director must separate and analyze. Nevertheless the corporate pay-off of all training activity is found in results evaluation. The results an organization looks for can be stated simply in terms of higher profits – the bottom line. The training department contributes to a favorable bottom line by reducing employee turnover, reducing workmen's compensation costs, reducing the number of grievances that must be arbitrated, reducing the amount of scrap, reducing inventory shortages, improving management decision-making, and a host of other factors that mean higher profits or lowered cost of operation to an organization. It is the responsibility of the training director to keep the eye of his department always fixed on the bottom line. He must find ways to relate his programs to the P & L statement for his organization.

11

What Can the Training Consultant Do for You?

A company's need for the services of a training consultant is not measured by its sales volume or its number of employees. The only real measure is the nature of the problem to be solved and the value the company can receive for its investment in a consultant. Even after some firms reach a conclusion on this basis, they reject the idea of using a consultant for such reasons as professional jealousy, dislike of outside interference, or fear of the exposure of operating weaknesses.

How does a company judge its need for a training consultant? A good answer can be found in a recent situation involving a firm that operates a $100 million sales organization with many decentralized locations and with various types of operations within these locations. The company had no internal training organization except in one local division. Faced with high employee turnover and increased labor costs, members of management decided to turn to training as a means of help. They had no internal expertise – only an awareness of a problem. Where did they start?

They could have hired a staff person to perform the task, but they were not certain training really was their problem. If they hired a new employee, would he be the right man for the future and could he objectively review the problem and needs? Because of these and other uncertainties, the company sought outside help to (1) review its operation as it related to training, (2) establish plans and budgets for an internal staff, (3) recommend courses of study with budgets, and (4) indoctrinate management on how and why training must be conducted.

How do you know when you need a consultant? Are there symptoms of training needs just as there are symptoms of illness that tell us when we need a medical doctor? We can only suggest signs to look for that may help you spot the need. Problems such as an over-worked staff; need for one-time projects (especially films, programed instruction, and sales training programs); or need for particular expertise in a new field like computer-assisted instruction may be economically and effectively handled by an outside consultant. Ask yourself the following questions:

1. Will hiring a consultant save more money than assigning an employee to the task?
2. Is his expertise of value to your problem?
3. Would management be more likely to listen to an outsider who can be more objective in his answers than your own employee?
4. Considering the consultant's cost, can he add value to your operation for his cost?

WHAT IS A CONSULTANT?

The classic description of a consultant is "the man who helps the businessman with all the problems he himself has avoided by becoming a consultant." The usual definition of a consultant is "an expert experienced in the specific problem area for which you need advice or help." A training consultant is a person whose experience qualifies him to recommend solutions to specific training problems through the application of specialized knowledge of training techniques and tools. The problem is to determine which consultant appears to have the background and experience you require to make him of value to you.

HOW DO YOU SELECT A CONSULTANT?

The selection of a consultant would seem to be a simple task at first thought. Everyone is inclined to feel that all training consultants are alike, that they are all equal in experience and the only difference is what they charge for their services and where they are located relative to the company. Nothing could be further from the truth. Let us take a look at one firm and how they went about the first steps of selecting a consultant. From this example you will see how this process actually functions.

In our illustration we will call the company the Chef Corporation. Chef owns and operates a chain of fast-food, 15¢ hamburger stores spread over the southern United States. The stores were intended to be identical in physical design, products sold, and type of service offered. Chef's goal was to have a chain of stores identical in food quality and service, but the concept was failing because of high personnel turnover, a low-grade labor pool, and a lack of centralized store procedures and methods. Chef also lacked a training department and training facilities. Management recognized the need to organize and develop a training capability if it ever hoped to overcome its deficiency. Chef did not possess the internal capabilities to solve the problems and consequently turned to outside consultants for help. To accomplish the selection of a consultant, the management of Chef followed a series of steps which ensured an organized, thorough search and selection method.

Step 1: Potential sources. Their first step was to ascertain which firms or individuals were engaged in training consulting. They developed a list of potential consultants from the following sources:

1. Consultants previously retained by the company in any capacity.
2. Professional journals.
3. Professional organizations.
4. Bibliographies.
5. Other firms in the industry which had previous experience with consultants.

While this approach did provide an opening for the Chef Corporation, you should recognize that often the best consultants are not found through the normal channels of promotion and advertising. Remember to judge them only on the basis of their accomplishments. Keep this in mind when you search the field and look for actual cases where a consultant has solved a problem in a professional manner.

Step 2: Training needs. Building the list of potential consultants is only a start. The next step is to write to these firms and/or individuals to determine which one might be suited to your need. To do this, however, requires that you have some idea of what you think your training problems are.

As you know, it is not easy to identify specific training trouble spots. Often the real problem is hidden. The more information you can supply concerning the symptoms of your problem, the easier the task of finding the consultant best suited to your needs. You are not expected to develop an intensive diagnosis of your problem at this point. This is what you expect the consultant to achieve. You must, however, have a clear notion of where the training problem is within the company. If you went to a medical doctor, for example, and told him "I don't feel well" or

"I have pain in my stomach and my head aches," which do you suppose would get faster, clearer results? The latter, of course. This is exactly what you are doing when you try to isolate the problem for the training consultant.

Chef was in need of a complete review of its training system with specific need to develop training materials and methods for both management and line workers. The company chose to limit its selection of a consultant to a list of firms and individuals experienced in broad training systems analysis and solutions and with experience in the food industry.

Step 3: Contacting selected firms. Once the Chef people were satisfied that the list of consultants had been properly developed and culled to contain only those they felt were most capable of meeting their training needs, their next move was to contact the selected firms to ascertain their interest and availability. For this purpose a general letter stating the purpose and scope of the task was drafted. The letter contained sufficient information for a potential contractor to determine whether he was interested and qualified to bid on the proposed project.

A basic letter should contain the following information as a minimum:

1. Name of the company requesting the bid (usually on the letterhead).
2. The type of business the company is engaged in.
3. Basic description of the proposed task and its relation to the company.
4. Scope and length of the proposed contract.
5. Any constraint imposed upon the contractor.
6. Location of the contract performance.

While the initial letter should be brief, it must provide the potential contractor with enough data to allow him to determine whether he wishes to bid on the task. This letter is not intended to elicit bids; its only purpose is to determine which consultants are interested in bidding. Following is an example of a letter illustrating this step.

Dear Mr. Consultant:

The Chef Corporation is engaged in the fast-food industry through the operation and management of a chain of 100 company-owned units. These units are located throughout the southern United States from Mississippi to Florida.

In recent years we were able to secure an adequate supply of labor from among older people who migrated to the South for health reasons or retirement. Now, however, the rise of new industry in the area has caused a labor shortage which necessitates our hiring teenagers as line workers, thus creating a need for training in proper work habits. At present we have no training program.

Our desire is to retain a firm such as yours to help us develop the necessary training program. We hope to accomplish this development task within the next six months.

The only restriction we would impose on the development phase of the project is to require that the contractor work on location for several weeks in the Florida area at our main office.

If you would be interested in bidding on this proposed training development task, we would appreciate hearing from you with a brief statement of your company's qualifications. When we receive your positive response, we will send you more detailed data from which you can draft a formal proposal.

Sincerely,
THE CHEF CORPORATION

The potential consultants will take anywhere from a few days to a few weeks to answer your letter. Some consultants not interested in bidding on the project may not answer at all. If you have planned your initial list wisely, you will receive a sufficient number of interested contractors' responses. Keep in mind that a lack of interest on the part of any one consultant is sometimes due to previous commitments which may conflict with the proposed project, and not his lack of ability or desire to work for your company. Some consultants will also send negative replies because they believe the scope of the proposed task is too small or too large for their staff or that it is not their specialty. In any event, do not get discouraged if you have only a few positive responses; it is the quality not the quantity that counts.

Having developed a list of potential consultants, and having written the initial letter to them and received replies, you are now ready to submit the request for proposal (RFP). This document is the most crucial phase in the cycle of contractor bidding, selection, and contract fulfillment. As a consequence great care should be taken to develop a clear and concise RFP.

Step 4: Request for proposal (RFP). A building contractor would not build a house without detailed plans. The more specific these plans, the greater the probability that they will result in a well-contructed building at a reasonable cost. The same rule applies to the hiring of consultants. If you draft a clear, concise set of plans in your RFP, describing the task and conditions under which you wish to retain and utilize a consultant, you are likely to receive clear, concise proposals and ultimately an effective performance by the successful bidder.

The RFP developed by Chef contained the following items:

1. The training problem defined in one or two sentences.
2. Data on the education, age, and background of the training population.
3. Outcome (objectives) desired from the project.
4. Work task

   a) Specific work task description.
   b) Schedule of delivery.
   c) Acceptance criteria.
   d) Testing criteria.
   e) Cost basis for bid (fixed price, cost-plus, or other).
   f) The form of the final report or materials, and the number of copies required.
   g) Constraints, logistics problems, or other inputs affecting the project.

An RFP serves as the basis for the writing of the proposal by the potential consultant and as your blueprint during the construction phase to be certain that the consultant follows the plan. It should be well designed and adhered to by all parties concerned.

Briefly review the items on an RFP and how you may construct them. In doing so keep in mind that this list is not all-encompassing and your RFP might include more or fewer items depending upon the task for which you are seeking proposals. As stated above, it should include the following:

1. *The training problem defined in one or two sentences.* The crux of your entire effort is boiled down into a one- or two-sentence description of what you consider the central training problem. This description should be clear and concise so that the reader has no doubt of your intent. If your problem is to produce a programed instructional course to train a specific group of employees, the description might read "To research, write, and validate a programed instructional course designed to train food-service employees in the proper methods of dishwashing."

2. *The education, age, and background of the trainee population.* Provide the most exact data you can regarding the trainee population's

background. Too often failure occurs in the development stage simply because this critical input was missing, ignored, or improperly applied.

You should be able to gather this information by talking with your personnel director, by observation, or by direct contact with members of the trainee group.

3. *Outcome (objectives) desired from the project.* While concise objectives are difficult to develop at this stage in the project, it is practical to at least state your desired outcome. What do you expect the learner to accomplish from this training program?

4. *Work task*

a) Specific work task description: Exactly what is the task you expect the consultant to accomplish? To some extent this will be an elaboration of your opening definition of the training problem. Be clear; don't hedge on this statement with fancy words. Do not leave any doubt in anyone's mind as to what you specify as the work task.
b) Schedule of delivery: When do you expect all or part of the package delivered? List dates; be specific.
c) Acceptance criteria: What is acceptable to you? Again, be specific about what you consider a test of acceptability. How will you and the potential contractor know when the final product has been adequately tested? If you won't be satisfied unless 90% of the students achieve 90% on the post-test, then be clear and state this as a criterion.
d) Cost basis for a bid: If you have a desired cost base such as fixed price or cost-plus, it should be stated. In the absence of such a statement, it is assumed that any cost method will be acceptable to you.
e) Form of final reports and number of copies required: Is the final report really a report or do you expect 100 copies, 10 copies, or some other amount? Is a product the anticipated result? State clearly the final form you expect. If, for example, the final report is to be a reproducible copy, state that "the final report shall consist of two (2) IBM Executive-typed copies, 8 × 11 format suitable for reproduction. Type face shall be bold face #1." Be clear on this point to avoid arguments at the end of the project.

f) Constraints, logistics problems, or other inputs affecting the project: Are there any constraints, location requirements, or material problems that might affect the project? If so, state them now. Do not leave this until later. It is best that the potential consultants be aware of any such problems before they bid.

If you follow this RFP format, the finished document will be similar to the following example.

Request for Proposal

1. Training problem

   To develop a programed instructional course to teach the backline operator's process in a fast-food store.

2. Student population

   a) Teenagers.
   b) High school students (non-graduates).
   c) No business experience or other work experiences.
   d) Male only.

3. Objective

   Given standard Chef equipment within a store, the inexperienced backline operator will be capable of producing a finished product as specified on page 10 of Chef's manual.

4. Work task

   a) With data, manuals, audiovisuals, and other materials available, the contractor is expected to develop the course. The contractor is expected to also teach the store managers how to use the completed course in local store training.
   b) Delivery: 90 days from date of contract.
   c) Acceptance criteria: At least 90% of the test students should receive 90% on the post-test.
   d) Test criteria: Same as above.
   e) Cost basis: Fixed price contract.
   f) Delivery format: Completed course will be delivered in three (3) reproducible IBM Executive-typed copies in Bold Face # 1 type face.
   g) Constraints: None.

5. Contractual data

   a) If you have any questions regarding the project, contact the undersigned.
   b) All bids are due 30 days from date of RFP.
   c) You must name project director and assistant and show their previous experience.
   d) Include a general plan for development of the course.

A copy of the completed RFP should be sent to all of the potential consultants who replied to your original letter stating an interest in bidding on the proposed project. Be certain to treat all potential consultants alike. If you offer to answer questions on the RFP to one consultant, make the same offer to all potential consultants.

Proposals (bids) from the consultants will be developed in many physical formats. Some will simply be letters; others will be very elaborate. Do not let the physical appearance of the proposal influence your decision. You are not buying paper work; you are buying expertise. Many firms will put more effort and expense into a proposal than it warrants simply to impress the prospective client.

Before the bids filter in it is necessary to establish a system for evaluating them. Again, if we follow our Chef case history, we will find that management had no way of knowing which bid would be acceptable unless it established criteria or a framework in which to judge the bids on an equal basis. For this purpose an evaluation form similar to the one in Fig. 11-1 was developed. This evaluation form is particularly effective if a committee or group is to make the selection from a large number of proposals.

While the evaluation form is an aid in selecting the desired consultant, you cannot rely solely upon this method in making your final selection. One major item that the reading and evaluation of a written proposal fails to reveal is the human qualities of the people you must work with. This is especially true when you are dealing with a large firm where the individuals selling the proposal are not likely to be the persons who will actually work on the job. It is necessary, therefore, to specify who will be working on the job. You could be very unhappy after signing the contract to find the consultant's second team showing up for work when you anticipated someone else.

Step 5: Selection. Chef has now reached a point in its selection cycle where it has received bids worth consideration from two or three contractors. All other bidders were immediately informed that another firm had been selected to perform the task. Do not fail to properly respond to the rejected proposals; failure to do so is not only professionally irresponsible, but is potentially damaging to your company's best interest should you need the services of one of the rejected firms in the future.

For this purpose a simple letter will suffice. It should consist of one or two paragraphs explaining that you were appreciative of their effort and considered their proposal to be of professional quality, but that another firm was selected because it came closer to filling your needs.

Fig. 11-1. Contract proposal evaluation form.

Project ______________________ Date ____________

Contractor Bidding ______________________ Total Rating Points ____________

<u>Measures</u> <u>Rating</u>

I. <u>Contractor Qualifications</u>

A. <u>Professional Qualification</u>

1. Project Manager ____________
2. Task Analysts and Programmers ____________
3. Technical Support Capabilities ____________
4. Related work produced by contractor ____________

B. <u>Other</u>

1. Financial capacity of contractor relative to task ____________
2. Proximity to company ____________
3. Has done previous quality work for the company ____________

II. <u>The Proposal</u>

<u>Qualities</u>

1. Proposal objectives clear ____________
2. Techniques proposed are clear ____________
3. Comprehensiveness ____________
4. General clarity of writing ____________
5. Cost of task in relation to others ____________
6. Administration considerations ____________
7. Show concern for company "systems" question ____________
8. Has evidence of specialized capabilities ____________

III. <u>Other</u>

Did contractor respond to all non-program requirements in RFP ____________

TOTAL RATING POINTS ____________

<u>Key</u>

<u>For Each Item Listed Rate</u>

5 for top quality
4 for very high quality
3 for medium quality
2 for average quality
1 for lowest quality

Close the letter by stating that you will keep them in mind for future jobs which may occur.

Depending upon the magnitude or complexity of the job, you may need to request further information from the remaining bidders by written or live interviews. Do not expect a potential consultant to travel long distances to discuss the project with you if the total contract is minor in value. After all, he must make a living and travel costs are extremely high, to say nothing of his time.

In our Chef case two bidders remained from the original group. They were selected because their proposed solutions to the training problem were logical and in keeping with management's view. Both firms were equally strong in staff quality and abilities, but one was better qualified because of its work experience in the food-service field. It was therefore selected as the contractor. At this point the tendency is to write off the other bidder. It is best to delay this action until after you complete the contract negotiation. Too often the parties fail to agree on terms in a contract and failure to have a runner-up proposal to turn to would force yoy to start all over again in the selection process. It is important, however, not to overdo your waiting game and expect bidder number two to wait weeks or months for you to conclude your negotiations. Play fair and answer as soon as possible, preferably within two weeks from the time you indicated to him that his bid was under final consideration.

Step 6: Contract. Once the decision has been reached as to the firm or individual consultant selected and letters have been sent to all other bidders indicating their failure to receive the job, it is necessary to negotiate the contract with the chosen consultant. On this single document hinges your entire working relationship. Great care must be taken to work out all details prior to the signing of the contract to minimize future friction. The essential details to be considered in drafting a contract are:

1. Task to be performed.
2. Length of time to perform the work task.
3. Acceptance clause.
4. Cost? Travel?
5. Form of payment; time of payment.
6. Who will work on the job? Where?
7. How much of your time is involved in the task?
8. To whom does the consultant report? When? Monthly? Final?
9. Validation test: When? How many? How?

Drafting a sound, adequate contract agreement is as essential to the consultant as it is to you. More problems arise from a badly drafted contract than from any other source in a consultant/client relationship. In drafting this contract, be fair in your dealings with the consultant. You are the one paying for the job and you may have trouble getting your money's worth if you treat him badly.

Since the contract is the critical working document, let us review each major item, what it means, how to administer it, and how to use the agreement to achieve your goals.

1. *Task to be performed.* Only you know what it is. You personally spelled it out in the RFP. Make sure the task is clearly defined in writing. Do not leave it to oral interpretation.

2. *Performance time.* Be realistic. Do not expect hours of work for which the consultant is not being paid. Remember you are buying his time so be certain you contract for enough time to get the job done.

3. *Acceptance of consultant's work.* Many times a consultant "completes" a job only to find he did not produce what the client thought he was producing. Do not make this mistake. It costs time, money, loss of sleep, and other difficulties. Spell it out. What constitutes acceptance? What do you want him to do?

4. *Cost.* What price are you going to pay for the consultant's work? How? When? How is he to account for his cost and time? Who pays the travel expense? These are but a few questions that must be answered. Be fair but be frank about this aspect of the contract.

5. *Cost guidelines.* How does one know what cost base to use in a particular situation? The best guide is common sense. If you plan to use a consultant sparingly and on a demand basis, it would be best to contract on an hourly base. If the task is to develop a programed course or other specified material, then a fixed price contract would be best because he has agreed to build a unit for which he has blueprints (RFP). Cost-plus might be applied where the client and contractor agree that the specific task is broad and undefinable at this time. In this case, however, you should stipulate a maximum amount.

What do you expect per dollar spent? If the consultant works eight hours, what will he accomplish? Unfortunately there is no formula answer. The only real guide is the consultant's reputation and your constant monitoring of his work.

6. *Form of payment; time of payment.* There are several standard methods which consultants use to charge clients: by the hour, day, week, or month; fixed price and/or cost-plus. An hourly charge may range from $15 to $30 per hour, or more, depending on the caliber of the personnel working on the task. This basic rate will apply regardless of whether the work effort is a few hours, days, weeks, or months. Be sure you specify what these costs are prior to signing the contract. Another form of costing is fixed price. In this method of charging, the bidder stipulates what he thinks the total charge for performing the task as specified in his proposal will be. There should be no added cost to the client beyond the one fixed price agreed upon. The cost-plus method, on the other hand, is an open ended arrangement whereby the client agrees to pay the contractor his actual cost of labor, materials, and travel plus a specified fee. These costs must be spelled out in the contract and will vary as the work task progresses.

If the contract is for a specific task such as development of a programed instructional course, it would be best to establish a fixed price contract. On the other hand, if you wish to use the consultant to review your present training program, training materials, or simply to advise you, it might be more economical to establish a cost charge by the hour or day. The payment schedule for these accrued costs should be based on the consultant's performance – pay for what you receive. Also hold back about 10% of the contract value for final payment to the contractor after he has met the final criteria of acceptance. Keep in mind that there are no bargains in buying consulting time; you get what you pay for.

7. *Specifically who will work on the job?* You may wish to specify a name or names and not simply job titles or numbers. This is up to you. If you do not specify a person, don't be surprised at whom you might have to work with on the actual job.

8. *How much of your time is involved in the task?* While at first thought this may seem to be a rather simple point and one where you may be inclined to say "So what; I'll do what I have to do," it can in reality be a very difficult matter to handle after signing the contract.

Be specific. What will you do other than monitor the work? Do you plan to write the course objectives and outlines or test the material? How much effort will be required on the premises, at another location, or at the contractor's? Spell out how you plan to participate beyond the role of monitoring the contractor.

9. *Reports.* Often failure to produce a satisfactory product is due to inadequate communication between consultant and client. Specify in the contract what type of reporting system will be employed and the frequency of the reporting. Use these reports to adjust or redirect the work task if necessary. Do not wait until the completion of the task to voice your opinions of the work effort.

The frequency of reporting will depend upon the difficulties and complexity of the project. In most instances a formal monthly report for projects lasting six months or longer is adequate. For projects shorter than six months, a reporting system based on milestones in the actual work is probably the best check system.

The establishment of a formal reporting system does not rule out or discourage the informal reporting which should take place throughout the life of the project between the contractor and the contract monitor. The prime function of the scheduled reports is to be certain that all facets of the project are reviewed periodically.

A final report on the project should be required regardless of the output of the contract. You will find this report of immense value in reporting to your management on how the money was spent and what the company got for its investment.

10. *Testing.* All projects regardless of their nature need some form of testing. Whether this testing phase is formal or informal depends partially upon the task and partially upon your desires. If you contracted for a programed instructional course, for example, you must require both developmental and validation tests. Your minimum acceptance criterion might be that 90% of the students achieve 90% or better on the tests.

It is best to write the validation requirements into the contract. Remember that anything is possible in writing and rewriting learning materials until a specified set of test results is achieved, but this takes time and time is what you are buying.

The validation test must reflect the preset course objectives. Did the student achieve these objectives? Check the tests and be certain they reflect these objectives.

While there is no such thing as an ideal contract suited to the needs of everyone, certain facts as previously discussed will help to establish a sound working relationship with the consultant, and will normally help you to avoid many problems on the job. The contract is actually a set of work rules. It clarifies in writing what each party expects from the other. The physical form of the contract will depend upon what you as the client desire. It may be a simple letter stating the terms, a formal contract written by a lawyer, or a middle-of-the-road approach wherein the terms are specified in letter form and both parties sign the letter to indicate their acceptance of its terms and conditions. The contract should be worked out as a joint document; it should not be a contract in which the client or consultant generates the agreement and the other party simply responds to the terms until they are mutually satisfied.

Step 7: Using the Consultant. Once you have signed a contract, the real work begins. Do not feel that by having hired a consultant you have done your job and now can sit back in your chair and let him wave a magic wand over the problem to produce results. Nothing is further from the truth.

It is the consultant's job to find solutions or to devise a plan or material to overcome your problem in training. But it is your job to direct this effort to be certain you receive a return on your investment in this consultant. You must be actively interested. Schedule informal and formal progress meetings to be certain that the consultant is on target. Remember that you are buying his time; make good use of this expensive commodity.

Keep in mind the fact that a consultant is an outsider to your group and is looked upon with suspicion. He represents change, problems, and possibly even the loss of jobs to some workers. Because of these factors, management must pave a smooth path prior to his actual appearance on the job. A good example of what happens when management fails to pave such a path was a recent consultation task.

In this instance the task was to survey the organization's present teaching program to determine ways and means to improve the output of the system. The line manager in one unit, however, was against the concept and chose to ignore the fact that a consultant was coming. He simply indicated to his subordinates that "management was sending someone to look at the operation." Without any more knowledge than that, the workers viewed this man with alarm because they thought he represented a threat to their jobs. Only when one employee stated this fact to the consultant was this lack of management preparation known. Up to that time the consultant had had difficulty working with the staff. Once he knew the situation he could state his purpose to the staff and help to resolve the problem.

The basic vehicle necessary to accomplish the work task is strong communication between client and consultant. The communication may take many verbal or nonverbal forms, formal or informal methods. Whatever method you employ is fine provided the system is kept open and the reports are frequent.

You should establish a specific formal reporting schedule as stated in the contract. The final report should be both written and oral to ensure a complete understanding of the project results.

Step 8: Follow up. The work of the consultant and the investment by the company are both wasted unless the findings, recommendations, or materials produced by the consultant are actually used by the client. If you are paying to produce a study, use the recommendations. Be certain that the personnel responsible for implementing these recommendations actually carry them through on schedule. It is best to have worked out an agreement with top management prior to the conclusion of consultant's work as to how the project will be implemented internally and to whom the line managers will be responsible if the recommendations are not implemented.

It is natural for most individuals to "forget" a task which is difficult, time consuming, or unwelcome because it was not their idea in the first place. You must therefore establish a rigid follow-up system. It may be patterned on the design in the example below.

Step	Time Scale	Task
I	30 days from time recommendations were received.	Each individual affected must report in writing what action he has taken.
II	90 days from date of recommendations.	Progress reports in writing.
III	Every three months thereafter until completed.	Progress reports in writing.

Step 9: Value received. The value of any consulting effort is determined by the quality of the consultant's work and the desire of the company management to implement the consultant's recommendations or to apply the developed training materials to the organization.

The value of the consultant is found in the measurable results attained. To be certain you have received value, check the following:

1. Were the recommendations and their implementation costs realistic relative to the situation?

2. Has your own management been stimulated to do its own thinking on future projects of this type?
3. Did you find his working relationship and quality of work satisfactory, and would you rehire him?

If we apply these checks to our Chef case we would note that the company selected a consultant who advised it of a need for (1) a new work procedures manual and a program to teach this material to management, and (2) the development of basic training materials for use by an internally developed training department.

Maximum value will come from your investment in a consultant if you can not only benefit from his original work effort, but also require him to return later to see how his recommendations worked and how well they solved the problem for which they were designed. In fact, adjustments may be necessary in the original report and materials prepared. Change is valuable only if it solves the problem.

Part 3

Basic Methods and Materials of Training

The purpose of the third part of this book is to describe some of the basic training media and the techniques for producing them at the lowest cost. Our intention is not to cover all of the available media or all of the ways of producing materials related to those media we cover. Instead we have selected some simple, inexpensive, but effective means of getting a job done. Chapter 12 begins with a discussion of some of the basic media of learning and progresses through materials requiring greater technical knowledge and skill.

12

Basic Verbal Training Techniques

The first impulse most people have when faced with a communications problem is to try to solve it by simply going forth and telling the people involved what they need to know. Similarly, in confronting training problems the immediate solution always seems to be to gather a group and begin lecturing. One wonders why this happens with such consistency. Possibly the school and university models we have experienced all of our lives have become so indelibly etched on our minds that we find it hard to break away and consider the myriad forms of verbal training available.

This chapter deals with the different kinds of verbal techniques, describes their advantages and limitations, and provides a brief discussion of how to use the techniques. Because of space limitations it is impossible to treat each technique in an exhaustive manner. Rather, we suggest that this chapter serve as a primer to this field.

PRINCIPLES OF EFFECTIVE ORAL PRESENTATIONS

Before describing the characteristics of the various basic verbal training techniques, here are some general suggestions to assist you in making any kind of oral presentation more effective.

1. Detailed preparation and rehearsal prior to any presentation is critical. Even informal discussions, if they are to be productive, need careful, advance planning in the form of provocative questions, resource materials, and alternative topics.
2. Begin preparation by defining for yourself the fundamental purpose

of your presentation. Is it to inform, persuade or instruct? Then keep your answer in mind as you go through all of the other stages of planning. Consider it when you evaluate the results of any oral presentation.

3. The next task is to develop clear objectives covering the major points that you want to cover in the presentation. These should be as detailed as you can make them. Usually it is easier to start by simply writing a list of objectives without regard to their final order. Once the list is complete, you can then go back and put them in the correct sequence.

4. Most oral presentations have three standard parts: an introduction, a body, and a summary. The introduction is used to establish the subject and deepen the audience's interest. The body is the heart of the presentation, containing your major arguments, descriptions, problem discussion, etc. The summary is used to restate major points and conclude the presentation. Following this three-part pattern in the preparation of any oral training technique can usually be counted on to achieve results.

5. Once the objectives have been set down in the proper sequence, the next step is to decide what illustrations, stories, examples, statistics, and so on will help you reach these objectives efficiently and effectively.

6. Once the presentation has been roughed out, it is imperative that you get some feedback on it. This will be of greatest value if it can be obtained from one or more representative members of the audience for whom it is intended. After receipt of feedback, it is then necessary to revise and polish.

7. The many principles of speech are a course in themselves and it is impossible to cover that material within a chapter of a book. Our suggestion to a training person who expects to devote a large portion of his time to public speaking is that he study thoroughly the principles of effective speaking. Public speaking is an acquired skill, which you must work at to become proficient.

Always keep in mind that your prime voice problem is to speak loudly enough so that all can hear; but too much volume is as annoying as too little. Gauge your audience and the circumstances of the presentation to strike a balance. When in doubt, ask someone in the back of the room if he can hear you satisfactorily. Clarity of voice is important simply because you want to be understood by the audience. Watch the pitch and the speed also, especially speed of delivery. Do not go so fast that no one can follow you, or so slowly that they will go to sleep. Vary the speed of your presentation.

8. Other factors to consider in speaking are gestures, platform habits, and dress. Too often we fail to realize that the audience must watch the

speaker as well as listen to him. His voice may be fine but his platform manners very bad. When you speak, dress appropriately, being careful not to overdress. Do not pace the platform, smoke, chew gum, or show nervous habits to the audience. Keep your gestures to a minimum. Most important, let your speech reflect your personality. Relax and be yourself, insofar as that is consistent with the principles of good public speaking.

LECTURE

The most common verbal technique employed in training is the lecture. Simply stated, a lecture is a prepared oral presentation of a subject by a qualified person. While this one-sentence explanation would make the technique seem simple, it is in reality quite complex to use and to evaluate. Why is this so?

More often than not the weakness in a lecture is not in the technique but in the lecturer himself. For one thing, it is not easy for an instructor to know if his lecture was a success. There is little or no audience participation or feedback. Normally the weakness occurs because either the lecture method was the wrong medium for the training problem, or the lecturer failed to properly prepare a lesson plan.

Step 1: Preparation. If we return to our definition of a lecture, we find that a lecture is a "prepared" presentation. The steps listed below, if followed, will normally allow an instructor to prepare an adequate lecture presentation.

a) Analyze the group to whom you will speak.
b) Establish how much speaking time you will have.
c) Determine the objectives of the lecture.
d) Establish main facts to be covered in the lecture.
e) Organize the main facts and teaching points in outline form (Chapter 9).
f) Keep the order of your presentation logical.
g) Develop opening lead paragraphs.
h) Develop adequate transitional steps between main facts to allow for a free-flowing speech.
i) Determine what audiovisual aids you need in support of your speech.
j) Decide how you will evaluate the results.
k) Check to be sure you allowed enough time for a question period.

After carefully preparing the lecture facts, practice the delivery. Pay attention to such aspects as the timing of your delivery, integration of the visual aids, speech qualities, and smoothness of the entire presentation. Rehearse as much as you can to ensure a smooth delivery. Avoid the "ahs" which only serve to distract the learner.

Step 2: Presenting the lecture. The key to a good lecture is preparation, but this will be wasted if the instructor fails to deliver an interesting presentation. Some ideas to remember are as follows:

a) Use "you" rather than the personal "I"; this will create a much better rapport with the audience.
b) Practice the transitional points in particular to ensure smooth coherent presentation.
c) Speak clearly, firmly, and slowly enough so that the audience can listen and take notes if they desire.
d) Use your aids properly and dispose of them or cover them up when finished. Nothing is more distracting to an audience than to look at such errors as a chart on fact one while the lecturer is on fact two or three.
e) Finish within the time allotted. The audience will appreciate you for this gesture.
f) Put variety in your speech with aids, jokes, gestures, rhetorical questions, and so on.

Step 3: Question period. Often used, seldom planned – the consequence is a series of disorganized questions from a few extroverts in the audience. To use a question period effectively requires preparation. The following suggestions should help you make better use of your classroom time.

1. Have the audience write questions down as they occur to them during the lecture. Be sure to provide pencils and 3 x 5 cards for this purpose. Collect questions and have them screened by an assistant for their group value.
2. Speak to the group rather than to a single person when you respond to the questions.
3. Read or repeat the question so that all can hear it.
4. Above all be brief in your response. They have already heard your lecture; don't repeat it.
5. Do not let the question period go beyond the scheduled close of the session. The audience will not pay attention when you "infringe" upon their time.

We have looked briefly at the preparation, presentation, and follow-up (question period) of the lecture technique under the assumption that the instructor and the course chairman were the same person. If, however, the lecturer is an outsider who is to present only one lecture on a portion of the course, then you must maximize this person's appearance through further planning. We suggest the following sequence of events to accomplish this purpose:

1. Meet the lecturer in person, not by telephone or letter only.
2. Know enough about this person to adequately introduce him.
3. Provide him with the lecture facts on:

    a) Objectives.
    b) Topics.
    c) Time allotted to present these facts.
    d) Audience facts.
    e) Physical facilities facts.
    f) Available aids.
    g) Time of the lecture.

4. Follow through to be certain he understands these rules and objectives.
5. Request a copy of his lecture or notes in advance to help him in shaping his speech and to be certain he is on the objectives.
6. One week prior to his scheduled appearance reconfirm his schedule.
7. One day prior to his appearance once again reconfirm date, time, place, as a reminder. These reminders need not be addressed to the man personally, but to his secretary or assistant.

If you are the chairman, you will have the task of introducing the lecturer, closing the program after he completes the lecture, relating his lecture to the overall course goals, and encouraging further student study as well as thanking the speaker for his presentation.

We have talked about the lecturer and his responsibilities, but you must also remember to consider the physical environment in which this lecture is to be presented. Failure to do so can ruin the entire effort. Keep the following points in mind when you are assessing the situation:

1. Adequate ventilation and lighting. Will the audience be too hot or cold during the presentation? It is also a good idea not to allow smoking during the lecture. This could destroy the advantage of having a well-ventilated room.

2. Seating is also critical. How many times have you sat through a speech on a hard uncomfortable chair, wishing you were somewhere else? Try to have chairs with padded seats and adequate writing space on the arm.
3. Use a public address system if required. Do not make the students strain to hear. They won't anyway.
4. If you plan to use films or other media, prepare for this in advance and make sure the room can accommodate them and the audience.
5. Remove all aids and film equipment, if possible, when you finish with them.

When Do You Use the Lecture Technique?

There are some rules on this question, but like all rules of this kind, they are not hard and fast. Your own experience, your own budget, and the physical classroom environment may dictate the use of lecturing when, in fact, it is not the best medium for the presentation. In any event, here are a few justifiable uses of the lecture technique.

1. To present facts, knowledge, ideas, and information in an organized way.
2. To identify or clarify issues or problems.
3. To stimulate or motivate the audience to greater effort.
4. To save time.

Advantages and limitations

Advantages

1. Direct, clear.
2. Conserves time.
3. Facts presented in orderly fashion.
4. Large number of students can be accommodated.
5. Training aids easy to use.

Limitations

1. May be dull, boring.
2. Lacks group participation.
3. Only one person's ideas expressed.
4. May use inappropriate vocabulary.
5. Effects on audience not easily determined.
6. Requires speaking ability.

How to Evaluate a Lecture

The best way to determine whether the lecture was the best instructional tool to employ and whether the specific lecturer and lecture were properly presented is to assess the results by using a checklist such as the example in Fig. 12-1.

Fig. 12-1. Lecture evaluation form.

1. Speaker
   a) Was he organized?
   b) Was he understandable?
   c) Did he relate to course goals?
   d) Did he read the course goals?
   e) Were appropriate aids used?
   f) Did he use question period?
   g) Did speech end on time?
2. Audience
   a) Was audience motivated?
   b) Was audience prepared properly?
   c) Did audience listen intently?
   d) Was there evidence of audience acquisition of knowledge?
   e) Did lecture move group toward their course goal?
3. Lecture technique
   a) Was the lecture the correct technique for this portion of the course?
   b) What other technique would have been better? Why?

GROUP DISCUSSION

A group discussion is a training technique where a group of from five to twenty persons with a mutual interest in a topic meet under the direction of a leader to converse or deliberate with the intention of arriving at a conclusion or direction for the group. The group discussion technique allows maximum opportunity for the individual learner to share his experiences and ideas with other members of the group. This technique is useful to encourage students to express their opinions, to identify, explore or solve problems, or to clarify or amplify a topic.

When using this technique, care must be taken to be certain the students (participants) are adequately prepared in the subject matter to be discussed to be capable of a meaningful exchange.

Step 1: Preparation. The discussion group leader must prepare his topic in advance by adequate reading, viewing of films, or other appropriate

Fig. 12-2. Preparation checklist for group discussion.

Have I:

_______ Read up, prepared on subject?

_______ Separated trainees into groups of similar interest?

_______ Set objectives for the discussion?

_______ Distributed appropriate information in advance?

_______ Prepared an agenda to follow?

_______ Prepared lesson plan?

_______ Prepared physical facilities for group discussion?

activities. From this effort, he will then be able to list the main ideas or facts he wants to have discussed. Later he can check the list to be certain they are all covered. For each main idea, he will develop a brief outline listing three to four subpoints to bring out from each topic or problem. He must also develop a list of questions designed to stimulate the group to participate.

The leader must always keep in mind that a group discussion is not a lecture. Consequently his task is to motivate the group to respond to questions so that they, not the instructor, build the right answers or solutions.

If you go over this checklist (Fig. 12-2) prior to the actual group discussion, you can tell if you have thought of all the factors necessary.

Step 2: Presentation. With this background, you are now prepared to conduct a discussion session. One key fact to keep in mind is that no matter how long your group members may have studied the subject to be discussed, you must still provide a period at the start of the discussion to review the topic by films, pictures, lecture, or other suitable media. Explain what will be discussed and why. Encourage the students to respond and participate. If you follow the sequence outlined in Fig. 12-3, you will find that the discussion will flow smoothly.

Fig. 12-3. Presentation checklist for group discussion.

_______	Use your outline as the script.
_______	Ask thought-provoking questions.
_______	Present illustrations; invite comments.
_______	Stay on the outline.
_______	Switch topics if group is wandering.
_______	Summarize from time to time.
_______	Keep arguments down.
_______	Relate topics to one another and to goals.
_______	Encourage everyone to participate.
_______	Close each topic when feasible. Do not regress.
_______	Direct attention to neglected topics.
_______	Conclude (summarize) discussion with results.

The group discussion technique has many uses, advantages, and limitations. As a training technique, it is especially suitable for use after a topic has been studied in the shop or practice session. It is also useful after lectures, audiovisual presentations, field trips, or similar situations where facts and concepts have been presented.

Advantages and limitations

Advantages

1. Provides an opportunity to share experiences and ideas with group.
2. Encourages individuals to work as team.
3. Helps students develop self-confidence.
4. Helps students gain group acceptance.

Limitations

1. Suitable only for 5 to 20 persons.
2. Requires study of topic before meeting.
3. Easy for one or two students to dominate discussion.
4. Requires topics which lend themselves to discussion.

DEMONSTRATION TECHNIQUE

A demonstration technique is a planned presentation that shows the student how to perform an act, skill, or procedure. Usually it is accompanied by appropriate visual presentations, student questions, and student involvement.

The prime uses of the demonstration technique are to teach students how to perform an act; to develop a skill; to use new equipment, machinery or products; and to build their confidence in performing in these circumstances.

Step 1: Preparation. This is a big step with many parts:

a) Prepare demonstration goals. What do you expect the students to know and be able to do afterwards?

b) Relate the demonstration to the course and course goals.

c) Prepare the means and allot the time to carry out the demonstration.

d) Arrange for proper equipment or settings. If using equipment, be sure it functions; test it prior to class.

e) Be certain that the equipment and class setting are arranged so all students can see and hear.

f) Prepare advance materials to be given to students, listing some of the following points.

What is the demonstration? Why was it selected?
How does it fit course goals?
How and where will the learner use this knowledge?
Where will the student practice the new skill?

g) Prepare demonstration steps to follow in class.

h) Develop step-by-step lesson plan.

i) Run through the steps in the plan to be certain they mesh and are complete.

j) Decide which steps, if any, may require another medium such as film to further describe an action or sequence.

k) Rehearse the plan to be certain that it is smooth and that you have included all steps in their proper sequence.

Step 2: Presentation. As is true in all training situations, there are certain fundamentals to remember or do prior to the presentation phase. These include the proper classroom preparations as noted earlier in this chapter and the assurance that all necessary equipment is in place and in good operating condition.

As the class assembles, put the students at ease. Motivate them to be interested and curious as to what mechanics will be demonstrated or what situation will be presented. Find out what they already know about the subject. Do not dwell on material they already know.

To start the actual demonstration, lead into the subject with a statement indicating how the demonstration is related to what has already been taught and then establish the purpose of the present lesson. State clearly your intentions regarding what you expect the student to do during and after the demonstration.

Stress key points or features. Do not move on to the next point until you are certain that all the students are with you and clearly understand the sequence. Go slowly but steadily. At critical points in the demonstration, summarize, repeat, and ask the students questions to determine whether they understand what is being taught. Let the students participate by having them repeat the step, and by asking them questions which are pertinent to the demonstration. Actual student handling of the equipment involved is important, especially if you are teaching a skill such as the assembly of a part. Repeat your instructions if you find the students are having difficulty understanding the procedures or steps.

As the students begin to show their ability to perform the skill being taught, gradually reduce your instruction to the point where the students are self-sufficient. This does not mean, however, that you should allow them to make repeated mistakes. Unfortunately, such negative learning can be just as easily acquired as the correct learning.

Step 3: Follow-up. The skill you seek to teach must be practiced by the students if it is to be retained. Offer them opportunities to practice on their own under supervision. Test their skills to determine whether they comprehend the entire cycle, not just small steps in the process.

Advantages and limitations

Advantages

1. Easier to visualize steps than if presented orally or in writing.
2. Learner has opportunity to test learning under guidance.
3. Steps in process easy to relate.

Limitations

1. Equipment may not be readily moved.
2. May be difficult to get audience to equipment site.
3. Lack of student opportunity to practice due to class size.
4. Limited to practical problems only.

CONFERENCE TECHNIQUE

The conference technique is a training method whereby a group of persons (usually 12 to 20) pool their ideas, examine facts, test assumptions, and draw conclusions. The conference is an open discussion designed to encourage group thinking on a problem, with eventual acceptance of the conclusion by the group.

Step 1: Preparation. The major task here is the preparation of a discussion outline. It should cover the following points.

a) Objectives.
b) Facts to develop.
c) Best approach for conference.
d) Ways to arouse and maintain interest.
e) Potential problems.

In addition, be sure to check and prepare facilities for the group.

Step 2: Developing a stimulating conference. To get maximum value from the conference, observe the following points.

a) Carefully plan all questions.
b) Create interest with films, charts, etc.
c) Encourage all conferees to express their opinions.
d) Assemble (record) facts as they are presented.
e) Evaluate facts presented.
f) Make certain all members participate.

There are several ways to encourage participation. It is wise, for example, to devise some method to acquaint the participants with each other. Perhaps coffee prior to the conference will achieve this. The leader's attitude is also important. He should not pose as a subject authority to the extent that he scares all the conferees from participating. The manner in which he handles all conferee responses will either encourage or discourage participation.

Fig. 12-4. Question types and their uses in conferences.

	Type	*Use*
1.	Leading	Suggest answer by question.
2.	Factual	Seeking data, information.
3.	Direct	Directed at specific person.
4.	General	Directed at group at large.
5.	Controversial	Where two or more answers possible.
6.	Provocative	Designed to incite an answer.
7.	Yes or no	To draw yes or no responses.

Step 3: Conducting the conference.

a) Make a good beginning by stating the purpose and objectives of the conference and presenting facts via appropriate media.
b) Encourage discussion by all participants.
c) The key to the conference technique is the judicious use of questions. The list in Fig. 12-4 suggests some of the types of questions useful in conferences. Use good questions to draw out the conferees and to keep conference progressing.
d) Maintain control.
e) Summarize occasionally.
f) Close the conference with a summary of results and a preview of the next step you plan to follow.

Advantages and limitations

Advantages

1. Verbal audience participation.
2. Active listeners.
3. Ease of student clarification.
4. Ability to use with moderate size (12 to 20) group.

Limitations

1. Needs skilled moderator.
2. Often lack of time for all participants to speak.
3. One or two people may dominate conference.

SEMINAR TECHNIQUE

The seminar technique is designed for a group of five to thirty people engaged in the study of a topic and is normally led by an expert in the field. The object of the seminar is to study a given subject under the guidance of an expert. Seminars are most commonly used where graduate or management level topics are concerned. The technique requires considerable preparation by all participants.

The leader of a seminar is expected to prepare the course of study for the group. He must prepare the objectives, outline the purpose, and assign each participant a study task. As in other trainee situations, the leader is also responsible for arranging the physical facilities for the group.

Students of a seminar are expected to prepare papers or materials on that segment of the subject assigned to them. At the seminar itself, the leader will call upon the students to present these papers. He will criticize these documents as well as integrate them into the total learning experience.

The normal order of events in a seminar is an opening speech by the leader, followed by reports by the members, a question period, group discussion, and a summary by the leader. The amount of time spent on these seminar segments will depend upon time available. Emphasis is on the expert/leader presentations and the question period. It is in these two areas that the greatest learning occurs.

The leader's role in conducting a seminar is the key to success. He is expected to present the opening speech, motivate the students, pose fruitful questions, and arouse the students' desire to provide sound, useful reports. He is not a teacher in the usual sense. His role is to provide information on the subject and guidance of the students' efforts.

Advantages and limitations

Advantages

1. Uses a recognized expert to lead.
2. Generates high, active student participation.
3. Develops in-depth systematic study of topic.

Limitations

1. May lack appropriate resources.
2. Leader may be difficult to obtain.
3. Requires extensive student preparation often not feasible in industry.

SYMPOSIUM TECHNIQUE

Several methods of the symposium technique can be employed. The "ancient" and the "modern" methods are both popular. The ancient method is just what the name implies. It echoes earlier days when this form of meeting to study a problem was also a social event.

The method employed was for a group of up to 20 people to meet in a home or diningroom to informally discuss a topic of mutual interest. It often became a systematic study of the topic after completion of the meal. You will see a version of this today in some companies that have periodic management breakfasts or lunches. It is also used by churches to gather people to discuss a topic.

For our purposes, the more meaningful version is the modern one. Under this technique, a group of similar size meets to discuss a common problem or topic of mutual interest. Some three to six people in the group are assigned the task of developing short speeches (5 to 20 minutes) for presentation to the larger group. Such speeches are designed only to present information to the audience. The meeting is presided over by a chairman.

The symposium is a valid approach for presenting information to a group in an organized manner, clarifying problems, or stimulating group thinking. Like all group techniques, the symposium has its advantages and limitations.

Advantages and limitations

Advantages

1. Short speeches stimulate group.
2. Technique guards against oversimplification of topic.
3. Short speeches tend to force speakers and group to stay on topic.

Limitations

1. May lack audience participation.
2. Difficult to determine audience learning.
3. May lack competent speakers.
4. Can be boring and uninteresting.

PANEL TECHNIQUE

A panel can be used in a wide variety of arrangements. It is normally composed of a group of three to six people assigned to discuss a specific topic. One person is selected to be moderator and leader. Quite often the panel appears before an audience to discuss a topic, and then involves the audience after the panel discussion in a question session.

The panel technique is often employed to help clarify or identify problems or issues, to present several different points of view on a given topic, or to stimulate interest in a topic for the students' benefit. Most often the panel is made up of experts, who because of limited time or lack of depth in the subject are willing to serve on a panel rather than present a lecture.

Advantages and limitations

Advantages

1. Possible to assemble a group of experts for single meeting.
2. Diverse group offers different views on topic.
3. Informal approach.

Limitations

1. May lack qualified members.
2. Poor moderator weakens procedure.
3. Audience may fail to understand or respond to experts on panel.

COLLOQUY TECHNIQUE

A first cousin to the panel discussion is the colloquy. In colloquy three to four members of the audience join an equal number of experts on a given subject to ask questions of these experts, who, in turn, respond to the audience as a whole. The technique requires a moderator to conduct the session. The general audience may or may not participate in the session, depending upon the rules the moderator wishes to follow.

This training technique is especially useful in allowing students an opportunity to understand or explore a specific topic. It is also useful for stimulating students' interest in a topic and for identifying and clarifying problems or issues.

Like all panel or group meetings, the chief burden for success in the colloquy approach is on the moderator. On him rests the responsibility to prepare the necessary material and outline for the colloquy, as well as to lead the discussion. To ensure a strong, effective colloquy, the moderator should know the following:

1. The basic topics to be covered.
2. Goals to be reached in each session.
3. Amount of time available.
4. His students' background to ensure their understanding of the colloquy and to know where to involve them in audience participation.
5. The physical facilities.

If your moderator prepares with the items noted in the above paragraph in mind, he is in a good starting position to effectively conduct the colloquy. Failure to prepare properly will undoubtedly make this a useless training technique. But preparation is only part of the technique. Effective presentation is equally important. In this phase, we suggest that the moderator proceed as follows.

1. Present introduction as to why the colloquy is being held; also the ground rules he plans to follow regarding audience participation.
2. Work to encourage the audience to participate.
3. As the colloquy progresses, relate all of the students' questions to the topic and the colloquy goals.
4. Maintain the pace to ensure covering the topic in time available.
5. Direct all discussions while remaining neutral himself.
6. Summarize the colloquy.

The roles of the other members of the colloquy are varied. The resource people, for example, are expected to contribute when called upon by the audience. In doing so, they should make brief, concise responses. The audience should be prepared to understand the topics under discussion and to provide thoughtful questions in response to the colloquy output.

Advantages and limitations

Advantages

1. Audience representation feature which allows large audience participation.
2. Motivated audience.
3. Easy audience participation.

Limitations

1. Experienced moderator not easy to find.
2. If audience representatives poorly informed, consequent poor participation.
3. Poor resource people lead to poor inputs.

FIELD TRIP TECHNIQUE

Some may debate the merits of classifying a field trip as a verbal training technique, but we feel it should be included in this chapter because it is a teaching technique that is primarily verbal during and after the trip itself. The field trip is a carefully planned tour or trip where a group (of any reasonable size) visits a location of interest, or travels from the normal classroom environment to observe and study an object or its operation.

This technique is best used in training to provide firsthand knowledge of something which cannot be brought into the classroom. The observation or study on location is particularly suited to helping the student relate theory to practice by observing the object or action in its natural setting.

Careful and thorough preparation is the key to the success of a field trip. This preparation should cover not only the physical details involved (transportation, timetable, etc.), but also the educational objectives, the order in which subjects will be studied, and development of a follow-up study program to maximize the training value of the field trip. The list in Fig. 12-5 is a good checklist to follow in preparing for a field trip.

Advantages and limitations

Advantages

1. Firsthand experience.
2. Creates class rapport.
3. Firsthand observation.

Fig. 12-5. Preparation checklist for field trip.

- ________ What is the exact time of arrival on site?
- ________ When and where to meet for departure?
- ________ What will be the total time for the trip?
- ________ What is the objective of the trip?
- ________ What are points to cover or stress on trip?
- ________ Are there any physically handicapped students who can't go along?
- ________ Make all necessary visit and luncheon reservations well in advance (several weeks).
- ________ What other resources do you need such as maps, guide books, and so on?
- ________ Check out your travel plans.
- ________ Prepare the students for the trip:
  - ________ Field trip objective.
  - ________ What do you expect of students?
  - ________ Cost/time of trip.
  - ________ Proper clothing to wear.
  - ________ What follow-up will be from trip.

Limitations

1. Depends on object availability.
2. Lack of student time to attend.
3. Relation to teaching objectives may not be clear.

OTHER TECHNIQUES

There are many other verbal approaches to training which cannot be classified as techniques in their own right, but are effective subtechniques. This group includes:

1. Buzz sessions.
2. Brainstorming.

3. Question periods.
4. Listening and observing groups.
5. Audience reaction teams.
6. Screening panels.

Such subtechniques are used within a particular training technique. They are not suitable alone. These subtechniques are used with groups in excess of 30 persons and often in groups of up to several hundred students. Let us review each one briefly.

Buzz session. The audience is divided into small groups to discuss assigned topic. This method is used to permit discussion in small groups and by all students regardless of audience size. It is most often applied during lecture or group presentations to allow small-group feedback to the full group.

The key to success in the use of this method lies in the preparation of the small groups prior to their assembly. Make certain that the purpose is clear and clarify the topic for each group. Keep the topic simple. Include in this preparation how and when you expect the buzz group to report back. Appoint a chairman for each group. Divide large groups into 5 to 15 members each. Keep total meeting time for group down to 15 to 20 minutes.

Brainstorming. This is a special subtechnique used with the lecture, group discussion, or similar technique to encourage a spontaneous outpouring of ideas relative to the topic being studied. The method often helps identify several alternative ideas for a group problem. It is usually limited to 5 to 15 minutes and done in small groups.

The key to this subtechnique is to open up the minds of the participants to fully express any and all ideas no matter how small or trivial they may seem. These thoughts should be recorded during the session and later sorted out and evaluated so that those of value can be applied.

This technique is often usable simply as a means of encouraging the students to think beyond the straight and narrow path. Give your students, for example, the brainstorming exercise of recording all of the possible uses of a glass ash tray. The odds are they will come up with a long list of uses, but will fail to consider that your input was *all* uses; therefore they might also consider breaking the glass ash tray into various forms for unconventional uses.

Question period. This is a commonly used segment of the lecture and group discussions. It is seldom, if ever, structured as a subtechnique within these techniques. As a consequence its value is often lost to the training program.

Specifically, a question period is from 5 to 20 minutes long, normally at the end of a presentation, and is designed to allow the students to question any point that needs amplification or clarification.

To maximize the value of this technique, you must first inform the audience at the start of a presentation that a question period will follow it. Then provide the audience with a means of recording their questions while the speech is in progress rather than waiting until the end. This can be accomplished by providing pencil and paper for the recording of questions.

Once the speaker has concluded his talk and the questions are passed in, they are screened. The appropriate questions are read to the audience and the speaker. This is especially necessary if your audience is more than 50 persons. If it is less than 50, you can probably allow oral questions.

The speaker should be brief but to the point in responding. He should speak to the audience, not the individual. No one person should be allowed to monopolize the question period. When presented orally from the floor, all questions should be repeated by the speaker for the benefit of the audience.

Listening and observing groups. This subtechnique is designed primarily to force audience participation and active listening in a lecture or discussion by assigning them a task to accomplish during the platform presentation.

Essentially the audience is divided into two or more groups. Each group is assigned the task of either specific listening or observation tasks. An example of one of these tasks might be listen for three definite solutions to the problem raised in the discussion and write them down. Another example might be to identify all of the supporting and opposing points for a given proposition and list them on paper. This approach is used to prepare students for the forum or a similar training technique which follows.

Audience reaction teams. This subtechnique is both useful and dangerous. Its prime value comes from the idea that a small group of audience representatives can interrupt the speaker at any point to ask for clarification or amplification of topics or ideas which it feels the general audience failed to understand. Often this technique is used when a person trained on technical subjects is speaking to an untrained audience.

Obviously this technique requires the approval of the speaker. It can backfire, however, if one team overreacts to the speaker and disrupts the speech.

Clearly there are a great number of verbal training techniques available to a trainer. Choosing the most effective technique for solving a given problem requires analysis, judgment, and planning. Getting the most effective technique is every bit as important as deciding whether you need a filmstrip or a field trip to do the job. While the lecture and group discussion are well known and widely accepted as conventional training procedures, they must be placed in perspective and selected for use only when they fit the situation.

13

Effective Use of the Training Billboard: Chalkboards, Demonstration Boards, and Flip Charts

Most training people have heard the old joke about the hillbilly farmer who refused the help of the Washington agricultural expert because he felt he wasn't farming at the present time as well as he could. Similarly, we do not always use the simpler media of learning effectively simply because we have lived with them for so long. In this day and age of computer-assisted instruction and closed-circuit television, who can justify his exalted position in the training department by simply suggesting a good flip chart or a better presentation at the chalkboard?

Not long ago a large firm in the business of selling film and projectors published an article telling how it used a simple series of handmade flip books to teach assembly work to its own operators. It seemed unusual to most of us that a sophisticated company such as this one would turn to a relatively unsophisticated way of training its employees. Upon closer examination of the training system, however, it became clear that the method was extremely effective in reaching the training objectives. And that, after all, is the purpose of any medium. High cost and complexity cannot guarantee success. Earlier we stated that the training director should search for the simplest medium which would accomplish the job. In the case of our sophisticated film company, the medium it had selected was correct for the job it wanted done.

In this chapter we will take up three variations of what we have arbitrarily decided to call the billboard type of teaching medium. This medium is characterized by words, phrases, charts, drawings, or graphs to illustrate points the speaker is attempting to make in his presentation. The stimuli are presented in billboard fashion, designed to make a quick, reinforcing impression on the learner. They are flashed on and off the board or paper as needed. They catch the attention and help direct the speaker's and the learner's attention to important points in the presentation.

CHALKBOARDS

Almost every meeting area has one of these. The only change over the years has been in the colors of the chalk and the board. If your company is avant-garde, it probably has a white board with blue chalk. But the purpose served has remained unchanged.

The chalkboard has the following advantages which should be taken into consideration in planning for the use of this medium:

1. Use of it can rivet attention to key words and ideas.
2. Whether or not you have planned its use before the presentation, it is always available and can be called into action to help clarify an explanation with a sketch, a phrase, or a hasty graph.
3. Students can easily respond to the instructor's work by using the board themselves to explain their ideas.
4. A group of students can work at the board simultaneously while the rest of the group looks on.
5. Because the chalkboard is usually available in a meeting area, you can depend on its being there if it is suddenly needed.
6. The cost of this instructional aid is very little.
7. It is a fairly flexible medium.
8. If preplanning is done, preparation is relatively easy.
9. Use of the board forces a certain amount of organization on the instructor and students during a teaching/learning period.

The chalkboard also has some disadvantages you will need to consider:

1. It is not easily transportable to other locations.
2. If it is not properly cleaned, it may be difficult to see from certain parts of the room.
3. It does not use vivid colors and therefore loses some of the impact more colorful aids can provide.
4. The instructor's printing is not always legible.
5. It is not easy to use when you wish to conceal some information from the learner until a certain point in the presentation.

6. It is not good for large groups. As a rule of thumb, use another medium for more than 20 people.
7. It is difficult to see from a distance of more than 15 feet.

Here are some ways in which you can improve your use of the chalkboard:

1. Be sure to have plenty of chalk on hand. Do not hesitate to continue your presentation with just a stub, however, if it becomes necessary. Sending someone out for a piece of chalk is too disruptive.
2. Try to talk to the group as you write. It is not, however, a sin to occasionally turn to the board to sketch or write.
3. Periodically move away from what you have written or drawn so that the entire group can see your work.
4. Keep your work on the upper portion of the board rather than the lower. If you intend to use a great deal of board space, start at the left-hand side and work clockwise around the room.
5. Prepare as much of your board work in advance as possible. By all means sketch figures, diagrams, and charts ahead of time so that you can develop the skill to do it quickly and see how the finished product will look to the student.
6. Develop complex points step by step. Be certain to put only key material on the board. Do not try to write everything you say.
7. Use colored chalk for differentiation of data.
8. Keep the board clean so that dust and previous work does not interfere with your current material.
9. Get creative in your use of the board. You can conceal work with pieces of paper and tape. You can combine the use of the board with colored construction paper letters, drawings, and charts.
10. Learn to do a few sketches. Remember the fascination with which you watched the cartoonist who could create a character on the spot. A few drawings in your stockpile of tricks will be useful in making your point.
11. Integrate your use of the board in your presentation. This may be difficult to grasp. What is meant is that the board should not appear to the student as something artificial to your presentation. Your use of the board should seem natural and easy.
12. We usually practice speeches and the use of more complex audiovisual materials. Why not rehearse the use of the chalkboard?
13. Consider the size of your audience and its distance from the board. As a rule of thumb, lettering should be at least 3/4 inch high to be seen from 20 feet.

DEMONSTRATION BOARDS

Demonstration boards are simply boards made of various materials designed to hold paper, board, and other objects of varying shapes and sizes. The various demonstration boards include cork boards, magnetic boards, hook 'n' loop boards, and flannel and similarly textured boards. Flash cards can also be included in the category. A short definition of each type of board follows.

Cork boards. A board of cork or similar soft substance like beaverboard or insulating board is used to display materials which are fastened with thumbtacks.

Magnetic boards. A magnetic board consists of a sheet of metal on a stand or fastened to the wall. Magnets are backed to whatever display material is desired.

Hook 'n' loop boards. The hook 'n' loop board is backed with nylon hooked material. Tape with countless tiny nylon loops is applied to whatever object is to be placed on the board.

Flannel boards. Flannel boards are made by mounting a piece of roughnap flannel on a frame and then backing the material to be placed on the flannel board with rough sandpaper or velour. Eldon F. Gunter reported in the *Training and Development Journal* that velour cover stock could be used for the board cover and the backing material.* This has the advantage of not requiring mounting, framing or stretching.

Flash cards. Flash cards are simply cardboard cards of whatever size is desired. They can contain words, diagrams, or pictures and are designed to be flashed before the class as they are needed.

Demonstration boards have the following advantages:

1. Some of the boards such as hook 'n' loop boards can hold heavy three-dimensional objects.
2. Instead of a representational diagram of the object, the real object can be used.
3. Materials for demonstration boards can be vivid and colorful.

---

*Eldon F. Gunter, "Flannel boards without flannel," *Training and Development Journal,* April, 1966, p. 36.

4. The trainer handles the objects he is discussing. This builds learner interest in the subject matter during the presentation.
5. Material can be placed on the demonstration boards at the right moment. The trainer can control the buildup of the presentation by withholding placement of the prepared word cards and objects until the correct moment in his presentation.
6. All of the demonstration boards and materials can be constructed by the training director and his staff.

The following disadvantages of demonstration boards should be given consideration:

1. The boards may be bulky to transport to distant locations.
2. The entire presentation must be prepared in advance. Answers to questions, additional explanations, and so on must be handled without the assistance of the board since no material will be prepared for it. Except for flash cards which have been covered with a piece of plastic or acetate beforehand, nothing can be written on the materials which will not destroy their later effectiveness. Demonstration boards tend to be static aids.
3. The adhesive quality of the boards must be checked in advance, otherwise they may fail during the presentation.

FLIP CHARTS

Flip charts are pads of paper mounted on easels. (See Fig. 13-1.) They are bound in such a way that each sheet can be easily flipped over so the next sheet is exposed.

Flip charts are available in a wide range of sizes from five inches to five feet. They can be commercially purchased or home made.

The advantages of the flip chart are as follows:

1. By flipping the page, the trainer can control the presentation of material.
2. Material for the flip chart can be prepared in advance or on the spot as is the case with a chalkboard.
3. The flip chart is highly portable. Even the larger ones have collapsible legs.
4. A variety of shapes, colors, and devices can be used with the flip chart.

Fig. 13-1. Standard flip chart. (Courtesy Oravisual Company, Inc.)

5. The flip chart, like the chalkboard, can be used to answer spontaneous questions from students.

The disadvantages of the flip chart are as follows:

1. Flip chart material is usually difficult to see beyond 15 feet.
2. Flip charts are not usually good for groups of students exceeding 20.
3. Pages are occasionally difficult to flip, causing some embarrassment during the presentation.

The following pointers will be helpful in producing your own flip charts:

1. Organize your material on small sheets of paper before going to the full-size flip chart.

2. Place one item on each sheet of paper. If you want to include more than one item, consider using the paper-strip, take-down method of presentation. This simply means that the other items on the sheet are covered by paper strips and tape. As the presentation is made, the trainer takes off a paper strip and reveals the next item on the sheet.
3. Condense the verbiage on the sheet as much as possible. The material on the page should emphasize your point; it should not be the point itself.
4. These points should not be read off the chart page to the audience. If more detail is necessary than can easily be remembered, it can be penciled lightly on the page itself. From a distance the writing will not be visible. The danger here is that the speaker will spend too much time reading his notes from the chart and lose contact with the audience. The notes should be in reminder form only.
5. The first sheet on the flip chart should be blank and function as a cover for the entire presentation. In this way none of the presentation will be given away before the speaker is ready to begin. The chart is a great attention holder and should be protected so that that function can be performed.
6. The second sheet should probably be the title of the presentation. This will give the whole procedure a professional look.
7. Most people are concerned over the lettering on charts and other display boards. There is no need to be a professional letterer today. There are about a dozen simple techniques that the amateur can use to achieve a professional look on his work. The following are a few lettering techniques which can be used on flip charts and the other billboard training materials described earlier in this chapter.

   a) Rubber stamp lettering sets are available in a variety of styles and sizes. Different color inkpads can be used. You will need a ruler and an aligning guide to position the letters so that they come out in a straight line.
   b) Stenso® lettering guides can be used to stencil a variety of letter styles.
   c) Precut letters are available in a wide range of materials such as cork, cardboard, paper, felt, plastic, and so on. Some brands are gummed; others have a pressure sensitive backing.
   d) Dry transfer letters are pressure sensitive letters printed on an acetate sheet and can be easily transferred to most clean dry surfaces.

®Stenso is a registered trademark of Stenso Lettering Co., 1101 E. 25th St., Baltimore, Maryland.

e) ®Wrico lettering sets consist of a transparent plastic lettering guide, guide holder, and a variety of lettering pens.

8. You can produce good art work without being a professional artist. Here are a few methods which can be used to achieve a professional look on your flip chart pages or any other demonstration materials mentioned earlier in the chapter.

a) Find a picture of the artwork you want reproduced. Place the picture in an opaque projector. Project the image on a sheet of paper on a wall and simply trace the image onto the paper.
b) Clip artwork and paste directly on the flip chart page.
c) Attach tracing paper to the original artwork. Trace the material with an ordinary pencil. Transfer the traced material to the flip chart sheet by turning the tracing over on the new surface and using the back of a teaspoon or the nail of the finger to rub down the pencil lines. The carbon from the pencil will leave a light guide line. Finally go over the light guide lines with a heavier pen or pencil.

9. Sometimes flip charts must be mass produced for use in remote locations or by many supervisors all doing training at the same time. Here is a method which is very inexpensive.

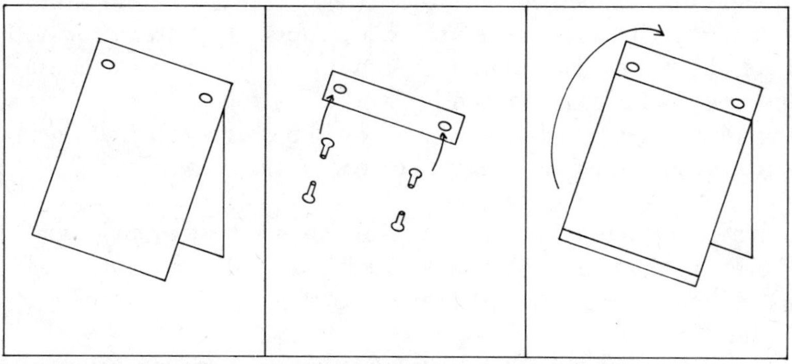

Fig. 13-2. Materials for constructing your own flip chart.

a) Have heavy cardboard backs cut by a stationer. Also have him cut strips which can be used to hold down the flip chart pages. Fasteners attached to the heavy backing board can be used to hold the strips over the pages. The pieces required will look like those on Fig. 13-2.

® Wrico is a registered trademark of Wrico Pen Co., Nutley, N.J.

b) At the same time have ozalid sheets cut slightly smaller than the backing board. When developed in an ammonia fed ozalid reproducing machine, these sheets will become the flip chart pages.
c) Take a sheet of tracing paper the size of the ozalid sheets. Have your drawing and lettering inked onto the tracing paper.
d) Place the tracing paper over the ozalid sheets and run them through the ozalid machine. In this way you can produce quickly as many sets of materials as you wish from one master copy at very low cost.
e) Your flip chart can be equipped with an easel type back by simply cutting out a stand and stapling it to the backing board.

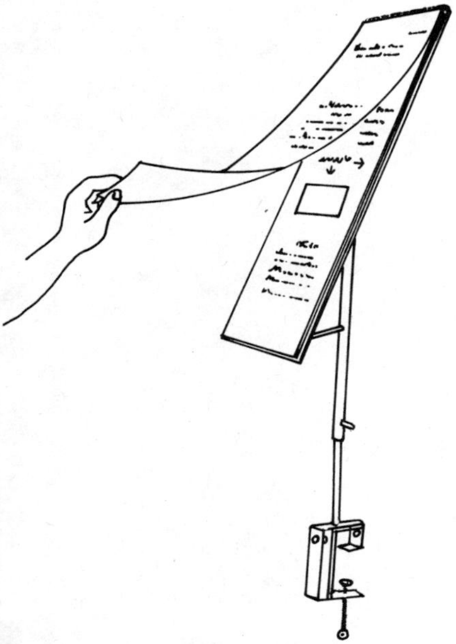

Fig. 13-3. Flip book attached to envelope machine. (Courtesy Envelope Manufacturers Association.)

10. Do not think of the flip chart strictly as a billboard that only a trainer can use to teach a group of students. The Envelope Manufacturers Association has developed a semiprogrammed flip book course which is clamped directly to the envelope machine by means of an adjustable easel.* (See Fig. 13-3.) Trainers, generally experienced machine operators, are provided with a trainer's guide,

*Envelope Manufacturers' Association, 1 Rockefeller Plaza, New York, N.Y. 10020

also clamped to their machines. The flip chart becomes a self-teaching device to be used while working on the machine and producing envelopes.

Sometimes just as much training can be bought for a few dollars as by spending thousands on an electronic monster. No medium is better than another. Each is designed to perform a specific training task. Your job is to match media to tasks and produce the necessary behavior change as economically as possible.

14

Overhead and Opaque Projection

OVERHEAD PROJECTION

Remember trying to learn the binomial theorem when you were in school? Somehow $(a + b)^2 = a^2 + 2ab + b^2$ was an impossible combination of letters and numbers to remember, let alone understand. You might have been lucky enough to have been able to regurgitate the formula for a test, but a day or two later the whole thing had evaporated and that was that. If you had to learn the formula all over in college, it was like meeting it for the first time.

Suppose, however, the teacher had tried to teach you the formula by throwing a line labeled *a* and *b* on a brightly lighted screen. The line looked like this:

The division of the line into parts *a* and *b* was arbitrary. All that was necessary was that one part be larger than the other. Suppose then, quick as a wink, she was able to add three similar lines marked off like the first, placing them in such a way as to form a square (Fig. 14-1).

Then as she repeated the formula, "a^2 . . ." and dropped a block of red, she formed a graphic illustration on the screen of a^2, which looked like the square in Fig. 14-2, and two brilliant yellow blocks of color representing $2ab$, which looked like Fig. 14-3, and finally a block of blue to complete the large square and represent b^2, which looked like Fig. 14-4.

You would have seen the binomial theorem clearly and quickly represented. And you would probably remember it for a long time to come.

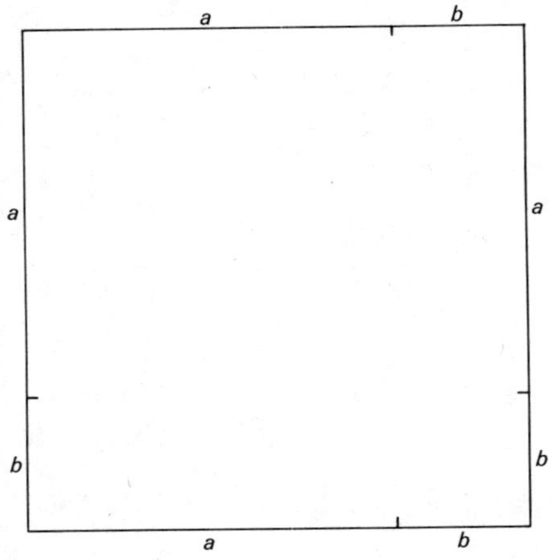

Fig. 14-1. First overlay.

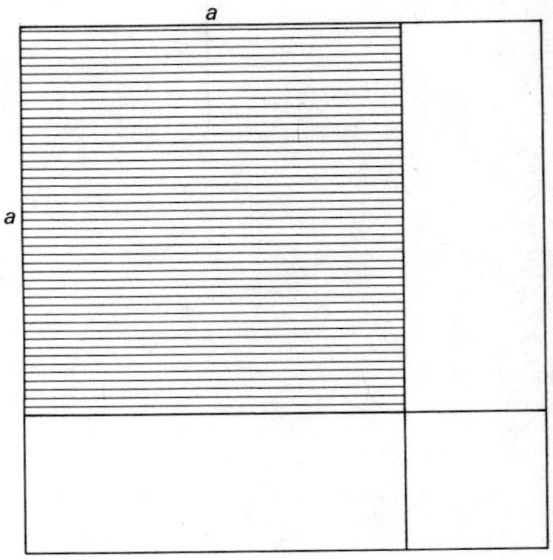

Fig. 14-2. Second overlay.

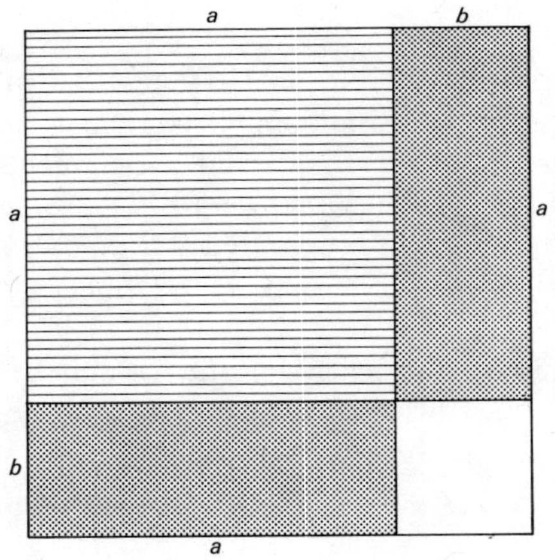

Fig. 14-3. Third overlay.

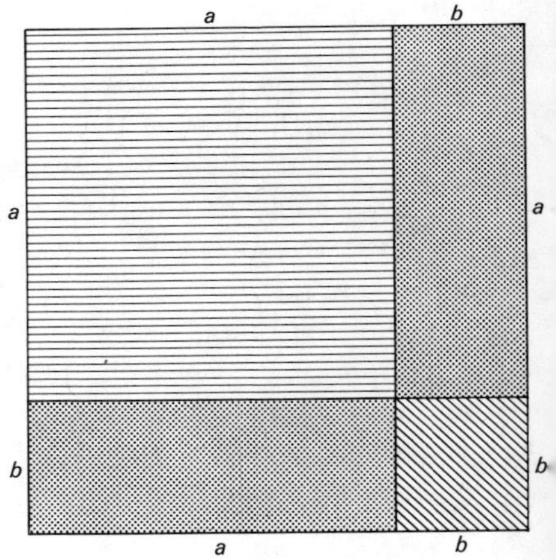

Fig. 14-4. Fourth overlay.

The overhead projector has been dubbed the "electric blackboard" or the "electric flip chart," but these nicknames short-change the usefulness of this tool. The overhead has come a long way since it was developed as a bowling alley score projector by the Navy in 1941. Briefly, the overhead will help an instructor because it has the following features:

1. It focuses the students' attention on specific material.
2. It permits the instructor to maintain eye contact with his students while writing on a transparency.
3. As a visual aid, it is easy to operate and to produce exciting and interesting visuals for.

4. The lights can be kept on in the classroom while the device is in use.
5. Transparencies are flexible. They can be written on or altered in a moment and then wiped clean.
6. Through the use of acetate overlays, teaching materials can be progressively exposed or covered. Complex concepts can be reduced to a series of simple steps.
7. Through the addition of certain mechanical devices, motion can be inserted into an otherwise static visual.
8. Portable models are available so that overheads can be used just about anywhere.
9. Cost of the overhead and materials is relatively low.
10. Students can create their own visuals in response to the learning situation.

Kinds of Overheads

A typical overhead projector is illustrated in Fig. 14-5.

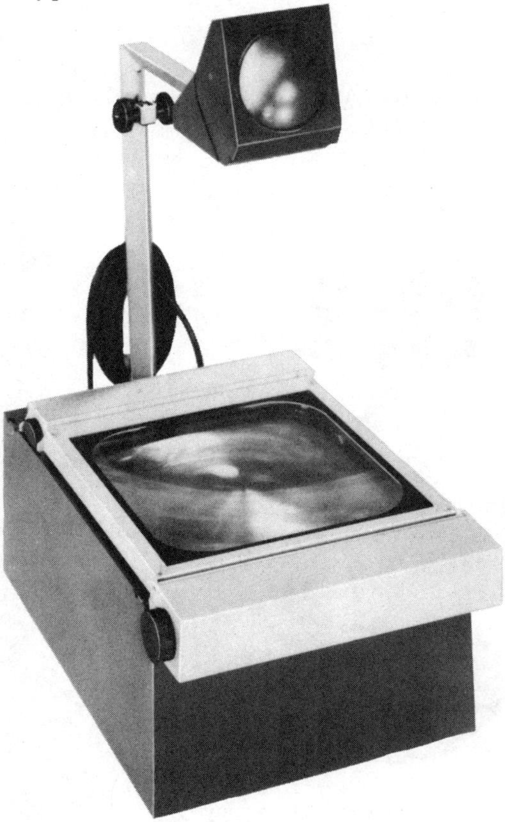

Fig. 14-5. A typical overhead projector. (Courtesy H. Wilson Corporation.)

Some models are built directly into desks as in Fig. 14-6. Others are designed to be truly portable as illustrated in Fig. 14-7.

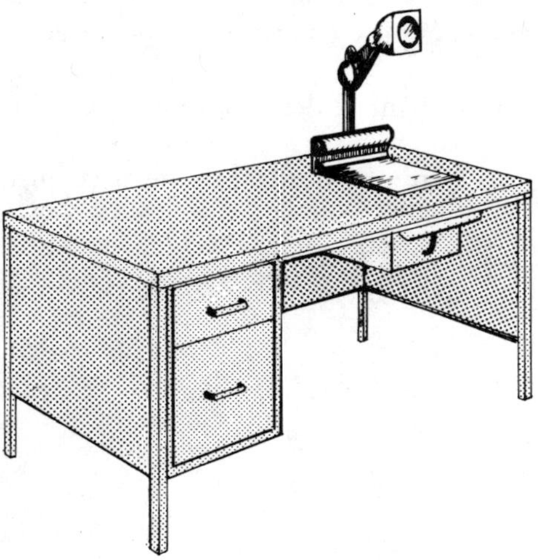

Fig. 14-6. Overhead projector built into desk. (Courtesy H. Wilson Corporation.)

Fig. 14-7. Portable overhead projector. (Courtesy the 3M Company.)

How to Prepare Overhead Transparencies

Overhead transparencies are easy to produce. Anyone can learn dazzling techniques in a few hours. Of all of the visual aids, the overhead transparency is probably the most satisfying to work with. Figure 14-8 shows a finished mounted transparency.

Here are some general principles suggested by Ray Wyman for organizing an effective transparency.*

1. The transparency must be capable of being understood quickly, accurately, and effortlessly.

2. The point of the visual (transparency) should be simple. Like the flip chart the visual is intended to reinforce the message. It is not the whole message. Only the pertinent information which is best visualized should be thrown on the screen. The rule for the maximum amount of printed material is six lines. If the message exceeds six lines, consider breaking the visual into two or three transparencies.

3. Your letters should be chosen for their readability. Printing is ordinarily much easier to read than cursive, if your letters are handwritten. Underlining should be used sparingly. Capital and upper-case letters are no more readable than lower-case letters. Letters should be one inch high for every 25 feet of viewing distance. For a distance less than 25 feet, reduce the size of the letter proportionately. Elite type is much too small; pica is barely acceptable. Primer typewriters, frequently found in elementary schools, are a little large but certainly acceptable. Commercial lettering methods were discussed in the last chapter.

4. The boldness of the letters is as important as their size. Boldness includes the line width, density, and sharpness. For maximum legibility, the width of the lines used to make letters should be about 15 percent of the letter height. It is as bad to have the lines too thick as too thin. The density of the print determines the contrast on the screen. Maximum visibility comes from completely opaque letters on a clear background. Truly opaque letters are easily produced from dry transfer letters. India ink on paper and typewriters with single-use plastic ribbons are next best. Pencils, felt pens, and ordinary ribbons make marks of low density in finished transparencies.

5. The organization of the message is also important to the understanding of the visual as a whole. Vertical lettering down the side of a

*Ray Wyman, "Creating readable transparencies," *The Instructor,* May, 1967, p. 104. Ray Wyman, "Choosing an overhead projector," *The Instructor,* February, 1967, pp. 120-121 and later pages.

transparency is particularly difficult to comprehend. We ordinarily look first at the upper left area of printed material. This is probably the best place to start a message. Avoid the bottom of the transparency as this may be one of the hardest places to see on the screen in the ordinary classroom.

6. The best test of the readability of a visual is to simply try it out in the training area where it will be used. To test it, sit in the corner of the room where the viewing is likely to be the worst. Then determine whether your transparencies aid the understanding of the student.

Quick Tricks for Producing Temporary Visuals

Here are a few quick and simple methods for producing visuals for temporary overhead transparencies.

1. Mark a sheet of clear acetate or plastic with a china marking pencil, felt tipped pen, or pen and plastic inks which you can later rub off.

2. Use frosted or matte acetate to sketch or trace on with black or colored inks. Apply color to desired areas with pencils, felt pens, or inks. Spray the frosted side with plastic spray. This makes the surface transparent to permit brighter projection.

3. Use a spirit duplicator to create transparencies. Prepare a duplicating master in the same way as you would for paper copies. Print a few sheets of paper with the master and when the print looks even, send through a sheet of acetate, matte (frosted) side up. Coat the frosted side of the transparency with plastic spray to protect the image. The transparency is ready to use.

4. If you have a Thermofax office copying machine around, simply use Thermofax heat sensitive acetate to create a transparency in a few seconds. Take an 8-1/2 X 11 sheet of paper with printed or inked material on it and place a sheet of heat sensitive film over it. Pass it through the copier, and through the process of heat transfer you will have your visual. Ball point pen and some printed materials do not work with this process. You may have to adjust the running speed of the machine to get the best exposure on the acetate.

Professional Methods for Producing Visuals

The previous transparency processes were simply hasty methods of getting some visual material for your screen. We did not even suggest mounting them. Let us now take a look at a few more complicated and professional

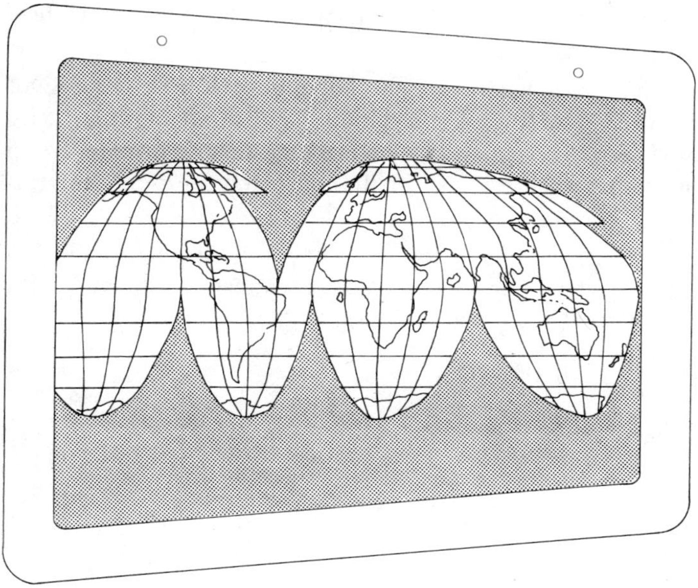

Fig. 14-8. A finished mounted transparency.

methods of producing transparencies. We will consider these as more permanent creations for your training files.

1. Use pressure sentitive materials to gain color and a professional look. Prestape® boasts over 9000 tapes for use on visuals. Tapes can be used for charts and graphs. Color can be cut in any desired shape and pressed into place on the acetate. Symbols, statistical tapes, reference tapes, and so on are available in a wide range of colors and textures.

2. Permanent type transparencies should be mounted to look like the one in Fig. 14-8.

3. Overlays of colored acetate can be used to convert a static to a dynamic projectual. Hinges are used to hold the overlays in place.

4. Diazochrome projectuals are diazo-sensitized sheets of acetate which produce brilliant colors. These sheets are developed through a simple ammonia and ultraviolet light process. To make a diazo transparency follow these steps:

a) Select the diazochrome film in the color you want.

®**Prestape**, division of Prestype, Inc., 136 West 21st St., New York, N. Y. 10011.

b) Draw your transparency material on tracing paper, or use a previously prepared clear piece of acetate.

c) Place it over the diazochrome sheet and expose it to a source of ultraviolet light. Sunlight will work, but you will have to experiment with the exposure time. If you have an Ozalid machine on the premises, you can pass it through that. There are specially constructed printers for this too.

d) Remove your master and develop your exposed diazochrome in a pickle jar or similar glass container. Place a sponge dampened with ammonia in the bottom of the jar (Fig. 14-9).

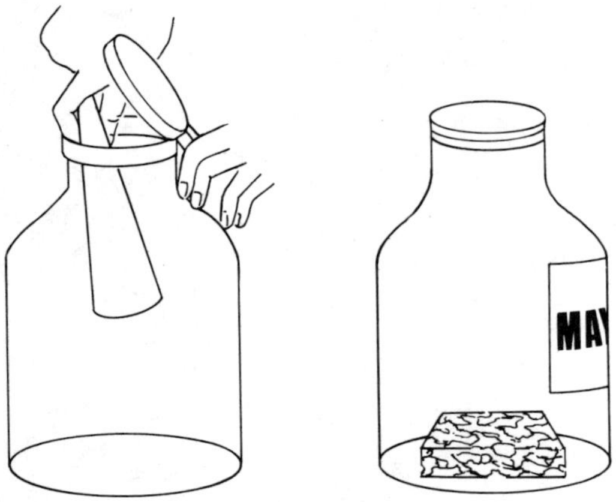

Fig. 14-9. Jars for developing exposed diazochrome.

If you have an Ozalid machine, you can use it for your ammonia source. Run the exposed diazochrome through the machine as you would any piece of Ozalid work. You will probably have to slow the machine down so that you have sufficient exposure time. The rubber rollers of the machine may scratch the surface of the acetate, however, and you might be better off simply placing your diazochrome in a pickle jar for development. Do not worry about the length of time you have the acetate in the jar. You cannot overdevelop. Furthermore, you need not wet the acetate with ammonia. The fumes from the sponge on the bottom of the jar initiate the development.

e) When the diazo is ready, the part of your visual with printing or other material will have retained the color. The rest of the acetate will be clear.

5. Your lettering can be made to look professional even though you know nothing about lettering. Pressure sensitive wax letters are easily applied to acetate (Fig. 14-10).

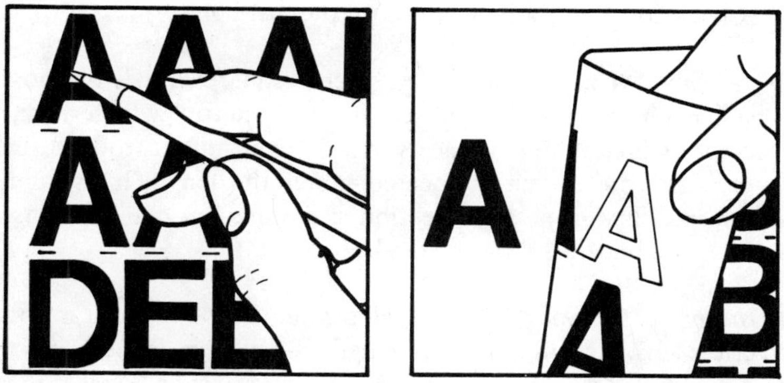

Fig. 14-10. Pressure-sensitive wax lettering.

Other methods of producing professional looking lettering were discussed in the last chapter.

6. Kits may be purchased to provide the illusion of motion to your transparencies. Dramatic effects may be achieved by using two polarizing light filters. Liquids can be made to appear to flow through pipe systems and so on. The kits contain a wide variety of motion materials including varying speeds of linear, rotary, and radial patterns; and blinking, gaseous, and turbulent effects. These polarization kits offer another element of sophistication that you can add to your bag of effects.

7. Another company has designed three-dimensional objects which can be used to demonstrate such principles as force-motion action and reaction, and the operation of levers, gears, pulleys, and so on. These are especially useful when large groups would be unable to see a demonstration. The effect is heightened by being projected on a lighted screen in silhouette.

These techniques by no means exhaust the possibilities of the overhead projector. There are, in fact, universities that give master's degrees in the subject. It would be good for the training director to consider attending a training seminar in the use of the overhead and the production of transparencies.

What to Look for in Buying an Overhead Projector

Ray Wyman has suggested some of the following considerations for investigation before investing in an overhead projector.*

*Ray Wyman, "Creating Readable Transparencies," *The Instructor,* May, 1967, p. 104.

1. *Safety.* Check for the UL designation on the nameplate.

2. *Working surface.* This should be ten inches square as it is on most models. Some machines are described as "low silhouette" which means that the mirror which directs the vertical light up through the transparency toward the screen is located under the lens. This system improves screen visibility in most projection situations but makes the use of overlays and special devices more difficult.

3. *Size of the projected image.* This is determined by the focal length of the projection lens. A common focal length is fourteen inches, which will change a ten-inch transparency into a sixty-inch screen image at a distance of seven feet. Twelve and one-half-inch lenses, which are standard on some machines and optional for others, fill the screen at a closer distance. The table below indicates projection distances for these two common lenses when used with the most common screen sizes.

	Screen Size				
Focal Length	50x50	60x60	70x70	84x84	96x96
12½″	5′	6′	7′	8′	10′
14″	6′	7′	8′	10′	11′

Focal lengths are generally marked on the lens barrel. A machine with the shorter focal length lens can be positioned nearer the screen and closer to the transparency, which makes a lower silhouette. It also decreases the working space above the transparency.

4. *Image brightness.* This is important if the screen will be used in a brightly lighted room. Brightness is determined by the type of lamp used, its wattage, its condensing optical system under the transparency, and the *f* number (the lower the better) of the projection lens in the head above the transparency. The light coming from the machine is properly measured in lumens, and such measurement provides the only real method for comparing relative brightness. The present range is from about one thousand to four thousand lumens. Machines are available for a wide range of situations, ranging from small groups or dark rooms to large groups or brightly lighted rooms.

The ratio of corner to center brightness is also important. The corners should be at least 50 percent as bright as the center. No variations should exceed this percentage.

5. *Resolution.* Resolution refers to the ability of the machine to produce sharp detailed images. It is usually expressed in lines per millimeter and will vary from the center (best) to corners (poorest). If most projection is to involve felt pen and grease pencil work on acetate sheets or rolls, then an inexpensive single-element or two-element lens will suffice. If detailed, prepared transparencies will be used, then a more expensive three-element lens is required. The better lens must be more carefully focused because its depth of field is less.

6. *Color fidelity.* This is of limited importance because full-color transparencies are as yet seldom used. The light should be reasonably white and the screen image free from noticeable colored bands or corners. Inexpensive lenses are apt to act like prisms and separate white light into colors.

7. *Light spillage.* This may cause discomfort that interferes with viewing. All light is supposed to go to the screen, but some of it may spill into the room. Many machines today use an inadequate plastic lens to condense light into the projection lens. Heavier glass lenses or a large concave mirror give better control.

8. *Steadiness.* The more portable the machine, the less steady it will be. No vibration should be allowed. You need a well-designed machine with firm support.

9. *Noise level.* The amount of noise a machine makes is measured in decibels but this specification is seldom available. Machines can easily be compared in any quiet location. A silent on/off switch is also desirable.

10. *Heat.* If the machine will be used for extended periods of time, the ability of the fan to cool the lamp is important. The fan should continue to run automatically after the machine is shut off and then automatically shut itself off after the lamp has been sufficiently cooled.

11. *Changing the lamp.* The lamp should be easily replaced, and located in a position that will allow you to switch in seconds. This is important so that a presentation will be interrupted as little as possible.

12. *Control of transparencies.* Several companies have developed projectors which permit pushbutton control of transparencies. The operator, by remote control, can draw each visual from the cartridge, project it, and replace it with another visual. This is useful if you do not plan to write on the transparency or use overlays or other devices.

Some Tips on Using the Overhead Projector

1. The projector should be turned on only when you are actually projecting a visual on the screen. As soon as you are finished showing the visual, the lamp should be switched off, even if it is only for a few minutes, before going on to the next visual. In this way you can focus the audience's attention on the screen when there is something there you want them to see. Their attention will automatically return to you as soon as the projector is switched off.

2. Use the pin registers to correctly position your visuals before turning on the lamp. In this way the visual will not be slipping around the stage while you find the best position for it on the screen.

3. Make your transparencies in a horizontal format whenever possible. Despite the fact that many commercially prepared master materials are organized vertically, square screens are not always available for projection. The trend toward meeting rooms with low ceilings frequently means either that information is lost from top and bottom of the screen or that the projected image must be made small enough for vertical transparencies to fit the screen.

4. The size of the screen is determined by the maximum viewing distance. The width of the screen should be not less than one-sixth of the distance from the screen to the last row of viewers. The projector should be placed so as to fill the screen with the projected image.

5. Ideally the trainer should be seated while operating the projector. The projector is then placed on a low stand below the line of vision of the viewers. The screen is raised to permit viewing over the head of the trainer. Because the projector stage is not visible to the viewers, they are not distracted by the trainer's operation of the projector. As a rule of thumb, the screen should be high and the projector should be low.

6. Like other projectors, the overhead is subject to the image distortion called keystoning. This can be corrected, as explained in a previous chapter, by tilting the top of the screen forward and the bottom backward.

OPAQUE PROJECTION

Pictured in Fig. 14-11 is an opaque projector which can do a few things an overhead cannot do.

Among its advantages are the following points:

1. Materials can be projected on the screen without copiers, chemicals, transparencies, or slides. You can, for example, project a piece of

Fig. 14-11. Opaque projector. (Courtesy American Optical Company.)

fabric, a page from a book, or a watch on the screen with equal ease and effectiveness.

2. Three-dimensional objects up to about 2-1/2 inches in depth can be accommodated on the stage.
3. Preparation cost is little or nothing for opaque projection.
4. Confidential materials can be projected without the possibility of duplication, thus reducing the security risk.
5. Materials can be spontaneously projected in response to the immediate needs of the learner.

You may be asking yourself why anyone would bother with the overhead. Here are some of the opaque projector's limitations.

1. For one thing, the opaque projector is heavier to lug around. There is no such thing as a portable opaque projector.
2. The bulk of the projector may obscure the trainer from the students.
3. Most opaques must be operated in a darkened room, although newer models permit some light.
4. Progressive disclosure of materials is not easily accomplished, although the roller device for changing material can be put to this use.

5. The vivid colors and illusion of motion characteristic of the overhead are not features of the opaque.
6. Materials tend to wrinkle and get out of focus if left on the hot projector surface too long.

The opaque projector has its place. If quick, simple, and unadorned projection is required there is no better tool. We have watched a fashion expert talk year after year with large groups of salespeople about the new fabrics and be able to clearly show actual swatches of material so that the color, texture, and weave were easily and quickly grasped. It just depends on what your objectives call for.

ADDITIONAL READINGS

Radiant Manufacturing Corporation, *Audio-Visual Guide to Better Projection.* Morton Grove, Illinois, n.d.

15

Producing and Showing Sound-Slides and Sound-Filmstrips

SOUND-SLIDES

My mother used to say that anyone could be a good cook on an unlimited budget. The real trick was to turn leftovers, sale items, and plain ingredients into a feast. This is the same problem that most training personnel face – how to produce professional results on a limited budget. One of the most effective and useful training tools is the 35mm sound-slide show. If you have checked the costs of having an ordinary 70- to 80-slide, 15 minute show produced by a professional company, you know that you will pay between two and five thousand dollars depending upon the photography and other production costs. By spending your money carefully and at the right time during a production, you can cut the cost of producing a high quality show to under $150 plus your own salary over the period of time involved.

This chapter is intended for the training person who is working with limited funds and has very little experience in the production of audiovisual materials. A single, simple, successful method is described. There are, of course, other techniques, more expensive equipment, and further refinements, but the following formula will provide you with a low-cost, useful training tool.

The Basic Equipment You Will Require

Let us assume that you want to produce a sound-slide show to be used on a Kodak Carousel-type slide projector (Fig. 15-1), with a stereo tape recorder (Fig. 15-2).

Fig. 15-1. Kodak Ektagraphic® slide projector. (Courtesy Eastman Kodak Company.)

Fig. 15-2. Emerson stereo tape recorder. (Courtesy Emerson Radio, Inc.)

You will need a camera capable of taking 35mm slides. A Kodak Instamatic Reflex (Fig. 15-3) will produce fine work, but there are many other models which will do as well. Your camera should also have a close-up lens attachment for close-up work.

Fig. 15-3. Kodak Instamatic® camera. (Courtesy Eastman Kodak Company.)

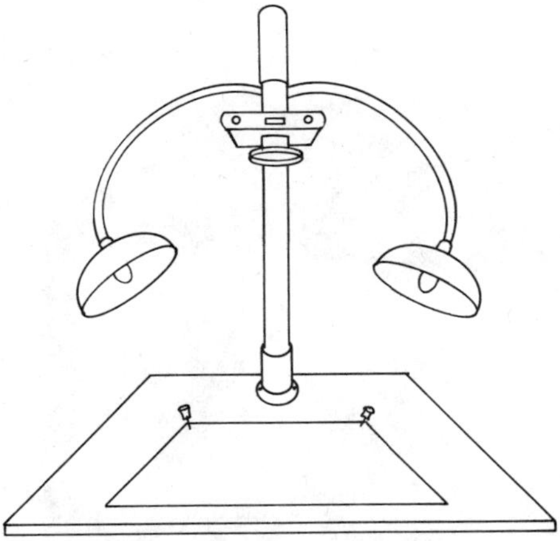

Fig. 15-4. Improvised copy stand with lights.

Bringing the necessary camera lighting into industrial locations often interferes with the on-going work. The simplest approach is to use a minimum of equipment requiring the shortest possible set-up time. For this reason, high-speed Ektachrome (assuming you will use color film) 35mm film is recommended. While Ektachrome does not produce the truest color, it can be used with the available light and no additional lighting equipment will be necessary.

Using a high-speed film and available light will in most cases mean that your exposure time will be longer. The longer the exposure time, the greater is the danger of camera movement and blurring of the subject. The

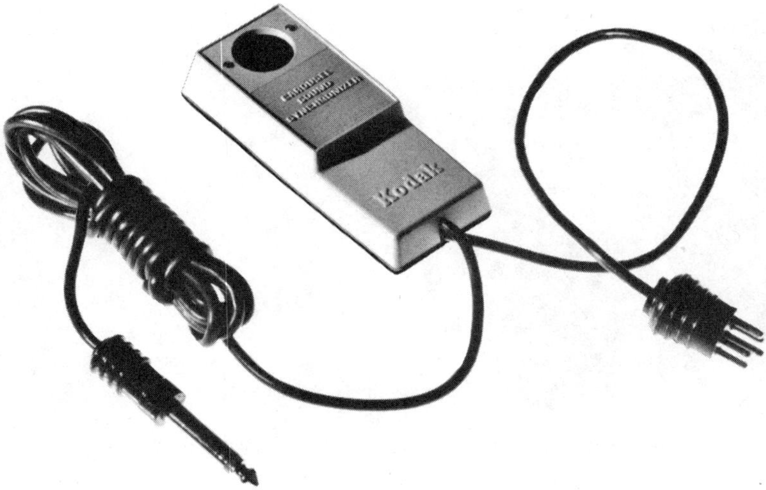

Fig. 15-5. Kodak Carousel © sound syncronizer. (Courtesy Eastman Kodak Company.)

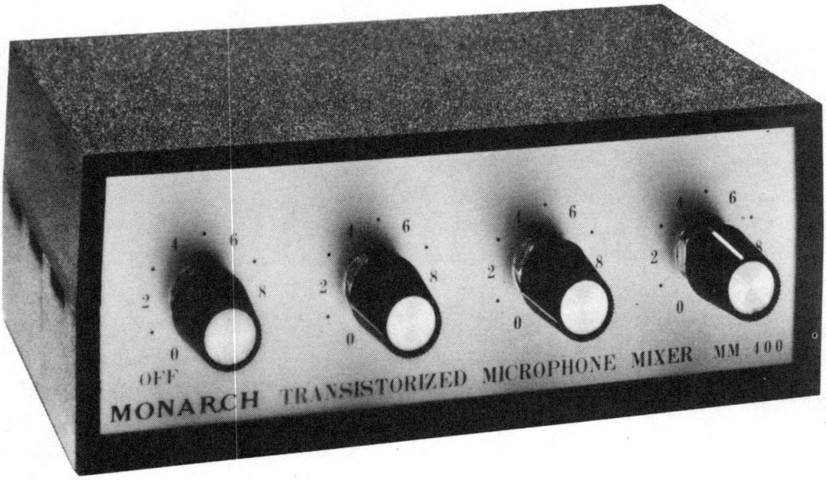

Fig. 15-6. Monarch four-channel sound mixer. (Courtesy Monarch International Electronics, Inc.)

best results therefore will be achieved with a camera tripod and a cable extension shutter release.

While some of your shots will be on location, many will be copies of charts, graphs, three-dimensional objects, or other photographs and artwork you may develop. For this work you will need a copy stand and

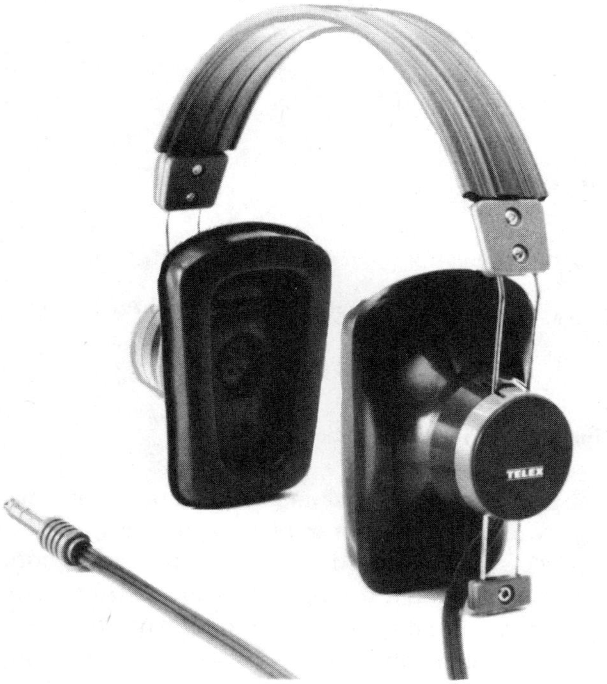

Fig. 15-7. Headphones. (Courtesy Telex.)

lights. (See Fig. 15-4.) You will also need two photoflood bulbs and reflectors, and an artwork template to frame your copy work. A translucent template which will serve for motion picture work as well is available from Kodak.

To record the sound and signals that will automatically advance the slides, you will need a stereo tape recorder, a sound synchronizer (Fig. 15-5), a four-channel mixer (Fig. 15-6), and a headset. The four-channel mixer will enable you to control the sound level of music, voice, and slide advance impulses all at the same time. You will be able to fade music in or out while maintaining the same voice level. The headphones (Fig. 15-7) will permit you to listen to the music while the narrator is speaking. The narrator will hear only his own voice and be unaware of your manipulations of the music or other sound effects.

To summarize, then, you will need to buy, rent, or borrow the following equipment:

Carousel-type projector with remote control.
Stereo tape recorder.

Carousel sound synchronizer.
Four-channel mixer.
Headphones.
Copy stand and lights.
Artwork mask.
Reflex 35mm camera with close-up lens attachment.
Camera tripod.
Cable extension shutter release.

The first three pieces of equipment listed will be required to show your finished production.

How to Write Your Script and Plan the Show

Once you have assembled your equipment and understand how to operate it, the next step is to prepare a shooting script or plan for the show similar to one which follows for *"The Making of a Merchant."* In the script, note that voice and sound effects are separated from a thumbnail description of each slide subject. The photographer and narrator can both work from the same script. Each has an opportunity to see how his work will fit with the other's.

Slide No.	Narrative (and Sound Effects)	Description of Slide Subject
1	*Music* (There's No Business Like Show Business!). Fade into background before dialogue begins.	Exterior of store.
2	At the heart of every big, successful, growing business, there are creative, ambitious, dynamic people.	Crowds streaming into the store.
3	These people are doers . . .	Young buyer on the selling floor, in the midst of shopping crowd, selling, etc.
4	They're leaders . . .	Buyer leading a sales meeting with sales force.

Slide No.	Narrative (and Sound Effects)	Description of Slide Subject
5	They're profit makers.	Buyer at the cash register.
6	Where do these people come from? From college campuses . . . *Music swells.*	Student crowds on a college campus
7	And by promotion from within our own organization.	Organization chart with arrow from picture to next level indicating promotion from within.
8	*No dialogue. Music fades just before dialogue begins in next slide.*	*Title slide:* "The Making of a Merchant"
9	Becoming a merchant is no simple job. It takes talent, skills, training, experience, and a generous measure of hard work.	Buyer and assistant studying unit stock plan.
10	These qualities cannot be developed overnight.	Clock and calendar symbolizing time.
11	But let's start a retailing career at its beginning. Suppose you joined our store as an executive trainee. *Music swells and fades.*	Direct shot of executive trainee who will be followed all the way through production.
12	*Music faint.* What does the view from the first rung of the ladder look like?	Trainee stands at the employee entrance to the store.

Assuming that you have already thought of the main points of the presentation, here is a simple plan that always brings results. The complete show can be divided into three sections: the "hook," the "message," and the "checklist." The hook is simply a gimmick for attracting attention to your subject. It should be accomplished swiftly and designed to deepen interest in what is to follow. In some cases it may provide an analogy or theme which you will wish to trace throughout the presentation. In a slide show used to train retail stock boys to handle large metal trucks more safely and reduce accidents to customers on the selling floor, the first few slides pictured lethal weapons such as guns and tanks and then made the point that stock trucks should also be treated as potentially dangerous weapons. This theme was carried throughout the show to emphasize the need for greater caution in pushing heavily loaded trucks through crowds of customers.

Slide numbers 1 through 10 in the following script are an illustration of the opening of a show used to retrain salespeople in departments having high register shortages. Most of these shortages are traceable to simple mistakes in operating the register or handling saleschecks. To emphasize the point that carelessness in handling sales media is like pouring money down the drain, the opening music to *The Sorcerer's Apprentice* was coordinated with slides of artwork showing increasing amounts of money going down the proverbial drain. The comparison was made throughout the film after each shortage cause was identified and its prevention explained.

Slide No.	Narrative (and Sound Effects)	Description of Slide Subject
1	*Music only.* "The Sorcerer's Apprentice." Change slide on strong beat. No voice.	Picture showing a small quantity of paper money dropping down the drain.
2	Continue *music only.* Change slide on strong beat. No voice.	Picture showing greatly increased quantity of paper money dropping down the drain.
3	Continue *music only.* Change slide on strong beat. No voice.	Picture shows a blizzard of paper money cascading down the drain.

Slide No.	Narrative (and Sound Effects)	Description of Slide Subject
4	*Fade music* to background level. Voice comes in the moment slide appears on screen. Register errors are the causes for thousands of dollars going down the drain each year at the store.	*Title slide*: Loss Causes.
5	Errors that pass unnoticed . . .	Employee ringing in on register, looking down at cash drawer and ignoring registered amount in the register window.
6	Or are ignored . . .	Employee at register throws away a sales check run in error.
7	Large errors . . .	Register window showing $75.00 amount.
8	Or small ones . . .	Register window showing $1.50 amount.
9	Accumulate to create an unnecessary amount of shortages for your department and to the store.	Three hands placing sales checks on a spindle full of incorrect sales-checks.
10	We are here to see how easy it is to cause a register shortage and how easy it is to avoid one. Let's take any normal working day, in any department, in any one of our stores.	Slide with words, "Opening the day" next to a magazine clipping of a bullfight arena. Bulls, like customers, are waiting to rush into the ring.

The "message" refers to the body of the production. It will form the bulk of the show and is usually presented in a straightforward manner. The "hook" is out, and hopefully the learner or audience is in a receptive state for training. The following is an illustration of the "message" section of the "*The Making of a Merchant.*"

Slide No.	Narrative (and Sound Effects)	Description of Slide Subject
22	After two months in the store, you'll be ready to move up to the job of Service Manager. It's back to the classroom for an intensive two weeks of training. The subject: how to supervise.	Service Manager teaching a group of executive trainees in the classroom.
23	As a Service Manager you'll be responsible for the selling floor.	Shot of busy selling area.
24	You'll have to be an expert in salesmanship to get the highest performance from your salespeople.	Shot of executive trainee training salespeople on the selling floor.
25	You'll need to know how to schedule your people to get maximum coverage and productivity from them.	Trainee scheduling from clipboard.
26	Of course you will need to know the various supervisory procedures.	Shot of supervisory documents and Service Manager insignia (a flower).
27	You must know how to run a department. Everything from ordering signs to the smallest details of housekeeping and maintenance.	Trainee adjusting merchandise on a rack.
28	The most challenging part of your job will be the supervising of people. Your formal training will help you to develop the required leadership skills.	Trainee mediating between irate customer and salesperson.

Slide No.	Narrative (and Sound Effects)	Description of Slide Subject
29	You'll learn the techniques of planning, organizing, directing, co-ordinating, and controlling. These are the tools of the retail executive.	Executive Training Director teaching from chart showing the Management Cycle.
30	A Service Manager is also a personnel executive. You'll help in selecting employees . . . reviewing their performance and improving their skills.	Poster with the words, "Selecting, Appraising, Improving."
31	After two weeks of classroom preparation, you will be placed in a supervisory position for a period of six weeks. This executive trainee has just been assigned as a Service Manager.	Staff Assistant pinning an S.M. insignia on E. T.

The third and last section of the show is a review or restatement of your purpose. The best way to arrange this section is in some kind of checklist format which asks the student or audience to take specific actions now that they have received the "message." Below is an example of the final portion of a show to train sales personnel to collect sales information for input to a computer.

Slide No.	Narrative (and Sound Effects)	Description of Slide Subject
64	What can you do to keep up the flow of merchandise to your customer?	Salesperson standing behind counter, looking into camera and waiting, as if for direction.

Slide No.	Narrative (and Sound Effects)	Description of Slide Subject
65	Here are a few simple steps you can take to be certain your buyer knows which merchandise our customers like best.	Same sales-person smiling, selling mer-chandise (with ticket exposed) to an obviously appreciative customer.
66	First of all, carefully remove one part of each multipart ticket at the point of sale. Place it face up on the specially designed, two-pronged spindle near your register.	Correct method of tearing stubs and placing them on the spindle.
67	All stubs must be placed on this spindle with three exceptions . . .	Close-up of spindle.
68	. . . marked-down stubs . . .	Close-up of hand holding marked-down stub.
69	. . . mutilated stubs . . .	Close-up of hand holding mutilated stub.
70	. . . and handwritten stubs . . .	Close-up of hand-written stub.

Here are a few additional tips to help you write a professional sounding script.

1. Think of your slides as billboards. They flash on the screen and either carry the message or reinforce the spoken dialogue. Their appearance will be as brief as the glimpse one catches of advertising billboards while driving in a car. A few slides in a show may require study, but the great majority will be quick and obvious.

2. Keep the quantity of your dialogue to a minimum The mistake that characterizes most amateur productions is too much narration per slide. The viewer looks at the slides, recognizes the image and is prepared for a new visual experience in a matter of seconds. If you keep him listening to a minute or more of dialogue, he will invariably take his attention from

the screen to something else in the room. The pace of a show should be about 5-10 seconds per slide.

3. Use the narrator's voice to help you make the transition from slide to slide. The momentary blackened screen will not be as noticeable if there is audio covering the slide change.

4. As you write the script, read it out loud from time to time to get a feel for the emphasis and style. Avoid complex sentence structure and awkward phrasing. Keep the dialogue as clean and simple as possible.

5. Vary the kind of subject matter you use in the visual presentation. Intermingle copy stand shots, title slides, and live action.

6. Use music and sound effects wherever possible.

7. Keep the action moving. If you find a lag in the presentation, work toward overcoming it with a striking visual or unusual audio.

8. Keep in mind your basic purpose – to train. Your decisions about the script should always be based on the premise that your aim is primarily to teach and secondarily to entertain. Professional shows may have the stamp of slickness on them, but will the student behave any differently after he experiences them? Follow the principles of good training practice rather than sales promotion gimmickry whose sole purpose is to get attention.

Some Slide-Taking Tips

Once you have laid out your shooting script and revised it to the point that you are satisfied with it, the next step is to take the slides. No attempt to explain how to use a camera will be made here; a good photography manual and some direct experience can help you accomplish this. Very little ability and experience, however, are necessary. Get yourself a good camera (rent one if you do not own one) with automatic features. Even a beginner can get usable results quickly.

The following tips will help through the slide-taking stage in your production.

1. Organize the shots you take so that all shots involving certain people or locations or props can be grouped and taken at one time. This will destroy the show's planned sequence, but you can reconstruct this later. Grouping shots will save a great deal of time and effort.

2. Contact your subjects and people responsible for the locations you intend to use well in advance. If you were hiring a professional photographer to take your shots, you would want him to waste as little time as possible getting talent lined up and getting permission to photograph people or props in a department. Treat yourself in the same way. Organize as much as possible before you take a single picture.

3. Take at least three shots of every subject. Do this from different angles using different exposures so that you will have a choice of shots later when you are putting the show together. The best time to get these shots is at the time of the original shooting. Most of the cost in reshooting is due to the time it takes to reset a shot. The cost of the film for additional shots when everyone and everything is present is negligible.

4. The copy stand provides an excellent opportunity to put variety and punch into your production. Not every shot need be of someone doing something in the industrial or business setting. With the copy stand you can arrange to photograph objects, photographs, artwork, letters – almost anything. Experiment with the lighting to get the most dramatic results.

5. Use your imagination with title and credit shots. Not all titles need appear at the beginning. The title in the "Making of a Merchant" appears as slide 8. If you would like to get something out of the ordinary, go to a professional and ask him to produce three or four slides for you. For a few dollars extra cost, you can get some special, highly creative work to add some additional sparkle to your production.

Arranging the Final Slide Set

As your slides are developed and returned to you, you can begin to select and sequence them. An inexpensive sorter (Fig. 15-8) with a bulb and translucent backing can be purchased for a few dollars. This will be a great help in sorting out the shot you want and putting a large number of slides into sequence. It is difficult to make a good selection using your slide projector or a single viewer. More expensive sorters are available, but they all serve the same purpose.

When the slide set you want has been selected, load it into a carousel tray and you are ready to record the sound.

Recording the Sound

Begin by assembling your equipment in an area free from distractions and noise. Be sure to avoid a room that has a ventilating system that cannot be shut off.

You will need the following items of equipment to do the job:

Carousel projector.
Sound synchronizer.
Stereo tape recorder and microphone.
Recording tape, splicing tape, white leader.

Fig. 15-8. An inexpensive slide sorter.

Four-channel mixer.
Headphones.
Record player or tape recorder.

Your set-up will look like the sound recording set-up in Fig. 15-9.

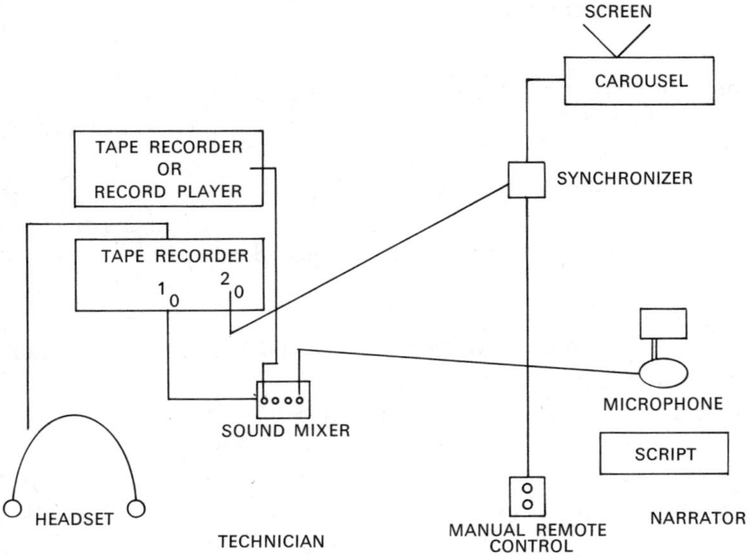

Fig. 15-9. Diagram of sound-recording set-up.

The operation of this set-up requires two people, but could be done by one person with experience in manipulating all of the equipment. The narrator or actors reading the script use a remote control button to advance the slides. The technician controls the tape recording and music or sound effects.

The voice, music, and sound effects are recorded on one channel of the stereo tape recorder. The electronic impulse from the carousel is recorded on the other channel. When the results are played back, one channel will carry the sound and the other will carry an inaudible impulse to the Carousel mechanism thereby automatically advancing the slide. However, if you use the automatic slide change feature you will lose the stereophonic effect.

Perhaps the easiest way to explain this set-up is to show how each piece of equipment is used and how it is connected to the other pieces.

1. Stereo tape recorder
   a) Connect power line to power source.
   b) Connect synchronizer to channel 2.
   c) Connect mixer output to channel 1.
   d) Connect headphones jack to external speaker for channel 1.
2. Carousel
   a) Connect power line to power source.
   b) Connect synchronizer.
3. Mixer
   a) Connect mixer output to channel 1 (as explained above).
   b) Connect the tape recorder playing music or the record player to mixer.
   c) Connect microphone to mixer.

To play back the results use the set-up illustrated in Fig. 15-10. To operate this set-up:

1. Connect the synchronizer to the carousel and the external speaker jack for channel 2.
2. Play back. Slide will advance automatically.

Using a Professional Narrator

The best investment you can make in producing sound-slide shows is in the narrator or actors. Fees range upward from $65, depending on the length

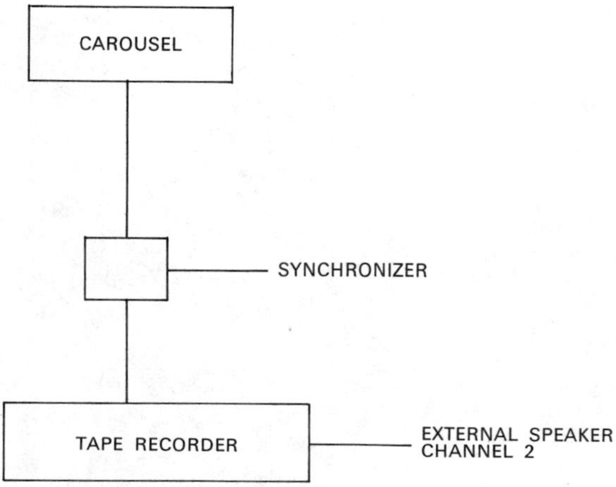

Fig. 15-10. Play-back set-up.

of the production and the number of people you use. A good narrator can cover a multitude of sins committed by the photographer, scriptwriter, etc. He can give the whole production a professional effect, and it is well worth the additional cost for his services.

A Few Projection Tips

The following tips will give your presentation a more professional appearance.

1. "Warm up" your equipment in advance of the showing so that you are ready to begin the moment the lights are dimmed.
2. Splice a white leader to your tape and cut off the unused portion of recording tape. Sound should begin immediately following the white leader. This will cut the lag between the slide's appearance on the screen and the start of the sound.
3. Put a 2 X 2-inch piece of cardboard in the first and last slots in the projector (unless all slots are used for slides). This will prevent the "unprofessional" white screen from flashing on before or after your presentation.
4. If you find it necessary to show more than 80 slides (one fully loaded carousel tray), put the 81st slide in the zero slot of the tray. Start the show on the first slide. At the end of the first tray, while the 81st slide is on the screen, quickly change to the second tray. Start the second tray on zero so that the 81st slide has somewhere to go

Fig. 15-11. Tape activated sound programmer. (Courtesy Pro-Gramo, Inc.)

when it pops up out of the projector. This device will permit you to change trays without having to break the continuity of the show.

5. Improvements in equipment are constantly being made. Pro-Gramo Incorporated, for example, has developed a single system, tape actuated sound programmer (Fig. 15-11) for Kodak Carousel projectors which combines pieces of equipment and wires into a single compact unit, thus making the entire set easier to operate and transport.

With a little time and patience you can produce sound-slide shows of a professional quality. Once the techniques described above have become routine to you, you will be able to create a high-grade show in 80 hours or less.

SOUND-FILMSTRIPS

A filmstrip consists of a series of illustrations photographed in sequence and prepared for projection on 35mm film. Filmstrips have the following advantages over slides:

1. Filmstrips are more compact and easier to handle.
2. Filmstrips are easy to load into the projector compared to the loading of individual slides into a tray.

3. There is no danger that the pictures will get out of order by accident.
4. The cost of duplication is much less than the cost of duplicating slide sets.

Some of the virtues of the filmstrip, however, also become some of its limitations.

1. While it is convenient not to have to worry about whether the picture is in order or whether it will appear right side up on the screen, it is a definite drawback not to be able to alter the order of the frames or update a frame. When one frame is unsatisfactory, the choice is either to live with it or to redo the entire filmstrip.
2. The filmstrip is more difficult to prepare than the slide show. It requires more skill with the camera and more patience to complete the process itself.

The preparation for producing a filmstrip parallels that of producing a slide show:

1. The basic equipment is similar. You need a 35mm camera, a close-up lens attachment, a tripod, a cable type extension shutter release, a copy stand, photo floodlights, an artwork template, a tape recorder, a mixer, a headset, and a filmstrip projector.
2. Your shooting script will follow the format described and illustrated earlier in this chapter.
3. You will need to prepare flats or take photographs of live situations. Flats are illustrations or photographs which are mounted in a frame of the appropriate size and are therefore ready for photocopying.
4. Once your photography has been finished, you add the sound and synchronize it with the movement of the filmstrip.

Single- and Double-Frame Filmstrips

There are two types of filmstrips, both produced on 35mm film. The most common is the single-frame filmstrip. It looks like the one pictured in Fig. 15-12.

Commercially produced filmstrips are usually single-frame filmstrips. Note the overhead alignment of the pictures. To prepare this type of filmstrip you need a single-frame 35mm camera. Most training departments do not have this kind of equipment.

The second type of filmstrip is the double-frame. Pictures on the double-frame filmstrip are the same size as those on ordinary 2 × 2-inch slides. These filmstrips look like the one shown in Fig. 15-13.

Fig. 15-12. Single-frame filmstrip.

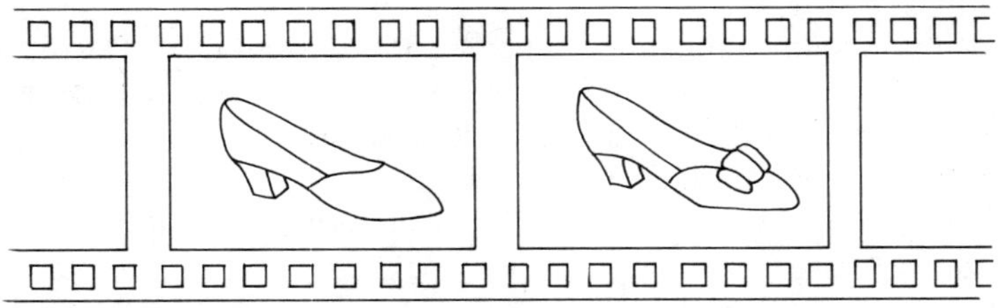

Fig. 15-13. Double-frame filmstrip.

Note that the pictures in a double-frame filmstrip run horizontally. A standard 35mm camera is used to prepare double-frame filmstrips. The distinction between the single-frame and the double-frame is primarily in the cost of the work on your filmstrip.

Basic Filmstrip Photography

There are three basic ways of making a filmstrip:

1. Go out and photograph live subject matter.
2. Prepare slides or negatives first.
3. Copy filmstrip flats.

Direct filming of live subject matter is not recommended for people who are not experienced with photography. You will be shooting the entire filmstrip in sequence, and one poor exposure could ruin the entire strip and force you to do the whole job twice. Your chances of producing an acceptable filmstrip, titles, artwork, and all are considerably less if you take shots outside the studio. If live shots are included, remember that the camera will have to be held in a horizontal position, as direct filming will produce a double-frame filmstrip unless a single-frame camera is used.

The simplest method for preparing a filmstrip is to put ordinary 2 X 2-inch slides or negatives – again, the format of all slides must be horizontal – in the sequence in which they should appear in the finished filmstrip, and send them off to a commercial laboratory. The cost of converting your slides is modest.

The third and most common method for preparing a filmstrip is to prepare a complete series of filmstrip flats. These can also be sent to a film laboratory for photographing and conversion to a filmstrip. The cost is minimal. You will use a single-frame mask as your guide for flats to be converted at a laboratory.

Basic Procedure for Making a Filmstrip from Flats

Let us assume that you are in the position of most training directors, i.e., a little shy on experience, yet forced into the assignment of preparing a filmstrip. We will assume that you have defined your objectives and have written your script. You are now ready to convert your script into the end product of the sound-filmstrip. Here are the basic procedures you will follow using the available, nonprofessional equipment.

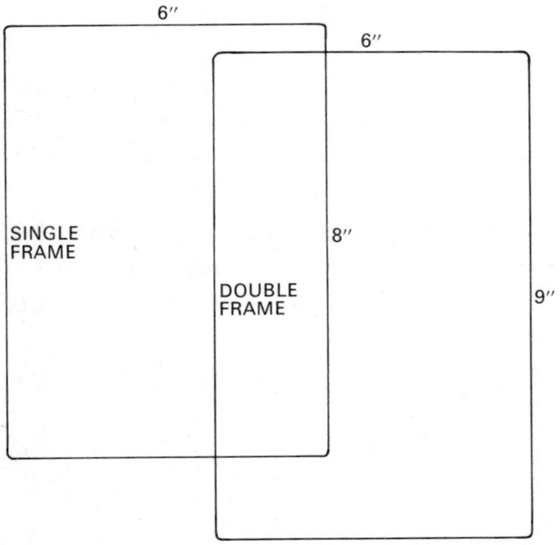

Fig. 15-14. Outline of single-frame and double-frame masks.

1. Begin by preparing either a single-frame or double-frame mask to be used as a guide in photographing all of your illustrations, photographs, artwork, or titles.

a) Use a single-frame mask if your filmstrip flats will be converted to a filmstrip by a film laboratory or photographed by a single-frame camera. The dimensions of a single-frame mask are 6- X 8-inches. An outline of the single-frame mask is pictured in Fig. 15-14.

b) Use a double-frame mask if you plan to photograph your filmstrip with an ordinary 35mm camera. The dimensions of the double-frame mask are 6″ X 9″. An outline of the double-frame mask is also pictured in Fig. 15-14.

2. Assuming that you copy your filmstrip flats with an ordinary 35mm camera, prepare them to fit the opening of a double-frame mask.

3. To prepare a filmstrip flat, follow these steps:

Step 1. Work on a registration board or other device for holding the material in position. First place a piece of cardboard down over the pins even with the outside dimensions of the mask.

Step 2. Line up your illustrations, photographs, or artwork to fit the horizontal 6 X 9-inch opening of the frame.

Step 3. Use acetate overlays with appropriate lettering for titles. Legibility standards can be roughly determined by reading the proposed lettering at a distance of five feet. If it is legible at that distance, it will probably be legible when projected in a normal room.

Step 4. Place the mask on the pins over the artwork and base board. Tape it on the edges so that it will not slip once it is on the pins. Be sure work is flat so that raised surfaces do not cause some of the material to be out of focus when photographed.

4. Load the camera with an ordinary 36-exposure roll of black and white or color film. Hold your hand over the lens and shoot the first few frames so that they will appear black after development and can be used for leaders. Do the same at the end of the roll.

5. Place all of your filmstrip flats in the sequence in which they are to appear in the final filmstrip.

6. Copy each one, using the copy stand as described earlier in the chapter. Photograph all material placed in the same direction in the horizontal position running toward you.

7. Shoot the entire film at one time to avoid variations in light and camera registration.

8. If only a few copies are needed, it will be less expensive and quicker to simply shoot the complete flat sequence again. If a large number of copies are needed, see the appendices for addresses of laboratories that duplicate filmstrips.

9. Sound may be recorded on a tape recorder of good quality. Duplicate disc recordings can be made by commercial companies from the master tape.

Some Tips for Successful Filmstrip Projection

The success of a filmstrip depends not only on its content and quality, but also on how well it is projected. Here are a few useful tips for showing filmstrips.

1. To insert the filmstrip roll correctly the first time, make sure the pictures are upside down with both ends of the strip curling toward the screen.
2. Adjust the framing knob for one complete picture at the time the lens is focused.

Fig. 15-15. Automatic tape sound filmstrip projector. (Courtesy Dukane Corporation.)

3. Select the proper aperture and carrier position before inserting the strip. Single-frame strips use the smaller aperture in a vertical strip. Double-frame strips use the larger aperture in a horizontal strip.
4. If you are using both a filmstrip and a tape or record be sure that the sound is synchronized with the picture. Nothing is more annoying to the audience than seeing a visual which does not match the soundtrack. Get in the habit of reviewing a few frames to test the coordination of the filmstrip and soundtrack before showing.
5. Like sound-slide projection equipment, filmstrip projectors are being improved. Figure 15-15 shows a filmstrip projector using a sound tape in a cassette instead of the conventional record. This simplifies the operation of the projector and improves the portability of the equipment. A special cassette recorder may be used to produce your own tapes with automatic advance signals.

16

Making and Showing Training Movies

"A long time ago when the earth was green,
There were more kinds of animals than you've ever seen. . . .*

Recently we heard of an instance in which some children in a third grade class took crayons and colored a series of pictures to illustrate a song about a unicorn. Later the teacher brought in her 8mm movie camera and showed a few youngsters how to use it so that they could make a short movie of their artwork. When it was completed, they played the record as they showed the film. For a few dollars they learned how to plan a project, work together, and express themselves artistically in two media.

This children's project is a good example of how the film medium can be used in a simple, inexpensive, yet effective way to solve a learning problem. No elaborate script, cast, or equipment had to be used. In fact, the whole project was so natural and easy that third graders handled the entire production by themselves with little direction from the teacher.

The short film has a message for training directors who tend to think of the motion picture as a complex, sophisticated medium of learning. We have all been conditioned by the Hollywood cinema to associate filmmaking with slickness and stardom. When we look at movies we expect a high degree of professionalism. Our bosses, peers, and trainees also have this expectation. However, the training film should not be looked upon as a 90-minute production, replete with talent and elaborate lighting and sets. While these may be important to films designed to entertain or to project the corporate image to stockholders, it should be of little concern to the training director who is responsible for carrying out a specific teaching/learning task. The children's film, lasting only three

*Shel Silverstein, *The Unicorn,* Hollis Music Corporation, N. Y.

Fig. 16-1. Fairchild Mark IV projector. (Courtesy Fairchild Industrial Products Division.)

minutes, did an effective job in providing the learning experience the teacher had planned.

One time after having made a 12-minute film to train salespeople in the collection of sales stubs from merchandise, we were called upon to show our work to the members of the company's management board. They viewed it, offered a few suggestions, and that was all there was to it. What made this situation unusual was that management had never asked to see our programed manuals, to attend our lectures, or to look at our filmstrips. The movie, however, was something entirely different. If the film had been less presentable, it probably would have been removed from the training curriculum even if it had been a useful training device.

During the last few years, films have undergone changes in format and use which are beginning to free them from the Hollywood stigma. Loop films for instructional purposes have proven to be useful. The Mark IV rear screen projector (Fig. 16-1), with its simple cartridge loading capability, has become popular. These particular cartridges hold about 20 minutes of film, thus forcing us to depart from the longer traditional format.

Single concept films have been developed or cut from longer films to teach one idea in two or three minutes.* Films are beginning to be looked upon as learning devices which can be integrated into a learning situation. It is no longer necessary to darken a formal viewing room and show a one-hour film from beginning to end. Training people are beginning to take rear screen projectors into the selling departments of retail stores, the assembly lines of factories, and the laboratories of research and development firms. There is a whole new way of looking at the film as a medium for instruction. The concern is not with the "Hollywood" quality but with the teaching/learning quality of the film and whether it meets the training objectives.

WHY A FILM?

Assuming that the training director looks upon a film as he would any other instructional medium, he must be able to answer the question, "Why a film?" We watched a training director squirm when his boss told him that he thought that a slide show would have done as well as the half-hour production he had just seen. It certainly would have been quicker and cheaper to produce.

The training director should answer the following questions to his own satisfaction before deciding on a movie as his medium.

1. Do I need motion to convey my teaching points?
2. Will the film be valuable to the company on a long-range basis? If the film is cheap enough and short enough, of course, this will not be a consideration.
3. Will a movie be the best vehicle for the types of learning problems my trainees face?
4. Can I solve the logistical problems of use and distribution once the film is finished?

If the answer to these questions is yes, then you are ready for the next step.

---

*Kodak has recently produced a free booklet called *Movies with a Purpose,* which provides practical help in making a single concept film using amateur equipment. The booklet may be obtained by writing Kodak, Motion Picture and Education Markets Division, Eastman Kodak Company, Rochester, N. Y.

SOME ESSENTIAL TERMS

Before we can begin to prepare our film we need to be familiar with a few terms. If you already know these, skip to the next section.

Scene. Each time you expose footage.

Take. Each time you expose footage on the same subject matter.

Sequence. A series of related scenes depicting one idea.

Cut. The instantaneous transition from one shot to the next shot which results in the splicing of two shots together.

Dissolve. An effect created when two shots are superimposed on the screen with the second shot gradually appearing as the first shot gradually disappears.

Dollying. Moving the whole camera when making a shot.

Fade. An effect created when a single shot gradually disappears into blackness (fades out) or appears out of blackness (fades in).

Close-up (C.U.). A shot taken with the camera close to the subject, often with the face filling the field.

Establishing shots. Usually long shots of exteriors to establish the whereabouts of a scene.

Long shot (L.S.). A shot in which the object of principal interest is far away from the camera.

Medium shot (M.S.). A shot showing a person at full height, or a scene at normal viewing distance.

Pan shot. A shot in which the camera head is panned across a scene.

Reaction shot. A shot inserted during a dialogue sequence to show the effect of a person's words on other participants in the scene; usually a close-up.

Two shot. A shot containing two characters. A three shot contains three characters.

Zoom shot. A shot taken with a zoom lens, usually by zooming in on or away from the subject

The language of film-making has a vocabulary of its own. The above terms will be enough to get you thinking about a film scene in terms of shots. One of the first experiences an amateur has when he begins to shoot a film is the sudden recognition that a scene is made up of many shots. As a viewer he accepted the camera changes without recognizing them as changes. The amateur finds that he cannot go out and simply point the camera at his action for three or four minutes and expect to come up with a film segment that is visually interesting. Rather, the segment will be made up of a series of shots, some of them lasting as little as two seconds or as long as thirty seconds. A ten-minute film usually consists of 75 to 100 or more individual shots.

Once the general objectives of the film have been established and agreed upon, a good deal of thinking will need to be done by the person responsible for the film's production. This thinking should take the form of visualizing the shots that will go into the scene or scenes.

A general approach to the whole project will need to be worked out. Here are a few approaches you might use in your film:

Ask a question and answer it.

Make a statement and expand on it.

Set up a puzzle and resolve it.

Set up a puzzle and do not resolve it.

Present a resolution and then the method used in arriving at it.

Pose two or more sides to a story and compare them. Then choose the best side or a compromise.

There are, of course, many other approaches you can use.

Having reached the stage where the thinking, visualizing, conceptualizing of the film have been roughed out, you can save time by making a storyboard of the film so that others can see, understand, criticize, and help you modify your plans before they become formalized on paper. In using the storyboard format, you simply sketch out the key shots in the various scenes. The story line and key scenes can be set up on large illustration boards, measuring approximately 2 X 3 feet. Along with these are the key instructions for the camera action such as zooming, cutting, fading, dissolving, and an indication of sound effects and music you might be planning to use.

PREPARING A MOVIE SCRIPT

Whether you need a script depends on how many people will be involved in your production, and the film's length and complexity. Obviously there is no need to write a script just for the sake of having something in writing to show your boss. The story board described in the previous section could be enough if everyone understood his part in the production. You may need only a listing of shots in the sequence you will take them and an indication of which scenes will contain the adlibbed dialogue.

The following portion of a script was designed for a 12-minute training film for which the training director did most of the shooting, editing, and sound work. The format is simple and workable.

Fifth Draft of Shooting Script: "Just the Ticket"

Intended audience: All sales personnel.

Overall objectives: To increase the percentage return of stubs from the selling floor to the data processing department.

Specific objectives:

1. To explain the sales reporting system.
2. To show why the stub is a critical link in the stock reorder chain.
3. To show the effect on the total system when the stub link of the chain is broken.
4. To explain the role of the salesperson in keeping the chain from being broken.

Film format: To be shot in 16mm color and reduced to 8mm cartridge load for Mark IV projector.

Time: Approximately 12 minutes.

	Picture	Sound
1	*Fade in.* C.U. Hand holding a set of automobile points.	*Narrator:* Recognize these? A set of automobile points . . .
2	M.S. Open hood. Motor exposed. Cap off distributor. Mechanic points to location of points as rotor spins.	
3	C.U. Same as 2.	. . . vital to the electrical system . . .
4	L.S. Overhead shot of stream of moving cars.	. . . of every car on the road.
5	M.C.U. Mechanic taking new set of points out of package and preparing to install them.	New points cost only three dollars and forty-nine cents.
6	L.S. Moving Rolls Royce.	

	Picture	Sound
7	M.S. Driver peers under hood of his stalled car.	Though the price is small . . . even the most expensive car on the market will not run if this part is worn or defective.
8	L.S. Woman and child shopping in fashionable department. *Fade in title over scene. Fade out title.*	
9	M.S. Same as 8.	However small and unimportant a part may seem, all complex systems depend on the smooth operation of their individual parts. Damage or omit one part and you may destroy the entire system.
10	C.U. Hand holding three-part ticket.	Like the points, this stub is a critical link in the successful buying and selling of merchandise.
11	M.C.U. Systems director points to each item of information on the ticket as it is identified by the narrator. (A specially prepared blow-up of the three-part ticket will be used for this C.U.)	On it is recorded the department number, the style, the class, the season, the manufacturer's number, the color, the size, and the price of a given piece of merchandise.

	Picture	Sound
12	M.S. Return to the close of transaction in 9. Salesperson removes stub from ticket, places it on spindle.	When this dress is sold, one part of the multipart ticket will be removed and sent to the data processing department.
13	M.S. Salesperson hands customer box. Customer exits. Pan to M.L.S. of rack of similar type dresses. *Fade out.*	In this way, the buyer will know exactly how many of these dresses are still in stock and how many will be needed to satisfy future customers.
14	*Fade in.* C.U. Kimball ticket machine producing chain of printed tickets. (Right side of the machine.)	These stubs can be compared . . .
15	M.C.U. Chain with large heavy links. *Pan* length of chain slowly from right to left.	. . . to links in a chain of activities required to successfully buy and sell merchandise.
16	M.L.S. Buyer in his office preparing purchases order.	The first link of this chain is forged . . .
17	C.U. Writing of order (seen from over buyer's shoulder).	. . . when the buyer writes the original order for the goods . . .
18	M.L.S. Same as 16. *Dissolve.*	. . . and sends it to the manufacturer.

The middle section of the script looked like the following.

	Picture	Sound
65	M.S. Same salesperson smiling, selling merchandise (with ticket exposed) to an obviously appreciative customer.	Here are a few simple steps you can take to be certain your buyer knows which merchandise our customers like best.
66	C.U. Correct method of tearing stubs and placing them on the spindle.	First of all, carefully remove one part of each multi-part ticket at the point of sale. Place it face up on the specially designed, two-pronged spindle near your register.
67	C.U. Spindle.	All stubs must be placed on this spindle with three exceptions . . .
68	C.U. Marked-down stub.	. . . marked-down stubs . . .
69	C.U. Mutilated stub.	. . . mutilated stubs . . .
70	C.U. Handwritten stub. *Dissolve.*	. . . and handwritten stubs.
71	M.S. Salesperson takes a green card from stack, and begins to fill it out. *Dissolve.*	Whenever you have a mutilated or handwritten stub, take a green striped card . . .

	Picture	Sound
72	C.U. Salesperson holds up filled out card.	. . . and record the required information.
73	M.C.U. Mutilated stub is thrown away and green card is placed in special envelope.	When you are finished, throw away the torn stub and place the green card in the data processing envelope.
74	M.C.U. Stub converter machine.	Remember . . . the machine can only read the holes in the stub. A re-stamped price is ignored.
75	M.C.U. Keypunch operator preparing punched cards. *Dissolve.*	All marked-down stubs must be processed separately.
76	M.S. Salesperson examining garment for three-part ticket. Does not find one. Takes green card.	If you are selling a garment without a ticket or just one part of the ticket, use the green striped card as you would in the case of a torn ticket.
77	C.U. Incompletely filled-out green striped card. *Dissolve.*	Fill in whatever information you have. A partial report is better than none at all.

	Picture	Sound
78	M.S. Salesperson accepting merchandise from customer. After customer leaves, salesperson takes a red striped card.	Whenever merchandise is returned for credit . . .
79	M.C.U. Salesperson filling out red card.	. . . complete the information required on this red striped card . . .
80	M.C.U. Completed card is placed in special envelope. *Dissolve.*	. . . and place it in the data processing envelope.
81	M.S. Salesperson approaching spindle with rubber bands and data processing envelope.	Each day at a time designated by your department manager . . .
82	C.U. Stubs being wrapped with rubber bands.	. . . an assigned person will wrap all of the stubs on your spindle with rubber bands.
83	C.U. Salesperson filling out envelope.	She will then print the necessary information on the face of the envelope.
84	M.S. Salesperson checks contents of envelope. *Dissolve.*	Before sealing she will check to be certain that the envelope contains all of the green and red striped cards, markdown stubs, and regular price stubs.

	Picture	Sound
85	M.S. Salesperson placing envelope in store mail pouch. *Dissolve.*	Sending the envelope . . .
86	Truck take pouches to city. *Dissolve.*	. . . to the data processing department in the city . . .
87	M.C.U. Chain. Repeat shot 15.	. . . is the final link in the chain of reporting sales to your buyer.

The final portion of the script was as follows:

99	M.S. Customer takes ad to salesperson. Salesperson shakes her head indicating that the merchandise is not in stock. Customer leaves, disappointed. Salesperson returns to straightening dresses on rack. *Dissolve, then zoom.*	Because of wrong or incomplete information, buyers unknowingly buy the wrong merchandise for you. This means that you have the wrong assortments. The end result is dissatisfied customers. Everyone loses—the store, the customer, and you!
100	M.S. Tab unit reading stubs. *Dissolve.*	Thousands of stubs will be fed into this machine today. Millions are processed each year.

	Picture	Sound
101	M.S. Buyer scanning sales report. *Dissolve.*	Each stub contains information vital to the successful buying and selling of merchandise.
102	M.L.S. Customer enters men's suit department. He pauses to look at magazine ad. Salesperson approaches. Customer shows him ad. Salesperson goes immediately to rack and selects the right suit.	Each stub is "Just the Ticket" you need to provide the highest quality of service to each customer.

CASTING

This chapter is written for the beginner, the training director who is more interested in producing a good teaching device than a slick production. The emphasis is on the simplest, least costly method of getting the job done. We take this point of view with the problem of casting too. For years professional casting directors have used what is known as the "type casting" system. But just what does a lawyer, teacher, doctor, foreman, or corporate president look like? The simple truth is that they look just like everyone else when placed in the desired picture environment. The training director should choose an actor who can do a convincing job; he should not worry about what the actor happens to look like.

Professional talent can be obtained through talent agents, radio and television stations, little theater groups, and university speech and drama schools. But it may not be necessary to use a professional. In fact, if possible, use employees who are already doing the work. They will enjoy a change from their routine and with their friends, will look forward to seeing the finished product. We have never known an employee to refuse the unpaid opportunity to be cast in a training film. If the part requires too much acting talent, have a professional narrator handle the speaking parts. If the whole film can be narrated, you can avoid the problems of synchronizing the sound and the film by putting the sound track on the film after it is completed.

For most training film purposes, your actors will not need makeup. In any case, avoid it if possible. Poorly applied makeup is always worse than no makeup at all.

Anyone who appears in your films or other audiovisual materials should be asked to sign a release form similar to the one below.

Date: ______________________

I hereby give permission to (insert name of individual, group, or institution making the audiovisual materials) to take pictures of me, of my minor child (insert name of child), or of materials owned by me, and to put the finished pictures to any legitimate use without limitation or reservation.

Signature: ______________________
Name (printed): ______________________
Address (printed): ______________________
City and state (printed): ______________________
Project (printed): ______________________
Director (printed): ______________________

WHERE TO SHOOT THE FILM

Forget about building elaborate sets or going to distant locations for a training film. Use your own environment whenever possible. If a special location is required, choose a relatively open area in a classroom, for example, and use one or two properties to help you suggest a location. If you must use an exotic locale in one of your shots, you may be able to buy the footage you want from a company that sells standard footage and then incorporate it into your film.

LIGHTING YOUR SET

The best lighting calls no attention to itself. When the lighting is right for the mood and subject of the scene, it goes unnoticed. On the other hand, good lighting is no accident. It will take some experimentation on your part to get the lighting to look natural. The typical lighting positions are as follows:

Key light. The apparent principal source of directional illumination falling upon a subject or area. The key light determines the exposure.

Fill light. Used to eliminate shadows, determine the contrast, and create the mood.

Back light. Used to highlight subject and separate it from the background.

Accent light. Sometimes called a kicker light. It highlights the subject and helps give three-dimensional effect.

Set lights. Separate illumination of background or set other than that provided for principal subjects or areas.

Always remember to use your light meter for balancing lights and determining exposure. One of a number of methods available consists of taking readings with a reflected light meter held at various parts of the scene and then averaging them.

Your basic lighting pattern should be as follows:

Step 1. Place one light about 45° to the side of the camera, somewhat closer to the subject and higher than the camera. This is the key light and should be twice as bright as any other source of light you use. (See Fig. 16-2.)

Step 2. Place a second light or two beside the camera on the side opposite the key light and at camera height. This light is called the fill light. (See Fig. 16-3.)

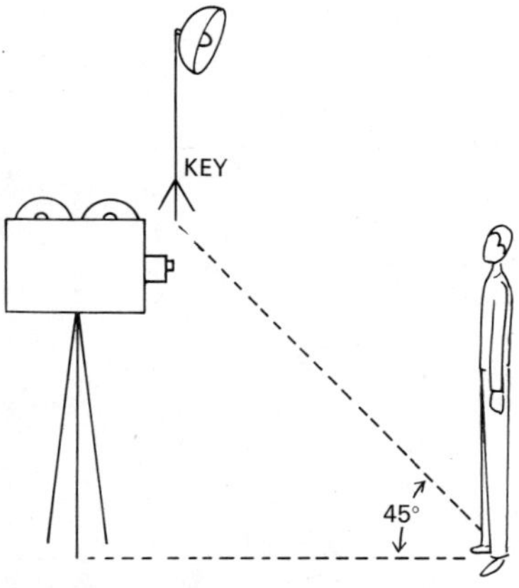

Fig. 16-2. Key light placement.

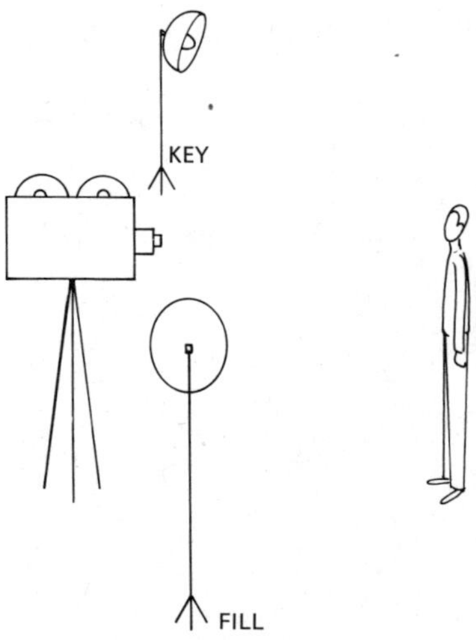

Fig. 16-3. Placement of fill light.

Step 3. Place a back light aimed evenly at the background to give the scene depth. Keep the subject two or three feet away from the background to minimize heavy shadows. (See Fig. 16-4.)

Step 4. Place a photo spot above the subject to accent the person or scene. (See Fig. 16-5.)

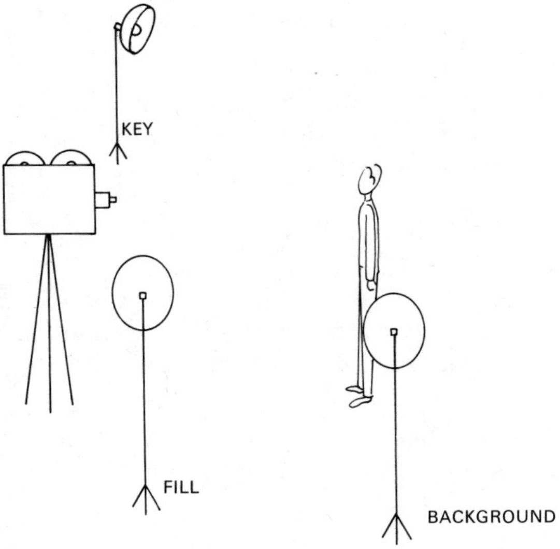

Fig. 16-4. Placement of back light.

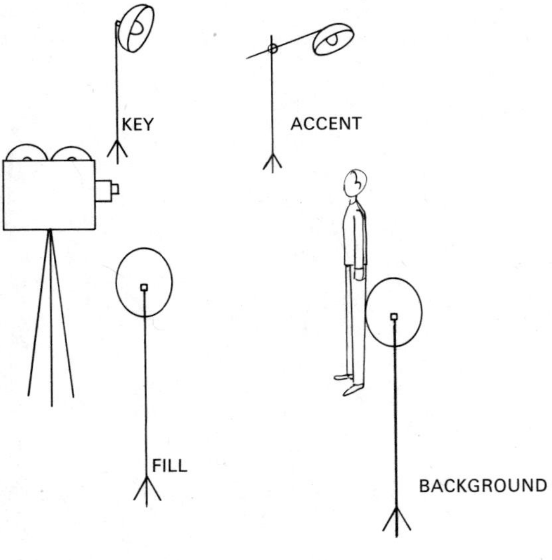

Fig. 16-5. Placement of accent light.

CHOICE OF FILM AND SHOOTING EQUIPMENT

Camera. Use as simple a camera as you can to do the job. Figures 16-6 and 16-7 show two cameras that are easy to operate and give good results. There are, of course, other good cameras.

Fig. 16-6. Fairchild's 8mm camera. (Courtesy Fairchild Industrial Products Division.)

It is suggested that you rent the camera and the other equipment if you do not already own them. Naturally, if you can get all of the necessary planning done before you start shooting and if you can organize your shots so that they are grouped by talent and location, you will be able to keep your rental costs at a minimum.

Fig. 16-7. Bolex 16mm camera. (Courtesy Paillard, Inc.)

Tripod. Most of your shots should be done on a tripod. You should hold the camera without support only when a tripod cannot be used because of the physical position you will be in.

Light meter. This is a must. Even if your camera has a built-in light meter, you will save time and money if you check every shot with your light meter before rolling the camera.

Lights. Use at least three photographic floodlamps. Be sure you have plenty of long extension cords. You will probably need to use several outlets on different lines so that you do not trip the fuse box with an overload.

Film. For 16mm color film use Ektachrome Commercial (7255). For 16mm black and white use any general purpose reversal type film. For 8mm, only color reversal films are normally available; special orders may be required for black and white. For films that will have magnetic striping for sound added, use single perforation film.

SHOOTING THE FOOTAGE

Once the general plan for the film has been accepted, your equipment assembled, and your talent briefed, you are ready to go out and shoot the footage. No one can tell exactly which angles to take or shots to make. You will have to experiment and develop your own style. Here are a few guidelines which you can use to get started.

1. Film is cheap compared to the cost of setting up. If you have the slightest doubt about a take, reshoot the footage while everyone is present on the set.
2. Start filming a scene just before the action begins and keep filming it until after it has stopped. In that way you will be certain of getting the complete scene and footage left over for optical effects and splices.
3. There is no set rule for the length of a scene. Film a scene just long enough to convey the idea but not so long that the viewer becomes restless.
4. L.S. – M.S. – C.U. – This is the fundamental sequence of shots but it need not be rigidly adhered to in every case.
5. Normal camera position is about eye level.
6. In most filming the camera is the eye of the audience, but this rule need not be always followed.
7. Tilting, panning, and zooming are generally used too often by amateurs.
8. If a sequence has a great many close-ups, occasionally reestablish the viewer's orientation with a medium or long shot.
9. To save confusion later, label every scene with the scene and take number. This information written on an 8-1/2 X 11 sheet of paper and held momentarily before the camera will help to identify your footage.

10. As you film scenes within the same sequence, the subject normally moves. Shoot adjacent and related scenes in such a way that a continuation of the movement is evident from one scene to the next.
11. If a subject moves across the frame from left to right, be sure he moves in the same direction in the next scene.
12. If action leaves a frame on one side, it must enter the next scene from the opposite side for continuity.
13. For possible use during editing, take cut-in and cut-away shots. A cut-in shot is a close-up of some part of the scene being filmed. A cut-away is a shot of another subject or separate action taking place at the same time as the main action.

WORK PRINTS

The process of editing a film requires a great deal of handling of the original film. Rather than take the chance of damaging the original from which many copies may be made, have a film laboratory supply you with a black and white work print. This is a cheap duplicate of the original. After the work print is made, the film laboratory will put matching edge numbers on every foot of the work print and the original. This will make it easy to transfer changes made in the work print to the original.

If copies are to be made of the film, the laboratory will give you an "answer print" which includes exposure corrections and optical effects (fades and dissolves). Once you accept the answer print after having corrected it if necessary, you can have duplicate or release prints made.

EDITING YOUR FOOTAGE

Editing the developed footage will take place in three stages: the string-out, the rough cut, and the fine cut. You will need the following equipment to do the job:

Projector	Grease pencil
Viewer	Splicer and scraper
Pair of rewinds	Film cement
Spare reels	Pair of cotton gloves
Scissors	

In the string-out follow these steps:

1. Cut all scenes apart.
2. Eliminate obviously unusable footage.

3. Splice usable takes of all scenes together in sequence and put on one reel.
4. Review reel and make notes.

In the rough cut stage follow these steps:

1. Using the rewinds and the viewer, eliminate all but the best take for each scene.
2. Remove unnecessary footage but do not shorten scenes at this stage without a good reason.
3. Splice remaining footage in accordance with script onto one reel.
4. Review on projector, reading script against normal projection. Average number of words for each foot of 16mm film is four.
5. Rearrange footage as necessary.

The fine cut is the most difficult and critical part of your production. It would be wise to have this stage of your work completed by a professional editor. The money will be more than well spent. A professional editor will know exactly in which frame to make a cut. He can also help you rearrange or insert other footage if necessary. If you choose to do this portion of the editing yourself, it is simply a matter of patience and eye-straining work to polish your film as well as possible.

ADDING SOUND

The simplest way to add sound to a film is by having the release print striped with a magnetic stripe by the laboratory. You can then borrow or rent a magnetic sound movie projector and record the sound directly on the stripe while the film is being shown. Mistakes can be easily re-recorded. Lip synchronization is very difficult, although with some patience it can be done for very short speeches. The easiest route for the amateur is to use a professional narrator to narrate the script once the stripe is on.

Fairchild has recently produced a Mark IV 8mm projector with a built-in recording device. You can record directly into microphone or transcribe tape recorded background sound or commentary directly to your own production or a purchased professional professional film. Any Mark IV or V can be modified at the factory.

Optical sound can be handled by a sound-on-film motion picture camera which records the sound either magnetically or optically onto the film in the camera while it is being shot. The problem of editing then becomes more complicated because picture and sound editing must be done at the same time.

USING FILMS IN TRAINING

The following applies to using your own films or other films in training. You will get better results from the use of film by following these guidelines.

1. Never simply show a film for the sake of filling in time. Do not show a whole film if a small portion is all you really need.

2. Before showing the film, direct the trainee's attention to specific points you want him to see and learn in the film.

3. Increase the anxiety and therefore the attentiveness of the learner by suggesting that the film's contents are important to his future, class rank, and so on.

4. Suggest that the trainees think of the answers to questions which may be posed in the film. Then ask for answers to these questions when the film is over.

5. Stop the film and have the trainees answer questions asked in the film before proceeding.

6. Do not have the trainees take notes during the film. Most of the time this is too difficult because of the lighting to be worth the effort.

7. Be certain that you have previewed the film before showing it to a group.*

8. Do not leave the projector during the showing. Too often something goes wrong that could be cleared up if the instructor were next to the projector.

9. Show the film over again if you think it is worth while. Films move along too rapidly for some learners. Make the film available for other students to review on their own time if necessary.

10. Thoroughly integrate films into your lesson plans. Films are too often permitted to stand alone when in fact they can carry only part of the teaching load. Films foster passive learning and need a live instructor to repeat points, reinforce responses and so on.†

---

*If you can't preview the film yourself, Olympic Training Film Profiles has a service which supplies fact sheets on about 240 films and filmstrips each year. For further information write Olympic Film Service, 161 West 22nd St., N.Y., N.Y., 10011.

†Roundtable Films Inc. 1321 So. Beverly Drive, Beverly Hills, Calif. 90212, will send you, upon request, a free evaluation form for evaluating your film training sessions. The form may be duplicated for use in your classes.

17

Instructing with Television

During the 1968 baseball season, the newspapers carried a story about Carl Yastrzemski, left fielder for the Boston Red Sox, and his miraculously improved batting average. Yaz's skill had slipped noticeably from the preceding year's level. Almost overnight, however, he made a comeback and was heard to remark, "For me the season begins tomorrow." When asked how he had managed to improve so quickly, Yaz replied that he studied videotapes which showed his swing the year before when his hitting was really hot. He went over and over these tapes in an effort to relearn what he had done so well the preceding year.

Yaz was able to capitalize on some of the unique teaching advantages of television. There are many. But TV is no "miracle whitener." It has its own set of drawbacks. Like other communications devices, it must be used in learning situations where its special features such as instant replay contribute to the attainment of specific teaching goals. Too often the task is determined after the tool has been selected. We begin with "let's make a movie" instead of "what must be taught and what is the best way to teach it?" In too many cases, instructional television has been used to duplicate the conventional classroom approach to learning. We have had an endless parade of screens filled with "talking faces." The only justification for using TV appears to be its gadget value. The lesson should be clear: the first job of the training person is to plan his learning objectives. If television will help the student to reach these objectives and no other medium will do as well for the cost and time available, then the use of television is justified.

PURPOSE AND SCOPE OF THE CHAPTER

Anyone who is interested in instructional TV will quickly find that there is a great mass of material at his disposal. Our purpose in writing this chapter is to introduce to this field the training person with little or no experience in using television as a teaching device. A few of the ways in which TV has been and is being used to train people will be summarized. We will assume that the reader is interested in learning how an instructional TV show is put together from writing the script to setting up the classroom so that everyone can see well. This chapter is not, however, intended as a technical treatise. It is simply an introduction to be used as a starting point by a training person who is considering the use of this medium.

HOW WELL DOES TELEVISION TEACH?

According to Wilbur Schramm, the director of Stanford's Institute for Communications Research, students do learn from television. This has been demonstrated in hundreds of public schools and colleges. "Instructional television is at least as effective as ordinary classroom instruction when the results are measured by the usual final examinations or by standardized tests . . . "* In 1964 Wilbur Schramm's institute compiled more than 350 research abstracts on instructional television (ITV). The majority of these studies were designed to measure the effectiveness of televised instruction compared to face-to-face instruction. The studies overwhelmingly indicated that there were no significant differences in the measured results of the two modes of instruction.

Much more research needs to be carried out. We need answers to the more difficult questions of how TV can be used most effectively and for what purpose. We need to know if it is more effective with some levels of student ability than with others. We need some conclusive results in the retention rates of televised and nontelevised instruction.

For the present we know that TV is an excellent medium to use to train large numbers of people at the same time, to overcome the physical problems of poorly designed classrooms, and to inexpensively record great teaching for posterity. It is also good for image magnification and instant visual feedback to a student. However, it makes class discussion difficult;

---

*Wilbur Schramm, "What we know about learning from instructional television," as quoted in Judith Murphy's *Learning By Television*, New York: The Fund for the Advancement of Education, 1966, p. 49.

it makes it difficult to use the drill technique; it does not allow for individual differences; and it tends to encourage passive learning rather than active seeking and responding.

SOME EXAMPLES OF HOW TELEVISION HAS BEEN USED TO INSTRUCT

There are hundreds of examples of the use of television for instruction in business and education. Here are three typical examples, one each from the fields of business, education and health.

The IBM office products division in White Plains, New York uses videotape for sales training.* Students are given an assignment to make a customer approach call. Each student is provided with a given sales situation and told to develop his presentation. The role of the customer is played by the class instructor, who interrupts with questions and, in general, behaves like a customer. The presentation takes 10 to 15 minutes and is taped. Immediately following the presentation, the tape is replayed and criticized by both the student and the instructor. The student has an opportunity to immediately see himself through the eyes of the customer. Together the student and the instructor can develop an appropriate set of sales behaviors essential to an effective call. Television in this particular situation serves as a mirror of the student's behavior. The image can be looked at as many times as necessary. Instead of the instructor's trying to remember what he has seen in the 10- to 15-minute presentation and then communicating it to the student, the machine does the work more accurately. With the help of the television, the instructor can concentrate on the job of coaching.

At Syracuse University, photography students in the school of journalism are taught darkroom procedures by television.† It had always been difficult to see these procedures because of the large number of students who had to crowd into the lab. Furthermore, the lab itself had to be lighted by infra-red lights because of the light sensitivity of the film and printing papers. Imagine trying to learn something while standing on your tip-toes, peering over someone's shoulder at objects dimly lighted by infra-red lights.

*"Videotape helps train IBM office products salesmen," *Training & Development Journal,* Vol. 21, No. 4, April, 1967, pp. 62-63.

†Robert L. Kerns, "Applying ITV in the teaching of photographic darkroom techniques," *Audiovisual Instruction,* December, 1967, pp. 1073-1078.

Syracuse now places a TV camera in the darkroom. The students view the equipment and darkroom techniques on monitors outside of the lab. The instructor communicates with the class via a two-way microphone. Not only is this a far more comfortable arrangement, but also, because of a special video tube in the transmitting camera which is sensitive to infra-red light, the picture transmitted looks as if it had been taken under normal light conditions. Darkroom techniques which previously required five hours to teach now need only one hour.

The third example comes from the field of health. At Montefiore Hospital in the Bronx, an experiment was conducted in order to determine whether large numbers of student nurses could be taught how to care for patients more effectively and more efficiently by television than by conventional instruction.* Fifteen cameras were mounted in fifteen patients' rooms. The instructor had two monitors, one which switched automatically every 12 seconds from room to room and another which could be controlled manually.

Each student wore a hearing device. The instructor used this device to teach or comment on the student's work. The patient was not able to hear the instructor's comments. This, of course, made it easier for the instructor to be candid about the way a student was handling a patient. If necessary, the instructor could leave the monitor and go to the patient's room.

This system proved to be as effective as conventional techniques had been. The real gain was in the number of students a single instructor could effectively teach. With TV an instructor was able to increase the number of pupils she was training by one third without reducing her training results.

These three examples have one element in common: each capitalizes on a feature or features of television to solve a training problem which no other medium could handle as well. This is a primary consideration for any training person considering the use of television or, in fact, any other medium.

THE LANGUAGE OF TELEVISION

The following is a brief list of terms which you will need to understand what you read and hear about television. If you are already familiar with this medium, skip this section. If not, glance over it now and come back to it as you need it.

---

*"TV focuses on the hospital room," *Training in Business and Industry*, Vol. 3, No. 7, July, 1967, pp. 33-35.

Aspect ratio. The proportional relationship of the width of the TV picture to the height. In TV as in motion pictures the aspect ratio is four to three. This must be taken into consideration when designing posters, lettering, etc. for use on TV.

Audio. That part of TV transmissions pertaining to sound.

Camera or cut light. The red reflector light on the front or on top of the camera which goes on when the camera is on the air.

Cans. Receivers and head phones worn by cameramen, stage managers, technical directors, etc. in the studio.

Closed circuit. A system for transmitting TV signals to receiving equipment directly linked to the originating equipment by coaxial cable, microwave relay, or telephone lines.

Coaxial cable. A special cable designed to carry one or more channels of television signals simultaneously.

Contrast. The brightness relationships between the different elements of a TV picture.

C.U. Close-up shot. Narrow angle picture. Usually bust or head shot of person.

Depth of focus. The field before the camera that registers in sharp focus.

Director. The individual in charge of all composition and action in a TV production.

Dissolve. The overlapping fade-out of one picture and fade-in of another.

Dolly. A movable carriage usually mounted on four wheels which carries either camera, or camera and cameraman.

Dolly in. To move in from a distance for close-up by means of a camera mounted on a dolly.

Dolly out. Reverse of dolly in.

Dolly shot. A shot taken while the camera is in motion.

Fade-in. Effect created when the TV screen is dark and the picture gradually appears to full brightness.

Fade-out. Effect created when from full brightness a picture disappears gradually until the screen is dark.

Focusing. Adjusting the optical lens in a camera to bring a scene into clear view on the mosaic, and consequently to the eye when viewed on the related camera picture monitor.

Gray scale. The achromatic color scale or table from white through grays to black, the intermediate grays differing from each other only through a proportional admixture of white and black. For practical printing and photographic purposes it is a ten-step transition from white through the grays to black.

Head room. The area between the actor's head and the actual top of the set. This area is important in relation to the amount of upward camera movement possible without overshooting the set.

Hot background. Term used when lighting of a playing area background is too strong or is of high illumination. Usually hot backgrounds are not desirable since there is not enough light contrast between center ground and background, causing the two areas to blend and giving a flat picture. A hot background could be useful in photographing a silhouette and other dramatic effects.

Image orthicon. A television camera pickup tube commonly used in commercial broadcasting and occasionally used in closed circuit installations.

Iris in. Also circle in. The gradual appearance of a picture from a small spot until it fills the picture with the constantly enlarging circle.

Iris out. Reverse action of the above. Circle closes down until it disappears.

Kinescope. The tube (currently used in receivers or monitors) on which the television picture is reproduced. Trade name ad developed by RCA.

Kinescope film. Technique developed by RCA to record complete TV programs on film.

Lap dissolve. Cross fading of one scene or image over another. Momentarily both pictures are visible. One picture disappears as another appears.

Lens turret. The plate on a TV camera on which are fastened several lenses, usually a wide angle, a narrow angle, and a telescopic lens. The plate can be rotated to facilitate rapid interchanging.

L.S. Long shot. A full view of set or background usually including a full-length view of actor or actors.

Mix. To combine by recording or re-recording various sounds to blend them together.

Monitor. A control kinescope used by producer, switcher, etc., to check and view camera pickup or on-the-air pictures.

M.S. Medium shot. A relative term, halfway between a close-up and a long shot.

Multiplexer. A specialized optical device that makes it possible to use a single television camera in conjunction with one or more motion picture, filmstrip and/or slide projectors in a film chain.

Pan. Move camera head right or left to follow action.

Resolution. The ability of a TV system to distinguish and reproduce fine detail in the subject televised.

Superimpose. To overlap an image produced by one camera with the image from another camera, both pictures being visible, but appearing finally as one picture.

Switcher. A control which permits the selection of one image from any of several cameras.

Talent. Live actors, actresses, or training people who perform in the show.

Tilt. A slow camera movement, up or down.

Truck. (right or left) Move camera with tripod right or left.

Video. The visual components of a television signal.

Vidicon. The camera pick-up tube in vidicon camera used in most closed circuit systems and filmed programs in broadcasting.

Viewfinder. A small monitor built into the TV camera enabling the cameraman to see exactly what his camera is focusing on.

Wipe. A transition in which a new scene gradually replaces the old one, in some gradually increasing geometric pattern.

Zoom. Move lens in or out.

HOW TO GET STARTED WITH INSTRUCTIONAL TV

Wars are usually productive of good slogans if nothing else. Remember gas rationing during World War II? The A, B, and C windshield stickers? Everyone asked "Is this trip really necessary?" before starting out.

The same kind of thinking should be rigorously applied to any consideration of using TV (or *any* medium) for instruction. The sixty-four dollar question every training man must answer is, "Will television help me to do a training job that no other instructional aid can do as well or as cheaply?" Once this question has been honestly answered – and that is not easy, with everyone else's training department acquiring videotape units and with your boss sending you literature and asking, "Should we have one of these?" – the next step is to select one or more staff people to be responsible for the selection, installation, and operation of the equipment.

This individual (or individuals) need not be an expert in electronics, but he should have some interest in and capacity for learning about the operation of the equipment. Major repair work will be done by professional technicians. What is needed is a responsible person with the desire and time to provide the necessary momentum to get a TV operation going and in use by an organization.

Fig. 17-1. Basic television equipment: camera, monitor, and videotape recorder. (Courtesy Radio Corporation of America.)

The second step is to see in operation some equipment of the type wanted. The person responsible can call in a consultant or simply call a manufacturers' representative. The trouble with consultants is that they cost money. The trouble with manufacturers' reps is that they push their own equipment. One of the best sources of advice can be another training function that has TV in operation. Training people tend to be very communicative about their successes and failures with a new technique. The professional journals are filled with training people telling their stories. A less objective way to try out some equipment would be to rent for a trial period and apply the rental costs to the purchase price. The trouble with this is that once the equipment is installed and operating, the desire to select alternate equipment or none at all is considerably reduced.

The third step is to select the appropriate system to fit your particular set of training needs. Chapter 4 covered some of the basic considerations in buying equipment.

The basic equipment will include a camera, a monitor, and a sound transmitter. (See Fig. 17-1.)

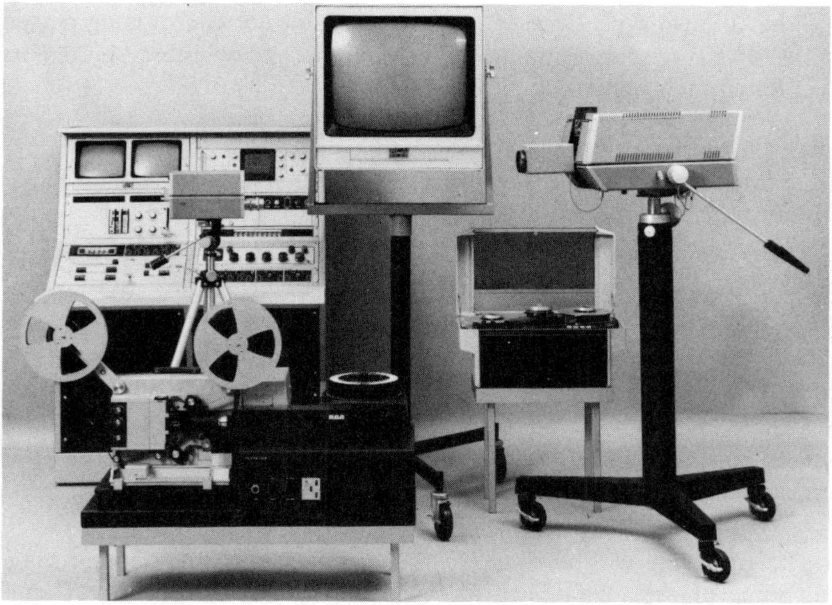

Fig. 17-2. Studio television set-up. Front: film system and cameras. Back, from left to right: console, monitor, videotape recorder. (Courtesy Radio Corporation of America.)

These basic elements can be expanded to include several cameras, a properly lighted studio, a control room containing monitors, a switcher, a film chain, sound equipment, and an internal communications system. (See Fig. 17-2.) The basics can cost less than two thousand dollars. A studio, control room, and more elaborate equipment can run up to several hundred thousand dollars. The complexity of your system should depend on the nature of your training problem.

Getting a salesman to see himself as his customer sees him can be accomplished with a videotape recorder costing less than two thousand dollars. No studio or control room is really necessary. On the other hand, if you intend to regularly produce training programs requiring film, special lighting, and sound effects, etc. you will need costlier, more professional equipment.

CHECKLIST FOR PRODUCING A TRAINING PROGRAM USING TV

This section and some of the following sections will give the inexperienced training person some guidelines for producing a training program using television.

The following checklist will serve as a guide for the training person responsible for producing the show. (The word "show" is used here in its non-entertainment sense.)

1. The first step is to determine the training objective of the production. Will television carry the entire program or will it be a part of a larger instructional situation?

2. The second step will be to determine the method or methods of presentation. Will the program require graphics? Other audiovisual materials? More than one instructor?

3. Step three is the preparation of a script to bring together the content, the method of presentation, and some of the technical directions for televising the show.

4. Step four will involve the set-up of the location of the show. Will this be in a classroom? Laboratory? Studio? Will more than one set be necessary for the entire production?

5. The fifth step will be to check the adequacy of the equipment to be used. Some of the methods of presentation may need to be modified if the existing equipment is not technically capable of achieving the desired training results.

6. Step six will be the production of the required graphics such as title cards, overhead transparencies, film segments, etc.

7. Step seven will be the selection and rehearsal of the talent and technical assistance required to produce the show.

8. Step eight will be to time the production, if this is important. Parts of the script may need expansion or reduction to meet time limitations.

9. The last step is to edit and review the entire finished program.

These steps can of course be expanded upon and worked out in detail to suit the complexity and formality of the actual program. The above checklist is meant to provide a rough framework of activity in which the training person will be working.

HOW TO PREPARE A TV SCRIPT

Scripts fall into two general categories, formal and informal. The informal script provides a framework for the show by blocking out the main segments of the program. Dialogue is merely outlined. Minor camera movement is left to the discretion of the cameraman. The following is an example of a portion of an informal script.

Video	Audio
Fade-in title. (Cam. 1)	Theme music.
Dissolve to L.S. of clerk and family at the reception desk in the lobby of a modern, well-furnished motel. Dolly in to M.S. (Cam. 2)	Music fade to background. A man and his family, anxious to be on their way, have been waiting for ten minutes at the registration desk while a clerk telephones ahead for a reservation. The children fuss, the wife is impatient, the man worries and time passes . . . Dialogue should fit the situation.
C.U. Clerk.	The clerk turns and apologizes to the family, telling them there are no rooms available.
M.S. of wife. Pan to other members of family.	Each member of the family is disappointed.
L.S. of family as they leave the motel.	They leave the motel, wondering where they will spend the night.
M.S. of narrator.	Narrator: "Did you feel that the clerk handled this situation in a professional way?. ."

Note that the script has been divided into two columns. The "video" column simply tells what is being done, while the "audio" column tells what is being said. The dialogue will be adlibbed and the video cues will be less specific as the script progresses. The advantage of an informal script is that it produces a more relaxed, spontaneous show. Control of the program is in the hands of the talent. Specific lines are not memorized. The show is worked out with the director and talent beforehand, but the exact action and dialogue are left open.

The formal script is set up in the same general way as the informal, the difference being one of detail. All video and audio cues are set forth. As little as possible is left to chance. Much more time is required for rehearsal. The following is an example of a formal script.

Video	Audio
T.C.U. (tight close-up of narrator. (Cam. 2)	*Narrator:* The usefulness of instructional television has been questioned by administrators, teachers, and students. How well does it teach? Is it worth the money? Does it force the classroom teacher into new and different roles?

Video	Audio
L.S. of school building exterior. (Cam. 1)	We will present a typical but imaginary system in which we can explore some of the ways in which TV is being put to work.
Superimpose title.	Fade-in music. (Music down.)
Zoom in on door of building. Children entering.	Let's follow some students through a typical day. Music out.
Dissolve to L.S. of classroom. Pan class to narrator. Zoom in on narrator interviewing student. (Cam. 2)	*Narrator:* What's going on here? *Student:* We're registering for next year. Boy, what a change from a few years ago. *Narrator:* Why? What do you mean?

A FEW GUIDELINES FOR PREPARING GRAPHICS FOR TV

The following comments will help the inexperienced person avoid some of the common pitfalls in preparing graphics for use on black and white television.

1. Material which looks professional and well done may not come across in the same way on the TV screen. On the other hand, material that does not rate an "A" in a graphics class may look excellent on the receiver. TV transmission can hide many of the faults in a graphic providing it has been prepared according to a few simple rules.

2. The TV picture has an aspect ratio of 3:4. This means that all graphics, if they are to fill the screen, must be constructed 3 units high and 4 units wide. The size does not matter, but the proportion does. The most frequently used card size is 11×14 inches. The information area on the card is usually 7×10 inches, thus providing the necessary margin of safety for framing the picture.

3. A particular color may look good in the studio but may come off poorly when transmitted. The basic rule to follow is to use colors that contrast well. The TV system reproduces only ten steps on the gray scale. Black is step ten and white is step one. There are eight shades of gray in between. All TV pictures are made up of these ten steps on the gray scale. Good visualization is obtained by using a two- to three-step minimum separation on the gray scale.

4. Glare is a problem with visuals. Instead of a white background use light gray.

5. Lettering on cards should be simple and have clean lines. This will avoid smeared or streaked letters on the receiver. Letter size should be one-tenth of the vertical size of the graphic card, or one-seventh of the information area.

6. To superimpose words on a picture, two cameras are used, one to shoot the picture and the other to shoot a black card with white letters.

7. As a rule of thumb, plan to use at least one graphic for every two or three minutes of dialogue.

HOW TO HANDLE THE CAMERA

You cannot learn to operate a TV camera by reading this section, but once you have tried to shoot with a real camera the following guidelines will help you get better pictures. The guidelines are divided into two sections, one telling you how to move the camera more smoothly, and the other telling you how to compose better-looking pictures once you have moved into the desired position.

Movement

1. Do not work with a jacket on. Extra clothing restricts movement and if you are working under lights you will get warm.

2. Unless you are going to do a dolly immediately, keep your friction head unlocked, your hands on the camera, and your head in the view finder. Then you will be ready to adjust composition as the talent or subject moves or rearranges itself – not after it.

3. Do not make any sudden moves on the air. You know you are going to move, but the viewer doesn't. If the framing must be adjusted after a change in subject composition, do it gently so that it will not be noticeable.

4. Before you make a move, look around. Cables, people, other cameras, and so on may be in the way. When you bump into something, it looks to the viewer exactly as if you bumped into something.

5. When you pan, do it smoothly and slowly. Start slowly, pick up speed, but slow down before you stop. This avoids jerky movements and backlash. If you make a panning error, do not stop in the middle and go back. It is less noticeable to finish the pan even if you are on the wrong subject.

6. Follow these steps for dollying with tripod camera support.

a) Pull the camera back to at least two feet behind the point where you want to begin the dolly.

b) Lock the pan head; unlock the tilt head.

c) Push the camera straight forward to the dolly starting position, making sure that it is pointed exactly in the direction in which you wish to dolly. This sets the wheels and avoids the lurching start common at the beginning of the dolly when the wheels have to readjust without help.

d) Put your left hand on the friction-head handle and your right hand on the camera-focus handle in a way that will enable you to turn the tube-focus section easily. Put your forehead against the view finder hood.

e) To start to dolly, push the base forward with your foot. After you start moving, your forehead provides the forward thrust, your left hand steers the camera, and your right hand is free to follow focus as smoothly as possible as you move toward the subject.

f) Dollying out requires practice; you must use both hands to operate the head and focus handles and still follow focus with the right hand.

g) Occasionally you will have to dolly in and out directly without an "off-the-air" opportunity to reset your wheels. To do this, get set for your dolly as usual. Shortly before you reach the end point of your dolly, begin to arc your camera to the right or the left so that at the point where your dolly is complete, your wheels have actually readjusted to a trucking position. Then slowly convert the trucking action to your dolly out by the same arcing movement you used to dolly in. When possible it is best to complete the action before resetting your wheels for the dolly out or before you stop at all. Otherwise there may be a lurch when you try to start again. This technique requires a good deal of practice but will pay dividends on the occasions when you have to use it.

Composition

1. Compose your picture as a unit. Keep the background and foreground as well as the subject in mind.

2. Remember that the viewer does not see as much of the picture as you do in the viewfinder. Do not put important video information too close to the edge of the frame.

3. Know the kind of shot you will get with which lens from from what distance and from what angle.

4. Depending upon other elements of the picture, a person looking to the right or left of the center of the frame (picture limits) usually has to be framed a little in the opposite direction to achieve a pleasing balance.

5. Many people with little experience in this area are able to compose "pleasing" looking shots from the beginning. If you have difficulty doing this, you may be able to help yourself by looking through photography magazines and studying what has been done with the elements in its pictures. The trick is to make yourself aware of good composition in whatever way possible so that the sense of what good composition is will become second nature when using the camera.

6. An inexperienced cameraman tends to move the camera and use the zoom lens too much. Much less movement is necessary than is normally supposed by people who have never handled a movie or TV camera.

7. If you are working with a camera without a viewfinder and must use a remote monitor to see what the camera sees, you will need to practice moving the camera each time the relative position of your equipment is changed.

WHAT WILL YOU NEED TO KNOW ABOUT LIGHTING?

Actually very little. Unlike motion picture work, you can produce acceptable programs with normal room light. If your picture is dark or shadowy you can adjust the lighting and improve the quality of the picture without having to wait for film to be developed. The general rule to follow in lighting a TV set is simply to do it in such a manner that the viewer will be able to see on the screen what he is supposed to see.

Depending on the complexity of your equipment and your need to establish a particular mood or atmosphere, you may need to learn more about lighting equipment and how to use it to achieve your desired effects. It is beyond the scope of this introductory chapter to cover that subject. There is an abundance of information available in technical books on the subject of lighting.

SOME GUIDELINES FOR THE TALENT

The following comments are basic instructions for the people who will be on camera. These comments will be especially helpful to someone who has never performed on television before.

1. Trainers who are used to pacing the classroom will need to consciously restrain their physical movement in front of the camera. The cameraman will have difficulty following a wandering lecturer.

2. An instructor who is used to keeping eye contact with his class will need to be reminded several times to look directly into the camera lens instead. If you are using more than one camera, he will also need to be reminded that he must play to the camera with the glowing red light on top. This, of course, tells him which camera is on the air.

3. Instructors who have little or no camera experience tend to develop nervous habits they never had before. One instructor begins to pace; another begins to wipe an imaginary speck of dust from his suit; another twists and retwists the lavelier microphone cord. This usually stops once it is brought to the instructor's attention and he becomes aware of this newly formed habit.

4. If a program is being filmed using an informal script, timing will be a problem at first. Most people tend to talk longer than they think they do. Without an audience it becomes difficult to imagine student response to the training. This realization by the instructor during a filming session often leads to repeating points made earlier during the presentation. Even an informal program will need to be walked and talked through once or twice before it is finally filmed.

5. Informal programs should be filmed after the first or second run through. Later dry runs become increasingly less spontaneous and shorter because the trainer tends to leave out details he included previously. Tapes made on the first or second try are usually superior to those made after four or five tries.

6. The following points may serve as a basic guide as to what performers should and should not wear in front of the camera.

a) Whenever possible check the appearance of a fabric and color on a monitor before doing a final production.

b) Avoid extremes in colors, fabrics, and accessories.

c) Do not wear jewelry or items which will cause a distracting reflection when televised.

d) Pastel shirts for men are better than white.

e) Avoid small repetitive patterns in cloth. They tend to appear "busy" on the screen.

f) In general, costuming should conform to the rule of two- to three-step gray scale contrast separations. You will probably want to give your performers some general advice before you produce a show.

7. The following points will serve as a basic guide to make-up considerations for your performers.

a) Most of the time you will not require make-up for training programs.

b) For nondramatic purposes you may wish to use television pancake make-up to cover a dark beard, reduce the reflection of light from the nose, forehead, and bald head, and play down skin texture.

c) Women usually require special make-up attention in only one area – the lips. Pale shades of lipstick may not give enough contrast for a good picture. Too much make-up should be avoided.

d) Of course, you may require make-up for dramatic purposes. For information on dramatic applications you will need to consult a technical book on the subject.

HOW TO SET UP A CLASSROOM FOR TV VIEWING

We turn now from the problems of producing a TV training program to the problems of setting up a classroom for optimum viewing. The ability to see and hear well are basic for effective learning. You will probably teach in a conventional classroom with trainees sitting one behind the other. In order for a group of 25 or more to see and hear adequately, it is best to use a TV set with at least a 23-inch tube. An additional advantage is that 23-inch sets are manufactured in large quantities and frequently subject to discount pricing.

The recommended minimum viewing distance for a 23-inch set is from six to eight feet. The maximum viewing distance is 19 feet. At a greater distance the students will not be able to see the picture easily. It is

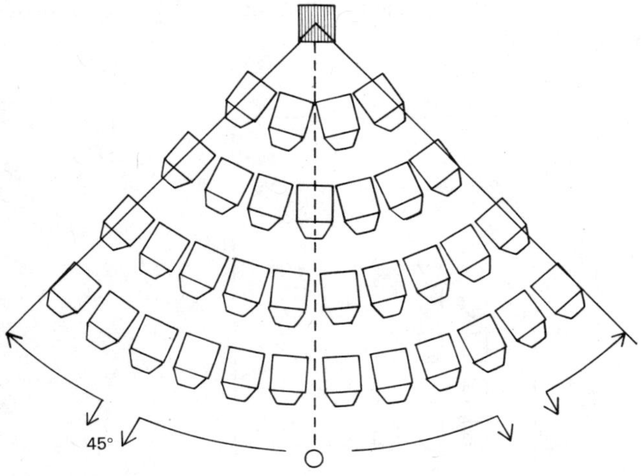

Fig. 17-3. Angles and distances for viewing legibility.

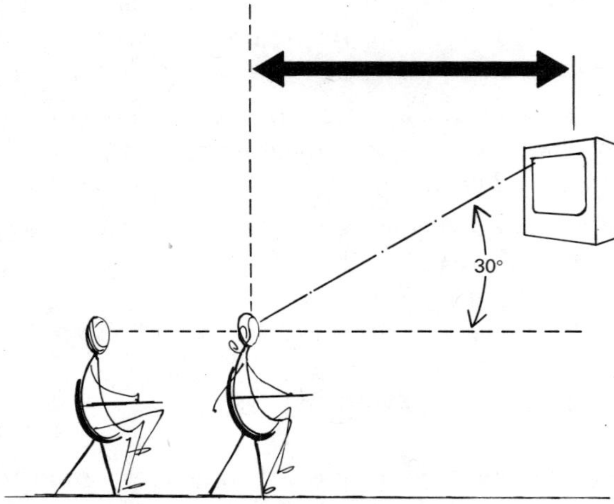

Fig. 17-4. Elevation of set.

also recommended that the students sit at no more than a 45-degree angle to the screen. The farther the viewer is seated from the center line axis perpendicular to the picture tube, the greater will be the image distortion and resultant loss of legibility. (See Fig. 17-3.)

So that students may see over the heads of those in front of them the receiver should be elevated, but not more than 30 degrees from eye level. A higher angle will result in neck or eye strain. If a set is placed on a stand that is between 41 and 43 inches in height, students will get the most comfortable view. (See Fig. 17-4.)

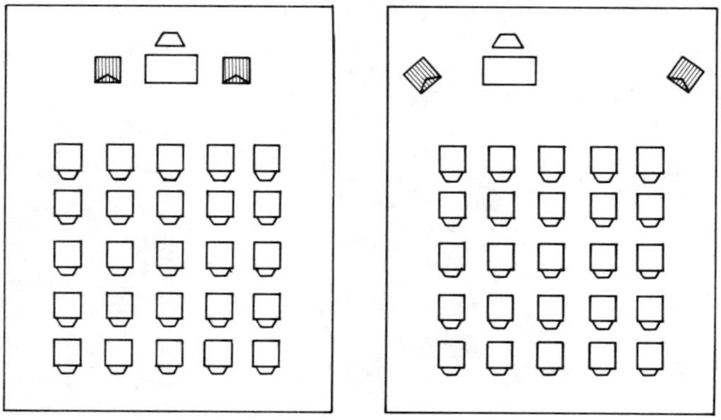

Fig. 17-5. Two examples of set placement.

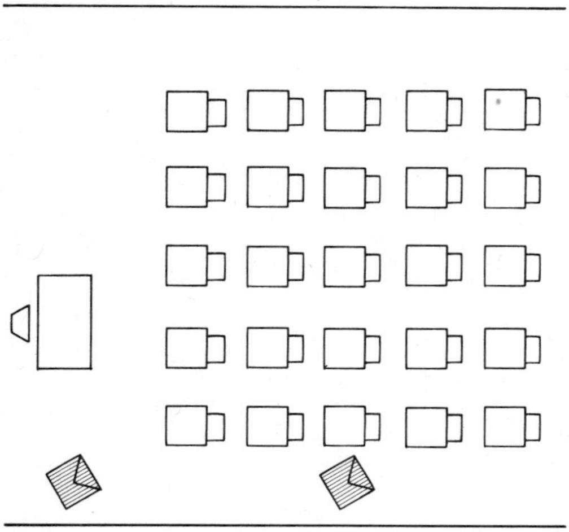

Fig. 17-6. Another example of set placement.

In larger classrooms with 25 to 40 individual desks and chairs permanently fixed to the floor, the arrangements shown in Fig. 17-5 offer possible variations for positioning receivers. These arrangements are designed for 23-inch sets.

The diagram at the left of Fig. 17-5 shows the most common arrangement, with two sets flanking the instructor's desk. This is particularly effective when the room is too wide for one set to be useful for all classes. The right side of the diagram shows two sets positioned in the corners. This arrangement has the advantage of leaving space in the front of the room for additional visual materials and for the trainer to speak during or after the program.

The set-up in Fig. 17-6 may be used if more space is needed at the front of the room or if the door opens directly into the front of the room. This arrangement is the least desirable because all of the students must watch at an angle. This could become tiring and reduce attentiveness.

For a really large room such as an auditorium, several sets or a large screen projection system for television will be needed. (See Fig. 17-7.) The number of television receivers to be used in any learning space will be determined by the number of viewers in the class group.

In situations where the desks and chairs are not permanently mounted there is greater flexibility in the arrangement of the receivers and viewers. The diagram in Fig. 17-8 shows the sets arranged so that the students have a good view from everywhere in the room.

In most cases normal lighting can be retained as long as there is no direct glare falling on the surface of the screen. A direct light on the

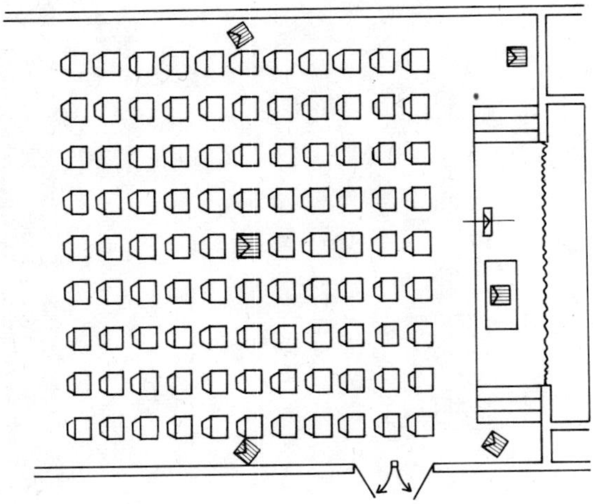

Fig. 17-7. Set placement for auditorium.

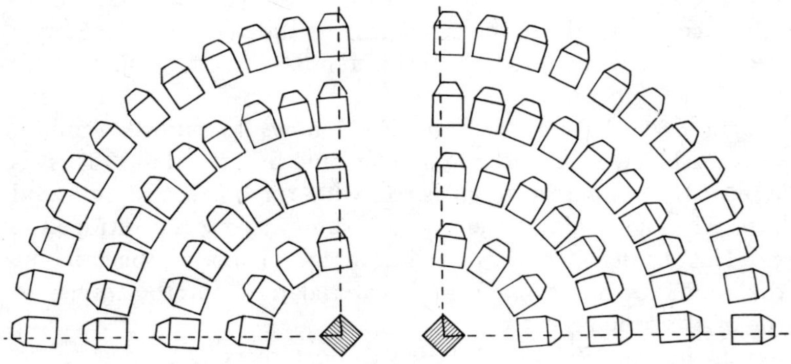

Fig. 17-8. Set placement in room with movable seating.

screen tends to soften the image definition, making it less legible. If you elevate the back legs of the TV stand slightly with a ruler, eraser, or pad of paper, you can usually avoid the glare.

If the classroom you are using has movable chairs and desks, your TV sets should be mounted on rollers or casters. The casters should be made of rubber and have a minimum diameter of three inches to support the weight of the set. If your receivers are on wheels, you can take advantage of the best viewing position at all times regardless of class arrangement or lighting conditions.

SOURCES OF COMMERCIALLY PRODUCED VIDEOTAPES

If you have a videotape playback unit, you may want to expand your library of tapes by purchasing or renting off-the-shelf programs. At the present time the number of sources is limited and does not seem to be growing. The following organizations can provide you with information about television programs for rent or purchase:

Great Plains Instructional Television Library
University of Nebraska
Lincoln, Nebraska, 68508

National Center for School and College Television
Box A
Bloomington, Indiana 47401

Educational Television Department
Pennsylvania State University
14 Hill Avenue
University Park, Pennsylvania 19610

National Project for the Improvement of
Televised Instruction
National Association of Educational Broadcasters
1346 Connecticut Avenue N. W.
Washington, D. C. 20036

National Educational Television
2715 Packard Road
Ann Arbor, Michigan 48104

Midwest Programs on Airborne TV Instruction, Inc.
Memorial Center, Purdue University
Lafayette, Indiana 47907

SOME INSTRUCTIONAL CONSIDERATIONS

The same learning principles apply to television as apply to other media. A behavioral analysis should precede a televised training program. Complete specifications of what the trainee will be taught must be made. There is ample evidence to indicate that students learn more effectively when a mechanism for active responding is built into the program. This could take the form of workbooks or oral exercises used during or after the televised portion of the program. Most training departments tend to let TV stand alone, to let it carry the instructional workload. However, television, along with films and records, must be incorporated into the training design for maximum effectiveness.

And one final note. Putting a classroom lecture on videotape does not exhaust the possible uses of this medium. Television is primarily a visual tool. It should therefore be used in ways that capitalize on its visual characteristics.

ADDITIONAL READING

Stroh, Thomas F., *The Uses of Video Tape in Training and Development.* New York: American Management Association, 1969. (*Note*: This is an exceptionally valuable study based on a November, 1967 questionnaire obtained from 482 companies. The results provide some very helpful insights for any organization considering the purchase of VTR. The booklet covers the major uses and misuses of VTR; what kind of equipment companies have purchased and why; special problems associated with VTR; and some ways in which the medium has been effectively used by companies participating in the survey.)

18

Preparing and Using Programed Materials

Programed instruction in one form or another has been with us since the time of Plato, but has only become a recognized medium of learning since 1954, when B. F. Skinner of Harvard University released his famous research paper. Today programed instruction can be found in use throughout public schools and training programs at almost all levels in various complexities.

Its versatility as a training medium has shown that programed instruction can be used to teach subjects ranging from those taught on the primary grade level to those taught on the postgraduate level. The only limitation on the use of this medium is the imagination and creativity of the program writers.

WHAT IS PROGRAMED INSTRUCTION?

Programed instruction has been given many different definitions by many people. To some it is a concept; to others a format. Within these definitions are many variations on the styles of programing. Essentially, however, programed instruction is a name given to any of "several techniques which have a common set of characteristics: the teaching material is designed to involve the student actively, the material provides immediate feedback, and the materials are tested and revised until they teach successfully.*

The term "program" is used to designate an arranged sequence of information, questions, and other materials to actively involve the student

*Robert E. Silverman, *How to Use Programmed Instruction in the Classroom*, Cambridge, Mass.: Bolt Beranek and Newman Inc., 1964, p. 1.

in the learning process. In actual program usage, the student will normally (1) read a statement or problem, study an illustration, or receive an audio stimulus; (2) make a response to these stimuli in some manner such as writing, speaking, or acting; (3) be shown immediately whether he is correct or incorrect; and (4) move on to the next "frame" of information at his own pace, insofar as it is practical in his particular educational environment.

Specific philosophies of programming and program formats and styles are often sources of considerable debate and confusion as to which are good and which are bad, and why. In reality they all can contribute to the goals of learning. From a variety of approaches we achieve a more balanced and interesting teaching program.

Over the years since Dr. Skinner first opened the field of modern programed instruction, two major kinds of programing have developed. These are referred to as intrinsic (branching) and linear (constructed response) programs. The intrinsic form is usually a program of large (full page) segments of information with multiple choice responses. The student will respond, and if incorrect, he will be "branched" – i.e., he will be instructed to turn to some other frame explaining the error in thinking, and then be put back on the correct learning path. These branches may be simple or complex depending upon the subject being taught. In some programs, the branches provide enrichment materials. In a linear program the student normally composes an answer which may be a single word, a paragraph, or even an oral response.

The key to the differences between the two program styles lies not in their formats but in their approach to teaching. The intrinsic programs usually provide less guidance to the student in that he is given large blocks of information and then corrected if he makes an error. In linear programs, the student is provided material in a carefully sequenced system arranged so that his potential for making the correct response is great and so that immediate feedback on his responses is provided. The concept is that exposure to an incorrect response may actually reinforce incorrect learning.

PROGRAMED INSTRUCTION AND LEARNING THEORY*

Since its introduction as a training tool, programed instruction has frequently been described as an educational revolution originating in the

*From Rollin O. Glaser, "Let's take the mystery out of PI!," *Training and Development Journal,* ASTD, Vol. 20, No. 5, May, 1966, pp. 36-42. Reprinted by permission of the publisher.

learning psychologist's laboratory. One psychologist has written, "Programed instruction is the first application of laboratory techniques utilized in the study of the learning process to the practical problems of education." Claims by manufacturers of teaching machines and purveyors of programed materials, of course, have been far less conservative. To the general public and the professional educator alike, it has seemed that at last the concerns of teaching have indeed become the concerns of science.

But in spite of the scientific aura surrounding the new "technology," there are at least two basic incongruities, disturbing to the professional educator who has taken the trouble to assess the theories and uses of PI. First there is the unsettled question of who is really qualified to create programed materials. A learning psychologist, or at least an educational psychologist, would seem to be the logical first choice. But while the initial practice was to employ a psychologist as a programer, most professionals are now recruited from within company ranks and have little, if any, background in learning psychology.

The authors of a recent report on the selection and training of programers have concluded that the ideal programer should have a high linguistic ability, high mental ability, a wide interest level, an ability to withstand confinement, and a few other personal characteristics. But nowhere in the study is it reported that it is necessary to know and be able to apply the principles of learning. In fact the summary of the report specifically recommends that any discussion of learning theory be delayed until the student has had experience in frame writing. Clearly there is a discrepancy between who *should* write programs and who *can* and *does* successfully write them.

Lack of New Technical Information

A second inconsistency is evident in the subject matter of current articles appearing in professional programing publications. There is an abundance of the type of article that expresses the opinion that PI is here to stay or that "programer" should be spelled with two "m's". But the technical articles discussing the learning psychology foundations and research on programing, so prevalent several years ago, can no longer be found. The serious programer is forced to conclude that either all that is to be said has already been printed, or that the scientific foundations of programed learning were more apparent than real.

Confronted by a formidable array of gadgetry and technical terms, the training director has a difficult task determining how and where and when PI will fit into the company's total training effort. In order to evaluate an individual program, employ and supervise programers, or even work with an outside programing firm it is imperative that the training director or training person responsible for the development and implementation of programing efforts understand the learning principles underlying programed instruction and be able to ascertain the extent to which these principles are crucial to the "art." Without this knowledge programed instruction and teaching machines can offer costly pitfalls to the unwary.

PI AND LAWS OF LEARNING

Because the great majority of programs studied and in popular use are of the Skinner or linear variety, the following discussion will be restricted to those learning fundamentals thought to be the bulwark of the linear program. There are six important generalizations fundamental to the teaching machine and programed instruction – operant conditioning, reinforcement, immediacy of reinforcement, operant discrimination, extinction, and shaping. An analysis of these six fundamentals and how they correlate with recent research will help us pinpoint the exact relationship between the laws of learning and programed instruction.

Operant Conditioning

Operant behavior, according to Skinner, is behavior which is emitted by the organism, but not elicited by the environment. In other words there is no particular, observable stimulus which will consistently elicit an operant response. The learning of operant behavior, called operant conditioning, consists of strengthening an operant by making a particular response more probable or more frequent. This is achieved by reinforcing the operant response when it occurs. The strength of operant conditioning is measured by its rate of emission. Raising or lowering this rate of emission, according to Skinner, constitutes learning.

By manipulating operant conditioning, pigeons can be trained to peck at different colored lights and rats trained to press bars or engage in any of a multitude of behavior patterns. Applied to human learning by programed instruction, operant conditioning takes the form of questions and answers. The question (or statement to be completed) provides the stimulus to which the learner responds by constructing an answer. According to Skinner and his followers, the activity of answering questions is the same as the activity of emitting responses. By reinforcing correct answers/responses, a particular operant can be strengthened.

In all cases the response must be overt, i.e., it must be written out. A covert response would violate the principle of operant conditioning. For this reason directions to early programs emphasized the need for the student to write his response in each frame. It was however not long before students found that thinking the response worked about as well as writing it.

The great majority of later studies undertaken to demonstrate the importance of the overt response have found no significant difference between the amount of learning produced by overt or covert responding. Taking into account both time and amount of learning, some studies have even demonstrated that the covert response is more efficient.

The translation of the principle of operant conditioning into student constructed responses appears inaccurate. When steps are made very small and the possibility of error held to a minimum, overt responding is probably unnecessary. Anecdotal records of student reactions to programs support this contention. A more important response requirement is probably related to the kind of response the frame requests. In an experiment by James Holland, it was demonstrated that students made the fewest errors on a posttest when the responses required were related to the critical information in the item. This suggests that mere activity is not sufficient, but that the stimulus question must force some kind of internal response which demands a high level of interaction between the student and the material.

Reinforcement

A second important generalization fundamental to programed instruction is the principle of reinforcement. The term reinforcement refers to any of a wide range of conditions which may be brought into a given learning situation to increase the probability that a given response will recur in the same situation. The list of conditions that may be introduced is long and diversified and includes such reinforcers as food, water, electric shock avoidance, money, grades, and trinkets. And although it is clear that the empirical operation of reinforcement is essential to learning, the exact nature of the mechanism of reinforcement is not. Reinforcement under one set of conditions may not be reinforcement under another.

By using the technique of reinforcing certain actions in the presence of certain stimuli and not reinforcing other actions, very complex behavior repertories can be built up in animals. Skinner's ping-pong playing pigeons are a good example of the application of reinforcement techniques used to develop a complex behavior repertory.

When translated into human learning and programed instruction, reinforcement is defined as response confirmation or telling the student that his response was correct. The student's "knowing" that he was correct is interpreted as providing that reinforcement which will increase the probability of the recurrence of a given operant.

Successful students report however that because step size is small and the error rate is low, it is a simple task to determine the answer in any given frame. Because it is easy, many students do not bother to check their answers. Whatever reinforcement properties the answers may have possessed is lost for these students. Yet they do as well as their reinforced counterparts. Knowledge of results is at best a questionable reinforcer.

Immediacy of Reinforcement

The third fundamental, immediacy of reinforcement, sets forth the time relationship of reinforcement to response. Increasing the delay of reinforcement after a response has occurred introduces an increasingly long chain of responses between the desired response and reinforcement which may interfere with learning. Wolfe, in a representative experiment, found that a delay of reward for as short as five seconds reduced the learning of a single T-maze by rats. Longer delays produced progressive decreases in efficiency, with the greater part of the decrease occurring within the first minute. The majority of studies with programed instruction support the principle of immediacy of reinforcement as contributing to learning. Scattered studies report comparable learning from students informed about their performance as much as twenty-four hours later.

A second aspect of the time relationship between response and reinforcement is concerned with the pattern according to which reinforcers follow responses. If reinforcement is given after every correct response, the schedule of reinforcement is said to be continuous. The majority of programs operate on a continuous schedule. Any other schedule of reinforcement given on a time-contingent basis or for a certain proportion of correct responses is referred to as an intermittent schedule or partial reinforcement. Each type of schedule affects responding in characteristic ways. In general more responses per reinforcer are obtained on an intermittent schedule than on a continuous schedule. If reinforcement is withdrawn, responses continue and resistance to extinction is greater after training with intermittent rather than continuous reinforcement. Human learning through programed instruction has not revealed any correspondence between posttest results and a particular schedule of reinforcement. This fact should not be surprising, however, if knowledge of results is a highly questionable reinforcer to begin with. No particular schedule of presentation can be expected to affect learning. Immediacy of confirmation also comes into question by this logic, for if the student already knows the answer before he receives reinforcement from the program, no delay of reinforcement can be said to exist.

Operant Discrimination

The fourth principle of programed instruction is concerned with operant discrimination. In an experiment where a pigeon is trained to stretch his neck when a light comes on, the light is said to have become the stimulus occasion upon which the neck-stretching response is more likely to occur. The process through which this behavior is produced is called discrimination. In a program the discriminated stimuli are the questions that almost always elicit appropriate responses. The use of operant discrimination is not, of course, the exclusive device of programed instruction. The mechanical agency of the frame serves the purpose of isolating the discriminative stimuli so that they may be more easily recognized, but beyond that, discriminative stimuli in programs deserve no special attention.

Extinction

A fifth principle is the principle of extinction. If a response has been developed to a high rate through reinforcement techniques, it can be extinguished or reduced to its original rate of emission by failure to continue reinforcement. In programed instruction the operation of extinction is implicit in the method. If a response is unreinforced, it will be extinguished. If response confirmation does not take place, the response will return to operant level. Extinction operates, however, in any educative situation when a given response goes unreinforced. Again, programed instruction can lay no special claim to its use.

Shaping

The sixth principle is referred to as shaping. Shaping behavior is the process of producing a learned complex sequence of responses. This is accomplished by reinforcing each unit of the sequence until the entire chain has been established. The laboratory concept of shaping has been translated into programed instruction by reducing information to very short steps and placing these steps in an ordered sequence leading to a specified terminal behavior. Each bit of information is presented separately and reinforced separately at first. Gradually the learner is led down a special path to a complex goal behavior. Step size is kept small to ensure a high probability of reinforcement.

In theory, shaping in a program appears to function in the same general way as shaping in the laboratory. In practice, however, complications arise in defining the meaning of step size and in determining what a logical sequence is. No one has been able to do either so that clear procedures can be laid out for programers. Size of step has been measured in a number of ways, none of which offers concrete guidelines. In general, programs with small steps measured in any of the devised ways have produced more efficient learning.

The exact nature of a logical sequence also eludes definition. Three of five experiments reported by Wilbur Schramm show no significant difference in learning when program items were placed in random order or in what the programer considered a logical sequence.

TASK ANALYSIS

In a paper presented by Robert M. Gagné at the 69th Annual Convention of the American Psychological Association, an attempt was made to focus on those principles of learning which could be applied to the practical problems of military training. After examining the well-known principles of reinforcement, distribution of practice, meaningfulness, distinctiveness of the elements of a task, and response availability, Gagné arrived at the conclusion that there was not much to be drawn from these principles in the way of practical advice. Instead he turned to the techniques of task analysis as providing the greatest usefulness in designing effective training procedures.

Gagné's conclusion is similar to the one to be drawn from the relationship of learning principles to programed instruction. In the final analysis, the most important outcome of the entire PI movement is the systematized attempt to prepare objectives and then teach in terms of them.

Although a learning psychologist was responsible for the teaching machine/programed instruction movement, learning psychology has not really provided the solid foundations of established learning principles some would like to believe it does.

It would be, however, just as incorrect to conclude that programed instruction has little or nothing to offer present training methods. Programed instruction has operated on American education and training as a positive force, focusing our attention once again on the learning process and the methods we use to aid this process. PI's success as a method of communication, however, only incidentally rests on learning theory.

EFFECTIVENESS OF PROGRAMED INSTRUCTION

Much has been said and written about the effectiveness of programed instruction in education and training. When questioning effectiveness, one should always keep in mind that programed instruction, like any other medium, is only as good as the quality of its construction.

There is significant evidence from a variety of studies which generally reaches the conclusion that PI is better than or equal to other forms of teaching. But this is only part of the answer of effectiveness.

Sufficient evidence also exists to prove that while PI may be equal to other training techniques in effectiveness, it is often highly significant in the dollar savings it can achieve. Two good examples of significant cost savings were illustrated in a pilot training program and a food service program.

The pilot training program was cut by a total of 22 classroom hours in the flight phase because of the introduction of programed instruction. This time saving could be translated into a total saving of $3000 per student. At the same time, an increase in the general quality level of the students was recorded.

In the food service case, several problems existed in a chain of restaurants, including lack of standardized training and over-involvement of the local managers in the training problems. Through the use of programed instruction in the first year alone, over 20,000 managerial hours were saved and a significant improvement in student performance quality was recorded.

The style of program which is most effective will depend upon the kind of training problem and the kind of student to be trained. Linear programs are effective in the teaching of basic educational skills and fundamentals, especially to students whose motivation is low or students who are fearful of the subject matter and who have had little learning success in the past.

Intrinsic programs are particularly suited to providing enrichment and for instructing mature students who are well motivated to learn. This type of student prefers the challenge of the large blocks of information and will often find the small-step, linear kind of program to be very boring.

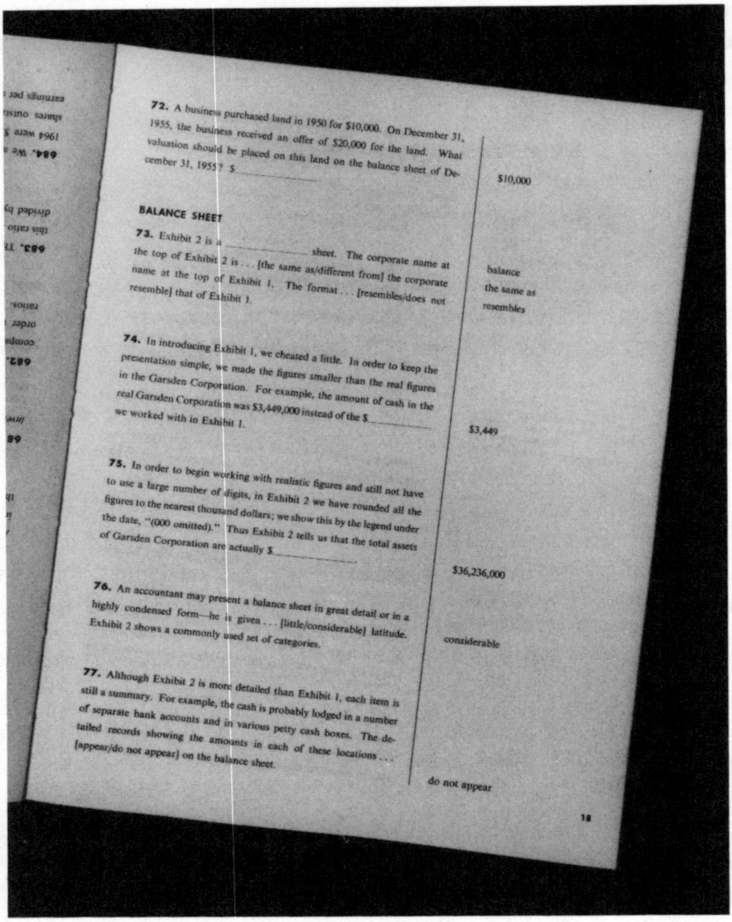

72. A business purchased land in 1950 for $10,000. On December 31, 1955, the business received an offer of $20,000 for the land. What valuation should be placed on this land on the balance sheet of December 31, 1955? $________ — $10,000

BALANCE SHEET

73. Exhibit 2 is a ________ sheet. The corporate name at the top of Exhibit 2 is . . . [the same as/different from] the corporate name at the top of Exhibit 1. The format . . . [resembles/does not resemble] that of Exhibit 1. — balance / the same as / resembles

74. In introducing Exhibit 1, we cheated a little. In order to keep the presentation simple, we made the figures smaller than the real figures in the Garsden Corporation. For example, the amount of cash in the real Garsden Corporation was $3,449,000 instead of the $________ we worked with in Exhibit 1. — $3,449

75. In order to begin working with realistic figures and still not have to use a large number of digits, in Exhibit 2 we have rounded all the figures to the nearest thousand dollars; we show this by the legend under the date, "(000 omitted)." Thus Exhibit 2 tells us that the total assets of Garsden Corporation are actually $________ — $36,236,000

76. An accountant may present a balance sheet in great detail or in a highly condensed form—he is given . . . [little/considerable] latitude. Exhibit 2 shows a commonly used set of categories. — considerable

77. Although Exhibit 2 is more detailed than Exhibit 1, each item is still a summary. For example, the cash is probably lodged in a number of separate bank accounts and in various petty cash boxes. The detailed records showing the amounts in each of these locations . . . [appear/do not appear] on the balance sheet. — do not appear

18

Fig. 18-1. A programed textbook.

PHYSICAL PROGRAM FORMATS

Over the years, programs have appeared in a variety of formats ranging from sheets of paper to elaborate teaching machines. These formats will also vary within their categories. For example, there are many varieties of programed books ranging from the simple linear program, where frames appear in consecutive order, to the very complex branching "tutor-textbooks." (See Fig. 18-1.)

Teaching machines also vary in size, kind, price, and purpose. These machines range from a simple cardboard concept in semibook form to a

Fig. 18-2. A typical teaching machine.

very elaborate electronic device. The value of the teaching machine compared to the book will vary in direct proportion to the quality of the programs it contains.

A teaching machine can add learning value if the device is designed to reinforce the learner. An early experimental classic model provided a piece of candy to a child when he selected the right answer. The only problem was that the child got sick on the candy. Today the reinforcer comes from the program or the teaching machine's mechanical attributes or both. In a machine, for example, where the student must discriminate between several answers, select one, and press a button to determine whether he is right or wrong, the reinforcement comes from the machine's ability to respond to the learner. In other words, it is a responsive system.

The selection of the "right" presentation format for programs will depend upon the students to be taught and the kind of program being employed. Linear or branching programs are suited to particular problems. On selecting the most appropriate program style or combination of styles, the selection of the presentation format will be determined by (1) the type of students, (2) the geographic dispersion of the student audience, (3) the time available for the training task, (4) the supervision available for the task, and (5) the budget available for the total program.

The most significant factor is the type of students to be taught. If the student group is composed of slow learners, poorly motivated and under-educated individuals, then a teaching machine would probably be more effective than a book format because the book may symbolize academic failure to this group. Economics is an important modifier to this decision, and you must consider the quantity required for the task, the mechanical problems you may encounter, and most important, whether you will continue this project with the development of more programs for the particular device selected. If the project is to be a one-shot approach where machines are appropriate, then consideration should be given to the use of an inexpensive "paper" machine like the "Programatic,"* which is a combined book and sliding-mask teaching machine bound together. (See Fig. 18-2.) The opposite of this inexpensive approach is the fixed installation like the "Auto-Tutor"† 35mm device.

PROGRAM PROCUREMENT

There are three means of procuring programs in either the book or teaching machine format. One approach is the purchase of commercially available mass-produced programs, which are bought in the same manner as textbooks. Another is to contract for custom development where a program is written to meet your specific needs, and the third is in-house development by your own staff. Commercially available programs will vary in quality and cost from the inexpensive book type to very expensive film type in teaching machines. The best source of data on what is available is C. H. Hendershot's bibliography *Programmed Learning: A Bibliography of Programs and Presentation Devices.*‡ This bibliography is updated periodically and provides the reader with data on the kind of program, number of frames, cost, and publisher. It makes no attempt to editorialize on the quality of the programs listed.

In using commercial materials in a training program, nothing is as suitable for checking the program's validity with your needs as an actual reading and criticism by the instructor. Prior to this, however, you can check the program against the following list of items to determine whether it is worth that effort in relation to your needs.

**Programatic* ®, Colortone Press, Washington, D.C.

†*Auto-Tutor* ®, Welch Scientific Corp., Chicago.

‡Carl Hendershot: Buy City, Michigan, 1967.

Checklist to determine validity of a commercial program

What are your training objectives? List them and compare them against those listed for the program being assessed.

Has the program been field tested and validated to show its effectiveness?

What is the language level used?

Check the criterion frames. Do they teach the subject as you need it taught?

How much time will be required for the students to work the program? Will it fit your course schedule?

Is the program in book format or will it require a special teaching machine?

Are teacher's guides and tests or other necessary materials available with the program?

Is programed instruction the best medium for your training task or would another be better suited to your needs?

In reviewing any ready-made program, keep in mind that perhaps only portions of the program may be suited to your needs rather than the whole course. It may be that it would be worth while to use these sections in your training program.

The preceding checklist will work to assess both book and teaching machine programs. With teaching machines, however, you have a second check to make on the device itself. For that purpose use the following list to assess the teaching machine.

Checklist to determine validity of teaching machine devices

Why do you propose to use a teaching machine rather than a book format? Check the audience to be certain this approach is valid. Does the teaching machine add to the learning?

Who is the manufacturer of the teaching machine? Is he likely to be in business tomorrow?

What is the cost per student of the device?

Will more than one student be able to use the device in class?

How complex (electrically and mechanically) is the device? Are breakdowns probable? How do you get the machines repaired?

If you need more teaching machines in the future, what is the probability of their being available at that time?

Who makes programs for the device and under what standards?

What is the cost of programs for the device?

Is this the best available device for your needs?

If possible, lab check a teaching machine in your environment to determine whether it will fulfill your needs.

Do not be taken by glamour or fads in selecting a teaching machine. Use a device only if it fulfills a training function no other medium can provide.

Custom Programs

Custom programs are those specially produced by an outside contractor to meet your specific training needs. Most often they are developed because the training department has determined that programed instruction is the best medium for the training situation and that no commercially produced program approaches the particular needs of the course. An example of custom programing would be a programed instruction course to teach a new product to salesmen or a course to teach company operating procedure. Both are peculiar to that company.

To contract for the development of a custom course, you should follow the guidelines established in Chapter 11. It has been estimated that the cost of having a program produced by an outside consultant will range from $10 to $30 a frame or even more in some instances. To quote cost, however, without knowledge of the specific training problem or circumstances is much like quoting the cost of building a house without knowing the house plans and specifications. Your best approach to this problem is to let a few consulting firms bid on the development phase to determine whether your budget can stand the cost and your training needs warrant the investment.

A safe way to assess the value of developing a custom program compared to another medium is to determine the cost per student hour. This will help you ascertain what value will be added for what costs. If, for example, the total project cost $5000 to produce, test, and apply, and you had 100 students per month or 1200 a year who would use the program, then the cost would average $4.16 per student. Is this more or less than the cost of other media when you consider effectiveness as well as administration costs and problems? A cost of $100 or more per student may be a low cost for your particular training problem. Only you can be the final judge on this question of cost effectiveness.

You must be careful in having outside contractors prepare a program to be certain the final product meets your specific needs. Again, if you follow the procedures outlined in Chapter 11 you will minimize your problem.

Another point to consider in custom development of programs is to be certain you have budgeted for *all* costs. Too often a client will simply contract to have a program written and completely ignore the costs of reproduction and implementation. Both of these costs can be substantial.

Judging the quality of the custom program will again require that you go back to your original objectives and criteria established with the contractor *before* work on the program had begun. Adhere to the criteria and demand that they be met. Test a final draft of the program on a population sample to be certain it meets your established requirements. You are the one who controls quality in a custom program, so do not blame the contractor if it is not met at the end of the project.

To be certain your custom program fills the needs of your training program, act as content editor for the program and read all items to see whether they cover the topics to be taught and whether they are in the right sequence and depth. You hired the contractor to write the program, not the content. If you keep this in mind and fulfill your role in custom designing, you will achieve your objectives.

In-House Programing

This is perhaps the approach to program development that is easiest in some respects and most difficult in others. It is easy in that a properly managed staff of quality writers can produce good programs economically. It is difficult because programers are hard to hire, difficult to properly train, difficult to manage, and equally difficult to retain once they become proficient in their art.

The first question to answer in establishing an in-house capability is, "Why do we feel the need for such a staff?" Cost is a critical item in this question. To hire and maintain even one person (plus supervision) can cost as much as $15,000 to $20,000 a year when the costs of salary, overhead, supervision, and materials are added together. The programer alone must be paid a salary of $8000 to $12,000 per year. The question of productivity must also be answered. Can you keep this person gainfully employed all year long? How much work (how many frames) can this person produce in a year? What is the real cost per frame for the in-house program compared to outside contracting for the programs as required? Will there be a need for a programer in the years to come or is this simply a one-shot task? These and other questions should be answered before you hire anyone.

If you decide to hire one or more programers, be certain you can supervise their work. Too often a training director without any knowledge of programing will hire programers and then is incapable of supervising them. Even highly creative people require some form of supervision.

RECRUITING PROGRAMERS

One of the hardest tasks in developing a programing group or even finding one qualified programer is the recruiting itself. To start with, the market for programers is high and the quantity of available programers is low. This is further aggravated by the fact that many of the so-called experienced programers are not well trained and consequently they are not adequate for their jobs. The most effective and the immediate solution is to hire an inexperienced program writer and train him or have him trained in the art of programing.

When interviewing experienced programers, begin by reviewing their previous work. Is it well written both in prose style and programing quality? How extensive is the writer's experience? Where and how was the individual trained? Is the programer a stable person as evidenced by his record? What is the cost of the "experienced" person compared to the cost of training one to fit your needs? There are other routine personnel questions to ask, but your primary concerns should focus on a candidate's ability to write programs and on the person as an individual.

If you are hiring an untrained writer, you need to look for the same traits, but at a different level of development. The two key elements to look for in the untrained program writer are the ability to write clear prose and the ability to analyze a problem in an orderly logical fashion. You must also seek a person who is patient and to some extent an introvert, because programing requires a great deal of slow methodical writing in an environment where the program writer is alone for long periods of time.

We have found that good potential programers are teachers, writers, and recent college graduates who were English majors. By far the best candidates will be experienced school teachers. Not only are they trained in teaching skills and learning theory, but they are usually eager for new careers which will pay better salaries.

The most effective means of recruiting programers is through advertisements in the Sunday editions of the metropolitan newspapers. The ads should stress the need for an "educational writer." Experience has shown that an ad for a "programer" will only result in a rash of incompetent applicants or computer programmers. The form in Fig. 18-3 has proved to be an effective advertisement.

EDUCATIONAL WRITER

A leading Cambridge R and D firm wants man to work on developing educational materials, especially programmed instruction. Background in teaching or technical writing or both. B.A., 5 years experience minimum. Salary open. Call 491-1850, ext. 403, before 5 p.m., week days.

Fig. 18-3. Example of recruitment ad for educational writer.

This ad, if placed on a Sunday, may produce 50 applicants, particularly if it is placed in late June or early September to recruit teachers. When the applicants write to you, it is a little easier to screen the material. When they telephone, your need is to verbally cull the group of individuals who are not suited to the task or who are misreading the intent of the ad. For the telephone interview, use a list of questions similar to the list below.

1. Applicant's name, address and telephone number.
2. Ask whether they fully understand what you are looking for in the way of applicants. You will find that 50% will drop off at this point.
3. Educational background.
4. Job experience – related or unrelated.
5. Married or single.
6. When available to start work if hired.
7. Assuming you get by these questions satisfactorily, arrange to have the applicant come in for a personal interview.

The personal interview and subsequent test should be conducted to again cull your list of applicants to a small group of acceptable individuals. The interview should cover what you are seeking in an individual, the strengths and limitations of the job, the usual facts on the company, salary range, and other pertinent employment details.

If the applicant still appears satisfactory for the job, your final screening phase is a brief programer's selection test. This should be given to the applicant after the interview. He should take the test home to complete and mail it back to you. By following this approach, you are going to find that 50 to 70 percent of the "interested" applicants will never follow through and complete the test. We have found that this approach helps to indicate individuals who are resourceful, interested, and potential self-starters on the job.

The test should be simple and direct. Its intent is to determine how well the person can organize material and write. You are not looking for programing skills since they are to be taught after employment. Ask that badly organized rules for a simple card game be put in readable form. The point is not to trick the reader but simply to force him into rewriting the material. An example of this test is shown below.

> This is a brief description of a card game called Chase the Ace. The description contains all the rules of the game, but does not necessarily present them in the best order or with the greatest clarity. Your problem is to write a set of instructions that will tell someone how to play the game. Write the instructions for an audience ranging in age from 12 years old through adulthood and assume that they are familiar with a standard deck of cards.
>
> Your instructions should be sufficiently clear, complete, and well ordered to allow a student who follows them to deal the cards and to play an expert game of Chase the Ace on the first try. The student should be able to discriminate between desirable and undesirable cards and to exchange an undesirable card when he is dealt one.
>
> **THE GAME**
>
> At the beginning of the game Chase the Ace, each player is given three tokens. When a player has lost his three tokens, he is out. The winner is the player who has at least one token when all the other players have lost theirs.
>
> One card is dealt to each player. The object of the game is to avoid holding a low card, ace being the lowest and king the highest card. Spades rank higher than hearts, hearts than diamonds, diamonds than clubs. So the highest card is the king of spades and the lowest card is the ace of clubs.
>
> The players look at their cards. Any player who has been dealt a king places it face upward on the table. These players cannot be asked to exchange cards. Now, beginning with the player to the dealer's left (player number 1), each player has the option of exchanging his card with the person on his left or saying "stand" if he wishes to keep the card dealt to him. Exchange means just that the first player passes his card (if it is a low one) to the person on his left. That person, in turn, gives the first player his card. Player number 2 can now exchange cards with player number 3 or can say "stand." All cards are exchanged face downward. If the person to the left of the player has exposed a king, no exchange can be made, but in that case, the player to the right of the king can exchange with the

player to the left of the king. A low card will probably be passed around the table until it reaches a player who has given an even lower one in exchange. He will, of course, say "stand." When it comes to the dealer's turn, he exposes his card and he can either say "stand" or take a card from the pack in front of him.
All the cards are then shown and the holder of the lowest card forfeits a token.

In the final analysis you must select the one or more programers from the remaining applicants who will give you an optimum blend of talent, education, attitude, and salary requirements, in that order.

TRAINING PROGRAMERS

The inexperienced programer, if properly selected, will probably be an intelligent, effective prose writer with organizational skills. Starting from this point, it is not difficult to train a person to start program writing.

If you need to train only one or two programers, the best approach would be to send them to a workshop such as those conducted by the University of Michigan and the University of Rochester. These workshops will range from one to three weeks in length. It is best to send a new programer to the longer workshops if time and budget permit. The workshops will provide a foundation in the basics of programing and its underlying theories as well as practical knowledge in writing frames.

If your budget or time scale will not permit the workshop approach to training, you can conduct an on-the-job course. In this instance you must be the teacher. Provide the new programer with material which is designed to teach him the background and methods of programing. If possible procure a programed course on how to write programs. These are effective both to show the concept in practice and to teach the concept itself. Use sample programs to show the forms, the formats, and the variations of style. Allow the new person to spend several days under your supervision in constructive reading, questioning, and, if possible, in seminars where all of this material can be brought into focus. Also, if you have experienced programers on your staff, let them work with the new person to pass on their thoughts and ideas about programing. After two or three days of background study, provide some problems in the analysis of a specific training problem, the development of objectives, and the organization of an outline. Be very careful at this point to ensure that the programer is on the right track and that his work measures up to standard. Do not be hesitant to ask for redrafting of his work. The only thing to keep in mind is that the person is new and must be handled as such.

Once the outline phase shapes up, you can start the actual writing of frames. We suggest the writer first read Markle's *Good Frames and Bad,* Rummler *et al.'s Programmed Learning – A Practicum,* and Silverman's *How to Write a Program.** Each will aid in shaping proper frame-writing habits. It is best to begin frame-writing by first doing a short sequence of 10 to 15 frames. The sequence must then be carefully reviewed by you and another experienced programer to determine its quality. Discuss your criticism with the individual and suggest ways to improve the frames. Have him rewrite and expand this sequence to include another 10 to 15 frames. Continue to expand the program until the writer has covered a unit of instruction of approximately 100 frames. Next monitor his work in the larger 100-frame segments until you are satisfied that the new programer is self-sufficient. After this stage, monitor his work as you would that of any program writer – at least once a month.

One of the more formal ways to train programers on the premises is to schedule full courses conducted by qualified teachers. Such courses can last one to three weeks and can include classroom work on theory and practice followed by the work phase of on-the-job program-writing. In using this approach, the two keys to success are the hiring of a good classroom instructor and the follow-up after the course has been completed.

We have found that the best approach to programer training under this method is to conduct a full (40 hours per week) two-week intensive workshop on theory and practice followed by a six-month "internship" composed of six one-day sessions spaced a month apart. The purpose of these follow-up sessions is to work with the programers individually to determine their weaknesses and to help correct any flaws in their work before they become habits. Also during this phase, each programer should have completed a program and tested, rewritten, and field-tested the unit.

The standard for program effectiveness is usually stated as 90/90, meaning 90% of the students achieve a test result of 90% or better. While this is a fair gauge of results, everything else being equal, one must remember that the test should meet the objectives of the particular programed unit, and should not simply be designed to achieve 90/90.

It is also difficult to measure the cost effectiveness of an in-house group. How much did it actually cost for each programer to produce

---

*Susan Markle, *Good Frames and Bad,* John Wiley, New York, 1964; Geary A. Rummler, David G. Markle, Dale A. Brethrower, Albert W. Schrader, and Donald E. P. Smith, *Programmed Learning – A Practicum,* University of Michigan, Ann Arbor, 1964; Robert E. Silverman, *How to Write a Program,* Honor Products, Cambridge, Mass., 1969.

programs? How many usable hours of instruction were completed? Would this same service cost less through a contract programing organization? You cannot simply measure a group's effectiveness by these facts or by the popular measure of "2400 frames a year per programer." None of these speak of quality. Rather, the rate of production should be measured by the total number of teaching hours produced by the programer in program form. If we accept the fact that an hour of programed instruction is at least equal to an hour of traditional instruction, then what did your "traditional" instruction system cost per hour compared to programing? This is your measure of cost effectiveness.

ADDITIONAL READINGS

Gagné, Robert L. (Ed.), *Prospectives in Programming.* New York: Macmillan, 1963.

Green, Edward J., *The Learning Process and Programmed Instruction.* New York: Holt, Rinehart and Winston, 1963.

Polin, A. Terrence, *et al., Selecting and Training In-Plant Programmers.* Swarthmore, Pennsylvania: The Personnel Journal, Inc., n.d.

Schramm, Wilbur, *The Research in Programmed Instruction.* Washington, D. C.: U.S. Government Printing Office, 1964.

Skinner, B. F., *Science and Human Behavior.* New York: Macmillan, 1953.

19

Simulation Techniques

An Aetna Life and Casualty ad makes our blood run cold, informing us that " . . . 15,600 young lives were lost in cars last year." To help reduce the accident rate among young drivers, Aetna has developed a driving simulator for high schools. (See Fig. 19-1.)

Fig. 19-1. Driving simulator. (Photo courtesy of Aetna Life and Casualty.)

The idea of constructing a learning environment which removes the risk to life and limb, yet parallels real situations, is not new. World War II veterans remember the famous Link trainer, a mechanical device that looked like the inside of an airplane cockpit and imitated actual flight conditions while the pilot was still on the ground. By the time the trainee pilot got up in the air, he had already had a chance to react and maneuver without putting his and the instructor's lives in jeopardy.

The Santa Fe Railway will soon be training enginemen in a mobile, computer-controlled system (Fig. 19-2) that will simulate actual locomotive and train operations. The trainee will look ahead at a screen on which will be projected exactly what an engineer would see during an actual trip. A unique lens system will provide realistic depth to the image on the screen.

Just as mechanical simulators are used to teach skills, a variety of verbal simulators have been developed to teach verbal behaviors. Again, the reason for providing a vicarious experience is to minimize the hazard of practicing poor verbal behaviors in a real life setting. This chapter covers some of the basic verbal simulation techniques and their potential applications to training situations.

ROLE PLAYING

Role playing is one of the best-known types of verbal simulators. It is the spontaneous acting out of a situation, condition, or set of circumstances by members of a learning group. The purpose is to emphasize relationships among people. The group members portray typical attitudes, problems, situations, and relationships which the learner may encounter in real life situations.

This method of teaching is valuable because of the emotional impact that comes from observing or participating in the presentation. Role playing allows the trainee to come closest to the actual experiences or feelings connected with the problem or situation being studied.

Role playing is best employed in training when the goal is to illustrate a dramatic aspect of a situation or problem in such areas as managing personnel, selling, or problem-solving under pressure. This method helps develop an understanding of the feelings and attitudes of people under certain circumstances, and also helps the trainee discover how people may react under certain conditions.

The role playing method has a number of advantages and disadvantages. Its prime advantage is its ability to stimulate students to listen and observe a problem, and to project themselves into a role by acting out their responses and then analyzing the entire situation.

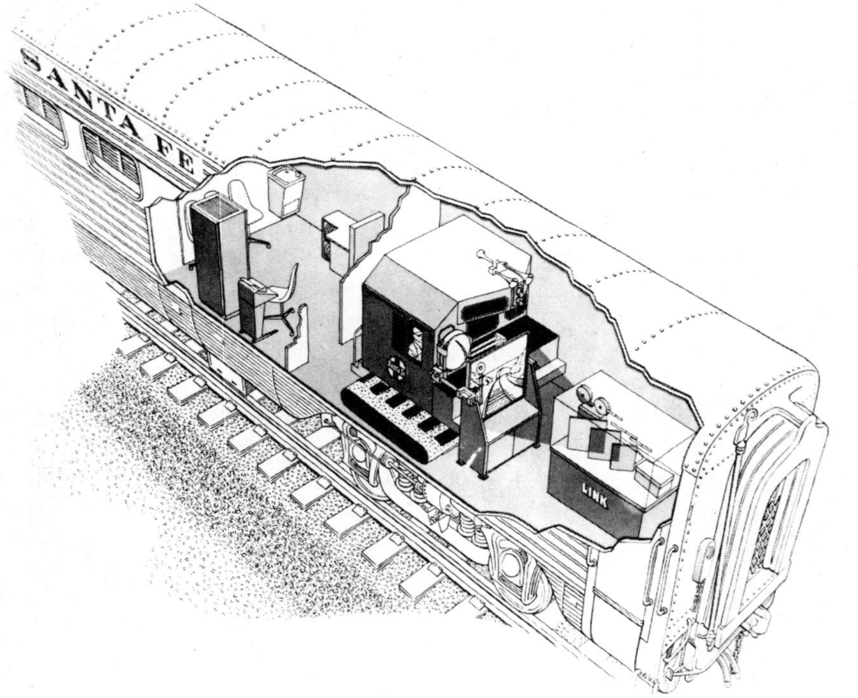

Fig. 19-2. The Santa Fe locomotive simulator.

One of the limitations of this method is the natural tendency for an instructor to use role playing as a gimmick rather than as an experience. Part of this problem stems from the uneasiness of the participants because of their lack of adequate preparation in the subject, the role playing itself, or both. If this condition exists the instructor is to blame. Too often he is not equipped to handle the method. Simply supplying the class with role playing problems does not ensure adequate results.

To prepare properly for the role playing method the instructor or leader should carefully study his students to determine their background, age, personal characteristics, and anticipated reactions to the role playing situation. He can be fairly certain that the group will feel uneasy at the prospect of role playing and that the instructor will need to work at reducing this fear. Some methods of preparation which will help alleviate students' uneasiness are as follows:

1. Clearly define the problem to be dramatized and explain why this approach is being used.

Fig. 19-2 (continued).

2. Keep the number of participants to a minimum (two to five). If possible, line up the students to participate in advance. Brief them on their roles.

3. Prepare an outline for each character but avoid unreal situations which can easily deteriorate into comedy.

4. Prepare an introduction to help the audience understand the goals of the role playing situation to be portrayed, the setting for the action, and background information on the characters in the roles. Also brief the audience on what you expect of them.

5. One method of quelling the general uneasiness is to require the audience to participate by recording on paper the key points (do's or don'ts) which the play depicts. These can form the basis of a discussion after the problem has been presented.

When the actual role playing situation is ready to start, give a final briefing to the players and present your introduction to the audience. Let the action begin, but do not let it get out of hand; control the play. When the appropriate time occurs or the play is failing to generate the proper audience response, cut off the action at a point where the players can summarize what they thought of each role and its meaning. Replay if appropriate with new players, but do not set up another run just to involve all of the students; do so only if it is appropriate to the learning situation.

After the players summarize their reactions, illustrate the points made and involve members of the audience in discussing their interpretations of what they have seen. This can be accomplished by group discussion or a forum, depending upon the purpose of the play.

CASE METHOD

Like role playing, the case method is often misused by the instructor, employed in name but not in reality. The inclusion of a case problem for example, in some form in a training situation would seem to qualify the program as having been taught via the case method. The case method, however, is a tool with its own set of rules and must be properly employed to be effective in producing the desired behavior change.

What is the Case Method?

A case may be a written, oral or filmed presentation of a problem associated with business operations. A case will usually be drawn in sufficient detail to give the student adequate data to understand the problem being presented. Cases may be presented in a few words or in many pages. They may be complex or shallow, but they will have one thing in common: they are designed to challenge a learner to solve the problem they present.

The prime objective of the case method is to provide students with the opportunity to analyze a business problem and to develop solutions to it. With this approach, a wide spectrum of student skills and abilities can be brought into play; likewise, a student's inabilities or weaknesses in problem solving will also be revealed.

Harvard Method

The Harvard case method is regarded as the granddaddy of the case problem technique. Its method is to use cases developed from actual situations in which the student will be able to learn from independent thinking how his skills may be used in solving the problems presented.

This method is nondirective in that the instructor presents the case problem to the students, allows sufficient study time, and then creates an environment for group discussion. The instructor guides the discussion and acts as a catalyst for the group. He helps the students discover for themselves what the answers or solutions may be. He assists the group through the use of skilled questions to draw out, direct, or guide the thinking of the group. In the final analysis the results of this approach may be a series of solutions to the same problem.

Other case methods differ mainly in the manner of their presentation, whether it be filmed cases, role playing, or "live" cases. The film approach presents an open-ended problem to be solved by the group. Its advantages include that of offering considerable detail about real life settings in which emotional reactions as well as facts and data are visualized. This approach is useful when the remote or unique setting of a problem is critical to the interpretation of the case.

Live cases are those which are still active in a problem context. The situation being studied is undergoing change at the moment of study. This is an effective method for an organization which is actually involved in the study problem and seeks to train its personnel to handle the situation.

Criteria for Acceptable Cases

To be effective as training devices, cases employed in teaching must meet minimum criteria in their construction. These criteria, which may be used to select commercially available cases or in the development of your own cases, are listed below:

1. The case is based on firsthand observation for realism.
2. It is based on facts, not opinions disguised as facts.
3. It shows more than it tells.
4. It provides organized information.
5. It shows formal and informal interpersonal relationships.
6. It describes key people in the case.
7. It reveals the effects of change.
8. It indicates that the situation was changing when observation stopped.

Case Analysis

Like the criteria for measuring the acceptability of a case, certain key factors should also be kept in mind in the analysis employed in the teaching of cases. Too often a case is ruined as a teaching device because the instructor fails to remember that he must be all of the following:

Realistic. When reading the cases keep in mind the question, "Can this be done by real people in real life?"

Thorough. In analyzing the facts and the factors affecting the problem the case must be considered in its totality.

Flexible. In the approaches to analysis flexibility is a key factor. Insistance on a rigid approach will only cause the students to arrive at a rigid answer.

Objective. What do you seek to achieve by this exercise? Your objectives will probably need to be repeated several times during the case analysis.

Ready to act. When you arrive at a solution, how will you translate this into action?

Limitations of the Case Method

The case method, like all other media, has its limitations. You must recognize that no case presentation, regardless of its form, can possibly portray all of the factors identical to the real situation, especially in relation to emotions, bias, and personal backgrounds. The problems of language often cause difficulties in comprehension. Added to these shortcomings is the possibility that your students may be apathetic to the case method itself and therefore may be unable to attain the degree of involvement required to successfully learn from this method.

Classroom Approach

Keep these limitations in mind when you use cases in teaching. Try to overcome some of these potential pitfalls by the proper classroom approach to the use of the case method technique.

The first rule is to keep the discussion focused. Do not let it get sidetracked for too long. Watch out especially for the one or two people who may try to monopolize the discussion. Also remember that you have only so much time to cover the *whole* case. Be careful that you do not waste 30 minutes of an hour class on 10% of the case and then have to compress the rest into the last 30 minutes. In guiding these discussions, be sure you keep the atmosphere free and fluid. Your goal is to seek as many diverse opinions, ideas, and potential answers as possible. Don't expect to come up with a single "best" answer to any case. Review inadequate and incorrect solutions for the benefit of the whole group so that each trainee will better understand why a certain solution was finally selected.

When to Use the Case Method

Like all techniques in training, the case method is better adapted to some specific types of training problems than others. Cases are well suited to the teaching of such a topic as supervisory training, where plant and personnel problems can be presented in case form. Cases are also useful in management training, complex union problems, or similar exercises where a student should be given the opportunity to apply his analytical and creative talents to solving problems.

The case technique is best utilized with small classes (20 to 25 students). This size group affords the opportunity for free, open discussion by all. Too large a group will stifle the desire of the quiet students to participate. It is best not to use the case method more than once a week as a technique to ensure adequate student thinking and responding to a given problem.

The Student in a Case Discussion

Too often we lose sight of the fact that the learner is the reason for our training activity. We must keep his needs, attitudes, and problems in mind when presenting cases.

The student will often read a case, looking for a single problem to fix or repair like a broken toy. He often responds with the following solutions: "Formulate a plan;" "Develop directives;" "Sell off the unit in question;" or "Fire someone." If these quick solutions fail to meet the need, you may hear broad generalizations such as: "The problem is one of leadership," or "Communications."

The student will often continue to interpret the cases in his own personal way with little thought to objective responses. He will give you his opinion of the person or persons responsible for this problem and tell you where their judgment was faulty. In short, you will receive a great deal of doubletalk and unclear thinking from students. Your job is to clarify the points and to help the students become adept at the analysis process.

Use of the case method is directed toward the development of the student's analytical abilities in case situations which simulate real life problems the student is likely to face after training. Therefore, care must be taken in the development and selection of cases to teach these skills.

INCIDENT PROCESS

The incident process is a variant of the case method. Its technique is to create self-awareness through a blending of clear thinking, practical judgment, and social awareness of people and their feelings. The starting point in this technique is the incident rather than the whole problem. A particular case is studied with the following questions in mind:

1. Where can I gather facts which pertain to this incident and how should they be organized?
2. What is my decision about this incident relative to the short term needs and long term ramifications?
3. Now that I have arrived at a solution, how do I test its validity?

In using this technique the instructor should construct his learning sequence to require each student to write his answers to the above questions. He then collects the answers and uses them in class discussion. If the answers represent considerable differences of opinion, small groups should be convened to develop support of the various points. Debate between the group leaders is useful at this point to focus on a series of acceptable answers to the solution of the incident. Following this the instructor should summarize the problem and give the historical answer, explaining how it affected the incident. No solution as such should be provided since no incident has a pat answer.

The important experience to be distilled from the incident process is for the individual to learn by leading. The large group is divided into two-man teams. Each team leads the group twice. In the first round, one teammate serves as leader and the other as observer. Then the roles are reversed. In their respective roles, the teammates prepare and present the incident from a prepared case. In the group discussion phase the team deals with the incident assigned to it again. The final summary is a written report submitted to the entire group.

EDUCATIONAL GAMES

Games are familiar to all of us. We participate in various forms of games no matter what our age. Games involve players, rules, objectives, and some kind of contest. Two or more players can participate in a game, depending upon the type of game and its complexity. Games are primarily useful as a device to teach cause/effect relationships and problem-solving techniques. They are secondarily useful for the teaching of working in groups.

There are four basic considerations that govern games:

1. What is the relationship between players and subject matter (realistic, historical, hypothetical, or fantasy games)?
2. To what degree do the players control the game (skill versus chance)?
3. To what degree does the outcome depend upon the interaction of the players (showdown versus strategy)?
4. To what degree is the action governed by a rules structure (free role playing versus rules)?

Games are a simulation of what we expect in the real world. The purpose of using the game method is to give the student the opportunity to make more and more decisions on a particular problem as he learns more about the process represented by the game. The group participating in the game functions as a group when certain actions taken by one player in a game affect others.

As in other simulation techniques, the goals of a game are usually stated, but the specific outcome is not. This outcome will vary depending upon the backgrounds of the participants and the setting for the game.

Criteria for Using Games

Games require more class time than most conventional training techniques. In fact, the average game requires three class periods to complete because of the need for pregame briefing, play time, and debriefing. The method is effective only if the students are highly motivated.

Physically, games require that the training set-up not be disturbed during the time between playing periods, a problem sometimes not easily overcome in business environments.

Advantages and limitations of educational games are as follows:

Advantages

1. Teach interdependence of the same elements and people.
2. Provide learner opportunity to test assumptions – solutions.
3. Motivate learner to be interested in related principles.

Limitations

1. Learners' attitude that they know the answers.
2. Mainly quantitative problems; overlook the qualitative skills.
3. Do not teach decision making as such.

Sources of Games

There are a few sources of off-the-shelf games today. Generally speaking if you wish to use the game technique you will have to either develop a game yourself or contract for its development. If you choose to develop a game, it is best to let the game model reflect your industrial world rather than a hypothetical situation. Some of the criteria to consider in developing or assessing a game are as follows:

1. Select an allied industry or product for the game.
2. Be certain that your model reflects real relationships.
3. Scale decision periods (time) to the real life game.
4. Have each team start the game in an identical position.
5. Determine the objective of the game exercise and decide whether this goal can be realistically reached with the game.
6. Ask yourself if you can afford the time and space for the game technique.
7. Be sure your instructors are qualified to use this technique.
8. Determine how you will integrate the game into the course.

Developing a Game

Game development can be as simple or complex as the problem demands. For those who have never used games in teaching, it is advisable to procure a ready-made game the first time and then to consider developing your own after that.

For those who wish to actually develop a game for the first time, we suggest you work with another person experienced in gaming techniques. In doing so keep in mind some of the criteria needed to formulate a game:

1. What elements will you include in your model? Some ideas include:

   a) *Product:* type, unit, and price.
   b) *Financial:* investment required, cash, capitalization, banking sources.
   c) *Materials:* supply problems, raw materials, government restrictions, transportation difficulties and timing, inventory costs and practices, depreciation policy, and others.
   d) *Marketing:* advertising-marketing costs, problems and timing, salesmen's needs, size of force, wages, etc.; also competition, size, type, etc.
   e) *Production:* plant capacity, tools, machines, scheduling, and others.

f) *Labor force:* labor problems, types and quality of labor, training costs and problems, recruiting programs.
g) *Other constraints* peculiar to your situation and problem.

2. Select the items you wish to use in your game and assign priority to each. Build a general model based on these priorities and make additions until the game is as complex as you desire.
3. Note the interdependency of all the selected and rated items in your model. Determine their cause/effect relationship.
4. Draft a model of the game including all variables, constraints, and limitations placed on participants. The more detailed you can get at this point the better the results will be. Do not overdevelop details for their own sake.
5. Begin the game with a clear set of instructions to the participants on the game procedure, constraints, background knowledge necessary to execute the game, and any information or data which the participant would normally have in a real situation.
6. Test the game on a small student sample to be certain all parts integrate and the desired goals can be achieved. Adjust if required.

Using a Game

When a game is either selected or designed and the actual use in class is to begin, be certain to completely explain what a game is, why it is being used, its limitations, review any necessary facts or factors about the game, and provide for a question period.

The question period should be limited to questions that will affect the game which has already been presented by the instructor or will clarify the materials. No questions which pertain to the game problem should be answered.

The teams are then sent to their meeting areas to set their long-range objectives before making any decisions. This opening round sets the goals for their strategy in the game. The participants may elect officers and so on if desired.

As the game unfolds, the rules may change, just as they sometimes do in real life. The control of such changes is vested in the umpire, who also is allowed to aid any team that gets too deeply into trouble to avoid complete failures.

When the game is completed, a postgame critique is held. This is one of the most valuable aspects of the process. It is particularly important that all players clearly understand the limitations of the game and the assumptions used in its creation. A "winner" can only be determined if a careful point scale has been designed for each decision made by the teams.

SENSITIVITY TRAINING (LABORATORY TRAINING)

What is the Laboratory Training Method?

A training laboratory is an artificial community designed to provide an opportunity to learn about the characteristics of groups and how individual members can operate effectively within the framework of a group. The laboratory is a place where participants can observe the behavior of other group members, experiment with their own behavior, and obtain candid feedback concerning the consequences of this behavior. The object of the training laboratory is to provide an environment, not otherwise available in our culture, where new patterns of behavior can be invented and tested in a climate conducive to change and growth, protected from the full consequences of the real world. The T group (training group) is the chief device of the laboratory method.

What Is the T Group?

The T group is an unstructured group in which the participants learn from their own behavior within the group. It can best be described as a microcosmic society in which the individual members struggle to create a productive organization – one which permits the growth and satisfaction of each of its members. The data for learning are generated by the group as a result of the interaction of its members. No leadership or definition of goals is provided. It is entirely up to the group to establish a process of inquiry, collect its own data, analyze its experience, and test its validity. Each individual in the T group learns about his own motives, feelings, and strategies in dealing with other members of the group. Each member of the group learns about group processes while trying to build a particular group. The hope is that each person will learn something of group behavior and his own behavior in a group which will enable him to operate more effectively in "real" group situations.

What Are the Goals of the T Group?

The T group has three general goals: to help individuals learn how to learn; to help individuals learn how to give help to others; and to develop an effective group membership.

The first goal, that of learning how to learn, is accomplished by exposing the individual to the experience of interacting with others in a group under conditions which permit exploration of personal feeling and motivation. The individual has a chance to observe how others react to his behavior and to get criticism or confirmation of this behavior. The group becomes a laboratory where the individual becomes sensitized to the reactions of others to himself. Gradually the T group member learns that he does not need an instructor or a formal program to learn. His own behavior and the behavior of others become the data from which he learns.

The second goal, learning how to give help to others in a group, is discovered by the participant to be one of the primary responsibilities of membership in a group. Giving and getting help through feedback within the group requires sensitivity and skill so that a climate of trust can be substituted for the usual climate of fear.

The third goal of the T group, developing an effective group membership, is aimed at teaching participants that successful membership depends on locating the barriers to openness and trust, understanding the motivations of others in the group, and solving the problems of communication.

How Does the T Group Operate?

The T group is usually composed of eight to twelve members and a trainer. The function of the trainer is to help create a climate of permissiveness and inquiry. He does this by avoiding the role of group leader whenever it is thrust upon him by the group, helping the group to open up avenues of inquiry, and occasionally illuminating directions the group may be taking. Whatever he does, he avoids taking sides, committing himself to a particular line of inquiry, or providing an agenda for the group to discuss.

In general, the T group usually progresses through six stages of development. The initial stage is characterized by joint searching for a subject and a leader. The group may try to pick a leader from its ranks or it may turn back to the trainer for guidance. Finding no help from the trainer, the group may resort to criticism of him. Usually someone in the group suggests that all of the members introduce themselves. After this the group drifts, still searching for direction which will prove satisfying to all of its members. The general feeling during this first stage is one of frustration and disturbance at not being able to utilize the traditional methods of functioning within a group.

The second stage is ordinarily characterized by a sharp difference of opinion within its membership. Two methods of approaching the group situation emerge, one advocating assigned topics for discussion and the other advocating an exploration of the personal problems of the group.

The third stage is characterized by attempts by various individuals in the group in one way or another to control it. During this stage the other members of the group, if they recognize these attempts to manipulate the group, come to resent individual attempts to control the group for selfish purposes.

Fairly soon in the life of a T group, members begin to recognize that if the group is to make any progress, there will need to be some modification of individual behavior. Some kind of feedback system must be developed so that the group can become a productive unit. There is a great deal of anxiety in both the giving and the receiving of criticism. None of the members at this point in time know exactly how the others will receive feedback or how to cope with it themselves when it is given to them.

In the fifth stage the group begins to build an effective organization where all members can learn and grow. No one feels any pressure to agree or conform. Individual contributions are explored and developed. The group has developed a high degree of cohesiveness.

In the final stage before the group is disbanded, members of the group usually intensify their efforts to help others in the group. A considerable amount of empathy and understanding is present.

A Condensed Laboratory Training Plan

A full scale sensitivity training program requires an experienced trainer. A brief experiment (similar to the one described below) to give a group a feeling for group dynamics can be performed without danger.

Stage 1. Trainer introduces method to entire group by explaining that next 45 minutes will be spent in a laboratory session. Two groups will be formed which will be called T groups (training groups). Each participant will have an opportunity to learn more about groups and being a more effective group member. The job of the group members will be to analyze what happens in the group during the training session. Each of the two groups will have a trainer, but no group leader.

The trainer then forms two T groups of an even number, with from eight to ten members. Additional class members will be observers and should seat themselves around the outside of either group.

Stage 2 (10 minutes). T group assembles and begins to seek its purpose. Trainer answers questions but does not provide the group with an agenda or fulfill the traditional leadership role.

Stage 3 (5 minutes). Trainer asks group to pair off and spend five minutes discussing their feelings about the group and what went on in it.

Stage 4 (10 minutes). T group reassembles and continues to plan its activities. The group may find some of its members in conflict as to what the group should discuss and who should be the leader.

Stage 5 (5 minutes). Trainer again asks group to pair off, this time with a different partner, and discuss how, as individuals, they might help the group develop a more effective organization.

Stage 6 (15 minutes). T group reassembles and possibly begins to establish a system of feedback between its members. The climate of the group may improve to the point where individuals in the group may feel secure enough to explore some of their own feelings and motivation and give help to others in exploring theirs. The group toward the end of this stage may begin to develop goals and work toward these goals.

Stage 7. Groups return to their original organization to discuss insights into group processes and their own roles as group members.

For more information on T groups, read *T-Group Theory and Laboratory Method,* ed. Leland P. Bradford, John Wiley, New York, 1964 or write to National Training Laboratories, Bethel, Maine.

IN-BASKET TECHNIQUE

As the title implies, this simulation technique presents the learner with samples of administrative work via the in-basket (mail box) to measure his actions and reactions in regard to this mail. Its prime purpose is to train learners to make decisions, prepare reports, handle correspondence, and generally become proficient at writing communications.

The essential approach to teaching is for each participant to be given an envelope containing prepared in-basket items which he must handle. Normally a specified time period is selected and the learner must handle as many pieces as possible within this time reference. At the end of the period his decisions are discussed and the class arrives at the best solution or action.

This training technique is useful for training in specific operational and administrative procedures such as training loan clerks in a bank, or giving practice in managerial processes and problems.

To construct your own in-basket training exercise, begin by defining your objectives. With the purpose of your in-basket exercise defined, develop your problem in a fictional but realistic framework. To do this consider some of the possibilities listed below and how they may apply to the development of the exercise.

1. What is the general type of problem you are concerned with in this exercise?

   a) Organizational relations.
   b) Outside relations.
   c) Organizational control or planning.
   d) Personal work habits.
   e) Operational decisions.

2. What is the best setting for the in-basket problem?

   a) Company – real or imaginary.
   b) Learner's managerial level or another.
   c) Subordinates' relationships to problem.
   d) Physical environmental factors.

3. What problems can be covered in the exercise?

   a) Specific types of material (letters, memos, contracts).
   b) Are the problems only at the learner's level or are they designed to teach him his boss's daily problems?

4. Other factors affecting the development.

   a) Time pressure.
   b) Long- or short-range response.
   c) Deadlines.
   d) Interruptions.

Developing an Exercise

By using the outline above, you can begin to isolate the specific types of items that pertain to your training problem. It would be advisable to use a content expert for the drafting of the materials. To start with, select some large basic problems to cover – problems such as relations with superiors, application of a new sales or credit policy, and so on. Then simulate the setting in which the learner will actually work. Is the student a new hire, a transferee, or simply an existing worker who needs further training? The in-basket items you employ in the problem would be far more meaningful if you could take actual examples from the work environment the students will be or are currently working in. The facts in this actual problem may be changed to avoid embarrassment later.

When you construct the in-basket problems, keep the paper work involved and heavy enough in quantity so that the learner must organize and schedule his time to the best advantage.

When you feel the concepts and basic data you wish to incorporate into the in-basket exercise are properly laid out, be sure you relate all of these items to one another to be sure that the problem has continuity. From this point construct an introduction to the lesson.

The introductory material must set the scene and provide for a backward and forward glance at the problem. The introduction must state all facts pertinent to the problem.

Be sure to allow sufficient time for the participants to finish the exercise and to discuss each item in the exercise, its purpose, meaning, and even the "right" response. Most students find the in-basket approach highly stimulating, so remember to capitalize on this fact with free discussion after the lesson.

In some situations it might be useful to allow students simply to work the in-basket problems and not to offer an opportunity for class response. They could save their response until after a series of lectures or other presentations which would cover the subject in depth. Such added information may change their decisions.

The advantages and limitations of the in-basket technique are as follows:

Advantages

1. Students are highly motivated.
2. Sample of learner's behavior in work environment.
3. Easy feedback on exercise.
4. Easy construction problems.

Limitations

1. Unreal relationship with situation. No past relations to hamper proper decisions.
2. Actual response on the job may be different from that given in class.
3. Limited to inexperienced correspondence handlers.

The in-basket technique, like other training media, is most useful if employed in moderation and not relied upon as the sole teaching method. It should be laced with a series of lectures, discussions, and similar techniques which will relate the in-basket problems to the whole subject being taught.

Commercially prepared in-baskets are available. Two of the most useful and stimulating we have tried are found in *Problems in Supervision,* by Cabot L. Jaffee.* The book is designed so that the perforated pages may be removed to simulate the actual documents one might find in his own in-basket.

*Cabot L. Jaffee, *Problems in Supervision,* Reading, Mass.: Addison-Wesley, 1968.

Part 4

Basic Training Applications

Part 4 takes some of the principles of program development covered in the first three parts and puts them to work. The training applications described are ones which most training managers are familiar with. These descriptions are meant to offer a jumping-off point for the training director as he goes forward to develop his own programs tailored to the needs of his particular organizational setting.

20

How to Develop and Present Employee Orientation Programs

You can put a man in a sailboat and tell him to sail around for a while, and eventually he will learn to handle the sails and take advantage of the wind. He may even win a race or two without any help from you. It is a lot quicker and safer, however, if the man is given a few minutes of training on shore on how to turn the boat, steer it, land it, and so on. Give him a little orientation in what he is about to do and he will be able to do it that much more efficiently and quickly. In a nutshell, that is the reason we bother to train at all. We think that we can shorten the time it takes to make a man effective and useful to the organization which he has just joined. Given enough time and latitude to make mistakes, most employees can learn the corporate ropes by themselves. Providing an orientation is simply a way of saving corporate assets by heading off mistakes, employee turnover, grievances, and so on. This chapter focuses on orienting a new employee to the organization's overall environment. Specific job orientation is taken up in Chapter 21.

GENERAL OBJECTIVES OF ORIENTATION PROGRAMS

As a general rule, all employees should be given some kind of orientation to an organization. This can range from a few minutes with the person responsible for personnel management activities to an elaborate lengthy program conducted in company classrooms by top management and the training department. New employees, from porters to executives, need exposure to what the company does, how it works, and what it offers for benefits. Even executives need an orientation, although we usually forget about them; we expect them to orient themselves. They can do it, usually more quickly than rank and file personnel, but that is just because they know how to get information more quickly and have greater freedom to move in the organization.

The general objectives of an orientation program should be as follows:

1. To introduce the new employee to the organization's reason for being, its structure, and its leaders.
2. To give the new employee a feeling of participating in and belonging to something larger than his individual work group will be. To relate the individual to the organization.
3. To provide an opportunity for the new employee to ask questions about subjects or interests which concern him.
4. To give a new employee the kind of basic direction he needs to be successful in his job.
5. To teach him enough of the corporate policy and procedures to keep him from making needless mistakes in his early life with the organization.
6. To introduce him to the physical facilities of his organizational life.

HOW MUCH ORIENTATION SHOULD BE GIVEN?

Like pieces of string, orientation programs come in all lengths. They range from ten minutes to two weeks or longer. Often the orientation program becomes loaded with "nice-to-know" information. One department after another expresses a desire for representation. The program grows over the years. Hour after hour is added. Seldom is anything deleted. One day management looks at the "academy" and wonders how much it costs to maintain it. Shortly thereafter the whole structure may be razed.

The only remedy for this is a careful development of the objectives of the orientation program and a periodic checking of what is being accomplished. Of all of the training department's programs, the orientation is most likely to get out of hand and is therefore most in need of watching. Knowing this the training director should be prepared to be challenged and ready to defend his program if it is defensible.

WHAT IS USUALLY COVERED?

Orientation programs should provide an employee with information about the following three basic subjects.

1. The organization as a whole and as a number of departments working together to accomplish a mission.
2. The ground rules for working in the organization.
3. The advantages of working for the organization.

The first area, an overview of the organization, should include such topics as:

1. History, growth, and future of the organization.
2. How the organization is structured to do the work.
3. Who the important leaders are.
4. Knowledge of the product or other end result of the organization's activities.
5. A tour of the facility or service.

The reasons for taking this up are as follows:

1. To give the employee an understanding of how his job and department fit into the total work of the enterprise.
2. To stimulate a sense of belonging to a larger group and loyalty to that group.
3. To develop a sense of appreciation in the employee for the effort that has gone into the development of the organization.

The second area, the ground rules for working in the organization, should include such topics as the following:

1. Absence - How to report it, what will be paid by the company, what is considered excessive and how it will be disciplined.
2. Work schedule - Starting and quitting time.
3. Time keeping - Time clock, time sheets, honor system.
4. Coffee breaks - Length, where to take them, how often.
5. Lunch periods - Length, facilities, where to take them.
6. Place for personal belongings. Lockers, coat rooms.
7. Official employee entrances and exits.
8. Parking facilities.
9. Pay. How paid, what day, where to go about pay problems, pay deductions.
10. Security regulations.
11. Lost and found.
12. Collections and solicitations.
13. Emergency provisions. Fire, civil defense.
14. Dress and grooming standards.

15. Smoking, chewing gum.
16. Accidents on the job. How and where to report them.
17. Causes for discharge.
18. Personnel records.

The third area, the advantages of working for the organization, includes such topics as the following:

1. Holidays. How many, how paid.
2. Discount privileges (if any) on company merchandise.
3. Insurance programs. Health, accident, life, disability, travel, eligibility, premium, employee/company contribution, etc.
4. Medical services.
5. House organ and other communications media. When issued, how obtained.
6. Jury duty. How reimbursed, how granted.
7. Leaves of absence. Military, personal, sickness, eligibility.
8. Restaurant facilities.
9. Retirement programs. Eligibility.
10. Profit sharing, stock option or purchase programs, bonuses.
11. Credit union.
12. Vacations. Vacation period, eligibility, length.
13. Training programs leading toward promotion.
14. Educational and recreational programs.

HOW TO DEVELOP A PROGRAM

Step 1. This involves an assessment of the employee audience to be oriented. Will you be training elevator operators, dishwashers, clerical employees, junior executives, or some combination of employee groups? Who will be taught will to a large extent determine how they will be taught. Orientation programs are generally for a mixture of organizational levels. This, of course, complicates the way you will organize and present your material. As a general rule, orientation programs should be geared to the lowest level employee in the group for whom the orientation is given.

Step 2. As with all programs, the objectives of the orientation will need to be nailed down and agreed upon. If you have not prepared objectives before, it would be well to review the chapter on performing a training analysis. Objectives which are less concrete and less measurable than those formulated for other programs are acceptable for orientation programs because the material presented probably won't be taught or tested in the traditional sense of these words. It is still advisable to pin these objectives down in as much detail as possible. Then you must operate on the basis of consensus rather than empirical evidence that your inclusions are absolutely correct.

Step 3. Give strong consideration to the wishes of management and department heads in deciding what to include. They generally have definite ideas about what they believe new employees should know. Ask relatively new employees what might have helped them get a better start in the organization if they had had the opportunity to attend an orientation program.

Step 4. Your major role in preparing orientation programs will be to decide how these materials should be taught. You are the expert in the preparation of media which are best designed to inform.

WHO SHOULD DO THE TRAINING?

As a rule of thumb, the training department should administer what we call "common denominator training." Common denominator training is given to large segments of the employee population and is repeated with reasonable frequency. The training department is best equipped to perform this service for the total organization. Who actually delivers a lecture or leads a discussion depends on a number of factors. Sometimes it is better to have a department head or a member of management take over a particular subject even though he is not as professional in his training ability. The weight of his authority and his practical experience with the material may more than compensate for weaknesses in his presentation. It then becomes the training department's responsibility to help the line manager organize his material, select media for communicating it, and prepare him before the final presentation. If a videotape recorder is available, it would be worth while to tape a manager's presentation for analysis and development.

WHERE SHOULD ORIENTATIONS BE GIVEN?

Because of the distractions of the work area, it is preferable to give new employees an orientation to the organization away from the location where they will ultimately work. If a classroom is not used, a foreman's cubicle or the coffee shop is more desirable than the employee's workbench or an assembly room filled with other workers. Giving the orientation elsewhere also minimizes the disruption of the working atmosphere of the present employees.

While the orientation facilities need not be elaborate, they are often the new employee's first introduction to the company. The facilities should give him a positive impression of the organization and its concerns for his welfare.

EMPLOYEE PARTICIPATION

One of the worst faults of most orientation programs is that they are one-way affairs. The material is simply presented with no opportunity for the employee to react with questions or discussion of points that interest him. The orientation period should present sufficient opportunity for the employee to explore his concerns, his interests, his future with the company. There should be time given to open discussion. Lecturers should allow room at the end of their presentations for questions. The instructor should stimulate questions from the group.

EVALUATION OF THE ORIENTATION

Orientation material is not really taught in the true sense of the word. It therefore cannot be legitimately tested. Employees are immersed in their new world – superficially exposed to many new territories of it. The real criterion of success is how much the employee was helped in adjusting to the organization's demands and how excited he is about the future as a result of what he sees.

It is vitally important that the training director attempt to evaluate these criteria. This is often done with evaluation forms handed out at the close of the program. A tabulation of the forms usually shows an overwhelming satisfaction with the material. Unfortunately the student is not in a good position to relate what he has just learned to what he will experience in his new environment. He will not be qualified to do this until sometime after he has actually worked in the organization. The training director must go back and seek these employees out in an attempt to assess how valuable the orientation experience was. Employee reactions may cause the training director and his staff to revise the material.

STANDARDIZING REGULARLY REPEATED MATERIAL

The orientation program offers opportunities to standardize materials used regularly. The history of a company may be economically put on slides. Basic safety training may be programed. The training director should look for those sections of the program that can profitably be set in the cement of an audiovisual presentation.

THE PROBLEM OF RETENTION

The problem of retaining orientation material can be serious. Because the content is not really taught, the employee has difficulty in discriminating which material should be learned and which should be simply acknowledged. If any part of the program is to be remembered, it will need to be presented in such a way that the employee can learn it and retain it.

Much of the detail of insurance plans, organizational layout, products, etc. should be omitted from the presentations and relegated to handouts. The employee should be instructed to read the material later.

HOW OFTEN RUN

The problem with orientation programs is that they can rarely be given at the time the employee first enters the organization. The training director must decide with what frequency orientations should be conducted, taking into consideration the costs of running the program and the needs of the individuals and the organization.

ORIENTATION SCHEDULES

One of the training department's important responsibilities in administering orientation programs is to develop a schedule of activities and to coordinate the use of space, equipment, and staff. It is important to give everyone concerned a copy of the schedule. A typical schedule format looks like the one in Fig. 20-1.

Fig. 20-1. Orientation schedule for new salesmen.

Time	Activity	Trainer	Location	Special equipment needed
9:00–9:30	Introduction to the Job of Selling	Training Director	Classroom	Overhead Projector
9:35–10:00	The Approach	Training Specialist	Classroom	Role Play Exercises
10:00–10:15	Coffee Break		Cafeteria	Exercises
10:30–11:30	Product Information	Marketing Manager	Classroom	Slide Projector

PROGRAM COSTS

The orientation program is at best a leaning tower, lovely to look at but threatening to fall because of its own weight. Management is prone to chop away at orientation programs early in a budget-cutting spree. It is important, therefore, that management have a full understanding of what its money is buying and how much it really costs. Orientation programs are best boiled down to a size and sophistication that can be easily understood and justified by the training director. Of all of his pet projects, the orientation program offers the least tangible and the fewest short-range benefits. Forewarned, training directors, is forearmed.

21

Job Instruction

"Joe, this is Harry, our new counterman. Show him the ropes and let him handle customers as fast as you can break him in. We're shorthanded, you know, and the lunch crowd will hit in half an hour!"

With dispatch, Harry is handed a white apron, shown the menu, and pointed toward the counter, behind which sit a row of hungry, demanding patrons. If his supervisor has a moment between customers, he'll blurt out an instruction or two. If he doesn't, Harry will learn on his own by trial and error. And if he fails to make the grade – oh well, what can you expect from the kind of help in today's labor market?

With slight variation, this scene is repeated in a great many organizations. It happens in spite of the hundreds of dollars a company may have spent initially to recruit, screen, and place an employee.

By any standard, it is penny-wise and pound-foolish to omit showing a man how to do his job correctly. He'll cost you many times what you might have spent on his training by increasing your scrap rate, having accidents, damaging machinery and tools, disturbing other workers, lowering the quality of your product, distracting your supervisors, and losing your customers. And in the end you will lose the employee too, either because you must fire him for poor performance or because he chooses to leave for what he thinks are greener pastures.

A FORMAL DEFINITION OF JOB INSTRUCTION

Any job, whether it be wiring and soldering television receiver parts, or entering credits and debits on a ledger, is composed of a series of related tasks. Each of these tasks must be performed collectively in such a way as to meet a prescribed standard for the job whether formally or informally applied. If a new employee has not previously learned to perform these tasks at the expected standard of quantity and quality, he must be taught them by his new employer. In short, the reason for job training is to help any employee, new or old, perform a given job at a given standard as quickly as possible. When we formalize job training, we hypothesize that job skills can be taught and learned more efficiently and effectively than through informal, chance methods.

WHO SHOULD GIVE JOB TRAINING?

In a small organization operating without the benefit of staff services, the alternatives are limited. The immediate boss or a competent long-service employee may give job training. In larger organizations, members of the training department may offer a third alternative.

There are strong arguments in favor of having the supervisor do the training. For one thing, he is accountable for the quantity and quality of the output of his work group. Theoretically, he knows the job better than anyone else and can readily tell when it is being done properly.

On the other hand, there are some clear arguments against the supervisor as a trainer. The supervisor may be a poor communicator. His explanations may be weak and his pace too fast for a man who is new to the job. In addition, he may be unable to organize his materials or to find the best method for presenting them, and he may not know when his pupil has actually learned.

Some organizations try to solve the problem by making the training department responsible for job training. The rationale usually goes like this. The training department is supposed to know the best methods for getting people to learn their jobs. By centralizing instruction, a uniformly trained work group will result. And finally, because personnel development is the fundamental objective of the training department, it will probably put greater effort into getting people to learn their work. Supervisors are continually interrupted by production problems, and so their full attention will not be on training their subordinates.

But the same reasons that argue for the supervisor to do the training, argue against a professional trainer. The training department does not have firsthand experience with the work. Both procedures and standards must be learned secondhand and then taught. Furthermore, the training department conducts programs. Programs have definite beginnings and endings. When the training department shuts the books and hangs up its cap and gown, that's the end of it. Who now monitors and corrects performance? Probably not the training department.

Obviously, the answer lies somewhere in between, in a situation that combines the advantages which both a boss and a professional trainer can bring to the job training situation. The supervisor, however, must always be the key figure. He is the man who really knows what the job demands. He is there day in and day out, working closely with the employee, judging his efforts, correcting his deficiencies, and doling out rewards to him when they are deserved. The supervisor and the trainer *share* the responsibility of employee job training.

Ideally, a job training program should be developed and executed in accordance with the following pattern.

1. The supervisor and the trainer jointly analyze the overall training problem. The supervisor brings his expert knowledge of the work to the analysis; the trainer brings his methods for performing analyses and his experience in analyzing other training problems.

2. Together the supervisor and the trainer develop the program's objectives. The supervisor knows what must be accomplished; the trainer is skilled in developing clear and workable training objectives.

3. Together the supervisor and the trainer organize the content of the job instruction. The supervisor contributes his understanding of the procedures and standards; the trainer applies his ability to organize instructional material in accordance with the principles of learning psychology.

4. The trainer helps the supervisor select the most effective and practical methods of training. The trainer assumes most of the responsibility for preparing the job training materials to fit the selected medium or media and coaches the supervisor in effective use of them.

5. The supervisor in most cases gives the actual instruction. The trainer coaches him in this role. In those cases where it is more expedient for the trainer to give the instruction, the supervisor plays an important follow-up part.

6. The supervisor and the trainer jointly evaluate the results of their training efforts and revise their work as required.

IS YOUR ORGANIZATION READY FOR A MORE FORMAL JOB INSTRUCTION PROGRAM?

All employees receive some form of job instruction, however informal it may be. Before considering a more formal program for your organization, it would be well to consider the following points.

1. How much time can you afford to spend on training? Regardless of the scope of the program, time is needed to prepare for and to perform the training. Furthermore, more extensive training means more time lost from work by new employees.

2. What about your budget? You will incur additional costs in developing training materials and personnel to do the training.

3. Have written job descriptions and job standards been established? You will need both to know what to train for and to measure how well you have done.

4. Will your present line managers need training themselves before they can administer a more formal program?

5. Can you create an environment for training, even though it is on the line, which is conducive to learning?

6. Can the mechanical scheduling of employees for training be accomplished without undue disruption?

7. Is your management convinced of the necessity to formalize the training presently being given? If not, you will need to develop a rationale and cost data to show what will be gained by the organization's investment in a job training program.

If you can answer "yes" to these questions, you are in a position to enter into development of a formal job instruction program.

PRELIMINARY PLANNING FOR JOB INSTRUCTION

Step 1. Analyze the job. The first step in developing any job instruction program is to analyze the job itself. This is a task which is ideally performed by both the supervisor and a training specialist. One method of analyzing a job is to follow it step by step through a check sheet such as the one shown in Fig. 21-1.

Take the check list to the site of the job and carefully observe the work being performed. Identify each element of the job and determine the reason for its existence. Have the present workers and supervisor explain the work to you and tell you why it is done the way it is. If necessary, immerse yourself further by attempting some of the tasks yourself.

When the on-the-job observation is complete, return with the supervisor to a place away from the work area and sort through the tasks. You may need to rearrange the sequence of the steps for the purposes of training. Your observations may even lead you to question established

Fig. 21-1. Job instruction task analysis.

Supervisor________________________________
Job title________________________________
Job station (location)________________________
Job description (thumbnail)____________________

Job objectives______________________________

Step no. (in sequence)	Why is this step necessary	Tools required	Equipment required
1.			
2.			
3.			
4.			
5.			

Notes:__________________________________

methods. Often what comes out of a job analysis is more uniform and improved work methods.

The final analysis should be rechecked for accuracy at the job site before the next step is taken.

Step 2. Write a job description. If a written description does not exist for a job which is to become the subject of formal job instruction, one should be prepared. A job description is simply a systematic identification of the major responsibilities involved in a given job. It should be based on the tasks which make up the job, stated as simply, clearly, and succinctly as possible. The training specialist and the supervisor can prepare a usable job description from the analysis worksheet, if necessary.

Step 3. Develop standards of job performance. While the job description lists the important duties for a particular job, it does not reveal how well these duties must be performed. A standard of acceptable performance must be developed. A job description, for example, might state that a clerk-typist was required to type routine correspondence. The standard which corresponded to that particular duty might specify that a minimum of twelve pieces of routine correspondence containing a maximum of two minor errors per hour is acceptable.

Job standards are vital to a job instruction program because they tell the trainer and his student how successful the training effort has been. The job analysis, description, and standards are the three preliminary steps to designing a job instruction program. They will provide the solid objectives for the next steps.

ANALYZING THE STUDENT

At this point, it is well to give some serious thought to the students who will be the recipients of your job instruction. Not all trainees fall into the category of new workers. If they did, it would be a lot simpler to construct a job training program. We have, in fact, several types of trainees.

1. "Green" workers or those who have never worked on any job.
2. Workers who have worked the job in similar conditions but must now be retrained or converted to your methods and procedures.
3. Older employees being trained to perform new, more complex jobs.

While the job requirements may be similar, differences in the backgrounds and skill levels of trainees call for differences in approaches. There may be differences in which job steps must be emphasized, why these steps are important, and how the job fits into the company as a whole. Your psychological approach will also differ according to the employee you are dealing with.

A "green" worker, for example, finds the entire work environment to be strange, alien, even hostile. He will normally enter a job in such a high state of anxiety that much of what is said to him is lost unless it is repeated many times. A considerable effort must be made to keep the work environment as simple as possible at least for the first day.

The worker who has gained experience elsewhere and must now be converted to your method of performing a given job is faced with different problems. He feels he "knows the job" because he has lived with it for a long time already. He will normally resent the implication that his previous way of doing a job was wrong. Your best bet is to try to understand the worker's desire to show what he knows from his previous experience, and then to build on his knowledge and show him how it will make his present employment more fruitful. Let the employee tell you what he already knows and how the job was done in his previous employment. Once you have this information and his confidence, you are in a position to explain how this varies in his new place of employment and why this variance is necessary. From this point on he will probably be very cooperative.

Perhaps the hardest of all is the upgrading of older employees to a more complex job. There are several problems that arise. The average person in this position feels he is suddenly in the backwash of technology, a misfit being retreaded to perform a skill. Quite often he is in the 40-to-50 age bracket. Upon entering a new job situation he may feel insecure and hostile. He may resent having a younger man train him. To achieve results in this situation, be careful to follow a few simple rules.

1. Set the person at ease by explaining why and how the training process will improve his position as a valued employee.

2. Build on his previous experience, regardless of his old job. Where will his knowledge be useful on the new job?

3. Don't downgrade the previous job or the person. Both acts will cut you off from the individual.

4. Be positive in training the man in the new job. Show him the task with confidence that your training will be beneficial to the employee.

5. Be patient. He will possibly take a little more time to reach peak efficiency because the behavior established on his previous job will interfere with the performance of the new task. Allow sufficient time for the person to reach peak production even though it may take him a little longer than it would a new employee.

The principles of learning discussed in Chapter 6, of course, apply to the development of job instruction programs. In general, the guiding principle that the student is the focus of the learning process – not the material, the trainer, or the organization – will serve as a solid base for your program development.

SELECTING JOB TRAINING METHODS AND MATERIALS

Section III of this book details the selection and production of the basic methods and materials of training. Here are a few suggestions specifically applicable to job instruction:

1. The training should not be dominated by the method. Whatever communication media are used should be directly related to the objectives

established by the job analysis, description, and standards. Don't begin by saying, "We need a movie to teach arc welding."

2. Keep the materials as simple as possible. If a book of line drawings will serve the purpose, don't introduce a complicated electronic device which may require other learned behaviors to operate.

3. Work the materials, tools, and equipment normally used to accomplish the job into the training.

4. Simulate actual procedures. Produce a real product.

5. Select a communications vehicle which forces continued and significant student involvement and response.

6. Any method, regardless ot its familiarity or simplicity, needs rehearsal. Questions need to be formulated in advance. Demonstrations need to be practiced.

WHERE SHOULD JOB TRAINING BE GIVEN?

There is no particular requirement that job instruction be given either in a classroom or at the work station. The choice, if one can be made, depends on the number of employees to be trained, the materials to be used, and other factors. Satisfactory training conditions can be achieved in a small, crowded stockroom, provided certain requirements are met.

1. The student needs to have a reasonable amount of freedom from noise distraction so that he can concentrate on learning.

2. He needs a degree of privacy from his co-workers so that he can practice, make errors, and receive correction without personal embarrassment.

3. He needs an atmosphere conducive to the creation of a rapport with his instructor or materials of instruction.

4. He needs to be comfortable enough physically to permit complete concentration on the learning process.

5. He needs to feel that he is at the center of the learning situation, that the instruction is seriously intended for his benefit.

A WORD ABOUT MOTIVATION

Everyone talks about this elusive force, but few people are able to control it and build it into a work situation. For the moment, forget the elaborate financial incentives, benefit programs, and erudite theories. The trainer's task during job instruction is to attempt to build in the worker a self-generating eagerness to do a good job for as long as he works. Real motivation grows out of the employee's interest in the work itself. It is this fascination with the work and this pride in the product produced or service rendered which the trainer must work to foster.

There are other useful motivational techniques, of course. But none is quite so powerful as the excitement that can be generated by work of any kind which is well done and in which the doer takes personal pride. Here are some additional means of motivating the employee during job instruction:

1. Convey to the worker your sincere belief in the importance of his job.
2. Build an attitude that this is "his" company and his "own" department.
3. Convey to the worker your sincere interest in his family, ambitions, problems, and even his weaknesses.
4. Show the employee that there is a real chance for him to move ahead in the organization.
5. Keep the employee informed of company events, changes, and plans on a regular basis.

THE JOB TRAINING INSTRUCTOR

Too often the supervisor is given the job training task without adequate preparation in the art of training. The consequences of this approach are simply a frustrated supervisor and trainee. In some cases relationships can deteriorate. The result is poorly trained personnel who are prone to leave a job at the slightest provocation.

The essential point to stress in the training of all personnel who must give job instruction is to keep all training student-centered. If this is accomplished, the actual specifics of a task will be readily taught in a manner conducive to learning. The key ingredients necessary for a job training instructor are thorough knowledge of the job itself and the ability to convey this knowledge to others, always keeping the student's point of view in mind.

These abilities can be acquired. The job trainer will probably be a first-line supervisor who was once himself a worker on the same job. However, such experience does not mean that he automatically possesses the ability to teach this job to others unless he himself has been trained to train.

If it is necessary to train a supervisor in the art of training, a formal program should be established. Ideally, this program should follow the instructor training program specified in this book. If time does not permit this, it will be necessary to provide the supervisor with an abbreviated primer dealing with the basics of how to communicate, organize, and supervise training.*

As preparation for the assignment, the trainer should be required to perform the following steps before he begins:

1. Check his own understanding of the job functions with a thorough reading of the job analysis.
2. Be certain that he has all the tools and equipment available for the training task.
3. Prepare a brief outline of the points he will cover in the training cycle. Decide how much material he will try to teach at any given time.
4. Rehearse the training with the training director or members of the training staff to be certain that the essential training points will be taught in the most effective manner.

PROCEDURE FOR TRAINING

When an employee begins a new job he is a complete stranger to the environment of the new organization. His response to the company will be affected by what the trainer does and says during his first day on the job and how his personal needs are satisfied. Because he is new on the job, he will be unsure of himself. The trainer must, therefore, be careful not to appear hostile toward the trainee; he should not, for example, convey the impression that he has been assigned to perform the training even though he doesn't like the task. Instead, he should try to create a strong, positive impression. He can do this by being friendly and by showing an interest in the man's family, background, and job experiences, whether related or unrelated to his new job. The training should not begin until the employee is at ease with the trainer.

Once the worker is at ease, he should be told the purpose of the particular job and why training is necessary. He should be told what training he will be receiving and why it is necessary for him to acquire this particular knowledge and skill.

---

*For a concise set of procedures for training, see Martin Broadwell's *The Supervisor As An Instructor* (Addison-Wesley, 1968) and *The Supervisor and On-the-Job Training* (Addison-Wesley, 1969).

The trainer should follow a prepared outline and objectives. These simple rules will be helpful:

1. Do not go too fast in the explanation. Remember it may be old hat to you, but it is brand new to the trainee.

2. Be certain the trainee can see all the operations you are explaining and how they relate to other steps in the training.

3. Use the show-tell-show-practice approach. Your task is to achieve a level of performance from the trainee. You are interested in teaching only enough theory to achieve this performance.

4. Do not forget the *why* for each step and how it relates to the previous step.

5. Test the trainee on each step as you go through the operation. Have him perform the step while you watch and analyze. Be careful, however, not to expect him to perform an operation you have not yet taught. To reinforce good work habits, be free with your praise when he makes the right moves; tell him "that's good," "excellent," and so on. By the same token, do not be too critical when he makes a mistake. You cannot get a person to learn if he is in a high state of anxiety brought on by negative instructor reactions.

6. The evidence of his acquired skill is his performance on the job according to preset standards. To further test his understanding, let the employee explain to the instructor why and what he is doing as he goes through the steps. You can make this more complicated by asking the trainee questions about the job in random order, disregarding the sequence in which he was taught. This should help to show whether he understands the job or simply remembered the steps.

7. As the medical prescription says on the label, "repeat as necessary" until you are convinced he can perform. Once you have trained the worker to your satisfaction, your next task is to establish a schedule to transfer him from instructional supervision to normal supervision. To begin with, you must put the trainee on his own to perform. Do not expect full quality or quantity from the start. Let him go through the operation a few times alone.

It is helpful if the new worker can be apprenticed to an experienced fellow worker. Caution must be observed to ensure that the veteran worker does not teach the new man "his" way which will only serve to confuse the new worker. Encourage your trainee to ask questions and to work slowly to be certain he is right.

Fade the training support from the learner until he is on his own and near the point where he can be expected to reach full production shortly.

In this period you should occasionally check with the trainee until such time as it is evident he no longer needs any help to perform his job.

REMINDING SUPERVISORS OF JOB INSTRUCTION PRINCIPLES

A small card summarizing the basic principles of job instruction can serve as a useful reminder for supervisors.

How to Get Ready to Instruct

1. Have a time table – how much skill you expect him to have, by what date.
2. Break down the job – list important steps and pick out the key points.
3. Have everything ready – the right equipment, materials, and supplies.
4. Have the workplace properly arranged – just as the worker will be expected to keep it.

How to Instruct

Step 1: Prepare the worker. Put him at ease. State the job and find out what he already knows about it. Get him interested in learning the job. Place him in the correct position.

Step 2: Present the operation. Tell, show, and illustrate one *important step* at a time. Stress each *key point.* Instruct clearly, completely, and patiently, but don't give the trainee more than he can master.

Step 3: Try out performance. Have him do the job; correct his errors. Have him explain each *key point* to you as he does the job again. Make sure he understands. Continue until *you* know *he* knows.

Step 4: Follow up. Put him on his own. Designate to whom he goes for help. Check frequently. Encourage questions. Taper off extra coaching and close follow-up.

22

Training Your Supervisors

Scott A. Greer, in his booklet *Social Organization,* calls the foreman or the front-line supervisor "the man between."* The training director must grasp this basic truth of supervisory work before he can proceed to develop meaningful materials for this segment of the organization.

The supervisor is like a fugitive caught between the crossfire of two warring groups. Whichever direction he takes, he is apt to draw the fire of one group. His job is to implement the plans, policies, and procedures of upper management. He does this by transmitting them to the rank and file employees in such a way that the mission of the organization is carried out as efficiently and effectively as possible. He must at all times straddle the fence between two camps, management and labor. He is expected to think like management for management, and to represent the labor point of view for labor. In all probability the supervisor has come directly from the ranks of the workers. With little or no preparation he tries to imitate what he has seen and heard his boss do in the past.

People are not born good bosses even though we promote employees as if they have a natural talent to manage others. According to Greer, if left to develop on their own, supervisors cultivate one of three strategies for handling their jobs. They may join the work group and rely on their personal prestige to supervise the workers under them. They may remain far on the fringe of the group, keeping their management-slanted viewpoint from being sullied by rank and file thinking. Or lastly, they may attempt to combine the two behavior patterns, remaining both a friend of the men and an arm of management.

*Scott A. Greer, *Social Organization,* New York: Random House, 1955, pp. 1-4.

All three approaches have their pitfalls. By joining the group, the supervisor is in danger of diluting his authority. By remaining too far outside the group, he may be identified as the enemy. By combining the two approaches, he may appear inconsistent and obtain inconsistent results from his efforts. Because conflict is built into his job, the supervisor always feels the pressure existing between management and the work group. There is no escape. Acceptance of the job indicates a willingness to accept this ambiguous role. Finding solutions to this dilemma is a main activity of the supervisor's daily routine.

Recognition of this "in between position" is the first step in the planning and development of materials to train potential supervisors or to improve the skills of those already on the job. All too often, the supervisor is left to work it out by himself through trial and error responses to daily problems. Before he becomes skillful at handling his people and getting out the production, the supervisor probably makes a number of serious errors in judgment and a vast quantity of irritating smaller mistakes. A little preparation can easily save the organization time, effort, and money. And considering the critical nature of the supervisor's role in the organization, the training director can have a significant impact on the operation of this part of the organization.

WHAT THE SUPERVISOR NEEDS TO KNOW

Like the training director, the supervisor must understand and accept his "in between" role. He must realize that he is paid to live with and resolve the ambiguity inherent in his position between management and the workers. His daily work will involve him in a great many problems not easily resolved. But this is his job – to live with conflict and to resolve it in the best way, after considering the needs and goals of the organization.

A second basic understanding the supervisor usually needs to be taught is his responsibility for getting work done through others. The supervisor is usually picked because he is an outstanding worker. If he is given no further definition of his supervisory responsibilities, he will go on doing the work he was doing before he was promoted. He will not delegate work to others. He will simply do the work himself. His direction of other people will be incidental. He therefore needs to learn how to best get others to do the work.

Given these two basic understandings, the supervisor needs to know about and be able to apply to his knowledge to the following areas.*

---

*Burt K. Scanlan and Brad B. Boyd, "Training first-line managers; does it fit the bill?", *Training in Business and Industry,* Vol. 2, No. 2, March-April, 1965, p. 22.

Selecting and training employees.

Maintaining effective discipline.

Controlling costs.

Handling complaints and suggestions.

Administering the union contract or labor policies of the company.

Getting people to follow safe practices.

Motivating people.

Improving work methods.

Understanding basic benefit and promotion policies.

Understanding company organization and policy.

Let us take a closer look at the content of each of these basic subjects.

Selecting and Training Employees

Although the supervisor will probably not handle the initial interview with an applicant, he will probably handle the second and determining interview. Too often supervisors have no idea of how to interview to really find out anything of value. He often does most of the talking and bases his final judgment on the applicant's appearance or other superficial characteristics. The supervisor needs to be taught how to probe, what to look for, how to describe the requirements of the job, and how to sell the company to an applicant. These are not difficult techniques, and most people arrive at them if they interview applicants long enough. There is, of course, no need to learn entirely by experience. A little training will go a long way.

Once a man has been selected, he will need to be trained. He will need training, not only on the first day, but as long as he works in the organization. The supervisor needs to know how to give a new employee his initial instructions, how to coach him, and how to help him grow on the job. The supervisor also needs to know how to use the resources of the training department.

Maintaining Effective Discipline

Most untrained supervisors equate discipline to punishment. They need to learn that the various disciplinary measures form a spectrum ranging from a simple verbal warning all the way to discharge, with many steps in between. The supervisor will need to learn both the company policies and procedures for administering disciplinary actions and the techniques for handling everyday problems so that effective standards of discipline will be maintained.

Controlling Costs

The supervisor is responsible for controlling the costs in his unit. His costs will include the man hours used to accomplish a job, materials, tools, supplies, and other facilities of the unit. Every time he signs a time sheet or requisition for supplies, the supervisor is spending the organization's assets. The supervisor needs to understand the three basic elements of cost – material, labor, and overhead – as they relate to his unit. He needs to know fairly precisely what constitutes a fair day's work for each of his subordinates; he needs to be able to identify and correct the causes of substandard parts production; he needs to be able to control supply costs and machine utilization. Because the supervisor is on the scene, he is often in a better position than anyone else to control and reduce these costs. He'll need help in developing cost control programs once he is made cost conscious.

Handling Complaints and Suggestions

Because of the supervisor's close relationship with his work group, he'll need to know how to handle complaints and suggestions from his subordinates. If there is a union contract, the grievance procedure may be spelled out in detail. If a formalized suggestion system is in effect, he'll have to know how it operates. In any event, the supervisor must be able to keep the communication channels open with his people. This sounds easy, but in fact requires a high degree of skill in interpersonal relationships.

Administering the Union Contract

If an organization is unionized, the supervisor will need to understand and be able to apply the provisions of the contract to the problems he will find in his daily work. Too often supervisors are afraid to do anything because they do not know their rights under the agreement. They need to know how far they can go and who to consult if there is a question. They'll need some information on how to deal with shop stewards and business agents.

If there is no contract, the supervisors will need to know the organization's informal and formal labor policies. If management is opposed to being organized, the supervisors will also need to know what to do and say in the event of a drive for an election.

Getting People to Follow Safe Practices

The cause of safety may or may not be furthered by slogans and programs. Nonetheless, the supervisor is responsible for the safety of his unit. He needs to know how to spot unsafe conditions and how to remedy them. He needs to know how to set safety standards and supervise them. He needs to know how to persuade his subordinates to develop safe working habits so that they are followed even when his back is turned. This is not easy, but the behavioral scientists are giving us fresh approaches to age old safety problems such as the prevention of strains caused by lifting.

Motivating People

Supervisors need the benefit of motivational research. There is much talk of motivating people to produce, but little in the way of usable knowledge and technique has been transmitted to the supervisor. Most supervisors still think that money is the most powerful motivator. Even the fundamental motivation studies have not been filtered down to front-line supervision.

Improving Work Methods

Supervisors need to be made conscious of the need to consistently work at improving work methods. This means they need to learn techniques for eliminating unnecessary steps in the work, by rearranging, simplifying, or combining elements of the work. Methods improvement involves making better use of people, machines, and material so that the work can be done more easily, more safely, more quickly, or more inexpensively. The supervisor is in the best position to initiate methods improvement because he is closer to the work that is being done than anyone else in the organization.

Supervisors can be taught to improve work methods by developing procedures that permit them to break down the job, question every detail, and then develop new methods. They need to learn principles and become involved in programs.

Understanding Basic Benefit and Promotion Policies

Because of his close daily contact with his work group, the supervisor is in a good position to answer basic questions about vacations, sick leave, insurance and retirement programs, and other fringe benefits of the organization. He can cut some of the administrative red tape by handling routine questions about benefit policies so that productive time is not wasted in wondering and waiting.

A supervisor should be familiar with the company's promotion policies and aware of jobs that become available. He should be in a position to recommend his people for better jobs if they are qualified. If they lack some qualifications, he should help them plan individual improvement programs. Ability to communicate benefits and promotional opportunities helps everyone – the company, the work group, and the individual.

Understanding Company Organization and Policy

Supervisors need to know and be able to apply company policy to the problems the work group will bring to him each day. They need to know the company's absence policy, its tardiness policy, its overtime regulations, and dozens of other work rules that keep a work force operating efficiently.

And finally, supervisors need to know their way around the organization. They need to know who runs what and where to go to get needed materials and services. This knowledge begins with the organization chart, but goes further than that into the unwritten mores of the organization.

The ten areas discussed above are basic to the supervisor's job. Without information and the ability to use this information to effectively guide his work group, the supervisor will be crippled. He will waste a lot of valuable time searching this information out as he needs it. The training director and his staff can make a real contribution by organizing this knowledge and communicating it to front-line supervisors or by helping someone else communicate it.

WHAT METHODS ARE MOST EFFECTIVE FOR TRAINING SUPERVISORS?

Supervisors, if they are given any training at all, are probably trained through on-the-job methods. We believe that a combination of on-the-job and off-the-job methods must be used on a continuing basis. Let's begin with a brief review of some of the typical on-the-job methods and their strengths and weaknesses.*

1. *Coaching.* Coaching is generally defined as learning by doing under the watchful and helpful guidance of an experienced superior. According to research by Sterling D. Huggens, Training Manager for RCA, supervisory trainees remember 75% of what they learn while working under supervision, compared to 10% to 15% learned from listening to lectures and 30% to 50% from participating in conferences.† There is ample evidence to support the notion that coaching is the best method for developing effective supervisors. The advantages of using coaching are as follows:

a) Instruction is geared to the needs of the individual supervisor.
b) Instruction is more or less continuous.
c) The supervisor is provided with a role model to imitate.

The disadvantages of the coaching method are as follows:

a) The quality of the coaching depends on the superior doing the coaching.
b) Production requirements are often placed ahead of training requirements.
c) Coaching may not be given in the best sequence for learning by the supervisor.

2. *Job rotation.* Job rotation as a method of developing supervisors is defined as a procedure for moving trainees from one part of a job to another or to different jobs in a relatively short period of time for the purpose of exposing them to as much of the supervisory job as possible. The effectiveness of job rotation can be increased by having the supervisor of the work group in which the trainee is temporarily assigned delegate most of his responsibilities to the trainee. In this way, the trainee is forced to use his own resources to operate the work group as he will eventually have to in operating his own. The advantages of job rotation as a method for developing supervisors are as follows.

*Material in this section was suggested by Fred A. Manske in "Supervisory training: an evaluation of on-the-job methods," *Training and Development Journal,* Vol. 20, No. 9, October, 1966, pp. 44-51.
†Sterling D. Huggens, "Through coaching: progressive training and development," *Advanced Management,* September, 1959, p. 26, as quoted in Fred A. Manske, *ibid.*

a) The risk of poor training from a single weak supervisor is minimized.
b) The trainee gets a broader view of the operation and supervisory skills.
c) Work groups benefit from the temporary assignment of a supervisor with a fresh viewpoint toward the group.

The disadvantages of job rotation are these:

a) Training tends to be more superficial because of the temporary nature of the assignment.
b) The administrative procedures to keep trainees rotating and evaluated can become cumbersome.
c) The morale of the regular supervisor may be affected if he knows that his weaknesses will be exposed and reported back to his superiors.

3. *Development assignments.* Developmental assignments are defined as those assignments given to a trainee for the purpose accomplishing certain tasks such as writing a policy manual or planning a college board training program in a department store. The assignment usually provides an opportunity to learn and develop skills which will later be useful. Developmental assignments can take the form of special projects, understudy assignments, and fill-in assignments during a supervisor's absence or vacation. The advantages of this method for training supervisors are as follows:

a) A developmental assignment gives the trainee an opportunity to sink his teeth into a project for which he alone will be held responsible and judged.
b) It is easier to observe and judge a man's strengths and weaknesses if he can be assigned to a piece of work which has definite boundaries.

The disadvantages of developmental assignments can be as follows:

a) Too much emphasis may be placed on the results of the assignment and not enough on the growth of the trainee during the assignment.
b) Developmental assignments are sometimes too narrow in scope to properly prepare a man for broader responsibilities.

Let's turn now to a brief review of some off-the-job methods for developing supervisors and look specifically at their relative merit.*

*Material in this section was suggested by Fred A. Manske in "Supervisory training: an evaluation of off-the-job methods," *The Training and Development Journal,* Vol. 20, No. 10, November, 1966, pp. 20-27.

Of all of the methods for developing supervisory personnel, the lecture is probably most frequently used, yet the least effective. It is probably the easiest one, from the standpoint of preparation. It is versatile and economical. Unfortunately, however, supervisors appear to benefit least from it.

The conference method is definded as a group discussion in which the participants learn from each other. Conference training is probably closest to the coaching method in its effectiveness for developing knowledge. The trainee has an opportunity to participate by thinking and planning. He also has the opportunity to learn far more than one individual. The conference method, however, has the same weakness as the lecture method. It does not provide the trainee with an opportunity to actually perform the tasks of the supervisor. Case studies and other simulation techniques can provide this important developmental opportunity.

The off-the-job methods normally used to train supervisors are not of equal effectiveness. A combination of off-the-job methods must be used to supplement on-the-job methods, to give the supervisor an opportunity to learn the basic skills of supervision and to continue to grow on the job.

WHO SHOULD TRAIN SUPERVISORS?

The answer to this question involves a number of factors. We have just argued that the supervisor needs to be trained by both on-the-job and off-the-job methods. The actual training then should be handled as a joint responsibility of both the training department and second-line supervision. The following general guidelines may prove useful.

1. Training which is designed to be repeated many times in the future should probably be provided by the training department.

2. Specialized knowledge such as that concerning work improvement methods is best handled by experienced supervisors. General principles can be taught by training department members.

3. Company policy and problem solving can be handled by articulate members of the training department.

4. On-the-job methods are best performed directly by experienced supervisors but should be coordinated by the training department. The training department should handle the administrative details of assignments, records, evaluations and so on.

HOW MUCH TRAINING SHOULD BE GIVEN?

Supervisory training should not be considered a one-time proposition. Once the basic skills are learned, the supervisor will need refresher courses and further development. He needs a continuing opportunity to share his problems and to learn from his peers. As he grows in his job, he will probably need more specific, more individualized training. He may need the help of a programed text on safety or a seminar on quality control. The training department can learn of supervisory needs through performance reviews, surveys, and feedback from other supervisors. If there is enough demand, training can be formalized and organized for group consumption. If needs are isolated, individualized programs can be prepared.

HOW DO YOU MEASURE SUPERVISORY GROWTH?

There are many ways to measure supervisory growth – or the lack of it. Here are a few ways to think about. Looked at another way, these insights also indicate areas where training may be necessary.

1. Are there a relatively large number of grievances which go beyond the first step, usually a meeting between the shop steward and the foreman, and on to arbitration? Your supervisors may not have sufficient know-how to resolve grievances before they become costly and time-consuming.
2. Is your employee turnover exceptionally high? Your supervisors may need help in selecting applicants, training subordinates, and a host of other related supervisory techniques.
3. Do you have a large number of disciplinary problems? Your supervisors may not know how to set and maintain an effective discipline system.
4. Does employee morale seem poor? Your supervisors may not know how to get action on complaints and suggestions.
5. Is your Workmen's Compensation Insurance rate high? A study of the causes of work-related injuries may reveal areas where training could help the supervisor to institute safer working habits for his work group.
6. Do large numbers of employees come to the personnel department for answers to simple employee benefits questions? Your supervisors may be sending them there because the supervisors don't have basic benefit information.

7. Are mistakes in judgment made because supervisors simply do not know the company policy? Does the same problem crop up in different forms and require executive time to solve and resolve? Your supervisors may need training in basic company policy and procedures.

These are a few of the measures you can use for judging the overall growth of your supervisory force. Your personnel director and others on the staff will be able to tell you about other symptoms that you can use to measure the training needs of your supervisors. Any reduction in supervisory influence as measured by these criteria would indicate need for further supervisory growth after training.

CREATING A SUPERVISORY POOL

Most supervisors are promoted to the job and then trained for it. If your company is large enough so that you can forecast the number of supervisors you will be needing within the next year as a result of natural attrition, retirements, leaves of absence, promotions, or other turnover factors, you should create a supervisory pool. By screening good candidates for supervisory positions for a special training class, you can stockpile candidates and use them as openings occur. Companies that have tried this system find that their employees are eager for the opportunity to join these training groups. The list of interested people is usually long, providing management with an opportunity for selection instead of appointment out of desperation. The presupervisory training period gives the employee's supervisors and the training department a chance to really evaluate his abilities well before he must take on the responsibility of being a boss.

GETTING A SUPERVISORY TRAINING PROGRAM STARTED

If your organization has no program at the present time, the following steps for getting started might be useful.

1. Begin with the supervisor's job description. The responsibilities listed on it can offer the starting point for your program. It will, for example, probably indicate that the supervisor is the one responsible for maintaining the discipline standards for his work group. Your program should probably include material which will help the supervisor improve his

performance of this responsibility. The supervisor is generally rated on the basis of how well he carries out the duties in his job description. The job description can also be used in this way to measure how effective training has been for the supervisor.

2. A second place to begin is with the company policy and procedure manual itself. The supervisor needs to have a working knowledge of those areas of information which affect his relationships with the work group and be able to apply the information to the practical problems he faces.

3. A number of good, off-the-shelf, commercial programs for training front-line supervisors can be purchased. These programs can be used as they are or modified to fit your requirements. Using a reputable program will give you an opportunity to observe your supervisors and perform a more thorough analysis to determine exactly what they need.

The job of bossing people in most organizations is basically the same. The problems will vary slightly, and the policies will differ in detail, but the job itself is similar at all levels. As Guy B. Ford put it in his book,* it's a matter of "building a winning employee team." The training director has a superb opportunity to help the supervisor in his efforts to build that team.

---

*Guy B. Ford, *Building A Winning Employee Team,* New York: American Management Association, 1964.

23

Getting Started in Management Development

The greatest opportunity the training director has to contribute to the success of his organization is through the training and development of its executives. The future of any organization is closely tied to the quality of its leadership. We think that the training department is in a key position to spark the continuing growth of the organization's present and future managers.

MANAGEMENT DEVELOPMENT DEFINED

Elton T. Reeves, in a book titled *Management Development and the Line Manager,* defines management development as "any planned, guided, or directed activity undertaken by a manager to help him become more competent in his present position, or to prepare him for heavier responsibilities to come."* The training director has the dual problem of improving the current performance of an organization's managers and preparing managers for future responsibilities. His first task depends on which group he chooses to work with first. For convenience we will call present managers "incumbents" and future managers "potentials."

INCUMBENTS: JOB DESCRIPTIONS AND PERFORMANCE REVIEWS

A good starting point for planning an improvement program for your present managers is the job description itself, assuming, of course, that

---

*Elton Reeves, *Management Development and the Line Manager,* New York: American Management Association, 1969, p. 10.

one exists. By looking at the duties listed on the job description, you will be able to gain a first level of understanding of what a man or group of men performing similar jobs is supposed to be doing. By looking over current performance reviews or appraisals, you will be able to get some impressions of how well these responsibilities are being carried out.

POTENTIALS: JOB DESCRIPTIONS AND PLANNED ORGANIZATION CHARTS

One of the training director's responsibilities is to work with management and the personnel officer on long-range manpower planning. What will the organization's objectives be ten years from now? How will this affect executive requirements? How will the young managers be prepared to take on greater responsibilities? How will retirements and normal employee attrition affect future openings?

The training and personnel departments share the responsibility for being ready to place fully trained men against these manpower requirements. Obviously no manpower forecast is static. Training and personnel people have a continuing job of identifying and developing managers so that the organization is not caught short just when it needs to expand. Organization charts and job descriptions anticipating future needs offer a logical starting point for preparing a management development program for potentials.

CONVINCING THE TOP MAN

One continually hears in training circles about the importance of convincing top management of the organization's need for your program. There is much truth in this hearsay. While you will not receive much resistance to training bank tellers or arc welders, you may run into strenuous objections as you begin to suggest programs for middle and upper management. Why? Because managers are supposed to be capable of improvement simply by working at their present jobs. Because it is more difficult to measure the long-range effects of management's work than it is to measure the recently acquired skills of the arc welder. Because training people are often not themselves considered a part of management. And because top management often takes the attitude that it already knows everything there is to know about the science of management. Isn't the organization already running at top efficiency? Didn't we net 5% profit before taxes last year? Convincing the top man then may be a tough, long-range proposition for the training director. It is nonetheless a worthwhile activity, since programs always have an easier time of getting acceptance if support comes from the top. Assuming your chief is not receptive, here are a few ways you might try to gain his interest.

1. Start in a nonthreatening way. Drop a challenging article on management development in his in-box and in a few days casually stop by to discuss it with him.
2. Leave an outstanding book on his desk. A basic list for management reading is included later in this chapter.
3. Discuss the interest and enthusiasm of one of his peers for a management program he attended.
4. Suggest his attendance at a one-day seminar that you know will be stimulating.

INDIVIDUALIZING THE MANAGER'S PROGRAM

While some developmental activities will be designed for groups, the management development program for each manager must be planned on an individual basis. It goes without saying that men have different experience and educational backgrounds. They differ widely in their developmental needs. Each man's growth must be charted separately. One man may need an elementary course in accounting; another may require training on the use of a sophisticated electronic data processing system for inventory control. The training director must be familiar enough with the work done by the organization and with what it takes to provide development experiences to bring a man to a required level of competence to perform this work. This is a large order and can provide a challenge for a lifetime.

In general, the following steps should be considered when individualizing a manager's program.

1. How is the manager doing at the present time? What are his strengths and weaknesses? This requires making a comparison between his job description and his performance.
2. What does the manager need to progress to the next job? Compare his performance on his present job to what will be required according to the job description for the next job.
3. Thoroughly analyze the manager's abilities and background through testing and an analysis of his personnel records. Interview his present and previous bosses for their opinions.

4. What is the timetable for this manager's development? Are there deadlines? The program will have to be adjusted accordingly.
5. How will the manager's progress be checked? Performance evaluation? Testing? Interviews? Committee assessment?

MANAGEMENT DEVELOPMENT IS A CONTINUING PROCESS

We talk of development programs as if they had definite beginnings and endings. The rapid expansion of technology requires that the manager continuously update his information to avoid technological obsolescence. The body of knowledge that constitutes management science is growing because of behavioral research. Clearly, the development of a manager never ceases. It is, in fact, an absolute requirement that it continue to maintain organizational health.

WHAT DO MANAGERS NEED TO KNOW TO MANAGE?

The following list is very general. There is no way to answer the question with specifics unless the organization and exact requirements of the job in which the manager functions or will function are known. Managers need to know and be able to apply the basic principles in each of the following areas:

1. Personnel administration.
2. Labor relations.
3. Business management.
4. Marketing management.
5. Business economics.
6. Finance.
7. Legal, social, economic, and political responsibilities of business.
8. Production management.
9. Public speaking and group dynamics.
10. Management art and science.

WHO SHOULD BE RESPONSIBLE FOR MANAGEMENT DEVELOPMENT?

The fundamental responsibility for developing people always resides in the immediate supervisor. The training director should serve as a consultant to the supervisor in planning individual programs for managerial development, but should avoid taking full responsibility for the whole program. The manager should create an appropriate climate and provide structured learning experiences for his subordinate. The training person will provide the expertise work necessary for the working out of the methods and materials for the program.

SIX BASIC METHODS FOR DEVELOPING MANAGERS

The following six methods are often used to develop managers. No one method *per se* is better than any other. The method you choose will depend on the level of the manager's responsibility, his present ability to perform his job, his future position in the organization and other important variables.

The Executive Reading List

The following reading list, divided into levels of supervision, has been compiled by Paul O'Rourke. He suggests reading 20 minutes a day for four weeks to complete the average book. If one could develop this habit, he could complete five or six books a year.* Regular reading will help provide a solid intellectual foundation for the manager. The material may not be of immediate use, but it can very well become a useful source of later wisdom.

A-Level, Supervisory

Incumbents

Human Relations at Work, Keith Davis, 2nd Ed., McGraw-Hill, 1962.
Principles of Management, C. J. O'Donnel and Harold D. Koontz, 3rd Ed. McGraw-Hill, 1965.
Managerial Psychology, Harold J. Leavitt, Rev. Ed., University of Chicago Press, 1964.
Electronic Data Processing, An Introduction, E. Wain Martin, Irwin, 1964.
The Techniques of Clear Writing, Robert Gunning, McGraw-Hill, 1952.
Process of Communication, David K. Berlo, Holt, Rinehart and Winston, 1960.

*Paul O'Rourke, "Managerial reading program," *Training and Development Journal,* Vol. 21, No. 2, January, 1967, pp. 46-49.

Trainees

Managers for Tomorrow, Staff of Editors, New American Library, 1965.
Evaluating Your Personnel Management, USCSC Personnel Management Series, No. 6, U.S. Government Printing Office.
Management for Modern Supervisors, Carl Heyel, American Management Association, 1962.
Personnel Administration, Paul Pigors and C. A. Myers, McGraw-Hill, 1956.
Administrative Behavior, Herbert A. Simon, MacMillan, 1951.

B-Level, Middle Management

Incumbents

Management by Objectives, George S. Odiorne, Pitman, 1965.
Communication – Patterns and Incidents, William V. Haney, Irwin, 1960.
How to Talk with People, Irving Lee, Harper, 1952.
The Managerial Grid, Robert R. Blake and Jane S. Mouton, Gulf, 1964.
Planning and Implementation, Preston P. LeBreton, Holt, Rinehart, Winston, 1966.
The Art of Clear Thinking, Rudolf Flesch, Harper, 1951.

Trainees

Tough-Minded Management, J. D. Batten, American Management Association, 1963.
Human Side of Enterprise, Douglas McGregor, McGraw-Hill, 1960.
Managing for Results, Peter Drucker, Harper & Row, 1964.
Introduction to Group Dynamics, Malcolm and Hulda Knowles, Association Press, 1959.
Developing Competent Subordinates, James M. Black, American Management Association, 1961.
Applied Imagination, Alex Osborne, Rev. Ed., Scribner, 1963.

C-Level, Executive

Incumbents

Organizational Psychology, Edgar Schein, Prentice-Hall, 1965.
Business and Its Environment, K. Davis and R. L. Blomstrom, McGraw-Hill, 1966.

The Staff Role in Management, Robert Sampson, Harper, 1955.
Interpersonal Competence and Organizational Effectiveness, Chris Argyris, Irwin, 1962.
Survival in the Executive Jungle, Chester Burger, MacMillan, 1964.
Administrative Action, William H. Newman, McGraw-Hill, 1960.

Trainees

The Rational Managers (Decision-Making), C. H. Kepner and B. B. Tregoe, McGraw-Hill, 1965.
The Ordeal of Change, Eric Hofer, Harper, 1952.
The Practice of Management, Peter Drucker, Harper, 1954.
Motivation and Productivity, Saul Gellerman, American Management Association, 1963.
Objectives and Standards, Ernest C. Miller, American Management Association, 1966.

Full-length Feature Films

Full-length feature films can be used to teach managerial style. The following films have been used successfully.*

Tunes of Glory
Executive Suite
Twelve Angry Men
Twelve O'Clock High
The Lifeboat
Rashomon
Mutiny on the Bounty
Lost Horizon
Treasure Island

The films can be used as the basis of a discussion or used in conjunction with some other method for getting managers to look critically at the way they manage.†

*William J. Reddin, "Feature films for management development," *Training and Development Journal,* Vol. 20, No. 9, October, 1966. pp. 18-24

†Allen A. Zoll, in *Dynamic Management Education* (Addison-Wesley, 1969), gives a good description of how to actually use films as cases in management education. He also covers some of the problems encountered in use of films and the special role of the teacher.

Job Rotation

A commonly used method of preparing managers for greater responsibilities is the system of job rotation. The jobs should be carefully selected so that a manager will grow in each experience. The manager will need coaching from his boss and feedback at the end of each assignment so that he can work on his weaknesses. The great difficulty with job rotation programs is their lack of preciseness. The manager must know specifically what he is expected to gain from the experience. He cannot simply be placed in a position and then evaluated when his time is up and he is supposed to be ready for his next assignment. His boss will also need some instruction in how to help his temporary subordinate get the most out of the experience.

Correspondence Courses

Courses of study by mail can be useful tools for training executives. Sales managers, for example, often travel so extensively that they are unable to attend regularly scheduled classes. A course such as the *Alexander Hamilton Management Course* can be studied at airport terminals or just about anywhere else. The trouble with all correspondence courses is the lack of pressure to complete assignments. This can be remedied by having the boss set deadlines, requiring that specific assignments be mailed in by specific dates.

The Research Institute of America has developed a unique format in a correspondence-type program called *The Program for Effective Management* (PEM).* The program covers executive approach, problem-solving, delegation, decision-making, resolving conflict, planning, leadership/motivation, criticism, time management, and managing change.

The material for each subject is in a separate notebook. Four principal devices are used for getting the material across to the student. The first device is that of analogy, used as a vehicle to get the manager to recognize the need for finding a more effective way to manage. The subject of criticism, for example, begins with a report by a marriage counselor on a marriage which is on the rocks because of the way criticism is used in the family situation. The report is in dialogue form, and the student is able to observe the subtle effects of criticism as it has been used by the husband, the wife, and the counselor. Because the subject is presented in a nonbusiness setting, the student's attention can be focused

*The Research Institute of America, Inc., 589 Fifth Avenue, New York, N.Y., 10017.

on a problem in a way which prevents him from using the rationalizations he might normally apply to business problems.

The second device used by PEM is an interesting business case. At several points in the case, the student is asked to respond to some open-ended questions which help him to begin applying the principles under discussion to his own organizational setting.

The third device is programed instruction. The programed materials teach the important points of the case. Branching is used so that a student who makes correct responses is able to proceed rapidly through the material, while a student needing greater exposure gets help from additional frames.

The fourth and final device is the specific application of the material through a series of checklists containing questions which the manager can apply to his own behavior in specific situations. Other kinds of material, such as a series of cartoons on the subject of resolving conflict, are used to reinforce the principles taught.

Other features such as an appraisal of management judgments, a leader's guide for company discussions of the material, and a monthly publication called a "Briefing" round out the program to provide a comprehensive approach to manager *self* development.

Simulation Gaming and Other "Dynamic Techniques"

James L. McKenney defines simulation gaming as "a competitive mental activity wherein opponents compete through the development and implementation of an economic strategy."* The advantage of gaming as a developmental tool for managers is that it generates a high degree of student involvement. It provides practice in business decision-making that can be obtained in no other way with the same degree of verisimilitude. Games are available that require or do not require the use of the computer. You can buy commercially prepared games, have a consultant tailor one for your company, or develop your own.

Simulation gaming is one of the many dynamic techniques available to the management developer. Allen Zoll defines dynamic techniques as those which require the active participation of the learner. Other dynamic techniques include cases, incident processes, in-baskets, and action mazes. These methods are described in detail in Chapter 19. If you are to help a manager to make significant changes in his way of looking and dealing

---

*James L. McKenney, *Simulation Gaming for Management Development,* Cambridge: Harvard University Press, 1967, p. 2.

with problems, you will need tools which force deep and serious emotional involvement.*

Pitting Managers Against Nature

While this may sound like nonsense, it is being done at Outward Bound Schools in the United States and abroad. The first Outward Bound School was founded in 1941 at Aberdovey, Wales, by Dr. Kurt Hahn. The objective of the school is to develop a man's ability and determination to overcome adversity by placing him in a series of situations where he is forced to rely on his courage and endurance to succeed. He runs a mile, swims in an icy mountain stream, spends three solitary days in the hills, walks 60 miles, scales walls, and performs other feats of physical endurance. He learns decision-making skills, cooperation, and a whole range of behaviors required of the tough-minded executive.†

SEMINARS AND WORKSHOPS

Seminars and workshops lasting from one day to one week or more are offered all over the United States. Most of them offer an excellent opportunity for stimulation and learning. The following agenda for the Louis A. Allen "Profession of Management" seminar is representative.‡

Management as a Profession

The elements of professionalism.

The evaluation of management.

The role of the natural leader.

Professional aspects of management.

Management in transition.

Distinguishing between management and operating work.

The functions and activities of a unified management system.

The common vocabulary of professional management.

---

*All of these dynamic techniques are described with examples of each in Allen Zoll's *Dynamic Management Education* (Addison-Wesley, 1969).

†North Carolina Outward Bound School, P.O. Box 817, Morganton, North Carolina, 28655.

‡Louis A. Allen Associates, 615 University Ave., Palo Alto, Calif. 94301.

Principles of management derived from the experience of the world's most successful companies.

Planning for Profitable Results

Using planning principles to master the future.

Securing understanding and acceptance of people who implement plans.

Forecasting to anticipate the future.

Setting realistic objectives.

Programming and scheduling for improved operating results.

Tested management approaches for more effective budgeting.

Using policies to secure coordinated management action.

Streamlining procedures for policy implementation.

Organizing the Work

New principles of organization: how they are used in leading companies.

The critical choice in organization structure.

Delegating for less work and better results.

Building effective line/staff teamwork.

The uses of assistants.

Reorganizing to make the most effective use of available people.

Leadership in Management

Making and implementing successful management decisions.

Problem analysis.

The development of logical alternatives for reasoned decisions.

Communications for improved understanding.

Understanding and using motivation techniques.

Effective methods of management appraisal.

Counseling for improved performance.

Selecting the right people for the right job.

Developing the knowledge, attitudes, and skills of subordinates.

Controls for Management Effectiveness

Avoiding the dangers of historical controls.

Using the principle of management by exception.

Essentials of a successful reporting system.

Realistic evaluation of results.

Creative use of controls to help people improve performance.

Limitations of management by results.

Usable performance standards.

Measurement and correction of performance.

The important considerations when choosing a seminar or workshop are who will be teaching and who will be participating. If you are unable to satisfactorily answer these questions, you'd better find out before investing your organization's money and your effort.

UNIVERSITY MANAGEMENT DEVELOPMENT PROGRAMS

The university management development program appears to have become a permanent fixture in business education since World War II. Kenneth R. Andrews reports in *The Effectiveness of University Management Development Programs*, that an overwhelming number of executives who had participated in university programs and responded to his survey gave a favorable evaluation of the programs they had attended. They further indicated that they would like to participate in the same type of program every three to five years. They reported the effects of the programs as follows:

1. A broadening of perspective.
2. An increased confidence in their own ability.
3. A sense of assurance that their subsequent performance would improve with time.
4. A wide knowledge of segments of business other than their own.
5. A deeper appreciation of the nature of the human and social problems of business.
6. An ability to look at old problems in new ways.
7. A realization that many different approaches to a problem were available.
8. A wider tolerance of differences of opinion.*

The most respected of all university programs is the Harvard Business School Program. As one recent graduate put it, "In my company everyone knows that if you're sent to AMP,† you're on your way to becoming a

---

*Kenneth R. Andrews, *The Effectiveness of University Management Development Programs*, Cambridge: Harvard University Press, 1966.

†*Harvard's Advanced Management Program.*

vice president." Certificates of completion are framed and proudly displayed in offices. Being given the privilege of going through the Harvard program is indeed a symbol of a man's status in an organization.

Harvard operates two programs, The Advanced Management Program and The Program for Management Development. AMP is designed for "experienced executives who are, or are already selected to be in, top management positions."* PMD is geared to younger, less experienced executives ". . . currently filling responsible positions at the operating level who have demonstrated by their performances that they are potential top-echelon managers."†

Both programs are highly selective of the managers they enroll. Applicants must have their credentials passed upon by a committee. The AMP program, for example, requires that a candidate be in a top management position in his company, that he have 15 - 20 years of experience in business or the military, that he be academically fit, and that he be fully sponsored by his own company.

The course content for the Advanced Management Program includes the following subjects: business policy, marketing, control and planning, business history, labor relations, business and world society, human behavior in organizations, and decision analysis. The course content for the Program for Management Development includes general management, finance, quantitative analysis, human behavior in organizations, and issues in business. AMP is 13 weeks in duration; PMD is 16. Both require a total commitment for the student of six days a week, starting at 8 a.m.

The principal means of instruction is the case method, which Harvard has pioneered. Cases are first studied individually and then explored in small discussion groups. Finally, in larger classes the participants have their analyses and recommendations for action criticized.

Northeastern University's Management Development Program is another example of the university program. It is scheduled to include six weeks of in-residence instruction spaced over five months. Participants devote their time to their regular jobs for three weeks out of every four. The program begins with two weeks of classes, and then the participant returns to his job, taking up classes again one week out of every four for four months.

The Northeastern program provides a graduate-level curriculum in marketing, finance, production, accounting, economic analysis, industrial relations, group behavior, capital budgeting, information processing, business forecasting, business policy, and business organization. The general aim of the program is "to enhance the manager's long term value

---

**Management Programs at the Harvard Business School,* Revised January 1, 1968, p. 6.
†*Ibid.*, p. 7.

to his organization by relating him more knowledgeably to it." The specific objectives of the program are as follows: to enhance the manager's grasp of management problems, to increase his immediate productivity and that of his subordinates, and to employ quantitative tools in reaching decisions and attaining goals.

The content of the program is represented as follows:

Functional management. The fundamentals of finance, production, and marketing are examined in lectures and discussions. Specific illustrations highlight the importance of coordinating resources to attain profit goals.

Policy and planning. Emphasis is on matters which cross functional lines. This leads to a critical review of plans for the immediate and more distant future. A continuing management decision exercise simulates the organizational environment and relates course work to it.

Managing human resources. The effective use of human resources demands constructive self-appraisal and an understanding of both individual and group behavior. Professional guidance is employed to explore the complexities of human relations. The manager gains enlightened attitudes, relevant skills, and the ability to anticipate potential problems.

Measurement and control. Case studies feature the advantages and limitations of modern techniques for measuring performance in financial control, forecasting, and budgeting. Regular classroom sessions are augmented by frequent small group meetings. During weeks away from class, each man is assigned occasional written projects. These relate academic content to situations within his own company or industry.

The business environment. The role of external forces is revealed through analysis of significant trends in the domestic economy, international business affairs, labor management relations, and government policies. Changing technology receives special attention, particularly the impact of recent developments in information storage and retrieval.

Unless you have actually been through a university program or know someone who has, it is difficult to evaluate its usefulness to your own managers. A consultant like George W. Bricker could be of help. He is a professional advisor on the selection of appropriate university executive development programs for specific management personnel, and has published the vital statistics on 52 university programs in the Prentice-Hall *Personnel Management and Policies and Practices* manual. He lists programs up to 16 weeks in length, ranging in price from $350 to $4500. In addition the listing includes a description of the program, sponsor, duration, tuition, and number of participants in the program.

WHICH METHODS ARE USED MOST OFTEN?

The question should really be, "Which method is most effective as a means for developing managers?" Unfortunately, that question cannot be answered because of the large number of factors that must be taken into consideration in planning any development program. Wayne J. Foreman sent a questionnaire to 75 corporations asking, among other things, which method was used most often.* Responses were received from 45 companies. The following table summarizes the results.

Training Methods According to Frequency of Use

Training techniques	Times appearing in top five	Percentage
On-the-job	43	96
Conference and discussion	42	93
Job rotation	34	76
Special projects	32	71
Case studies	22	49
Problem solving	22	49
Management games	8	18
Role playing	8	18
Programed instruction	7	16
Sensitivity training	4	9
Brainstorming	3	7
Other	3	7

Mr. Foreman further reported that there was no significant difference in the kinds of training used by various industries.

MANAGEMENT DEVELOPMENT NEVER ENDS

The above methods for developing managers represent only a few of the many ways available. You will probably not want to rely on a single

*Wayne J. Foreman, "Management Development in Large Corporations," *Training in Business and Industry,* August, 1967, pp. 22-29.

method. Each manager will require a slightly different program to keep him operating at peak effectiveness in his present position and to help him continue to climb the corporate ladder. A program for development cannot be laid out once and for all. It must change with the individual manager's changing needs. The training director's responsibility for management development is clearly a challenging one; he must perpetually prescribe learning experiences or help others to prescribe them to keep his organization in good health.

Epilogue: Training and Training Directors in the '70s

If present signs are right, the 'soaring '60s,' marked by dynamic growth and change, in another six months will give way to the dawn of a 10-year period that will be even more awesome – the 'spectacular '70s.'*

In Edward Bellamy's utopian novel *Looking Backward,* the main character, Julian West, awakens in the year 2000 from a 113-year sleep. Of course, he finds a totally different society, one which does not correspond socially, economically, or politically to his 19th century memory.†

But one does not need to sleep for a century to experience the kind and magnitude of change Julian West encountered. It is happening *now* in this decade, and willing or unwillingly we are all partners to it. The quality of that partnership depends, however, on our ability to help shape the course and character of some important trends gaining momentum at the close of the sixties and start of the seventies. The effective training manager of the seventies will be the man who has anticipated these changes and turned them to the advantage of his organization.

That's what this chapter is all about – what's in store for the nation in the "spectacular '70s," the effects of what is to come on organizations, and how the training director can prepare himself and his staff to cope with these effects. The preceding chapters have been written for use by the practicing training manager. This chapter has been prepared in the same spirit. In the last section of this chapter you will find a checklist to

---

*"The Spectacular '70s," *U.S. News and World Report,* Vol. LXVI, No. 25, June 23, 1969, p. 42.

†Edward Bellamy, *Looking Backward*, New York: Random House, 1951.

assist you in assessing the impact of the future on your organization and developing a proposal to help management establish a philosophy and provide guidance for training function activities in the decade ahead.

MAJOR TRENDS IN THE SEVENTIES

Population growth. Projections tell us that our population will grow to 225 million by the end of the seventies. That's an increase of 22 million over the census at the end of the sixties. This increase in population will swell the demand for all kinds of consumer products and services.*

Increased family income. While the population itself is increasing, so is the money it will have available to spend on goods and services. The typical consumer in 1979 will have 32% more income to spend. One-half of the households will earn $15,500 a year, compared to one-quarter at the close of the sixties. The average annual individual income in 1980 will be $3600, compared to $2800 today. The income for a family of four will be $14,400. This increased affluence will, of course, increase consumer buying power.

More comfortable living. From all indications it appears that life will be easier, if we consider the anticipated increase in two-car households from 17 million in 1969 to 26 million in 1979 as representative. More of the increased standards of comfort will be available to everyone.

More education. In the sixties, 70% of all high school graduates went on to college; in the seventies, that proportion will rise to 80%. Everyone will be entitled, by virtue of his citizenship, to a minimum of fourteen years of education. One out of four employees will be a college graduate.

Lower average unemployment rate. The unemployment rate averaged 4.8% during the sixties. During the last few years of this decade, the rate dropped further and is expected to hold at about a 3.5% average for the seventies.

Increased governmental control. During the seventies, governmental regulations and control of business is expected to increase.

---

*The statistics presented in this section and the following one are taken from *U.S. News and World Report,* "Changes Facing Business in '70s," Vol. LXVI, No. 25, June 3, 1969, pp. 92-94, and "The Spectacular '70s," Vol. LXVI, No. 25, June 23, 1969, pp. 42-45.

In general, our unprecedented 30-year period of economic growth is expected to continue, sparked by the increase in population. Despite inflation and taxes, the American public will continue to prosper and enjoy more of the good things of life.

IMPORTANT EFFECTS ON ORGANIZATIONS

All of the foregoing, of course, will have a decided impact on the organizations presently in existence and those about to be brought into being. The following observations represent a few of the more important effects expected to be felt during the seventies.

Increased labor force. As a result of the population growth, an additional 15 million people will be added to the labor force during the next decade, bringing the total to 99 million.

Increased production. To meet the increased needs of the population of the seventies, production of U.S. goods will climb 100% to two million dollars. Individual output in the sixties rose 36.5%. Individual output in the seventies should equal this gain.

Increased expenditures for facilities and equipment. Spending on business facilities and equipment will increase by 70%, to a total of about 172 billion dollars.

Changes in the composition of the work force. By 1975, 4.5 million more professional and technical workers will be needed. By the same year white-collar workers will comprise 54% of the work force. In industrial jobs the number of women and Negroes will increase half again as fast as the number of men and whites. And finally, the entire work force by 1975 will on the average be younger. Forty percent of the increase in the size of the work force will be in the 20-35 age group. In the 35-44 age group there will be a 5% decline.

Increases in managers needed. An increase in the rank and file, of course, generates a corresponding increase in the need for managers. According to George J. Berkwitt in *Dun's Review*, nearly 750,000 top jobs open up every year.* Mason Haire, Professor of Organizational Psychology and Management at Massachusetts Institute of Technology, estimates that by

*George J. Berkwitt, "Building tomorrow's executive staff," *Dun's Review*, February, 1969, as condensed in *Management Review*, May, 1969, pp. 52-53.

1975 there will be a deficit of more than 40% in the number of people needed to fill managerial jobs currently projected.

Changes in the attitude of the work force. From previously quoted statistics, it is evident that the work force will be on the whole better educated. They will expect increased individual treatment, be more impatient with organizational constraints, and have greater expectations from their jobs. The belief in work as a duty will weaken. The paycheck will not have the motivating effect it once had. There will be greater emphasis on time away from the job as an earned right and not a privilege. While there will be little change in the length of the workweek (35-36 hours by 1975), the number of holidays will increase, vacations will become longer, and retirement will come earlier.

Increased automation. An increasing number of sophisticated applications will be found for the computer. Inventories will be leveled, removing the dips and rises required in production. This will serve to stabilize employment.

Increased cost of employee benefits. Insurance costs, retirement costs, and a host of benefits no longer regarded as "fringe" benefits will continue to proliferate, improve, and rise in cost to the employer.

CHANGE AND THE TRAINING FUNCTION

Given these forces shaping our society and its organizations during the decade of the seventies, what are the implications for the training director and his department?

First, the number and quality of programs, equipment, and facilities will need to be increased to meet the requirements of an enlarged and more sophisticated work force. In addition, training technology will become more sophisticated. A few of the expected advances are discussed below.

Technological Changes and Their Implications

Super 8mm. While 8mm film is not a new medium, super 8mm deserves some mention in this chapter because it is new and will soon have a significant impact on training departments. Super 8mm film is a format which provides a viewing frame 40% larger than the conventional 8mm frame without any increase in the film size. The secret to this format is in the maximum utilization of the film surface.

At the present time certain drawbacks to extensive use of this format have been created by competition. To alter the present market for 8mm or 16mm films is extremely difficult, especially in the area of prepared films. Converting 16mm film production equipment and existing 16mm films to 8mm equipment is costly. We can anticipate that more and more films will be produced in super 8mm, and eventually it will claim its place next to 16mm as one of the primary film media for training. In addition to commercially produced films, the super 8mm is also usable for home-made productions. Because it's easy to use and relatively low in cost, we can anticipate greater home use of super 8mm in the decade ahead.

Random access systems. Random access, sometimes referred to as dial access, is a method of storing programs and data by which any item can be brought forth immediately. Random access can bring forth visual images, sounds, or a combined audio-visual program. The range and variety of material handled by such a retrieval system depends upon the particular installation and its purpose. Normally a random access system is not practical for use with less than 50 students.

There are many brands of random access units on the market today. In most instances they represent first generation systems. We are bound to witness a vast improvement in quality, compactness, and cost. This field will probably develop much like the language labs of the 1950's, which began with modified tape recorders and then gave way to specially designed and engineered equipment.

Cost is also a major problem in random access systems. Student carrels, programs, central equipment, and personnel are needed to maintain this sophisticated equipment. The cost per student depends upon the complexity of the installation. Even a simple system could cost $1000 per student for the installation and several hundred dollars per student per year to maintain. The real question is whether the random access approach is the ideal solution to your specific training needs.

Computer-assisted instruction. Computer-assisted instruction (CAI) has been praised and condemned by many educators and trainers. Some view it as the "greatest technological breakthrough of this century." Others see it simply as a more refined form of programed instruction. It is praised for its speed and capability and for individualizing instruction, but condemned for its impersonal and machine-like qualities. Just what is CAI and why does it draw these types of responses from the educational field?

CAI relies upon the following basic elements to form its conceptual base:

1. Active student participation.
2. Positive reinforcement at each learning step.
3. Adaptation to individual's learning rate.
4. Adaptation to individual's method of learning.

You will readily note that these same concepts are the basis of programed instruction. The basic difference is that CAI can provide these elements in an infinite pattern and in microseconds while responding to the individual's variable patterns of learning.

The mechanical mode of CAI is the computer. Like any medium of learning, however, the computer is only as good as its programer. Many organizations and firms have conducted extensive research on the best programing approaches and methods of time-sharing, as well as the technical questions associated with the computer and education.

One experiment in the use of CAI, for example, revealed that seventh-grade students learned more from CAI than from the standard presentation of mathematical concepts, formulas, and problems by a human instructor. In this particular experiment, students began to use CAI to develop their own problems and ideas. In another experiment, CAI was to teach medical students to diagnose the ailments of a patient. The student had to react to the computer as though the computer were the patient. Failure to seek out the proper answer resulted in the "death" of the computer patient. Proper handling, on the other hand, "cured" the patient. Similar problems have been developed for training in business decision-making.

The computer is a multi-media device. As a learning center it is capable of presenting visual, audio, and printed media from a single output center.

We can also anticipate that CAI will alter the traditional trainer/student patterns. The trainer will not continue as a presenter of information and facts. He will spend his time diagnosing the individual's learning problems, helping to eliminate these problems, and working with the group to further their expertise through group discussions and similar techniques. CAI will, in short, make the trainer become more involved in individual students and their learning needs.

The major difficulties with the use of CAI today are (1) the need for research to develop mechanically better computers to meet the economical and functional needs of schools and (2) the lack of a sufficient number of CAI programs to make utilization economically and academically practical.

The cost of CAI is very difficult to pin down. To begin with, the basic cost of a computer can vary so much that it is impossible to generalize. Added to the basic computer cost are the costs of student centers, programming, and special integration into the training program. When the cost obstacle is finally overcome, we can expect CAI to become a real part of most training programs, whether it is fed by a company's computers or from a service center where the computer is used on a cost basis similar to that of our present telephone services. We don't anticipate rapid development of inexpensive CAI systems. We believe it will be another decade or more before everyday use of CAI will be practical.

Thermo tape. An experimental method of recording visual images inexpensively and quickly is the so-called thermo tape method. With this approach, the visual image is "burned" into the tape. Then the thermal image is ready for instant playback. The cost and key technical problems will probably take many years to solve before this method will be practical. When thermo tape becomes a reality, its application to training will be in the areas of recording training events, simulation training, role-playing, and similar situations where video tape is now used.

Record-based video programming. Several major broadcasting companies are close to a major breakthrough in the development of an economical and mechanically practical system of audio and visual recording which resembles the standard phonograph record in format.

While this approach will be similar to videotape and the audio-record, it will clearly be a departure from anything that is presently available. Indications are that this visual disc approach will be as practical and simple to use as the present phonograph records. Technological and cost problems currently hinder the marketing of this device, but it seems reasonable to anticipate an audiovisual disc recording within the next five to ten years.

Most innovations in media such as programed instruction, super 8mm films, and the like which will affect training are already with us in one form or another. Few additional innovations are likely to appear in this category in the next decade. What we are most likely to see is a refinement, upgrading, modification, and integration of these media into their proper place in training programs. Not that we have invented all that there is to invent! But so many practical systems and media currently available have not been properly evaluated and/or integrated into our training systems that we are likely to enter an era of the "let's use what we have before we develop something new" attitude.

We can see this today in the systematic organization of materials in schools and colleges. Systems to teach skills such as reading, mathematics, or science are being developed. The purpose of these new systems is to make better and more creative use of all available educational technology. As we enter this era, men will be called upon to use their time and materials more effectively.

If any "new" developments in media are to appear in the next decade, they will probably be in electronics, primarily in visual and audio data transmission. The electronic media will compete with the current photographic media (films, etc.), to bring about faster, less expensive, and wider dissemination of data.

Other Changes

In addition to the implications of the technological changes just discussed, the following will be of importance to the training director.

1. There will be greater insistence that the results of training undergo rigorous evaluation. Expenditures for training and development will continue to increase, but management will be more demanding in wanting evidence of success. More careful budgeting and expense control are coming and more elaborate attempts to relate expenditures to results achieved will be required.

2. The relatively low unemployment rate of 3.5% for the seventies implies a continued inadequate labor supply. More marginal employees will be hired out of necessity. The need for effective training and integration of minority groups into the work force will increase. Pressure from the government to increase the percentage of minority employees, especially at supervisory and managerial levels, will increase, again stepping up the demands on the training function.

3. Low birth rates during World War II and the increased size of the rank and file work force will place terrific strains on our supervisory and management reserves. Supervisory and management development programs will be mandatory even for small companies.

4. Learning environments will become more sophisticated. The four-walled classroom and blackboard will give way to learning centers of various configurations. Industry has already revealed its willingness not to be hemmed in by traditional approaches to learning. Large corporations will invest large sums in the construction of training facilities.

5. More effort will be put into teaching people to increase their personal effectiveness through small groups. Much work, for example, has already

been accomplished in T-groups and other forms of laboratory human relations experiences.

6. The need for research, consultants, and management development courses will place the business community in closer touch with the university. The separation of the practical world of business and the ivory-tower world of academia should diminish.

7. Training and development programs will be designed to deal with the career-long problems of the worker rather than occasional efforts to correct certain problems. Employees will undergo continuous formal and informal development in one form or another.

8. The great influx of administrative and professional workers will increase the demand for appropriate technical training. Continuing technical advances will require frequent retraining.

9. Greater effort will be made to tailor individual improvement programs for employees whose performance is substandard. The cost of replacing a worker will far outweigh the training gamble.

10. Individualized instruction will be preferred, especially by those employees with some college background. Greater effort will be made to deal with the problems of an individual rather than a group.

11. There will be a greater interest in both studying educational research and conducting it. We are in the process of building a solid body of usable learning theory.

12. The training director will have an increasingly strong voice in top management in planning for and developing the organization's human resources. More and more human development programs are being accepted on a par with other organizational investments rather than expenditures.

WILL YOU BE READY?

Technically, the training field is moving ahead at a dizzying rate of speed. But what about the training director? There is an old addition to the proverb that opportunity only knocks once: even if we hear the knocking, we are no better off if we are unable to open the door.

Many training people lack even minimum credentials. So far the universities and the professional training organizations have not offered much help. Fortunately there appears to be some evidence of change, even among these conservative bodies. The journals are becoming more informative. An increasing number of books are being published. Consultants exclusively concerned with training problems are becoming more numerous. It's looking better, but there is a considerable distance to travel before we are ready to meet the challenge of the seventies.

A case in point is the recent failure of training organizations to meet the challenge of developing hard-core unemployed individuals into productive, stable employees. Federally funded programs have sprung up all over the country, but by and large, these programs cannot be judged successful, notwithstanding the claims to the contrary. The fundamental techniques for designing programs are not understood or if they are, they are not widely applied.

This challenge and others are still with us. We will have to stop seeing ourselves, however, as public school principals presiding over faculties and industrial classrooms. We will have to look beyond the gadgetry, the lecture, and the four-walled classroom as the answer to all training and development problems if we are to come anywhere near meeting that challenge.

Appendix

Like prefaces, most appendices in books go unread. That may be because they are too scholarly, too all-inclusive, or just not very useful. We have tried to overcome these problems by including only a few general categories of information necessary to the daily work of most practicing trainers. Instead of listing hundreds of film distributors, for example, we give you only the major source directories. For the most complete list of media products and producers, see the McGraw-Hill *Encyclopedia of Media* – just seventeen volumes long.

We do not necessarily endorse items included in our list, nor disapprove of those excluded from it. These are simply a few representative books, people, and training bric-a-brac that we have found useful in solving everyday training problems.

SELECTED BOOKS FOR THE TRAINING DIRECTOR'S SHELF

Bergevim, Paul, *et al., Adult Education Procedures.* New York: Seabury Press, 1963.

Bienvenue, Bernard J., *New Priorities in Training.* New York: American Management Association, 1969.

Broadwell, Martin, *The Supervisor and On-the-Job Training,* Reading, Massachusetts: Addison-Wesley, 1969.

Bugelski, B. R., *The Psychology of Learning Applied to Teaching.* Indianapolis: Bobbs-Merrill, 1964.

Craig, Robert L., and Lester R. Bittel (Eds.), *Training and Development Handbook.* New York: McGraw-Hill, 1967.

Ferguson, George A., *Statistical Analysis in Psychology and Education.* New York: McGraw-Hill, 1966.

Graham, Robert G., and Clifford F. Gray, *Business Games Handbook.* New York: American Management Association, 1969.

Hill, Winfred F., *Learning.* San Francisco: Chandler, 1963.

Hilliard, Robert (Ed.), *Understanding Television.* New York: Hastings House, 1964.

Jaffee, Cabot L., *Problems in Supervision: An In-Basket Training Exercise.* Reading, Massachusetts: Addison-Wesley, 1968.

Kemp, Jerrold E., *Planning and Preparing Audio-Visual Materials.* San Francisco: Chandler, 1963.

Kimble, Gregory A., *Hilgard and Marquis' Conditioning and Learning.* New York: Appleton-Century-Crofts, 1961.

Mager, Robert F., *Developing Attitude Toward Learning.* Palo Alto: Fearon Publishers, 1968.

Mager, Robert F., *Preparing Objectives for Programmed Instruction.* San Francisco: Fearon Publishers, 1962.

Mascelli, Joseph V., *Five C's of Cinematography.* Hollywood: Cine Graphic Publications, 1965.

Minor, Ed, *Simplified Techniques for Preparing Visual Instructional Materials.* New York: McGraw-Hill, 1962.

Payne, David A., *The Specification and Measurement of Learning Outcomes.* Waltham, Massachusetts: Blaisdell, 1968.

Reeves, Elton T., *Management Development for the Line Manager.* New York: American Management Association, 1969.

Sanders, Norris M., *Classroom Questions: What Kinds?* New York: Harper & Row, 1966.

Spottiswoode, Raymond, *Film and Its Techniques.* Berkeley: University of California Press, 1964.

Staton, Thomas F., *How to Instruct Successfully.* New York: McGraw-Hill, 1960.

Stokes, Paul M., *Total Job Training: A Manual for the Working Manager.* New York: American Management Association, 1966.

Tracey, William R., *Evaluating Training and Development Systems.* New York: American Management Association, 1968.

Warren, Malcolm W., *Training for Results.* Reading, Massachusetts: Addison-Wesley, 1969.

Zoll, Allen, *Dynamic Management Education.* Reading, Massachusetts: Addison-Wesley, 1969.

MOTION PICTURE FILM DIRECTORIES

8mm Film Directory, Comprehensive Service Corporation, 250 West 64th Street, New York 10023.

Systems Film Catalogue, 245-87 Bagley Road, Cleveland, Ohio 44138.

Free-Loan Catalogues

Association Films, Inc., 600 Madison Avenue, New York, New York.

Modern Talking Pictures Service, Inc., 1212 Avenue of the Americas, New York, New York.

Sterling Movies, U.S.A., Inc., 375 Park Avenue, New York, New York.

Educators Guide to Free Films, 28th Edition, Educators Progress Service, Randolph, Wisconsin 53556
(*Note*: These are the three largest companies. There are hundreds of others, many of them listed in the MPE Audio-Visual Source Director, see reference below.)

Educational Film Library Association, 250 West 75th Street, New York, New York 10019. (This organization charges a $10 annual membership fee to cover their costs in searching for any film you may need.)

TRAINING CONSULTANTS

Bolt Beranek and Newman Inc., 50 Moulton Street, Cambridge, Massachusetts 02138, Attention: Calvin Otto, Manager.

Education and Training Consultants Co., 815 Moraga Drive, Los Angeles, California 90049, Attention: Dr. Leonard Silvern.

Maynard Research Council, Inc., 718 Wallace Avenue, Pittsburgh, Pennsylvania.

International Correspondence Schools (ICS), Industrial Training and Development, Scranton, Pennsylvania 18515.

Management Programs Inc., P.O. Box 72, Glen Ellyn, Illinois, Attention: Dan Kedzie.

Briarcliff House, 27 Briarcliff Road, Mountain Lakes, New Jersey 07046

Learning System Development Corporation, 365 Northland Boulevard, Cincinnati, Ohio, Attention: Marvin King.

Arnold S. Daniels, Management Consultants, 131 Mount Auburn Street, Cambridge, Massachusetts 02138.

USEFUL PERIODICALS

Training in Business and Industry, published monthly, 33 West 60th Street, New York, New York 10023.

Audiovisual Instruction, published 10 times a year, Department of Audiovisual Instruction, National Education Association, 1201 16th Street, N.W., Washington, D.C. 20036.

A-V Guide, published monthly, Educational Screen, Inc., 434 South Wabash, Chicago, Illinois 60605.

National Society for Programmed Instruction Journal, published 10 times a year, Trinity University, 715 Stadium Drive, San Antonio, Texas 78212.

Training and Development Journal, published monthly for members of American Society for Training and Development, ASTD Subscription Department, Box 5307, Madison, Wisconsin 53705.

Educational Television, published monthly, L.S. Tepfer Publishing Company, Inc., 140 Main Street, Ridgefield, Connecticut 06877.

Educational Technology, published semimonthly, Box 508, Saddle Brook, New Jersey 07662.

Personnel Journal, American Management Association, 150 West 50th Street, New York, N.Y. 10020.

Audio-Visual Communication Review, Department of Audiovisual Instruction, National Education Association, 1201 16th Street, N.W., Washington, D.C. 20036.

Business Screen, 7064 Sheridan Road Building, Chicago, Illinois.

More Effective Meetings, 3M Business Press, Visual Products Division, 3M Company, 3M Center, St. Paul, Minnesota 55101.

Dartnell Videotape Newsletter The Dartnell Corporation, 4660 Ravenswood Avenue, Chicago, Illinois 60640.

Meetings and Conventions, Gellert Publishing Company, 33 West 60th Street, New York, N.Y.

GUIDES TO PRODUCTS AND SERVICES

Photo Methods for Industry, PMI Directory, 33 West 60th Street, New York, New York (Film labs and services.)

Audio-Visual Source Directory, Motion Picture Enterprises Publications, Inc., Tarrytown, New York 10591. (Services and products.)

AVI Guide to New Products, contained in the September issue of *Audiovisual Instruction,* Department of Audiovisual Instruction, National Education Association, 1201 16th Street N.W., Washington, D.C. 20036.

Buyer's Guide. in December issue of *Training in Business and Industry* 33 West 60th Street, New York, New York 10023. (Comprehensive listing of products and services.)

Annual Red Book, A-V Equipment Guide, (published in November), 434 South Wabash, Chicago, Illinois 60605.

Audio-Visual Equipment Directory, National Audio-Visual Association, Inc., 3150 Spring Street, Fairfax, Virginia 22030.

National Directory of Adult and Continuing Education: A Guide to Programs, Materials and Services, Steven E. Goodman, Education and Training Associates, Dept. T, P.O. Box 9894, South Town Station, Rochester, New York 14623.

AUDIO TAPE DIRECTORIES

National Audio Tape Catalogue, National Education Association, 1201 16th Street, N.W., Washington, D.C. 20036.

TRAINING SEMINARS

The Addison-Wesley Seminar Program, Addison-Wesley Publishing Company, Inc. Reading, Massachusetts 01867.

American Management Association, 135 West 50th Street, New York, New York 10020.

Industrial Education Institute, 221 Columbus Avenue, Boston, Massachusetts 02116.

American Society for Training and Development, P.O. Box J307, Madison, Wisconsin 53705.

Calvin Productions, 1105 Truman Road, Kansas City, Missouri. (Three-day workshop on motion-picture making.)

Management Center of Cambridge, 87 Terrace Hall Avenue, Burlington, Massachusetts 08103.

University of Michigan, Bureau of Industrial Relations, 508 E. Williams Street, Ann Arbor, Michigan 48108. (Workshops on programed instruction.)

Up-to-date training calendars of programs to be presented are carried by both the *Training and Development Journal* and the *Training in Business and Industry* magazine. These are referred to in the periodicals section.

PROFESSIONAL ASSOCIATIONS

American Society for Training and Development, P.O. Box 5307, Madison, Wisconsin 53705.

A society for the promotion of professionalism in training. Produces a monthly journal, holds an annual convention and provides specialized seminars in training techniques.

Department of Audiovisual Instruction, National Education Association, 1201 16th Street, N.W., Washington, D.C. 20036.

DAVI is devoted to furthering both educational and training use of new instructional techniques and media. The organization publishes a monthly magazine and a quarterly journal. It also holds an annual convention.

National Society of Programed Instruction, San Antonio, Texas.

The NSPI is a limited-objective group devoted mainly to promoting the development and use of programed instruction in education and training. This group also produces a monthly journal and holds an annual convention.

Index